A His
of Renaissance Rhetoric 1380–1620

PETER MACK

OXFORD
UNIVERSITY PRESS

OXFORD
UNIVERSITY PRESS

Great Clarendon Street, Oxford, OX2 6DP,
United Kingdom

Oxford University Press is a department of the University of Oxford.
It furthers the University's objective of excellence in research, scholarship,
and education by publishing worldwide. Oxford is a registered trade mark of
Oxford University Press in the UK and in certain other countries

First published in 2011
First published in paperback 2013

Impression: 1

British Library Cataloguing in Publication Data
Data available

Library of Congress Cataloging in Publication Data
Data available

ISBN 978–0–19–959728–4
ISBN 978–0–19–967999–7 (Pbk)

OXFORD-WARBURG STUDIES

In Memory of
J. B. Trapp
and
Michael Baxandall

Acknowledgements

I am very grateful to the English Department, its then chair Thomas Docherty, and the University of Warwick for granting me study-leave in 2008–9, which enabled me to draft this book. I could not have contemplated writing the book without Lawrence D. Green and James J. Murphy's *Renaissance Rhetoric Short-Title Catalogue* (Aldershot, 2006). I am most grateful to the librarians who, and libraries which, made it possible for me to read so many early printed books, especially the British Library and the Bodleian Library, but also the Rare Books Library of the University of Illinois at Champaign-Urbana, the Huntington Library, the Newberry Library, the Warburg Institute, and Warwick University Library. An increasing number of the books I needed became available on the internet through Gallica at the Bibliothèque Nationale, Paris, the digitization programme of the Bayerische Staatsbibliothek, Munich, Googlebooks, and Early English Books Online. I am grateful to Dana Sutton for the bibliography of Neo-Latin Texts on the web at www.philological.bham.ac.uk, which helped me find electronic texts of many works not available to me in libraries.

Several of my previous publications discuss material included in this *History*, including my books *Renaissance Argument* (Leiden, 1993) and *Elizabethan Rhetoric* (Cambridge, 2002) and several articles, including 'Rhetoric, Ethics and Reading in the Renaissance', *Renaissance Studies,* 19 (2005), 1–21, 'Rudolph Agricola's Contributions to Rhetorical Theory', in P. Bizzell (ed.), *Rhetorical Agendas* (Mahwah, NJ, 2006), 25–40, and 'Vives's Contributions to Rhetoric and Dialectic', in C. Fantazzi (ed.), *A Companion to Juan Luis Vives* (Leiden, 2008), 227–76. I am grateful to the publishers and editors involved for permission to reuse information, arguments, and phrases.

I must especially thank Lawrence Green, Marjorie Woods, and Maté Vince for careful critical readings of the whole typescript. Martin Camargo, Kees Meerhoff, Lucia Montefusco, and James J. Murphy were always ready with help and suggestions concerning their wide fields of expertise. For information, advice and support of many different kinds, I warmly thank Fokke Akkerman, Jonathan Bate, Gibson Burrell, Gualtiero Calboli, Thomas M. Conley, Rita Copeland, Brian Cummings, Philippe Desan, Luc Deitz, Mike Edwards, Charles Fantazzi, Brian Follett, Roberto Franzosi, Simon Gilson, Tony Grafton, Judith Rice Henderson, Paul Hills, Sarah Holmes, Alfonso Martín Jiménez, Craig

Kallendorf, Dilwyn Knox, Manfred Kraus, Jill Kraye, Peter Larkin, Neil Lazarus, David Lines, Martin Loughlin, William Mack, Ian Maclean, John Monfasani, Lodi Nauta, Belmiro Fernandes Pereira, Alessandra Petrina, Marc van der Poel, Jennifer Richards, Jane Robson, Carol Rutter, Patrick Spottiswoode, Quentin Skinner, Ingrid de Smet, John Stokes, Simon Swain, Brian Vickers, John Ward, Christiania Whitehead, and Harvey Yunis.

For their support over the very long period in which I have written the studies leading up to this book I must thank students, colleagues, and administrative staff in the Department of English and Comparative Literary Studies, University of Warwick, and the Warburg Institute, University of London. Two of the people there who taught me most about scholarship, rhetoric, and writing are acknowledged in the dedication, but this is a place where I should also like to remember Paul and Dorothy Behm, R. W. Burchfield, John Goode, June Mack, Anne Marie Meyer, Charles B. Schmitt, and William V. Whitehead. Once again I must express my profound personal gratitude to my wife Vicki Behm, to Johanna and Mike, William and Naomi, Emily, and Rosy, and to our extended family, especially Bill, Brian, Carolyn, and Katie.

Contents

List of Tables

1

Introduction and Origins

This is the first comprehensive history of renaissance rhetoric.[1] It is largely a history of the development of new ideas and texts, and of their circulation, in print and through systems of education. Larger historical changes, which affect the support that a society gives to the discipline, are an essential foundation for the story, but my main focus will be on a host of individual thinkers and their works. Renaissance rhetoric was created by numerous individual contributions, such as Trapezuntius's incorporation of Greek rhetoric, Valla's critique of Aristotelian logic, Agricola's use of the topics to analyse classical literature, and Erasmus's exercises in the possibilities of expression. Later textbook writers like Melanchthon, Ramus, Soarez, and Caussin made new syntheses of the subject, adopting some classical and earlier renaissance ideas and rejecting others. We shall see that there are common themes, but the individual interventions take priority. I hope that this book will enable anyone who wants to read a particular renaissance rhetorician to find out about the historical development of the subject, to identify sources and comparable texts which should be read, and, in many cases, to obtain an outline of that writer's contribution. I hope it will provide a reliable basis for further studies of the impact of rhetoric on renaissance culture and history.

Rhetoric is a training in writing and delivering speeches, which originated in the Greek city-states and which became the principal form of higher education throughout the ancient world. As a subject rhetoric is characterized by the breadth of its concerns. Rhetoric manuals typically

[1] Earlier helpful studies to which I am indebted include J. Monfasani, 'Humanism and Rhetoric', in A. Rabil, jun. (ed.), *Renaissance Humanism: Foundations, Forms and Legacy*, 3 vols. (Philadelphia, 1988), iii. 171–235; B. Vickers, *In Defence of Rhetoric* (Oxford, 1988), 254–93; T. Conley, *Rhetoric in the European Tradition* (New York, 1990), 109–62, 181–6; G. A. Kennedy, *Classical Rhetoric and its Christian and Secular Tradition from Ancient to Modern Times*, 2nd edn. (Chapel Hill, NC, 1999), 226–58; M. Fumaroli (ed.), *Histoire de la rhétorique dans l'Europe moderne 1450–1950* (Paris, 1999), 45–517, M. DeCoursey, 'Continental European Rhetoricians 1400–1600', in E. Malone (ed.), *British Rhetoricians and Logicians 1500–1660*, 1st ser., *Dictionary of Literary Biography*, 236 (2001), 309–43; M. Hinz, 'Rhetorik II.3 Humanismus', in G. Ueding (ed.), *Historisches Wörterbuch der Rhetorik*, vii (Tübingen, 2005), 1505–23.

cover and connect an enormously wide range of doctrines, including the training of the memory, the use of voice and gesture, the ways to discover and present arguments, the arousal of emotions, self-presentation, selection of vocabulary, the organization of a speech, patterning of words and sounds within a sentence, metaphor, and allegory. Because classical rhetoric presents so many different elements for the speaker to consider, the manuals suggest only a small number of variables in each case, so, for example, they say that there are two types of audience or three levels of style.[2] Once pupils had mastered the basic syllabus, their practical training, as apprentices to an established advocate, would presumably have broadened their sense of the different possibilities at each stage. Another consequence of the breadth of rhetoric as a subject is that manuals of the whole subject tend to be quite conservative, as if they feared that omitting or altering one of the elements might cause unexpected problems elsewhere in the complex subject. Perhaps for this reason it was only in the renaissance that new manuals of the whole of rhetoric came to be composed.

Rhetoric and the renaissance are inextricably linked. The origins of the Italian revival of classical Latin are to be found among the teachers of rhetoric and letter-writing in northern Italian universities around 1300. In Paul Kristeller's influential definition, rhetoric is one of the characteristics of renaissance humanism.[3] Rhetoric appealed to the humanists because it trained pupils to use the full resources of the ancient languages, and because it offered a genuinely classical view of the nature of language and its effective use in the world. Between 1460 and 1620 more than 800 editions of classical rhetoric texts were printed all over Europe. Thousands of new rhetoric books were written, from Scotland and Spain to Sweden and Poland, mostly in Latin, but also in Dutch, English, French, German, Hebrew, Italian, Spanish, and Welsh. A few of these new works went through more than a hundred editions. This *History of Renaissance Rhetoric* will concentrate on the changes in rhetorical doctrine which these new publications announced.

As well as describing the most important individual contributions to the development of renaissance rhetoric, this history aims to analyse the new ideas which renaissance thinkers contributed to rhetorical theory. Renaissance writers rethought the way in which argument works, refining the tools of argument and testing the strength of different types of argument.

[2] K. Spang, 'Dreistillehre', in G. Ueding (ed.), *Historisches Wörterbuch der Rhetorik*, ii (Tübingen, 1994), 921–72.

[3] P. O. Kristeller, 'The Humanist Movement', in his *Renaissance Thought and its Sources* (New York, 1979), 21–32.

They reconsidered the relationship between narrative and argument and found new roles for argument within speeches. Renaissance writers rejected the division of rhetoric into three genres, proposing a range of different purposes, forms, and structures for discourse. They found new uses for the principles of logic and rhetoric as tools of textual analysis. They re-examined classical rhetoric's analysis of style, using the figures and tropes but incorporating the competing theory of ideas of style and giving new attention to amplification, *copia*, and brevity. Renaissance rhetoricians gave new emphasis to the role of proverbs, maxims, comparisons, and examples in writing. They reconsidered the place of emotion and play in the effective use of language. Writing a manageable history of rhetoric over 240 years and many different countries requires considerable simplification and omission but I want this history to give students of writing in other periods a reasonably full idea of the new doctrines of renaissance rhetoric, even where these were not widely taken up later.

It is now possible to write a comprehensive history of renaissance rhetoric because of the labours of Lawrence D. Green and James J. Murphy in producing a reliable *Renaissance Rhetoric Short-Title Catalogue*. Since it would be impossible to read all the 3,842 titles, their listing of all editions provides a defensible statistical basis for selecting a corpus of the new rhetoric manuals written in the renaissance. At the same time one needs to be aware of two problems which Green and Murphy point out.[4] In the first place their figures are only as good as the library and union catalogues they have worked from. My suspicion is that Italian and Spanish provincial libraries will eventually be found to contain a fair number of editions (especially Italian editions) not so far listed. Secondly there are problems in the definition of an edition. Some of the items which appear in the *Renaissance Rhetoric Short-Title Catalogue* as separate editions will turn out to be variant title-pages of the same edition.[5] Furthermore it would be wrong to assume that all editions comprised the same number of copies. But Green and Murphy's work has been sufficiently comprehensive that the rough groups into which I have mentally sorted the different texts (one to two editions, around ten editions, twenty or more, fifty or more, 100 or more) will not be altered much if all these problems are ever resolved. The figures one can derive from their book must be used with

[4] L. D. Green and J. J. Murphy (eds.), *Renaissance Rhetoric Short-Title Catalogue 1460–1700* (Aldershot, 2006), pp. xi–xii, xvii–xxi.

[5] e.g. Green and Murphy list forty-nine edns. of Montaigne's *Essais* before 1620; D. Maskell and R. Sayce, *A Descriptive Bibliography of Montaigne's Essais* (London, 1983), pp. xxviii–90, reduce this figure to twenty-one.

appropriate caution, but they are the best we have and at present it would be impossible to write a history without their help.

This history will have four main themes: the consequences of greater knowledge of ancient literature and the classical world; the place of rhetoric in education; the impact of ideas from dialectic on rhetoric and vice versa; and the adaptation of the tenets of classical rhetoric to a changed world. The growing availability of printed books was an important factor in the development of renaissance rhetoric. Where fifteenth-century authors like George Trapezuntius, Lorenzo Valla, and Rudolph Agricola wrote mainly for their pupils and friends and the spread of their ideas depended on personal contacts, later rhetoricians like Erasmus, Melanchthon, and Ramus composed their works for booksellers who had the means to provide them with a large readership throughout northern Europe. Not coincidentally the latter three were involved (sometimes indirectly) in the founding of new schools and the reform of existing ones. Printing also meant that teachers throughout Europe could easily own several different classical rhetorical texts instead of being dependent on one or two.

While printing helped circulate humanist ideas and rhetoric textbooks throughout Europe, humanist study of the Bible and the printing of religious pamphlets and propaganda also spread the Reformation which eventually divided Europe into two largely distinct intellectual camps. Later sixteenth-century rhetoric manuals tended to take on a confessional flavour so that textbooks by Protestant authors could not be printed in Catholic countries and vice versa. Once Erasmus's works were put on the Index devout Catholic authors could not even refer or acknowledge their debts to him. The religious wars between small German states, the Dutch revolt against Spanish domination, and the civil wars of religion in France further disrupted intellectual life and polarized opinion. Within each camp rhetoric was cultivated as a means of promulgating correct belief and suppressing heresy.

The classical rhetoric textbooks which were most used in the renaissance (*Rhetorica ad Herennium* and Cicero's *De inventione*) were well-known in the middle ages but new textual discoveries and a wider knowledge of different aspects of classical culture altered the way they were read in the renaissance. The rediscovery of Greek ideas about rhetoric, through translation and commentary on Aristotle's *Rhetoric* and the works of Hermogenes, was first felt in the mid-fifteenth century but it took almost 150 years to establish a consensus about the way in which Greek rhetoric could be absorbed within a mainly Ciceronian Latin tradition. The new emphasis which many renaissance rhetoricians placed on arousing emotions in an audience was partly a result of reading

Aristotle's *Rhetoric*. In the later sixteenth century Hermogenes's *On Ideas of Style* prompted a rethinking of approaches to style, always regarded as one of the most useful parts of rhetoric. Because my descriptions of renaissance textbooks often emphasize their debts to particular classical manuals I give outlines of the contents of the latter in Chapters 2 and 3. Main discussion of a particular text appears in bold in the index.

The history of rhetoric is inevitably a history of textbooks, but textbooks only really make sense in relation to the syllabuses and schools in which they are taught. Schools are always local, yet humanist educational theory spread across Europe and the textbook market in the sixteenth century was essentially international.[6] In my previous book I analysed Tudor rhetoric in terms of the skills which pupils learnt from the texts they read and the exercises they did in schools and universities.[7] I lack the knowledge to conduct the same sort of study for the whole of Europe over 240 years but from time to time I consider the role which textbooks I am describing played in particular school and university syllabuses. Rhetoric was usually given an important place in humanist educational programmes, as the culmination of the study of Latin language and literature which occupied the years of schooling. It seems that the boundary between school and university operated differently in different places. Some colleges in universities were in effect attached grammar schools whose job was to ensure that students were properly prepared in reading and writing Latin. On the other hand some schools progressed far into what would elsewhere have been considered the territory of the university, teaching not just logic but even theology, medicine, and law. Equally it seems that teachers with humanist leanings could introduce courses in rhetoric and rhetorically influenced dialectic in places where the statutes prescribed Aristotelian logic. The amount of emphasis given to Greek varied considerably, but Guarino, Sturm, and the Jesuits aimed at a thorough training in Greek.[8]

[6] Some general works on renaissance education: W. Woodward, *Studies in Education during the Age of the Renaissance* (Cambridge, 1906); E. Garin, *L'educazione in Europa 1400–1600* (Bari, 1957); E. Garin (ed.), *Il pensiero pedagogico dello Umanesimo* (Florence, 1958); J. Simon, *Education and Society in Tudor England* (Cambridge, 1966); A. T. Grafton and L. Jardine, *From Humanism to the Humanities* (London, 1986); P. Grendler, *Schooling in Renaissance Italy* (Baltimore, 1989); N. Hammerstein (ed.), *Handbuch der deutschen Bildungsgeschichte*, i (Munich, 1996); H. de Ridder-Symoens (ed.), *A History of the University in Europe*, ii. *Universities of Early Modern Europe* (Cambridge, 1996); C. Kallendorf, *Humanist Educational Treatises* (Cambridge, Mass., 2002).

[7] P. Mack, *Elizabethan Rhetoric: Theory and Practice* (Cambridge, 2002), 11–75.

[8] A few works on specific schools and universities: E. Vinet, *Schola Aquitanica (1583)*, ed. L. Massebieau (Paris, 1886); T. W. Baldwin, *Shakspere's Small Latine and Lesse Greeke* (Urbana, Ill., 1944), Peter Sharratt, 'Petrus Ramus and the Reform of the University', in P. Sharratt (ed.), *French Renaissance Studies 1540–1740* (Edinburgh, 1976), 4–20;

While the main aim of the grammar school was to teach Latin language and literature (and often Greek as well), the highest form of the school quite often studied a classical textbook of the whole of rhetoric, usually *Rhetorica ad Herennium*. From the earliest stage of learning grammar there was an emphasis on elegant phrasing and on techniques for composing Latin prose. In many schools the pupils were taught letter-writing and the tropes and figures before any other part of rhetoric. Teachers of literary texts often reinforced pupils' understanding of rhetorical theory by commenting on the use of tropes, figures, amplification, and structure. Some schools read a wide range of classical texts but there was a core of texts in which most schoolboys across Europe would have done some reading: Cicero's *Epistles*, *De officiis*, and *Orations*, Terence, Virgil's *Eclogues* and *Aeneid*, Ovid, Horace, or another lyric poet, Caesar or Sallust. Composition exercises were linked both to pupils' reading (for example in Cicero's earlier letters) and to composition manuals (such as letter-writing manuals, *progymnasmata*, and Erasmus's *De copia*). Modern rhetoric texts, such as those by Melanchthon, Talon, and Soarez, were often used as a preparation for reading the classical manuals and sometimes replaced them. While for most of the sixteenth century most Italian schoolboys would have read a classical manual of the whole of rhetoric before leaving school, in some northern countries modern manuals would be read at school, with the classical manuals left for the university.

Logic remained far more important to the university syllabus than rhetoric but there is strong evidence for some teaching of rhetoric at most universities. University was the most likely place for people to study Quintilian, Aristotle's *Rhetoric*, and Cicero's *De oratore*. The professor of rhetoric often taught classical Latin and Greek texts, partly as illustrations of the practical application of rhetorical theory. Many university students were trained in the rhetorical and logical reading of classical texts. The study of Aristotelian logic was often introduced by a modern dialectic manual which in many cases emphasized the connections between logic and rhetoric.

J. K. McConica (ed.), *The History of the University of Oxford*, iii. *The Collegiate University* (Oxford, 1986); D. Knox, 'Order, Reason and Oratory: Rhetoric in Protestant Latin Schools', in P. Mack (ed.), *Renaissance Rhetoric* (Basingstoke, 1994), 63–80; L. W. Spitz and B. Sher Tinsley, *Johann Sturm on Education* (St Louis, 1995); Francisco Javier Alejo Montes, *La Universidad de Salamanca bajo Felipe II: 1575–98* (Burgos, 1998); R. Black, *Humanism and Education in Medieval and Renaissance Italy* (Cambridge, 2001); P. Grendler, *The Universities of the Italian Renaissance* (Baltimore, 2002); A. Bianchi (ed.), *Ratio atque institutio studiorum Societatis Iesu* (Milan, 2002); Luis E. Rodríguez-San Pedro Bezares (ed.), *Historia de la Universidad de Salamanca*, ii (Salamanca, 2004).

Some types of renaissance rhetoric textbook were written to fulfil the demands of the school syllabus. For example Erasmus's *De copia*, the most printed of all renaissance rhetoric texts, which introduced a highly influential new approach to writing, owed its origin primarily to his own private teaching practice and secondarily to his wish to provide a textbook for his friend John Colet's foundation of St Paul's School. His much printed *De conscribendis epistolis* and *Adagia* were also intended to assist schoolboys express themselves more effectively in Latin.

Late antique theories of the division of knowledge and medieval university syllabuses meant that at the higher level rhetoric was always studied alongside dialectic (equivalent to logic).[9] Rhetoric encouraged dialecticians to concentrate on the practical application of persuasion, while dialectical principles opened up questions about the traditional divisions and rules of rhetoric. In the mid-fifteenth century textbooks on dialectical subjects by Lorenzo Valla, George Trapezuntius, and Rudolph Agricola introduced new ways of thinking about arguing in everyday language and in literary texts. In the early sixteenth century influential authors like Caesarius, Melanchthon, Ramus, Talon, and Wilson wrote coordinated textbooks on both subjects. Renaissance dialectic was an important driver for change in rhetoric.

Like their medieval predecessors renaissance rhetoricians questioned some of the underlying assumptions of the rhetoric textbook, which were based on the conditions in which speeches were given in Greek city-states: that there were only three kinds of speech, that every text should have four basic sections, that only certain types of argument could be effective in each genre. Some authors insisted on the range of possible model structures in which the general principles of rhetorical invention and organization could be applied, while others wrote detailed instructions for the arguments and structures of different genres of writing or different types of letter. Letter-writing manuals and preaching manuals, which developed from medieval textbooks, were places where the principles of classical rhetoric could be adapted to early modern conditions of writing and oratory.

Renaissance rhetoric textbooks can be divided into five main genres. Alongside the manuals covering the whole of rhetoric (1) and dialectic (2), we find a small number of textbooks which bridge the two subjects or which deal with both within a wider encyclopedic treatment of the trivium or the seven liberal arts. The main historical narrative of this book, running from Chapter 3 to Chapter 9 is concerned with manuals of the

[9] E. Eggs, 'Argumentation. 1. Rhetorik', in G. Ueding (ed.), *Historisches Wörterbuch der Rhetorik*, i (Tübingen, 1992), 914–86.

whole of rhetoric and dialectic, beginning with fifteenth-century Italy (Chapter 3), especially Lorenzo Valla and George Trapezuntius of Crete, and continuing with Agricola (Chapter 4), Erasmus (Chapter 5), Melanchthon and northern Europe 1519–45 (Chapter 6), Ramus and northern Europe 1545–80 (Chapter 7), southern Europe in the sixteenth century (Chapter 8), and ending with Keckermann, Vossius, and Caussin (Chapter 9).

Two very popular genres associated with the schoolroom, the handbook of tropes and figures (genre 3) and the letter-writing manual (4), are the subjects of Chapters 10 and 11. Other grammar-school texts are discussed in Chapter 5. Finally an extensive group of preaching manuals (genre 5) is discussed in Chapter 12. Since they also belong to the higher university faculties I have also included here some consideration of the much smaller group of dialectics adapted to the use of the legal profession.

One of the most important fields of literary production within renaissance rhetoric consisted in writing commentaries on classical rhetoric textbooks (particularly on the works of Aristotle, Cicero, Hermogenes, and Quintilian) and rhetorical and logical commentaries on classical literature (especially on Cicero's speeches, on Terence, Virgil, Horace, and Ovid). I have given some discussion of these works in Chapter 2, on the diffusion of classical rhetoric in the renaissance, in Chapter 6, in relation to Melanchthon's commentaries, and in Chapter 8, concentrating on Italian commentaries on Aristotle's *Rhetoric*. This is an area in which there is room for much more work.[10]

The History of Renaissance Rhetoric is a Europe-wide history and it takes place largely in the Latin language. Latin rhetoric textbooks printed in Venice, Paris, Lyon, Basel, or Cologne quickly found readers across the whole of Europe. At the same time, with the growth of printing in the vernacular, more of intellectual and practical life was taking place in the modern European languages. This history must respond to both these demands. The new ideas almost always originated in the Latin tradition and the main historical narrative of this book will consider in detail the innovative ideas of the major Latin rhetorical thinkers between Lorenzo Valla and Gerardus Vossius, but vernacular rhetorics, which were never produced in so many editions as Latin ones, can tell us a great deal

[10] J. O. Ward, 'Artificiosa Eloquentia in the Middle Ages', Ph.D. thesis, University of Toronto, 1972, 'Renaissance Commentators on Ciceronian Rhetoric', in J. J. Murphy (ed.), *Renaissance Eloquence* (Berkeley, Calif., 1983), 126–73; V. Cox and J. O. Ward (eds.), *The Rhetoric of Cicero in its Medieval and Early Renaissance Commentary Tradition* (Leiden, 2006); L. D. Green, 'Renaissance Commentators on Aristotle's *Rhetoric*', in W. Fortenbaugh and D. Mirhady (eds.), *Peripatetic Rhetoric after Aristotle* (New Brunswick, NJ, 1994), 320–48; M. Pade (ed.), *On Renaissance Commentary* (Hildesheim, 2005).

about the adaptation of rhetorical ideas to a more socially diverse audience than the well-off males who attended grammar school and university. In Chapter 13 I discuss the general characteristics of vernacular rhetoric and some particular features of the traditions of renaissance rhetoric in Italian, French, German, Spanish, and English, considering some examples in detail. This is another area where I could have done more but in this aspect at least the interested reader is at present better served by the national literary histories than is the person who wants to understand the Europe-wide Latin tradition.[11] In Chapter 14 I summarize the main developments in renaissance rhetoric and offer suggestions and bibliography on the impact of rhetorical training on renaissance reading, practical behaviour, and culture.

On issues of chronology I have tried to be practical and inclusive. Later in this chapter I shall say something about the origins of renaissance rhetoric and the slow process by which it began to differentiate itself from medieval rhetoric, but my narrative proper begins at the turn of the fifteenth century with Loschi, Bruni, the school of Guarino, and the rhetorical theories of Lorenzo Valla and George Trapezuntius of Crete. A group of late sixteenth- and early seventeenth-century rhetorics suggest themselves as the terminus, because of their importance in the seventeenth century but also because they do not yet exhibit the new features which one associates with the response to Cartesianism and the concentration on a more stylistic rhetoric. Soarez's *De arte rhetorica libri tres* (1562) was the most successful rhetoric of the second half of the sixteenth century and became the textbook of choice in the Jesuit schools established across Europe and in the new worlds of America and Asia. Keckermann's *Systema rhetoricae* (1606) was an encyclopedic survey of the state of rhetoric which provided the basis for seventeenth-century teachers of writing at the universities at the margins of Europe. Vossius's *Institutiones oratoriae* (1605) and his adaptations of it in 1621 and 1626 provided pupils with a primarily Aristotelian rhetoric textbook, supplemented with Ciceronian elements, while Caussin's *Eloquentiae sacrae et humanae parallela* (1619) collected together the teachings of classical rhetoric likely to be useful to the emotive preacher of the *grand siècle*.

I have decided to exclude some types of textbook from this study. Sometimes the basic grammar textbook, alongside the rules of accidence (the largest part of the book, to be learnt by heart) and syntax, included

[11] W. S. Howell, *Logic and Rhetoric in England 1500–1700* (Princeton, 1956); M. Fumaroli, *L'Age de l'éloquence* (Geneva, 1980); K. Meerhoff, *Rhétorique et poétique au XVIe siècle en France* (Leiden, 1986); L. López Grigera, *La retórica en la España del Siglo de Oro* (Salamanca, 1994).

the tropes and figures and also rules for letter-writing. In general I have excluded grammar books and texts on usage and elegance from this history on the ground that they belong to the history of grammar, but I refer to some grammar texts, notably Perotti's influential *Rudimenta grammatices*, in Chapters 3, 10, and 11. It would be possible to argue for the inclusion also of works on poetics, which undoubtedly show many debts to the rhetorical tradition (though there seems to be relatively little influence in the other direction, from poetics to rhetoric), but these would considerably complicate the narrative and have generally been thoroughly studied within the separate national traditions.[12] I have avoided discussion of works on memory (one of the five skills of the orator), though I mention the presence of a discussion of memory in the minority of rhetoric manuals which include it. The renaissance art of memory has been thoroughly examined by Frances Yates and Mary Carruthers.[13] Since rhetoric manuals in general do not discuss emblems, I have omitted any account of emblem books, even though there are probably similarities of approach and rhetorical assumptions may have influenced the way emblems were used.[14]

I shall end this introductory chapter with an outline of the origins of humanism and of renaissance rhetoric. Paul Kristeller describes renaissance humanism as a movement rooted in grammar and rhetoric which gave new impetus in a number of different fields. Renaissance humanism encouraged the study of texts, the learning of Greek and the analysis of Greek texts, and translation from Greek and Latin into the vernacular languages of Europe. Outside classical scholarship, humanists established new ideals of eloquence and new standards for Latin expression. They made important contributions in poetry, history, and moral philosophy.[15] Kristeller saw this new movement as originating especially in the fields of grammar and rhetoric, notably among teachers of *ars dictaminis*.[16]

[12] M. T. Herrick, *The Fusion of Horatian and Aristotelian Criticism 1531–1555* (Urbana, Ill., 1946); *Comic Theory in the Sixteenth Century* (Urbana, Ill., 1950); B. Weinberg, *A History of Literary Criticism in the Italian Renaissance*, 2 vols. (Chicago, 1961); B. Hathaway, *The Age of Criticism: The Late Renaissance in Italy* (Ithaca, NY, 1962); O. B. Hardison, *The Enduring Monument* (Chapel Hill, NC, 1962); G. Norton (ed.), *The Cambridge History of Literary Criticism*, iii. *The Renaissance* (Cambridge, 1999), P. Galland-Hallyn and F. Hallyn (eds.), *Poétiques de la Renaissance* (Geneva, 2001).

[13] F. Yates, 'The Ciceronian Art of Memory', in *Medioevo e Rinascimento: Studi in Onore di Bruno Nardi*, ii (Florence, 1955), 873–903; *The Art of Memory* (London, 1966); M. Carruthers, *The Book of Memory* (Cambridge, 1990).

[14] See P. M. Daly, *The English Emblem and the Continental Tradition* (New York, 1988); M. Bath, *Speaking Pictures: English Emblem Books and Renaissance Culture* (Harlow, 1994); and the Glasgow emblem website: http://www.emblems.arts.gla.ac.uk/.

[15] Kristeller, *Renaissance Thought*, 88–98.

[16] Ibid. 91.

While Kristeller's description of humanism has been very widely accepted, because it combines a well-defined focus with a picture of the wide range of activities to which humanists contributed, his account of the origins of humanism has been modified by Ronald Witt, who has pointed out the relative belatedness of humanist reforms in rhetoric. Witt showed that the earliest humanist writing was the Latin poetry of Lovato dei Lovati (1240/1–1309) written in Padua in 1267/8, with classicizing prose writing following only with the historical works of his compatriot Albertino Mussato (1261–1329) from 1315. Lovato's Latin poetry was prompted by competition with French poetry and a wish to assert the relevance of the Roman cultural heritage to the political situation of Duecento Italy.[17] This also explains the group of Italian translations of Cicero's rhetorical works and orations which Brunetto Latini (*c.*1225–93) and other Florentines made in the Duecento and which continued to circulate in the Trecento.[18] It was in poetry and in private forms of prose that classicizing Latin composition first took root. Public speaking and official letter-writing remained tied to the medieval *ars dictaminis* until, under the influence of Coluccio Salutati (1331–1406), Giovanni Malpaghini (1346–1422?) taught the fifth generation of humanists rhetoric in Florence.[19] Manuscripts of commentaries suggest that while *Rhetorica ad Herennium* and Cicero's *De inventione* were widely lectured on in Italy in the scholastic manner from about 1250, the new classicizing movement did not take hold much before the commentary by Guarino Guarini, written around 1420 and widely circulated thereafter.[20]

According to Witt, Pier Paolo Vergerio (1368/70–1444), among those attracted to Florence by the revival of the Studio in 1385, will serve as an example of this fifth generation, the first to aspire to fully classical standards in oratory.[21] In his *De ingenuis moribus* Vergerio regards history, moral philosophy, and eloquence as the proper studies of free-born youth.

> Through philosophy we can acquire correct views, which is of the first importance in everything; through eloquence we can speak with weight

[17] R. Witt, *In the Footsteps of the Ancients: The Origins of Humanism from Lovati to Bruni* (Leiden, 2000), 1–3, 17–19, 95–101.

[18] Witt, *Footsteps*, 178–93; Cox, 'Ciceronian Rhetoric in Late Medieval Italy', in Cox and Ward (eds.), *The Rhetoric of Cicero in its Medieval and Early Renaissance Commentary Tradition* (Leiden, 2006), 112–13.

[19] Witt, *Footsteps*, 292, 338–70.

[20] J. O. Ward, *Ciceronian Rhetoric in Treatise, Scholion and Commentary* (Turnhout, 1995), 205–9; Cox, 'Ciceronian Rhetoric', 109–36.

[21] Witt, *Footsteps*, 370–87. J. McManamon, *Pierpaolo Vergerio the Elder: The Humanist as Orator* (Binghamton, NY, 1996).

> and polish, which is the one skill that most effectively wins over the minds of the multitude; but history helps us with both.[22]

He singles out rhetoric as the discipline which used to be part of a nobleman's education but has been most neglected. Instead of the glory which used to be obtained through forensic oratory or the benefits to the state of wise deliberation, we now favour the trading of laws or unadorned reasons. Perhaps prophetically he notes that only demonstrative oratory is much practised at present.[23] But Vergerio's pessimism was premature and may have been adopted for tactical purposes. Within a generation and for more than two hundred years afterwards, rhetoric would return to the centre of liberal education.

[22] 'Per philosophiam quidem possumus recte sentire quod est in omni re primum; per eloquentiam graviter ornateque dicere qua una re maxime conciliantur multitudinis animi; per historiam in utrumque iuvamur.' Kallendorf, *Humanist Educational Treatises*, 48–9.

[23] Ibid. 50–3.

2

Diffusion and Reception of Classical Rhetoric

The textual discoveries of the early humanists and the recovery of direct access to Greek rhetorical texts prompted considerable changes in renaissance rhetoric. Where medieval study of ancient rhetoric had focused on *Rhetorica ad Herennium* and Cicero's *De inventione*, assisted by parts of Quintilian and *De oratore*, and from the thirteenth century by William of Moerbeke's Latin translation of Aristotle's *Rhetoric*,[1] renaissance scholars had the benefit of additional orations by Cicero found in the fourteenth century, of the *Vetus Clunaciensis*, containing better texts and further speeches found by Poggio in 1415, of the complete Quintilian and Asconius discovered at St Gall in 1416, of the eight new speeches found in 1417, of the discovery of the complete *De oratore* and *Orator*, and the unknown *Brutus* by Gerardo Landriani in 1421, and of the Greek rhetorical texts brought to Italy in the fifteenth century.[2]

The *Renaissance Rhetoric Short-Title Catalogue*, 2nd edition, edited by Green and Murphy shows beyond doubt that the major rhetorical works of Aristotle, Cicero, and Quintilian were widely available in fifteenth- and sixteenth-century Europe.[3] The pattern of publication, together with what we so far know about ownership, of the major texts suggests that rhetoric books could be produced in a few major centres of printing (such as Venice, Paris, Lyon, Cologne, and Basel) for distribution throughout Europe.[4] In the fifteenth century rhetoric works were printed

[1] L. D. Reynolds and N. Wilson mention 98 surviving manuscripts of William's translation of Aristotle's *Rhetoric*: *Scribes and Scholars*, 2nd edn. (Oxford, 1974), 234. B. Schneider, *Die mittelalterlichen greichisch-lateinischen Uebersetzungen der Aristotelischen Rhetorik* (Berlin, 1971), 5–9.

[2] Reynolds and Wilson, *Scribes and Scholars*, 116–23, 131–4.

[3] This chapter depends entirely on the bibliographical labours of Green and Murphy, and indeed this book would have been impossible to write without theirs.

[4] M. Lane Ford, 'The Importation of Printed Books', in L. Hellinga and J. B. Trapp (eds.), *The Cambridge History of the Book in Britain*, iii (Cambridge, 1999), 179–201; Julian Roberts, 'The Latin Trade', in J. Barnard and D. F. McKenzie (eds.), *The Cambridge History of the Book in Britain*, iv (Cambridge, 2002), 141–73; E. S. Leedham-Green, *Books*

mainly in Italy. From about 1520 northern European editions became more numerous. Green and Murphy's lists suggest that the printing of Ciceronian rhetoric started to decline around 1570 and became rather rare after 1590.

In the later chapters of this book I shall sometimes note that particular renaissance textbooks omitted certain doctrines which previously formed part of the rhetoric textbook. Because the major classical texts were printed so frequently teachings omitted from modern textbooks remained available to teachers and readers. So, for example, in Chapter 10 I shall point out that the most printed early sixteenth-century handbooks of the tropes and figures omitted the figures of thought. This may suggest that the figures of thought were not taught in grammar schools. Nevertheless at the same time large numbers of editions were produced of *Rhetorica ad Herennium* and *Institutio oratoria*, so the figures of thought remained available and were later incorporated in other, less often printed, handbooks of the figures. Modern handbooks were often taught before the classical manuals so they may have directed pupils' attention to certain doctrines more than they prevented access to others. In the case of the topics of invention, a new emphasis on the topics in renaissance textbooks seems to prompt a higher level of printing of Cicero's *Topica*.

The most successful rhetoric text remained the *Rhetorica ad Herennium*, which was generally attributed to Cicero. This continues the trend noted by John Ward of the increasing numbers of *Rhetorica ad Herennium* manuscripts in the early fifteenth century.[5] Even after Regio's proof that this work was not by Cicero, first published in 1491, gradually gathered currency, with the result that the text began to be ascribed to *incertus auctor*, it continued to be printed in collections of Cicero's rhetorics. Most commonly *Rhetorica ad Herennium* appeared with Cicero's *De inventione*, sometimes alongside other texts as well. Green and Murphy record a total of 143 editions of this combination between 1460 and 1620.[6] In addition there were forty editions of *Rhetorica ad Herennium* without *De inventione*, whereas *De inventione* appeared only four times without *Rhetorica ad Herennium*.

in Cambridge Inventories, 2 vols. (Cambridge, 1986); R. J. Fehrenbach and E. S. Leedham-Green (eds.), *Private Libraries in Renaissance England*, 5 vols. (Binghamton, NY, 1993–8).

[5] J. O. Ward, 'Renaissance Commentators on Ciceronian Rhetoric', in J. J. Murphy (ed.), *Renaissance Eloquence* (Berkeley, Calif., 1983), 128–46.

[6] In arriving at these figures, as in all the numbers cited here, I have ignored multi-volume complete-works editions, which tell us more about the importance of the author than about the demand for particular works. For the record Green and Murphy list forty-nine editions of Cicero's complete works before 1620.

The pattern of production is very steady. Between 1470 and 1509 there were generally ten to fifteen editions in each decade (the majority of the editions before 1501 were Italian). Between 1510 and 1569 there were generally around twenty editions per decade (in which an even division between Italy and the North gives way to a predominance of northern printings, especially from Paris, Lyon, Basel, and Strasbourg), with a tailing off to around ten editions per decade in 1570–89, before two final editions in 1590. It would be interesting to know why there were no editions of *Rhetorica ad Herennium* between 1591 and 1642, but we should remember that the second-hand book-market in a text so often reprinted would have ensured its availability through the early decades of the seventeenth century. There were also eleven editions (1475–1566) of three Italian translations.

Because it was so well-established and because it gave a complete account of the subject, *Rhetorica ad Herennium* provided fifteenth- and sixteenth-century readers with their understanding of the structure of rhetoric and its principal doctrines. It outlined and then described the three genres of rhetoric established by Aristotle (judicial, deliberative, and epideictic: 1.2), the five skills which the orator had to master (invention, disposition, style, memory, and delivery: 1.3) and the six parts of the oration (*exordium*, narration, division, confirmation, refutation, and conclusion: 1.4).[7] These three initial divisions generate the organization of the whole book. The overarching shape is provided by the five skills, though with a slight change of order: invention (1.4–3.15), disposition (3.16–18), delivery (3.19–27), memory (3.28–40) and style (4). The section on invention is organized according to the genres, concentrating on the judicial or courtroom speech (1.4–2) and treating the deliberative or political speech (3.1–9) and the epideictic speech, dispensing praise or blame, generally on a social occasion such as a wedding or a funeral (3.10–15), as variants. Each of these sections is organized according to the six parts of the oration. Thus the author begins by explaining that the exordium should aim to make the audience attentive, receptive, and well-disposed, and suggesting ways of achieving these aims depending on

[7] In general I will write about the four parts of the oration (introduction, narration, argument, and conclusion) as outlined by Aristotle. Other versions, like that in *Rhetorica ad Herennium*, observe the same structure but treat subdivisions as separate sections. Thus narration is divided into narration and proposition (or division) and argument into confirmation (arguments in favour) and refutation (of opposing arguments) to give a six-part oration. Renaissance authors who write of four parts may be aware of Aristotle, while those who write of six may be following *Rhetorica ad Herennium*. The key difference is the division, where the speaker explains where he agrees with his opponent and what the points of disagreement are. This section suits judicial oratory more than other genres and is found in *Ad Herennium* (1.10.17) and *De inventione* (1.22.31–3), but not in Aristotle.

whether the audience is hostile or favourable (1.6–11). Then he moves on to the narration in the judicial speech (1.12–16), which should be brief, clear, and plausible. In the division (1.10.17) the speaker should state what he and the opponent agree on, set out the main issues of disagreement, and list the points he will make.

Within his account of invention the unknown author gives most attention to the method of constructing arguments in judicial cases, in which he sets out the theory of status. In any law case the speaker must determine the point of disagreement between himself and his adversary. It will be the duty of the speaker to address all his arguments to this. Such points of disagreement can be organized into types and the student of rhetoric is provided with suggestions for arguments which should prove effective for each type of dispute. So, for example, the prosecutor and defender may disagree about whether the defendant committed the crime (this would be an example of the conjectural issue) or whether the action that he agrees that he committed was in fact a crime (issue of quality). In conjectural cases one may argue about the nature of the evidence or about whether it is likely on the basis of his character that the defendant would have performed the action alleged. Some types of status are helpful in thinking about arguments in a wide range of situations; others appear to be restricted to technicalities of Roman law. As well as offering suggestions for the kinds of argument one might make, this section of the work also describes a preferred five-part form in which an argument should be expressed (2.28–30) and various errors which should be avoided by a speaker or exposed by his adversary (2.31–46).

The conclusion to the speech should consist of a summary of the main points made, followed by an appeal to the emotions of the judges. The unknown author sets out ten arguments designed to elicit anger at a crime committed and a contrasting set of ways of arousing pity for the accused (2.47–50). This discussion of emotion is brief and entirely devoted to tactics appropriate to prosecutor and defender in a judicial case. Deliberative orations should be devoted to promoting the advantage of the state, which may consist either in security (including financial as well as military power) and honour (which is subdivided into what is right and what is praiseworthy) (3.1–7). These topics, which are discussed at greater length in Cicero's *De inventione* and *De officiis,* formed a foundation for many later discussions of ethical behaviour in practical life. Invention for demonstrative oratory consists of a list of headings for describing a person which were also much drawn on by later writers: external circumstances (including family, education, and wealth), physical attributes (such as strength, beauty, and health), and qualities of character (for example, wisdom, justice, courage, and their contraries) (3.9–15).

Because *Rhetorica ad Herennium*, like other classical rhetorics, organizes the treatise on invention around the parts of the oration, the treatise on disposition has, in effect, been pre-empted. We already know what the structure of the oration will be and the only issues left for disposition are to suggest occasions on which for tactical purposes one of the elements may be omitted or the order may be changed and to make a few comments on the ordering of arguments (start and finish with strong ones) (3.16–18). That every speech will have six sections is taken for granted; other possible forms of arrangement are never discussed. As rhetoric became a training in writing in general (rather than a training in making speeches fitted to the city-state), the limitations of its theory of disposition became increasingly evident. Renaissance rhetoric manuals and rhetorical training find ways of broadening the approach to disposition.

Rhetorica ad Herennium is justly famous for its treatment of Latin style. It gives examples of the three levels of style (grand, moderate, and plain) and of the faulty styles related to each (4.11–16). It outlines the characteristics of a good style: correctness, clarity (together conveying *elegantia*), artistic composition, and distinction (4.17–18). Most particularly, though, as contributions to distinction, it lists, explains and exemplifies thirty-five figures of speech, ten tropes, and nineteen figures of thought.[8] With its clear definitions, its many examples, and its advice on the use of many of the figures, book 4 of *Rhetorica ad Herennium* was an invaluable resource for renaissance readers and writers. It spawned the numerous renaissance manuals of tropes and figures which I shall discuss in Chapter 10.

De inventione (*c.*90 BC), Cicero's youthful summary of what he was taught, covers much the same ground as the first two and a half books of *Rhetorica ad Herennium* and was probably based on similar sources. After praising rhetoric as a primary factor in the establishment of civilization and setting out the three genres and the five skills, the first book surveys the sections of the six-part oration. The second book is devoted to status-theory, the arguments suited to the four principal kinds of issue, to the topics for analysing written documents, and to the special topics of deliberative and epideictic oratory. Since 143 of its 147 editions were of the combined volume with *Rhetorica ad Herennium*, there is no need to repeat the publication figures just given. *De inventione* was easily available throughout the period up to 1570. Students probably used it to supplement their understanding of the contents of the different parts of the oration and of status-theory.

[8] I follow the count given in H. Caplan's excellent Loeb edn. (London, 1954), pp. lvi–lviii.

The commentary on *De inventione* by Marius Victorinus (fourth century AD) which was enormously popular in the middle ages,[9] was printed a total of sixty-four times (first edition Milan 1474). It was mostly printed with *Rhetorica ad Herennium* and *De inventione* or with collections of commentaries on Cicero's rhetorical works. Thirty-three editions were from Venice, ten from Cologne. After ten incunable editions there were roughly seven editions in every decade between 1500 and 1570, with the exception of 1520–9 (two editions) and 1550–9 (ten editions). After 1570 there were only seven editions, the last in 1599. While the quantity and regularity of production is notable (and perhaps surprising) it may owe many of its printings to the custom of some (particularly Venetian) printers of including it with their most popular pairing of rhetoric texts. As a result of John Ward's immense labours on the medieval tradition of commentary on *Rhetorica ad Herennium* and *De inventione*, work has started to appear also on the renaissance commentary tradition.[10]

Cicero's mature rhetoric *De oratore* (55 BC) was printed in 133 editions between 1465 and 1610. Up to 1520 there were on average four to five editions per decade. There were thirteen editions in 1520–9, the increase apparently partly prompted by publication of Melanchthon's commentary. In the mid-century there was a considerable increase in production (twenty-seven editions 1540–9; eighteen editions 1550–9, nine of them from Paris; seventeen editions 1560–9), followed by a reduction to more normal levels and a petering out of publication between 1590 and 1610. Most of the early editions of the text were Italian. Later, northern Europe took a greater share, though Italian production was still important. Of the 110 editions produced after 1520, thirty-three were from Paris (the last Paris edition was 1564), twenty from Venice, and thirteen from Lyon.

De oratore is more an investigation of the nature of rhetoric than a textbook and it takes the form of a dialogue. Book 1 is given over to debates on the importance of rhetoric and on whether the orator needs a broad general education or merely a specialized training in public speaking. After explaining that the rules of rhetoric are much less important than talent, imitation, and practice, book 2 begins a survey of the principal doctrines, organized around Aristotle's three kinds of proof:

[9] Ward, *Ciceronian Rhetoric in Treatise, Scholion and Commentary* (Turnhout, 1995), 64, 72, 83, 88–90, 97; M. Victorinus, *Explanationes in Ciceronis Rhetoricam*, ad. A. Ippolito (Turnhout, 2006).

[10] See J. Ward, '*Artificiosa eloquentia* in the Middle Ages', University of Toronto Ph. D. thesis, 1972; Ward, 'Renaissance Commentators on Ciceronian Rhetoric', in J. Murphy (ed.), *Renaissance Eloquence* (Berkeley, Calif., 1983), 126–73; V. Cox and Ward (eds.), *The Rhetoric of Cicero in its Medieval and Early Renaissance Commentary Tradition* (Leiden, 2006).

rational argumentation (*logos*), character or self-presentation (*ethos*), and emotion (*pathos*) (2.114–15). So *De oratore* adds to the material presented in *Rhetorica ad Herennium* a short summary of the topics of invention (on which more below) (2.162–77), an important practical discussion of emotional persuasion, presented as an account of Antonius's tactics in the case of Norbanus, alongside a summary of the methods of eliciting different emotions (2.185–215), and a survey of the different types of joke which a speaker might make (2.216–90). Book 3 is devoted to style, arguing that distinction of style depends as much on the subject-matter as on the words. It includes interesting discussions of metaphor (3.155–65) and prose rhythm (3.173–98), together with a very brief listing of the figures of speech (3.206–7). The third book also includes a debate on active and contemplative life (3.82–90) and a discussion of the way in which consideration of general questions can be used to give distinction to arguments about a specific case (3.96–125). Studying *De oratore* provided a model for the possibilities of the dialogue form for many renaissance writers, notably Castiglione in *Il Cortigiano*.[11]

Several of Cicero's later (and shorter) rhetoric texts were also widely available, though as they tended to be printed in collections as Cicero's rhetorical works volume ii (volume i being *De inventione* and *Rhetorica ad Herennium*) there is room for doubt as to which particular texts were in demand. Including appearances in these selections in the count (as I think one must) may give an inflated idea of the importance of some of these works.

There were 152 editions of *Partitiones oratoriae* (45 BC),[12] a short work in which Cicero outlines the divisions and main headings of the whole subject of rhetoric for the benefit of his son. Only seven of these editions appeared before 1501 and only eight in the first two decades of the sixteenth century. Between 1520 and 1569 a total of 108 editions appeared. It appears that this extraordinary increase in the rate of publication was driven by large numbers of Paris editions, though the work was then taken up in other centres of printing such as Strasbourg, Cologne, and Lyon. There were fifteen editions in 1520–9, nine of them from Paris; twenty-two editions in 1530–9, fourteen of them from Paris; thirty-four editions in 1540–9, fourteen of them from Paris; twenty-one editions in 1550–9, eight of them from Paris; and sixteen editions 1560–9, six of

[11] D. Marsh, *The Quattrocento Dialogue* (Cambridge, Mass., 1980); V. Cox, *The Renaissance Dialogue* (Cambridge, 1992).

[12] *Partitiones oratoriae* appears to have been rediscovered in the 15th cent. Wilkins in Cicero, *Rhetorica*, ii (Oxford, 1903), p. iii, mentions two 10th-cent. manuscripts and numerous 15th-cent. copies.

them from Paris. The work continued to be printed regularly in the 1570s and 1580s (twenty-one editions in total), with seven editions also in 1590–1609. *Partitiones oratoriae* is a work well-suited to commentary, and the commentaries by Giorgio Valla, Strebaeus, Latomus, and Sturm seem to have played an important part in its diffusion. While the text provides a strongly logical outline of the subject as a whole which can thus be mastered quickly by a student, the commentator can add fuller explanations of particular points. Thus the text has some of the pedagogical advantages of the Ramist textbooks whose initial success in Paris dates from shortly after many editions of *Partitiones* were first printed there.

Cicero's *Topica* (44 BC), which was well-known in the middle ages and for which we have 140 manuscripts,[13] appeared 129 times before 1620, often alongside *Partitiones oratoriae*, and the pattern of publication is similar: relatively few editions before 1520, a large number (especially from Paris) between 1520 and 1559, regular publication between 1560 and 1589 (total of twenty-nine editions), tailing off in the 1590s. The peak of publication for *Topica* is lower than for *Partitiones oratoriae* and it comes a little earlier: fourteen editions 1520–9 (one from Paris); twenty-six editions 1530–9 (eighteen from Paris); twenty-one editions 1540–9 (ten from Paris); and nineteen editions 1550–9 (six from Paris). Between 1534 and 1545 there were sixteen Paris editions (out of a total of twenty-one). Following on from this explosion of localized publishing, printing of *Topica* spread to Lyon, Strasbourg, and Venice (but there were only two Cologne editions: 1530 and 1593). *Topica* sets out the method of discovering material appropriate to a given question by considering its key words in relation to a series of headings (such as definition, genus, cause, effect, adjacents, contraries, testimony). This technique of topical invention belongs to logic as much as to rhetoric. The burst of Paris printing in the 1530s and 1540s appears to be related to a reform of the Paris logic syllabus as a result of which humanist logic, with its emphasis on topical invention (see Chapters 3 and 4 below), replaced the scholastic logic in which Paris had previously specialized. Since the University of Paris furnished teachers to universities all over northern Europe and the Iberian peninsula, sixteenth-century Parisian intellectual fashions tended to be copied (with an appropriate time-delay) elsewhere in Europe. The pattern of Paris printing of *Topica* is rather similar to that for Rudolph Agricola's *De inventione dialectica*, the most important renaissance treatment of the topics of invention. It is quite likely that the decline in printing of *Topica*

[13] Cicero, *Topica*, ed. T. Reinhardt (Oxford, 2003), 73–9.

after 1580 is related to a revival in importance of scholastic logic (at the expense of humanist logic) in the last two decades of the sixteenth century.

The printing of Cicero's remaining rhetorical treatises was even more strongly involved with the collections mentioned above for *Topica* and *Partitiones*. *Brutus* (46 BC), which gives a history of Roman oratory intended to assert the importance of the expansive (or Asiatic) style against critics who preferred a briefer and more pointed way of writing (Atticism), was printed a total of sixty times between 1469 and 1608, but there were only eight editions of the work on its own. *Orator* (46 BC) portrays the perfect orator, asserting the importance of general education and summing up Cicero's ideas on invention. The greater part of the treatise is devoted to style, defending the Asiatic style, with a short account of the figures and detailed instructions on sentence composition and prose rhythm. *Orator* was printed in a total of eighty-two editions (often with *Brutus*, *Topica*, and *Partitiones*), including twenty-one editions on its own, accompanied by commentaries by Melanchthon, Strebaeus, Amerbach, and Ramus. Over half of the separate editions came from Paris between 1530 and 1555.[14] It seems safe to assume that, while both works were easily available to anyone who wanted to read them, *Orator* was somewhat better known than *Brutus* and considerably less well-known than *Partitiones* and *Topica*, whose pattern of publication is similar (though the quantity is greater). There is some textbook evidence that people were aware of the controversy between Asianism and Atticism but arguments about it did not play a significant role in the development of sixteenth-century rhetoric.

The publication figures suggest that the *Rhetorica ad Herennium/De inventione* combination was printed much less often after 1570 and that Cicero's other rhetorics were in less demand throughout Europe after about 1590. The relative infrequency of new editions may be a consequence of the large numbers of copies already in circulation but it may also reflect changes in the emphasis of the university syllabus. It may well be that across Europe as a whole rhetoric became a more important part of the syllabus from the 1530s onwards with the fashion for humanist logic and that after 1580 scholastic logic reasserted its former predominance. Alternatively one might argue that the large numbers of editions of modern guides to rhetoric, such as those by Soarez and Talon, in these decades, imply that these works were now replacing the Ciceronian manuals rather than being used as introductions to them, as previously happened.

[14] K. Meerhoff, *Rhétorique et poètique au XVIe siècle en France* (Leiden, 1986), 6, 8, 28–9, 52–7.

For many renaissance rhetoricians, starting with Lorenzo Valla, Quintilian's *Institutio oratoria* (*c.* AD 95) was the ultimate authority. Quintilian as professor of Latin rhetoric in Rome set out to write a comprehensive and reflective synthesis of the subject. After discussions of the grammatical education which should precede the study of rhetoric and the nature of rhetoric (books 1–3), Quintilian teaches invention (3–7), disposition (7), style (8–11.1), memory, and delivery (11.2–3). Book 12 describes the ideal orator, the orator's career, and the development of oratory. Quintilian often notes divergences between different authorities on a particular doctrine, weighing up the advantages of the different positions and determining which is to be preferred. In comparison to *Rhetorica ad Herennium* his book is more questioning in approach. He gives far more material on argument, including a full treatment of the topics of invention (5.10), some discussion of ways to present and order argument (5.11–13), and more thorough accounts of emotion (6.2), amplification (8.3–4), reading, imitation and practice (10), and decorum (11.1).[15] His treatment of style and of the figures (book 9) and tropes (8.6) is even more exhaustive. Quintilian also adds discussion of sentence composition and prose rhythm (9.4) and of jokes (6.3). *Institutio oratoria* is a very substantial work, roughly four times as long as *Rhetorica ad Herennium.*

Institutio oratoria was printed a total of ninety-five times between 1470 and 1620, either on its own or with the *Declamations* which were then attributed to Quintilian, but the pattern of printing is surprisingly uneven. As befitted an important recently restored classical text there were nine incunable editions, all Italian, six (out of eight datable) before 1483. Then there was a growth of printing activity from 1510 to 1555, followed by a decline. Between 1560 and 1620 there were only eleven editions, with a fairly regular rhythm of one edition per decade at the end of the period. Between 1520 and 1550 about half the printings were from Paris but we do not find the pattern of a Parisian fashion gradually taking over elsewhere which we observed for *Topica* and *Partitiones.* There were nine editions 1510–19 (three from Paris); sixteen editions 1520–9 (seven from Paris); eighteen editions 1530–9 (ten from Paris); twenty-two editions 1540–9 (eleven from Paris); and five editions 1550–9 (one from Paris). The implication that relatively low numbers of editions could satisfy European demand for most decades draws our attention to the heavy concentration of fifty-six editions between 1520 and 1550. We might imagine that a number of university teachers across Europe were teaching or recommending Quintilian in these decades. Perhaps the fashion

[15] Russell gives a helpful plan of the work in Quintilian, *The Orator's Education*, 5 vols. (Cambridge, Mass., 2001), i. 12–18.

for Ramism or the production of other modern rhetoric textbooks edged out demand for Quintilian or perhaps the number of editions produced during the thirty years from 1520 meant that the second-hand market could supply the demand for this long and advanced rhetoric text thereafter.

The *Declamations* attributed to Quintilian were certainly available in the renaissance. Fifty-two editions of *Institutio oratoria* included the declamations, usually or perhaps always the major declamations. But there were only eight separate editions of the major declamations and eight separate editions of the minor ones, so it is difficult to know how much they were really read, but presumably there must have been some interest in the works in order to justify printing them alongside the already lengthy *Institutio oratoria.* There was a definite falling off of publication of the declamations after 1565, as with *Institutio oratoria.*

Tacitus's *Dialogue on Orators* only became available in the mid-fifteenth century. It was first printed alongside Quintilian's *Institutio oratoria* in Paris in 1530. There were five further northern editions of this combination (1580–1618) and one edition of Tacitus with Cicero's *Brutus* (Basel, 1564). In comparison with the attention given to it today, renaissance scholars undervalued this work.

The pattern of publication for Seneca the Elder's *Controversiae* is most unusual. Undoubtedly the work was available for those who sought it, notably in twelve editions of the philosophical works of both Senecas (first published Naples 1475), which was printed in Basel roughly every fifteen years throughout the sixteenth century. The *Controversiae* alone (total of nineteen editions, first published Paris 1527) were printed irregularly in the sixteenth century, but after 1600, with the appearance of Schottus's recension in Heidelberg, there were twelve editions before 1620 (especially from Geneva and Paris) and many more later in the seventeenth century. This seems to indicate both a significant growth of interest in the work and the consequences of an improved edition of the text. The principal texts of Roman declamation were made available from about 1475, but significant interest in Seneca's *Controversiae* (and possible use of it as a teaching text) seems to date from around 1600.

Minor Latin rhetoric is represented in print by editions of the works on figures of speech and thought by Rutilius Lupus, Aquila Romanus, and Rufinianus. Rutilius Lupus (first century AD) gives the Greek names of forty-one figures together with definitions and examples in Latin. The examples are translated from Greek speeches. Rutilius Lupus's *De figuris sententiarum et elocutionis libri duo* was printed twenty-two times before 1620 (first edition Venice 1513). Several of these editions included the work of Rufinianus and modern treatises on the tropes and figures such as that by Peter Schade (Mosellanus). Most of the printings (eighteen) of this work occurred between 1519 and 1542, six of them from Venice, five from Paris, and four from Lyon. There were sixteen editions of Aquila Romanus's *De figuris sententiarum et elocutionis* (third century), mostly together with Rutilius and Rufinianus (and often others), mostly in the period 1519–42. There were thirteen editions of Rufinianus's *De figuris sententiarum et elocutionis liber* (fourth century) which expands Rutilius's work, adding many additional figures and giving Latin examples, mostly from Virgil. In twelve of the editions Rufinianus's work accompanied Rutilius Lupus. Eleven of the editions were printed 1521–41 (five Paris, three Lyon, one Venice). The first edition and the only one in which the work appeared on its own was Leipzig 1521. The interest in these works can be linked with the general increase in editions of rhetoric texts in the 1520s. Their history clearly belongs with that of the renaissance manuals of tropes and figures (see Chapter 10), which to some extent replaced them after 1540.

The first Greek publication of Aristotle's *Rhetoric* was as part of the Aldine edition *Rhetores Graeci* (Venice, 1508–9) which also introduced the Greek text of Aphthonius, Demetrius, and Hermogenes. The next Greek edition was printed in Basel in 1529. Thereafter there were six editions 1530–9, four editions 1540–9, and two editions in each decade thereafter until the final Greek-only edition, Frankfurt 1584. The major centres of production were Basel with five editions, Paris with seven, and Venice with five. The Greek-only editions had been increasingly replaced by Greek and Latin editions which first appeared in 1551 and continued until 1619 and then throughout the seventeenth century. In total up to 1620 there were nineteen Greek-only editions, seventeen Greek and Latin editions, and fifty-five Latin-only editions.

Combining the Latin-only editions with the Latin and Greek editions a reasonably regular pattern emerges. Between 1476 and 1539 only twelve editions appeared (three of them in the 1530s). Even this level of production would have been sufficient to ensure the availability of the text to scholars throughout Europe, a fact which library catalogues and book inventories thoroughly confirm. After 1540 there is an average of ten editions each decade until 1600, with a tailing off until 1620 (only six editions in twenty years). The principal centres of production were Venice (twenty editions), Lyon (fourteen), Paris (seven), and Basel (seven), with further editions from Geneva, Frankfurt, Strasbourg, Cracow, and elsewhere. This pattern suggests that, in spite of the difficulties which commentators found in applying their Ciceronian understanding of rhetoric to Aristotle's text, after 1540 the *Rhetoric* was in regular strong demand throughout Europe. That demand for Aristotle's *Rhetoric* held up after

1570 when most other rhetoric texts started to lose ground may even indicate a switching away from Cicero and Quintilian towards Aristotle in the final decades of the sixteenth century, which could be connected with the emphasis which Jesuit teachers placed on the work. The pattern of printing of Aristotle's *Rhetoric* is unusual in two other ways. It is the only classical rhetoric text for which Italian production remains as important as that in northern Europe throughout the sixteenth century and for which Paris is not the most significant centre of production in the mid-century. In spite of the international market in printed rhetoric (mentioned above) it is therefore possible that strong and long-lasting Italian use of the work may explain part of its continued success. Both in Italy and in the North Aristotle's was the rhetoric textbook best adapted to a return to scholasticism and Aristotelianism in the universities.

Because renaissance scholars read Aristotle's *Rhetoric* (*c.*335 BC) within a discipline already framed by his Roman successors it can be difficult for us to appreciate their understanding of his role. Many of the central ideas structuring later rhetoric (such as the genres of rhetoric and the parts of the oration) were first codified by Aristotle. Other important ideas (for example, the three kinds of persuasion: *logos*, *ethos*, and *pathos*) were absorbed in Cicero's later works as a result of his reading of Aristotle. So there are ways to incorporate Aristotle's *Rhetoric* within the Ciceronian scheme but at the same time those approaches tend to diminish some of what later readers see as most characteristic of Aristotle's work.

Aristotle begins the first book by defending rhetoric against philosophical attack, stating that it is the counterpart of dialectic and defining it as the ability to find the available means of persuasion in each case (1.1–2). He divides rhetoric into three types and sets out arguments appropriate to each of the three kinds. Thus deliberative rhetoric, which he treats first, will be concerned with money, war and peace, defence, provision of food, and framing of laws, each of which he discusses. It will also need to argue from ethical topics such as the different aspects of the good, and to compare greater and lesser advantages and goods (1.4–8). Epideictic rhetoric will be concerned with the honourable, with praise, and with amplification (1.9). The book ends with arguments about evidence specific to court-cases: laws, witnesses, contracts, torture, and oaths (1.10–15). Where book 1 is primarily concerned with rational argument the first half of book 2 is concerned with emotion, examining the different types of emotion and suggesting arguments for arousing each of them (2.2–11). It moves on to discuss *ethos*, ways of presenting character and the characters appropriate to different ages and circumstances (2.12–17). The book ends with a discussion of arguments suitable to all types of rhetoric (maxim, example, enthymeme, and the topics of invention) and of ways of answering false arguments (2.18–26). The third book is concerned with style, focusing on the qualities of good prose style (appropriate metaphor, amplification, prose rhythm, the periodic style, vivid presentation) (3.2–12) and arrangement, setting out the contents of the four parts of the oration (3.13–19).

In comparison with Roman rhetoric, Aristotle says nothing about status-theory, memory, delivery, or the figures of speech but tends to be fuller on probable argument, types of argument appropriate to each case, emotion, and general theories about character. Where Cicero emphasizes judicial rhetoric, Aristotle gives more attention to deliberative and epideictic.

Developing an understanding of Aristotle's *Rhetoric* was one of the most important tasks for renaissance rhetoricians. Already in the fifteenth century George Trapezuntius of Crete had found a place for some of Aristotle's doctrines within a framework based on *Rhetorica ad Herennium.*[16] Green and Murphy list twenty-two renaissance commentators on the *Rhetoric*, primarily in Italy. By the beginning of the seventeenth century Soarez, Caussin, Keckermann, and Vossius had established ways for northern readers to take advantage of Aristotle's teachings without abandoning the model of rhetoric which they had taken over from Cicero and Quintilian. While awaiting Lawrence Green's comprehensive study of renaissance commentaries on the *Rhetoric* we must attend to the impact which reading the text had on the major rhetoricians of the later renaissance. I shall discuss some renaissance Italian commentaries on Aristotle's *Rhetoric* in Chapter 8 below.[17]

Some renaissance rhetoricians, notably George Trapezuntius of Crete and Johann Sturm, attempted to promote the study of later Greek rhetoric, represented by the corpus of works attributed to Hermogenes, in western Europe. There were at least nine Latin editions of Hermogenes's *Art of Rhetoric*,[18] particularly from Paris in the 1530s, with separate editions of some of its components: *On Invention* (three editions, all from Paris and Strasbourg); *On Ideas of Style* (seven editions, three of them from Strasbourg); *On the Method of Forcefulness* (five editions, all from Paris and Strasbourg); *On Status* (four editions, two from Strasbourg) and *Progymnasmata* (nineteen editions). The Hermogenean corpus had been made available, perhaps largely through its promotion by Sturm in Paris and

[16] L. D. Green, 'The Reception of Aristotle's *Rhetoric* in the Renaissance', in W. Fortenbaugh and D. Mirhady (eds.), *Peripatetic Rhetoric After Aristotle* (New Brunswick, NJ, 1994), 323–8.

[17] See also Tom Conley, 'Some Renaissance Polish Commentaries on *Aristotle's Rhetoric* and Hermogenes' *On Ideas*', *Rhetorica*, 12 (1994), 265–92.

[18] The title of the three edns. of RR1966 suggests that they may contain the *Progymnasmata* alone rather than the whole collection. I discuss Hermogenes in more detail in Ch. 3 below.

Strasbourg, but the figures do not suggest that it was in wide demand (apart from the *Progymnasmata*).

In contrast to most of Hermogenes's works, the *Progymnasmata* (writing exercises) of Aphthonius was a great publishing success in the renaissance, going through 122 editions up to 1620. Similar works were also successful, the *Progymnasmata* of Hermogenes achieving nineteen editions and those of Priscian thirty-eight editions. Of these editions of Aphthonius, five (appearing 1515–50) were Greek only (four of them from Paris) and twenty-two (appearing 1507–1616) had Greek and Latin together (ten of them from Paris, six from Leipzig). Taking the Latin-only editions together with the Greek and Latin editions, the following pattern emerges: there were seven editions up to 1529; in 1530–1620 there was a regular production of on average ten to twelve editions per decade. The vogue for Aphthonius emerges relatively late (the popular edition with Lorichius's additional examples and commentary was first produced only in 1542) but once established production remains remarkably consistent up to the middle of the seventeenth century. Nine editions were produced in 1530–9, thirteen editions 1540–9, ten editions 1550–9, eight editions 1560–9, eleven editions 1570–9, fourteen editions 1580–9, twelve editions 1590–9, twelve editions 1600–9, and thirteen editions 1610–19. Publication was spread widely across northern Europe, with twenty-seven editions from Paris, twelve from Frankfurt and Lyon, ten from London, nine from Cologne, six from Leipzig, four from Geneva, three from Venice, and two each from Salamanca, Barcelona, and Marburg. There is good external and internal evidence for thinking of the *Progymnasmata* as a school (rather than a university) text, especially in northern Europe and in Spain. This may help explain why demand does not become reduced in the way that it seems to for university-level rhetoric texts.[19]

The Greek *Methodus conscribendarum epistolarum* by Libanius (314–93) went through nineteen editions, mostly in Latin translation and accompanied by other letter-writing manuals. Of these editions nine appeared 1548–58, seven of them from Basel. Its history must be understood alongside the Latin letter-writing manuals (Chapter 11 below), which were composed and published in very large numbers, as one of the staples of grammar-school education throughout Europe.

[19] Manfred Kraus is preparing a study of Aphthonius in the Renaissance. His preliminary studies include 'Progymnasmata, Gymnasmata', in Gert Ueding (ed.), *Historisches Wörterbuch der Rhetorik*, vii (Tübingen, 2005), 159–91, and 'Aphthonius and the Progymnasmata in Rhetorical Theory and Practice', in David Zarefsky and Elizabeth Benacka (eds.), *Sizing up Rhetoric* (Long Grove, Ill., 2008), 52–67.

Other Greek rhetorics which are famous today were relatively little known in the renaissance. There were nine Greek editions of Demetrius, *On Style,* but only one Greek and Latin edition (Basel 1557) and two Latin-only editions (first edition: Padua 1557) until it was reprinted in 1591 with Lipsius's *Epistolica institutio*. This Lipsius/Demetrius text was reprinted a total of thirteen times up to 1618. Menander Rhetor, so important to present-day understandings of classical epideictic, was printed only once each in Greek (1508), Italian (1553), and Latin (1558), but exercised further influence in manuscript and through Poliziano's lectures and Scaliger's *Poetices libri septem*.[20] Pseudo-Longinus, *On the Sublime* was printed three times in Greek (first edition: Basel 1554), once in Latin (Venice 1572) and once in Greek and Latin (Geneva 1612). It was much more successful later in the seventeenth century. In the early seventeenth century Keckermann and Caussin refer to and use the work in their rhetoric manuals.[21]

St Augustine's *On Christian Doctrine* was printed only nineteen times (excluding the numerous editions of his *Complete Works*). Nine of these editions included the complete text; ten consisted only of book 4, which contains much of the strictly rhetorical material. Most of these editions were northern, though none was from Paris. There were eight incunables, five editions in the 1520s, and four in the 1550s. Outside this there is very little: only one edition appeared between 1560 and 1620. The text was certainly available, particularly through Augustine's *Complete Works*, to those who sought it out in libraries, but the lack of editions suggest that it can only rarely have been used as a teaching text. Probably the main impact of Augustine's book would have been on preaching manuals, where, as we shall see in Chapter 12, the total numbers of editions are generally lower than for other types of textbook, reflecting the fact that they would have been used mainly in theology faculties and seminaries.

Marjorie Curry Woods's *Classroom Commentaries* supplements the assumptions of this chapter by showing how one medieval Latin rhetoric, Geoffrey de Vinsauf's *Poetria nova*, was used by several of the earliest Italian humanists and was taught in European schools and universities in the fourteenth and fifteenth centuries, even though it did not appear in print until 1721, when it was included in an anthology of Latin poetry.

[20] P. Harsting, 'The Golden Method of Menander Rhetor. The Translations and the Reception of the *Peri epideiktikôn* in the Italian Renaissance', *Analecta Romana Instituti Danici,* 20 (Rome, 1992), 139–57; 'More Evidence of Menander Rhetor on the Epithalamium: Angelo Poliziano's Transcription in the Statius Commentary (1480–81), Re-edited with a Discussion of the Manuscript Sources and Earlier Editions', *Cahiers de l'Institut du Moyen-Age Grec et Latin,* 72 (2001), 11–34, with further bibliography.

[21] See Ch. 9 below.

The *Poetria nova* teaches a selection of rhetorical doctrines which will make letters and poems more effective: good openings, the use of proverbs and examples, eight methods of amplifying (including apostrophe, personification, and description), abbreviating, metaphor, nine other tropes and fifty-four figures, many of them examples without explanations. Some of these were sometimes excerpted separately.[22] Woods discusses a number of fourteenth-century Italian commentaries, notably that of Pace of Ferrara, which continued to be copied in the fifteenth century and several commentaries which were composed, copied, and taught in central Europe during the same period.[23] She also shows that there is good evidence for the teaching of Geoffrey's text in the fifteenth century even where no manuscripts survive. As we shall see later, both Barzizza and Erasmus were influenced by Geoffrey.[24]

Alongside these manuals of rhetoric, Latin orations played an important role in rhetorical education. This is reflected in the numerous editions of Cicero's speeches and in commentaries on them. The Roman historian Asconius (d. AD 76) wrote commentaries on five of Cicero's speeches, which provide helpful historical background and explanations. This work was rediscovered by Poggio in 1416 and was printed complete twenty-one times up to 1620 (first edition: 1477 Venice). It was printed regularly between 1519 and 1554 (total of seventeen editions in thirty-five years), with printing split evenly between Venice and northern Europe. Several editions of Asconius's comments on individual speeches (particularly *Pro Milone*) were printed in collective commentaries on individual works.[25] Prior to the rediscovery of Asconius, Antonio Loschi had composed his *Inquisitio super XI orationes Ciceronis* (early 1390s), which analyses the rhetorical techniques Cicero employed. This work was included in the first Venice printing of Asconius and was printed complete a total of four times (never alone). Loschi's comments on individual orations were quite frequently printed in collective commentaries on the particular speeches.

Because of the numerous reprints of commentaries on Cicero's speeches in different collections and because of the variety of items produced (from a single-author commentary on an individual speech to massive volumes

[22] Marjorie Curry Woods, *Classroom Commentaries: Teaching the* Poetria nova *across Medieval and Renaissance Europe* (Columbus, Ohio, 2010), 238–43, 16–26; M. Nims (tr.), *Poetria nova of Geoffrey of Vinsauf* (Toronto, 1967). E. Faral, *Les Arts poétiques du XIIe et du XIIIe siècle* (Paris, 1924), 197–262, and E. Gallo, *The Poetria nova and its Sources in Early Rhetorical Doctrine* (The Hague, 1971) include edns.

[23] Woods, *Classroom Commentaries*, 94–162, 168, 179–222.

[24] Ibid. 136–7, 228–33, 258, 261–3.

[25] In several renaissance edns. there is a commentary attributed to Asconius on the first of Cicero's speeches *In Verrem*, which is not included in modern edns. of Asconius.

collecting the commentaries of numerous writers on a large selection or even all of the speeches), it is hard to produce reliable estimates of the number of editions. Green and Murphy list 160 editions of a range of different multi-author commentaries (pp. 128–35); to that must be added at least 139 (and probably in reality more like 250) editions of single-author commentaries (cross-referenced under author at their p. 127), so it seems safe to assume that more editions (a total of 300–400) were printed of commentaries on Cicero than of any classical or renaissance rhetoric manual. This reminds us that the teaching of the textbooks was reinforced by the reading of classical orations (and other texts), with the rhetorical structures and techniques pointed out by the teacher. The leading centres of production were Paris in the 1530s and 1540s and (somewhat less important) Cologne between 1540 and 1570. A number of editions were also produced in Venice and Strasbourg. The most popular orations for commentary were *Pro Milone*, *Pro Archia Poeta*, *Pro Ligario*, *Pro Marcello*, *Pro Lege Manilia,* and *In Verrem*. The most printed authors in single-author commentary were Asconius, Dubois, Latomus, and Melanchthon. Beumler, George Trapezuntius, Lenicaerus, and Paolo Manuzio are the next most important in this category.[26] These are also the authors most represented in the multi-author commentaries, in which the following commentators also appear in large numbers: Beroaldo, Bolerus, Bucoldianus, Bugelius, Curione, Hegendorff, Loschi, Merula, Omphalius, Schütz, Sturm, Tislinus, Walther.[27] I shall note the commentaries of only a few of these authors. Green and Murphy's lists give an idea of the work still to be done on Ciceronian commentary in the renaissance.

The most important texts of classical rhetoric were widely available throughout the sixteenth century, but Green and Murphy's figures also indicate that in total modern rhetoric textbooks were printed far more often than classical texts. A small number of renaissance manuals of the whole of rhetoric achieved publication figures equivalent to those of the classical manuals. For example, Soarez, *De arte rhetorica libri tres* (first printed 1557) went through seventy-five editions up to 1620 and 114 editions in all; Talon, *Rhetorica* (1545) 115 editions; and the three versions of Melanchthon's *Rhetoric* (first version first printed 1519) 122 editions. More specialized manuals which were also printed very frequently include Erasmus's *De copia* (1512) with 169 editions, Perotti's *Rudimenta grammatices* (1473), which includes a letter-writing manual, with 133 editions, Erasmus's *De conscribendis epistolis* (1520) with 149 editions of

[26] Green and Murphy, *Renaissance Rhetoric Short Title Catalogue* (Aldershot, 2006), 127.
[27] Ibid. 127–8.

Table 2.1. Editions of Classical Rhetoric Textbooks 1490–1620

Date	*RAH*	*De O*	*Partits*	Aphthonius	Quintilian	Aristotle
1490–9	6	2	2	0	3	2
1500–9	16	2	2	1	2	1
1510–19	19	6	6	1	9	3
1520–9	12	13	15	6	16	0
1530–9	17	8	22	9	18	3
1540–9	23	27	34	13	22	10
1550–9	22	18	21	10	5	8
1560–9	20	17	16	8	3	7
1570–9	11	7	8	11	2	15
1580–9	9	12	13	14	3	6
1590–9	2	3	3	12	1	9
1600–9	0	2	3	12	1	4
1610–20	0	1	0	13	1	3
TOTAL	157	118	145	110	86	71

two different versions, Negro's *Modus epistolandi* (1487) with sixty-two editions, and Vives's *De conscribendis epistolis* (1536) with about seventy editions. Preaching manuals and manuals in the vernacular were rarely printed more than ten times.

Tables 2.1 and 2.2 compare the production decade by decade of the most frequently printed classical and renaissance manuals between 1490

Table 2.2. Editions of Renaissance Rhetoric Textbooks 1490–1620

Date	Agricola (+ epits)	Erasmus *Copia*	Erasmus *Cons Ep*	Melanch *All Rhets*	Talon	Soarez
1490–9	0	0	0	0	0	0
1500–9	0	0	0	0	0	0
1510–19	1	27	0	2	0	0
1520–9	7	33	19	36	0	0
1530–9	29	41	22	25	0	0
1540–9	19	27	19	14	7	0
1550–9	10	21	14	9	13	1
1560–9	5	16	6	15	6	7
1570–9	4	3	2	7	16	17
1580–9	0	0	1	7	14	17
1590–9	0	1	0	2	19	12
1600–9	1	0	0	1	13	12
1610–20	0	0	1	1	13	9
TOTAL	76	169	84	119	101	75

and 1620. All the figures are based on Green and Murphy's lists of editions.

While the production of *Rhetorica ad Herennium* is consistently high from 1500 until its relative decline after 1570 and absolute decline after 1590, the other Latin rhetorics have a period of high production in the earlier part of the century (1520–50 for Quintilian; 1520–70 for Cicero's *De oratore* and *Partitiones*, with a revival in the 1580s). Quintilian was much less printed after 1550 and classical Latin rhetoric generally has few editions after 1590. By contrast Aristotle's *Rhetoric* and Aphthonius's *Progymnasmata* have a lower peak of production in the mid-century but continue for longer at a more consistent level. Printing of Aristotle's *Rhetoric* declines after 1600, while the *Progymnasmata* remain successful well into the next century.

The renaissance rhetorics generally share the pattern of very high peaks followed by steep declines. Erasmus's *De copia* was very successful 1512–70; his *De conscribendis epistolis* 1521–60; Agricola 1520–60. Printing of Melanchthon, which had reached a very high level 1520–70, declined steeply after 1590. The peaks of production for Erasmus, Agricola, and Melanchthon coincide fairly closely with those for Cicero and Quintilian. By contrast, the work of Talon and Soarez grows in success after 1560 and continues strongly into the seventeenth century.

Large-scale printing of rhetorical texts to some extent altered the balance between classical texts and new textbooks. It meant that improvements to a text could be spread much more reliably and quickly. Teachers and students could easily own and compare a range of classical texts instead of having to treat one text as authoritative. A new textbook could achieve a moderately large circulation relatively quickly and over a couple of decades could become as widely available as the classical texts.

It is possible that the decline in the number of editions of Ciceronian rhetorics from around 1570 can be explained in part by the rising numbers of editions of new manuals of the whole of rhetoric, such as Talon and Soarez (seventy-five and sixty-seven editions, 1570–1620); but it may also be that rhetoric became a less important subject in European universities in the final quarter of the sixteenth century.

3

Italy 1390–1480

Although Italy produced few rhetorical textbooks in the fifteenth century, and although those few books mostly achieved only a relatively restricted circulation, nevertheless many of the guiding ideas of renaissance rhetoric are expressed (sometimes for the first time) in these texts. Italian rhetorical works of the fifteenth century introduced: (1) a close critical reading of Cicero's orations to understand his tactics and his methods of achieving his aims (particularly in Loschi, Guarino, and George Trapezuntius); (2) the attempt to teach boys to achieve an acceptable classicism of expression, leading at a more advanced level to the ability to handle the full resources of the Latin language in an elegant way (Barzizza, Guarino, and Valla); (3) bringing the gains of Greek rhetoric (especially Hermogenes) over into Latin (George Trapezuntius); (4) a new understanding of the relationship between rhetoric and dialectic (Bruni, Valla, and George Trapezuntius); and (5) taking advantage of the textual discoveries, especially Quintilian (Valla). Whatever the importance of city republics for the initial growth of humanism,[1] the different allegiances of the writers discussed below (to republic, city tyrant, university city within empire, regional monarch or pope) show that in the fifteenth century rhetoric could flourish within different types of political system.

ANTONIO LOSCHI (1369–1441)

Antonio Loschi from Verona studied briefly in Florence with Salutati (1387) and then in Pavia (1388–90) before joining the Visconti court, first as *scriptor* and from 1398 as Chancellor to Giangaleazzo Visconti. He went on to become a papal secretary between 1406 and 1436.[2]

[1] R. Witt, *In the Footsteps of the Ancients: The Origins of Humanism from Lovati to Bruni* (Leiden, 2000), 174–5, 499–501.

[2] G. da Schio, *Sulla vita e sugli scritte di Antonio Loschi* (Padua, 1858); D. Girgensohn, 'Antonio Loschi und Baldassare Cossa vor dem Pisaner Konzil von 1409', *Italia medioevale e umanistica*, 30 (1987), 1–93; Germano Gualdo, 'Antonio Loschi, segretario apostolico (1406–1436)', *Archivio storico italiano*, 147 (1989), 749–69.

His *Inquisitio super XI orationes Ciceronis* (*c.*1395) divides its commentary on each oration into six sections. Loschi begins with the argument, which briefly explains the context and aim of the whole speech. Then he assigns the speech to its genre (judicial, deliberative, or demonstrative). In the third section he discusses the status of the speech and in the fourth comments on the disposition of its parts. In the fifth section he divides the speech into parts and describes the contents of each part, with particular attention to the topics of invention. Finally in the sixth section he discusses the style of the speech, quoting short passages, labelling figures of speech, and commenting on their use.[3] Although section 6 tends to treat the text in a rather fragmented way, section 5 can sometimes give a powerful sense of the way the different arguments of the speech work together.[4] In the commentary on the first two orations treated (*Pro lege Manilia* and *Pro Milone*) Loschi recapitulates a good deal of basic rhetorical theory (e.g. how to determine status, the five parts of rhetorical argumentation, the qualities sought in the narration[5]) before applying it to the speech he is discussing. This means that his book functions as a manual of rhetoric as well as a commentary showing how Cicero's speeches use the techniques set out in the rhetoric textbooks. Loschi's work was widely diffused in manuscript and was printed (usually as part of an omnibus volume of commentaries on Cicero) complete seven times. In addition Parisian printers issued nine editions of omnibus commentaries on particular orations which included Loschi's (four of them of *Pro lege Manilia*). Loschi's work was both a notable feat of thoughtful close reading and the beginning of a renaissance rhetorical genre which achieved more editions overall than any individual textbook.

LEONARDO BRUNI (1370–1444)

Leonardi Bruni from Arezzo studied with Malpaghini in Florence and enjoyed the patronage of Coluccio Salutati there. He translated many Greek authors into Latin, including a famous translation of Aristotle's *Ethics*. He became papal secretary (1405–14) and Chancellor of Florence (1427–44). He wrote a Latin *History of the Florentine People* in twelve books (1415–42), which survives in sixty manuscripts and three printed

[3] This plan, which Loschi carries out, is outlined at *In orationes Ciceronis enarrationes Q. A. Paediani, G. Trapezuntii et A. Luschii* (Venice, 1477), sig. 5^{r}.

[4] e.g. ibid., sigs. d3^{r}–4^{r}, at the end of the commentary on *Pro Milone*.

[5] Ibid., sigs. a5^{v}–7^{v}, b1^{v}, b7^{r}–8^{v}.

editions, and numerous letters and orations.[6] His *Laudatio Florentini urbis* (1404), an imitation of Aelius Aristides's *Panathenaic Oration* (*c.* AD 150), according to Witt attains new standards of Latin style in a public oration and argues for Florence's unique role in the defence of republican liberty.[7] Bruni's *Dialogus ad Petrum Paulum Histrum* (i.e. Vergerio) (1408) imitates Cicero's dialogues in presenting an unresolved debate and in allowing one member of the group to display his rhetorical skill by arguing on both sides. In the first book Niccolò regrets the decay of learning and argues that recent writers (specifically Dante, Petrarch, and Boccaccio) are far inferior to the ancients. In the second book he explains that he was dissembling his true views in order to provoke Coluccio into making a defence. Failing in this attempt he rebuts his own charges against the famous Florentine poets of the Trecento, while still expressing his great admiration for the classical authors. He does not retract his attack on education in the present day, contrasting the usefulness of reasoning from causes and effects with the stupidity of the new logic written by the *barbari Britanni* and the complacency of the Aristotelian establishment.[8] This type of attack on modern logic became a general humanist theme, which can be linked back to Petrarch's letter to Tommaso Caloria and forward to Thomas More.[9]

In contrast to such logical technicalities Bruni's *Dialogus* presents a model of the courteous exchange of elegantly expressed views between political equals. Civil society it implies is enhanced by literary education and by rhetoric. The praise of the Florentine poets in the second book, which seems sincere to me, is founded on argued admiration for their imagination, eloquence, and teaching, treating the poets as historians or orators with an extra quality of imagination (*artem fingendi*).[10] The dialogue reiterates the splendour of the city, flourishing in people, buildings, works of art, and ideas.[11] Bruni's balanced raising of questions of political culture is illustrated by the three times the dialogue turns to consider the example of Brutus: at first Niccolò attacks Dante for placing this defender of republican liberty alongside Judas Iscariot in the lowest

[6] L. Bruni, *History of the Florentine People*, ed. and tr. J. Hankins, 3 vols. (Cambridge, Mass., 2001–7)

[7] Witt, *Footsteps*, 404–15.

[8] E. Garin (ed.), *Prosatori Latini del Quattrocento* (Milan, 1952), 58–61.

[9] Petrarch, *Familiares*, 1. 7; Cesare Vasoli, *La dialettica e la retorica dell'Umanesimo* (Milan, 1968), 9-27; More, *The Complete Works of St Thomas More*, xv (New Haven, Conn., 1986), 1–149.

[10] Garin, *Prosatori*, 84–9, 92, 94. Witt, *Footsteps*, 432–40; D. Quint, 'Humanism and Modernity: A Reconsideration of Bruni's *Dialogues*', *Renaissance Quarterly*, 38 (1985), 423–45.

[11] Garin, *Prosatori*, 44, 76, 82.

circle of hell; then Coluccio denies that Caesar was the parricide of his country but insists that his virtues should be considered along with the vices, which in the Florentine view outweighed them; finally Niccolò argues that Dante understood Brutus's virtues but that the overall design of his work compelled him to present Caesar as the legitimate ruler of the world, leading to a presentation of Brutus as a treacherous butcher, which should be considered as a sort of poetic licence.[12]

Humanist scholarship in the fifteenth century recovered many manuscripts of hitherto unknown works of Latin literature. Rhetoric was a particular beneficiary of the efforts of the manuscript hunters. In Cluny in 1415 Poggio found manuscripts of Cicero's orations *Pro Roscio Amerino* and *Pro Murena*, which were previously unknown, alongside good texts of other orations. In 1416 at St Gall he found a complete text of Quintilian's *Institutio oratoria* (which had been known only incomplete in the middle ages) and Asconius's commentary on five orations by Cicero. In 1417, the year of his discovery of Lucretius, Poggio found another eight unknown orations by Cicero. In 1421 in the library of Lodi cathedral Landriani found complete texts of *De oratore*, *Orator* and *Brutus*. Poggio discovered Tacitus's *Dialogue on Orators* in 1425.[13]

GASPARINO BARZIZZA (1360–1430)

Gasparino Barzizza was born into a family of Bergamo businessmen and notaries, studied in Pavia (1387–92), and may also have worked in the chancery of Giangaleazzo Visconti, where he would have met Antonio Loschi, whose work he admired.[14] He taught grammar and then grammar and rhetoric at Pavia (1403–6) before being appointed as lecturer in rhetoric and moral authors at Padua (1407–21) where he also established a large household school.[15] His official university post required him to lecture on Priscian, *Rhetorica ad Herennium*, and Cicero's *De inventione*. He gave extraordinary and voluntary lectures on a wide range of Latin texts, including Seneca, Cicero's orations, letters, and philosophical works, Terence, and Valerius Maximus.[16] His commentaries generally follow

[12] Garin, *Prosatori*, 70, 78–81, 88–91.
[13] Reynolds and Wilson, *Scribes and Scholars*, 2nd edn. (Oxford, 1974), 120–4, 236–7; R. Sabbadini, *Le scoperte dei codici latini e greci*, 2 vols. (Florence, 1905–14; corr. repr. 1967).
[14] R. G. G. Mercer, *The Teaching of Gasparino Barzizza* (London, 1979), 24–6, 32–4, 93.
[15] Ibid. 26–7, 38, 44–5; Witt, *Footsteps*, 462–6.
[16] Mercer, *Barzizza*, 41, 80–2, 91.

medieval models, though he gives more attention to textual emendation and to collecting historical facts about antiquity.[17] He also used Geoffrey de Vinsauf's *Poetria nova* (*c.*1200) in his teaching of rhetoric.[18] Many of his works reflect his private teaching, supplementing what the classical texts had provided in several areas of grammar (for example, orthography and punctuation) and rhetoric.

He wrote a schematic treatise on letter-writing, which sets out the aims of the letter, its principal parts, and different ways of inflecting each of those parts.[19] He wrote a *De compositione*, which draws together principles of sentence construction from *Ad Herennium*, Quintilian, and Martianus Capella, to promote a return to classical models of the sentence.[20] His *Praecepta de partibus orationis componendis* discusses thirty-six precepts on grammatical constructions to 'show how different parts of speech are used in various parts and types of oration to give the best stylistic effect'.[21] His most successful works were model compositions intended for imitation by his pupils. *Epistolae ad exercitationem accommodatae*, a group of familiar letters on historical and moral topics set in republican Rome, is found in thirty-four Italian manuscripts and was printed at least twenty times in northern Europe (starting in Paris, 1470) mostly in the fifteenth century. His collection *Exempla exordiorum* (Padua, 1483) gives sixty-five examples of the classical *exordium*, covering every genre and approach. These works offered his pupils relatively simple first models of style and approach which could lead them on to the direct imitation of classical orations and letters. They aimed to show the variety of styles in which similar points could be made.[22] Mercer characterized Barzizza's published works as the occasional by-products of a lifetime of teaching.[23] More than that they inaugurate three important elements of renaissance rhetorical teaching: the lists of rules intended to assist in the composition of sentences in a plausible classical Latin style, collections of model texts and phrases, and guides to the imitation of Cicero.

[17] Ibid. 77–9, 91–3.

[18] Marjorie Curry Woods, *Classroom Commentaries* (Columbus, Ohio, 2010), 136–7. For the influence of Geoffrey's work on other early Italian humanists and for its numerous Italian manuscripts ibid. 94–162.

[19] Mercer, *Barzizza*, 94.

[20] Ibid. 93, 95. The work was edited by R. Sonkowsky in an unpubl. University of North Carolina dissertation, 1958. G. W. Pigman III, 'Barzizza's Studies of Cicero', *Rinascimento*, 21 (1981), 123–63.

[21] Mercer, *Barzizza*, 94.

[22] Ibid. 96–8.

[23] Ibid. 37.

GUARINO DA VERONA (1374–1460)

Guarino da Verona, who studied in Padua, Venice, and Constantinople, is most famous as an educator. He ran a private school in Verona (1419–29) and then established a court school in Ferrara and taught at the university there (1429–60). Guarino's school, whose curriculum was described by his son Battista Guarini, aimed to provide a wide-ranging education in classical literature and history, culminating in a thorough study of rhetoric, based on *Rhetorica ad Herennium*, but moving on to Cicero and Quintilian. He analysed Cicero's orations to demonstrate the operation of rhetorical doctrines in practice. Even at the grammatical stage his method of reading texts focused on style, and on collecting vocabulary, maxims, and flowers of rhetoric for use in pupils' compositions. Guarino placed great emphasis on writing exercises and on Greek.[24] Guarino lectured on *Rhetorica ad Herennium* for more than thirty years; his commentary survives in more than twenty fifteenth-century manuscripts and (anonymously) in six printed editions.[25] According to Cox and Ward, Guarino's major innovation was to simplify the commentary, setting aside the apparatus of divisions and explanations that had characterized the commentaries of Alanus and Bartolinus. By contrast Guarino focused on exposition of the general sense of the text, commenting in detail on its language and style, providing contextual information from classical history and literature, giving parallel examples from literary texts, and commenting on points of grammar and usage.[26] In order to elucidate the text and teach the subject more thoroughly he makes many references to Cicero's other works and to Quintilian. Many of the doctrines are illustrated by references to Cicero's speeches, especially *Pro Milone*. All these reforms link the text closely to the teaching of Latin language and literature and classical culture which we associate with the humanist movement. *Rhetorica ad Herennium* was offered both as a classic text in its own right

[24] E. Garin (ed.), *Il pensiero pedagogico dello Umanesimo* (Florence, 1958), 440–62. C. Kallendorf, *Humanist Educational Treatises* (Cambridge, Mass., 2002), 268–300. A. Grafton and L. Jardine, *From Humanism to the Humanities* (Cambridge, Mass., 1986), 8–16.

[25] J. O. Ward, 'The Medieval and Early Renaissance Study of Cicero's *De inventione* and the *Rhetorica ad Herennium*', in Cox and Ward (eds.), *The Rhetoric of Cicero in its Medieval and Early Renaissance Commentary Tradition* (Leiden, 2006), 3, 57, and 427. Cicero, *Rhetorica nova et vetus* (Venice, 1483), RRSTC 900.

[26] Ward, 'Medieval and Early Renaissance Study', 61–3; Ward, *Ciceronian Rhetoric in Treatise, Scholion and Commentary* (Turnhout, 1995), 205–9; Cox, 'Ciceronian Rhetoric in Late Medieval Italy', in Cox and Ward, *Rhetoric of Cicero*, 127–9, and appendix, 427–30. See also Grafton and Jardine, *From Humanism*, for a translation of part of the gloss.

(and as such a model of expression) and as a guide to effective writing. In similar vein Guarino gives far more attention than his medieval predecessors to the moral issues surrounding rhetoric and to the need for the orator to be a good man. It is such a helpful commentary that it is surprising that it was not reprinted more often. Guarino's often printed *Carmen differentialia*, by offering elementary advice on Latin usage for pupils to memorize, helped to establish acceptable standards of classical diction.[27]

Guarino's commentary on *Rhetorica ad Herennium* was absorbed into and replaced by new commentaries first published in the 1490s. Antonio Mancinelli (1452–1505), who taught grammar in Velletri and Rome, is best known today for his successful poem on the tropes and figures, discussed in Chapter 10 below.[28] He wrote a commentary on the first book of *Rhetorica ad Herennium*, which is usually printed together with the commentary on the whole work by Francisco Maturanzio (1443–1518), a humanist from Perugia who also wrote a chronicle of the city, a treatise on writing Latin poetry and a commentary on Cicero's *Philippica*. The combined commentary (1496) was printed a total of twenty-one times, mainly in Venice, Milan, Paris, and Lyon. Maturanzio's commentary summarizes and explains the teaching of *Rhetorica ad Herennium*, gives references to parallel teaching in Quintilian, adds examples from Cicero's orations to illustrate the principal doctrines and elucidates historical and cultural references in the text.[29]

GEORGE TRAPEZUNTIUS (1395–1472)

George Trapezuntius from Crete first came to Italy in 1416 to work as Greek copyist for Francesco Barbaro. Through studying with Vittorino da Feltre he soon achieved an excellent command of Latin and an admiration for Cicero.[30] In 1433–4 when he composed his summa of rhetoric, *Rhetoricorum libri V*, he was working as a private teacher of Latin grammar and rhetoric in Venice.[31] George makes available to Latin readers the

[27] W. K. Percival, 'A Working Edition of the *Carmina Differentialia* by Guarino Veronese', *Res Publica Litterarum*, 17 (1994), 153–77.

[28] R. Sabbadini, *Antonio Mancinelli* (Velletri, 1877); L. Franco (ed.), *Antonio Mancinelli (1452–1505), Quaderni della Biblioteca Communale di Velletri*, 10 (2005).

[29] Cicero, *Rhetoricorum ad C. Herennium libri*, with the commentaries of Maturanzio, Mancinelli, and Badius (Lyon, 1517); J. O. Ward, 'Commentators on Ciceronian Rhetoric', in Murphy (ed.), *Renaissance Eloquence* (Berkeley, Calif., 1983), 129, 150; Cox and Ward, *Rhetoric of Cicero*, 135–6, 460–4.

[30] J. Monfasani, *George of Trebizond* (Leiden, 1976), 4, 9, 11–12.

[31] Ibid. 25–6, 298.

fruits of Greek rhetoric, especially the corpus of works attributed to Hermogenes.

The corpus of five rhetorical works attributed to Hermogenes of Tarsus (fl. second century AD) was the most influential body of Greek rhetorical texts from the sixth to the fifteenth century.[32] Rabe, the modern editor of the corpus, lists over 100 manuscripts.[33] Hermogenes probably only wrote two of the five texts: *On Status* and *On Ideas of Style*, but he mentions now-lost texts of his own corresponding to *On Invention* and *On the Method of Forcefulness*.[34]

Taking the texts in the order in which they appear in manuscripts, the *Progymnasmata* is a version of the *Progymnasmata* of Aphthonius, discussed in Chapter 2 above.[35] *On Status* presents a highly developed, intricate, and thoughtful discussion of the arguments available on both sides, depending on the strategy adopted by the defence.[36] Hermogenes developed his version of the theory of status from the work of Hermagoras (fl. *c.*150 BC), which underlies the accounts given in *Rhetorica ad Herennium* and Cicero's *De inventione*, discussed in Chapter 2 above.[37] *On Invention* is a highly original survey in four books, probably written by a sophist at the beginning of the third century.[38] The first book is devoted to the exordium, identifying four types of exordium and three sections. The second is concerned with narration and exposition, describing the preparation for narration in five types of speech and discussing three kinds of narration: simple, with confirmation, and with representation.[39] Book 3 describes some ways of responding to arguments while book 4 provides a very unusual account of style, incorporating many of the figures of speech within two kinds of style: the compact and the spirited.[40] The work seems to belong within the context of declamation and may have been written by a teacher of declamation acquainted with Hermogenes's views.[41]

32 G. A. Kennedy, *Greek Rhetoric under Christian Emperors* (Princeton, 1983), 54–103. Hermogenes, *L'Art rhétorique*, ed. M. Patillon (Geneva, 1997), 7–128b; *Hermogenis Opera*, ed. H. Rabe (Leipzig, 1913).

33 Kennedy, *Greek Rhetoric*, 73–4.

34 *On Status*, ed. Rabe, 319, 378–9; Kennedy, *Greek Rhetoric*, 101–3.

35 Hermogenes, *L'Art rhétorique*, ed. Patillon, 40–2.

36 Malcolm Heath, *Hermogenes On Issues: Strategies of Argument in Later Greek Rhetoric* (Oxford,1995).

37 L. Calboli Montefusco, *La dottrina degli status nella retorica greca e romana* (Hildesheim, 1986).

38 Hermogenes, *L'Art rhétorique*, ed. Patillon, 77–83; Kennedy, *Greek Rhetoric*, 86–96.

39 Rabe edn., 119–25; Patillon edn., 82, 86–9, 223–37.

40 Kennedy, *Greek Rhetoric*, 87–93; Hermogenes, ed. Patillon, 98–105, 278–303.

41 Kennedy, *Greek Rhetoric*, 93–6.

Hermogenes's most original and influential work is found in the fourth treatise, *On Ideas of Style*, which discusses techniques for producing twenty-one different types of style.[42] Hermogenes identifies seven characteristics of style (subdivided in some cases): clarity (divided into purity and distinctness), grandeur (divided into solemnity, asperity, vehemence, brilliance, florescence, and abundance), beauty, rapidity, character (divided into simplicity, sweetness, subtlety, and modesty), sincerity (which also involves indignation) and force (which requires the appropriate deployment of all the other types).[43] For each of these types Hermogenes specifies thoughts, approaches, and aspects of style (among them diction, figures of speech, clauses, word-order, cadences, and rhythm), which contribute to the overall effect. Hermogenes illustrates each type with examples from Demosthenes. At the end of the work he discusses the styles of other Greek orators and historians.[44] Some of the characteristics he identifies are alternatives but he also recognizes that all speeches will require (for example) clarity, distinctness, and some kind of grandeur.[45] All speakers will need to convey some sort of character to the audience.[46] Hermogenes does not offer a comprehensive account of the figures of speech but many of them are mentioned as appropriate to a particular type of style.[47] The approaches (methods), which he mentions as suiting particular types, often resemble the figures of thought.[48]

Towards the end of *On Types of Style* Hermogenes regrets not having completed the separate treatise *On the Method of Forcefulness*,[49] to which earlier in the work he has sometimes deferred further comments. The compiler of the Hermogenean corpus added a treatise of this name, which discusses 'miscellaneous devices of style'.[50]

George Trapezuntius based the structure of his rhetoric on *Rhetorica ad Herennium*, adding a new book (2) based on Hermogenes's account of status theory, replacing some sections of the Latin rhetoric with Greek elements and basing his account of style on Hermogenes's *On Types of Style*, as Table 3.1 shows. Throughout the work George finds his own examples from Cicero's speeches.

[42] Ibid. 96–101; Hermogenes, ed. Patillon, 105–24. A. Patterson, *Hermogenes and the Renaissance: Seven Ideas of Style* (Princeton,1970).
[43] These English terms are taken from Cecil Wooten's translation, Hermogenes, *On Types of Style* (Chapel Hill, NC, 1987), which provides a useful diagram, p. xii.
[44] Rabe edn., 395–412.
[45] Ibid. 226, 235, 241; tr. Wooten, pp. 8, 14, 18.
[46] Rabe edn., 320–1; tr. Wooten, 70.
[47] e.g. Rabe edn., 287, 302, 304, 306, 361; tr. Wooten, 48, 58, 59, 61, 95–6.
[48] e.g. Rabe edn., 258, 266, 282, 312–14; tr. Wooten, 29, 34, 44–5, 65–6.
[49] Rabe edn., 379.
[50] Kennedy, *Greek Rhetoric*, 102; Hermogenes, ed. Patillon, 124–28b.

Table 3.1. Plan of George Trapezuntius, *Rhetoricorum libri V*

Bk	Outline of contents	Pages	Main sources
1	Introduction	1–4	Cic. *De oratore*
	Definitions and divisions	5–9	*Ad Her.*, Quint., Cic. *Partits*
	Exordium	9–33	*Ad Her.*, Herm. *De inv.*
	Narration	33–59	*Ad Her.*, Herm. *De inv.*, Quint
	Confirmation	60–94	Herm. *On Status*, *Ad Her.*, Cic. *De inv.*
2	Theory of status	95–205	Herm. *On Status*, and commentators, Cic. *De inv.*
3	Argumentation	206–94	Herm. *De inv.*, *Ad Her.*, Cic. *De inv.*, Boethius, Peter of Spain
	Confutation	294–320	*Ad Her.*, Maximus, *On Insoluble Objections*
	Conclusion	320–38	*Ad Her.*, Cic. *De inv.*
4	Deliberative oratory	339–68	*Ad Her.*, Cic. *De inv.*
	Demonstrative oratory	368–89	*Ad Her.*, Cic. *De inv.*
	Ductus	390–8	Fortunatianus, Herm. *De inv.*, Quint.
	Disposition	399–431	*Ad Her.*, Quint.
	Memory	431–8	*Ad Her.*
	Delivery	438–50	*Ad Her.*
5	Style	451–93	*Ad Her.*, Cic. *De oratore*, Dionysius, *De compositione*
	Seven ideas of style	493–607	Herm., *Ideas of Style*, *Ad Her.*
	On true *gravitas*	607–35	Cic. *De oratore*, Herm., *Ideas of Style*, original
	Ideas of style in parts of oration	636–45	

Note: Page nos. are taken from the Paris 1538 edn., now repr. with introduction by Luc Deitz (Hildesheim, 2006).
Sources: Monfasani, *George of Trebizond*, 266–94, and two articles by Lucia Calboli Montefusco, 'Ciceronian and Hermogenean Influences on George of Trebizond's *Rhetoricorum libri V*', *Rhetorica*, 26 (2008), 139–64, and 'Les Catégories stylistiques du discours dans les *Rhetoricorum libri V* de George de Trébisonde', in Montefusco (ed.), *Papers on Rhetoric IX* (Rome, 2008), 165–83. See also Luca D'Ascia, 'La retorica di Giorgio Trebisonda e l'umanesimo ciceroniano', *Rinascimento*, 29 (1989), 193–216.

My diagram risks understating George's originality. Even when the main thread of doctrine is taken from a single source we always find George adding in further explanations, refinements, and examples. So, for example, while it is true to say that George's doctrine of status rests firmly on Hermogenes, a comparison of George's text (111 pages) with Hermogenes's (64 pages) shows that after translating a sentence or two from Hermogenes, George typically adds another page or so of his own explanations and examples from Cicero before returning to his source.[51]

[51] e.g. at the top of p. 115 George translates a sentence from Hermogenes, p. 48.10; after twenty-three lines of his own explanations he resumes at the foot of the page adapting

George's account is very thorough in definition, division, and explanation. He gives many examples, both taken from Cicero and constructed on the basis of declamation subjects (some of these are taken over from Hermogenes). By using pseudo-Hermogenes George is able to give a fuller and more nuanced account of the exordium than was usual in the Latin tradition. On narration he explores the implications of the Latin rhetorical tradition by analysing examples of Cicero's practice but then incorporates material from pseudo-Hermogenes. As Monfasani points out, George draws important lessons from his close analysis of Cicero's practice, especially in *Pro lege Manilia*, *Pro Milone*, and the *Verrines*.[52]

George's lengthy account of confirmation and refutation follows the Latin tradition in incorporating status theory, though his version, based directly on Hermogenes, is more elaborate. His innovation comes in the account of argumentation. Where most rhetoricians outline two to four ways of setting out arguments (such as syllogism, induction, enthymeme, example), George suggests ten forms of argumentation drawn from a range of rhetorical sources.[53] So he starts with dilemma (*complexio*), in which a speaker offers his opponent two alternatives and shows that whichever is chosen loses the argument. He gives an example from Demosthenes's *On the Crown* and another from *Rhetorica ad Herennium*.[54] If this argument is well-formed it can never be refuted.[55] Then George describes argument by elimination, in which a number of possible explanations is set out and all but one are shown to be false.[56] Then he gives a simple conclusion ('If the accused was with us at the time the murder was committed, he could not have committed the murder') and *subiectio* (a figure of thought in which you examine what can be said on the opponent's side and show that in fact it supports your argument), giving an example from *Rhetorica ad Herennium*.[57] It is easy to see how each of these types of argument might be effective in an oration. Monfasani and Montefusco have shown how George has gathered them from different places, from pseudo-Hermogenes, from sections of Cicero's

two more sentences from Hermogenes, p. 49.8, and using one of Hermogenes's examples (George, p. 116.11) of letter and spirit. On p. 119.5 George returns to Hermogenes, p. 50.20, for *Inversio* and an argument about a presumed tyrant.

52 Monfasani, *George of Trebizond*, 289–90.

53 Ibid. 275–6. L. Calboli Montefusco, 'Les Formes d'argumentation dans les *Rhetoricorum libri V* de George de Trébisonde', forthcoming.

54 Dilemma and the next two arguments George gives appear to be taken from a section of *De inventione* in which Cicero explains how certain arguments can be refuted (1.42.78–9, 45.83–6).

55 George, *Rhetoricorum libri* V, 207–9. Montefusco, 'Les Formes'.

56 George, *Rhetoricorum libri* V, 210–11.

57 Cicero, *De inventione* 1.45.86. *Rhetorica ad Herennium* 4.23.33–24.34.

De inventione connected with refutation, and from parts of *Rhetorica ad Herennium* concerned with figures of thought, adapting what he takes in his own way.[58]

Having discussed status theory and forms of argumentation George turns briefly to the topics of invention, which he treats as a second kind of topics.[59] These include both the circumstances (person, thing, cause, place, time, manner, things assisting) and the traditional list of topics of invention, which George takes from Boethius's *De differentiis topicis* and Peter of Spain's *Tractatus*.[60] Then he describes a series of sub-topics for investigating circumstances and links them back to Cicero's theory of the attributes of actions.[61] Finally he tackles refutation of arguments, basing his general instructions on *Rhetorica ad Herennium* and then deriving fifteen *solutiones* from the *On Insoluble Objections* by Maximus the Philosopher.[62] He includes a declamation replying to Quintilian's arguments on the claim which the Thebans made for a hundred talents owed them by the Thessalians, which debt Alexander had cancelled when he conquered Thebes.[63] This subject was later taken up by Agricola and Erasmus.

George introduces a section on *Ductus*, the art of organizing a whole oration either in a straightforward way or with the intention of leading the listeners to a conclusion different from what it seems to be. George bases his account on Fortunatianus and Martianus Capella, and on hints in Quintilian and pseudo-Hermogenes's *De inventione*.[64] George notes that previous accounts of disposition have been rather brief. His fuller account relies on careful analysis of Cicero's speeches. He shows that within the confirmation the strongest arguments should be placed at the start, in order to seize the audience's attention, and at the end, in order to leave a strong impression, with the less striking arguments placed between them. Arguments that prove a case should be placed before those which amplify; arguments which depend on other arguments will need to be placed after the ones on which they rely.[65] In confutation, on the other hand, we should deal with our opponent's weakest arguments first and last, putting our replies to his strong arguments in the middle.[66]

[58] See plan and note on p. 42 above.
[59] George, *Rhetoricorum libri* V, 236.
[60] Ibid. 240–1, 256–78. Monfasani, *George of Trebizond*, 276–8.
[61] George, *Rhetoricorum libri V*, 279–94; Cicero, *De inventione* 1.26.37–29.43.
[62] Monfasani, *George of Trebizond*, 279.
[63] George, *Rhetoricorum libri V*, 311–17; Quintilian, *Institutio oratoria* 5.10.111–18.
[64] George, *Rhetoricorum libri V*, 390–9; Monfasani, *George of Trebizond*, 280–1.
[65] George, *Rhetoricorum libri* V, 400, 409–14.
[66] Ibid. 415.

George's version of Hermogenes's *Ideas of Style* provides Latin readers with a new and impressive resource. He fills out Hermogenes's advice on the thoughts, approaches, and stylistic features appropriate to each of the twenty-one types of style. He replaces Hermogenes's examples from Demosthenes with well-chosen excerpts from Cicero. Where Hermogenes discusses figures of speech appropriate to each style, George supplements his account with phrases and ideas from *Rhetorica ad Herennium* book 4. In some of the types he includes additional figures taken from the Latin tradition.[67] Some of his comments on sweetness may inspire later work on pleasing; some of what he says about abundance seems to feed into discussion of *copia*.[68] At the end George adds the section on true *gravitas* which Hermogenes never wrote. He bases himself on remarks earlier in *Ideas of Style* and on Cicero's *De oratore*. For George the key to true eloquence is the ability to adapt to different circumstances.[69] In his section on the true method of *gravitas* he includes comments on the styles of the Roman historians in imitation of Hermogenes's remarks on Greek historians, with Livy taking the starring role.[70]

George deserves a place of honour in this history as the first renaissance author of a textbook teaching the whole of rhetoric, for his contribution to making Hermogenes's doctrines of status and ideas of style available to the Latin world, for the innovative way in which he combined Latin and Greek sources, and for his thoughtful choice of and commentary on Cicero's orations. But it is a very long book and there are times when one fears that inclusiveness has got in the way of clarity. Monfasani lists twenty-four fifteenth-century Italian manuscripts of the work,[71] which indicates an impressive initial diffusion. Green and Murphy list thirteen editions (beginning in Venice *c.*1472), two of them incunables, six from Paris (1519–38), three from Venice (one of them doubtful; the latest the Aldine edition of 1523), ending with Lyon 1547. López Grigera notes the use of the book in sixteenth-century Spain, including a 1511 reprint with notes by Fernando Alonso de Herrera.[72] This pattern suggests a good availability in the first half of the sixteenth century but not a great success. Monfasani suggests that George's work was displaced by the publication of direct translations from Hermogenes but, as we saw in Chapter 2, these were not notably more successful and the Paris printings of Hermogenes

[67] e.g. ibid. 569–74, 587–9, drawing on *Rhetorica ad Herennium* 4.14.20, 25.34, 32.43–4; 4.20.27–21.29.

[68] George, *Rhetoricorum libri V*, 556–68, 583–9.

[69] Ibid. 607–23; Montefusco, 'Catégories stylistiques', 179–81.

[70] George, *Rhetoricorum libri V*, 623–35; Hermogenes, ed. Rabe, 404–12.

[71] J. Monfasani, *Collectanea Trapezuntiana* (Binghamton, NY, 1984), 459.

[72] L. López Grigera, *La rétorica en la España del siglo de oro* (Salamanca, 1994), 56, 75–7.

tend to overlap with, rather than succeed, their printings of George Trapezuntius. George's work was listed in the 1529 statutes of Salamanca and influenced Sturm and Scaliger.[73]

A few years after finishing *Rhetoricorum libri V*, George, still working as a school-teacher, now at Bagno di Romagna, completed a short summa of dialectic, *Isagoge dialectica*.[74] This work provides a brief, clearly expressed summary of the main principles of Aristotelian logic, without the scholastic additions. It is a cleaned-up version of Peter of Spain's *Tractatus* or Paul of Venice's *Logica parva*, which conveys the essence of logical teaching without the metaphysical implications, the semantic explorations, or the doctrine of consequences. After its tour of the predicables, the categories, the proposition, and the syllogism (to which he gives most space), George adds short accounts of definition, division, and the rules of disputation. He praises the usefulness of the topics for orators, logicians, and writers on all subjects,[75] but he does not include a full treatment of the topics. George writes of including only the parts of dialectic which are necessary 'for speaking and for investigating topical arguments', rejecting more recent additions as not really useful.[76] Monfasani interprets this as meaning that George intended to write a dialectic for the use of orators,[77] but George had already devoted much of *Rhetoricorum libri V* to confirmation and confutation and his section on argumentation there is completely different from his discussion of syllogism, conditional syllogism, enthymeme, and simple conclusion in *Isagoge*.[78] It seems better to assume that George deliberately provided a summa of logic suited to the humanists who wanted to do without the additions introduced by the *barbari Britanni*.

Monfasani finds eighteen fifteenth-century Italian manuscripts of *Isagoge dialectica*.[79] Green and Murphy list fifty-three Latin editions and one edition of an Italian translation (Venice, 1567). After one Venice incunable (*c.*1472) the editions are all northern, beginning in Paris in 1509 with a total of eighteen Paris editions (mostly in the 1530s and 1540s), fourteen from Cologne (1524–60), and eight from Lyon (1539–60). Monfasani suggests that *Isagoge dialectica* succeeded in the North because it covered exactly those parts of the traditional logic syllabus not included in Agri-

[73] José Luis Fuertes Herreros (ed.), *Estatutos de la Universidad de Salamanca 1529* (Salamanca, 1984), 175; Monfasani, *George of Trebizond*, 318–27; George, *Rhetoricorum libri V*, ed. Deitz, pp. xxvi–xxix.

[74] Monfasani, *George of Trebizond*, 37. Vasoli, La dialettica, 81–99.

[75] George Trapezuntius, *De re dialectica* (Cologne, 1539), sigs. J8^{v}–K1^{r}.

[76] 'ad dicendum et ad inspiciendum rationem topicam', George Trapezuntius, *De re dialectica* (Cologne, 1539), sig. A6^{r}.

[77] Monfasani, *George of Trebizond*, 300–1, 313.

[78] George Trapezuntius, *De re dialectica* (Cologne, 1539), sigs. E6^{r}–L1^{v}.

[79] Monfasani, *Collectanea*, 473–7.

cola's *De inventione dialectica*,[80] which sounds plausible but may underestimate George's achievement in producing a short clear manual which could be used in schools or as an introductory text prior to the study of Aristotle's logical works.

At more or less the same period George composed his commentary on Cicero's *Pro Ligario*, partly as a confirmation of the method of analysis practised in *Rhetoricorum libri V*, and partly to win his argument with Guarino.[81] This work goes into rather more detail than the pioneering analysis of Loschi and was frequently reprinted in collections of commentaries on Cicero's works.[82] Hence George must be regarded as one of the innovators in what became an important sixteenth-century genre. George completed his contributions to rhetoric early in his stay in Rome when he translated Aristotle's *Rhetoric* into Latin. This translation was highly successful. Monfasani lists twenty-three manuscripts and twenty-five editions, printed between 1475 and 1603–14.[83]

LORENZO VALLA (1407–1457)

Lorenzo Valla was probably the foremost Italian humanist of the first half of the fifteenth century.[84] For the sixteenth century he was the revered author of *Elegantiae linguae Latinae*, the authoritative guide to Latin usage, and the first humanist to work on the text of the New Testament. He grew up in Rome in a family associated with the papal court, where his first well-known work, *De voluptate* (1431), was set.[85] He never attended university and was primarily self-taught, though he learnt Greek from Rinuccio di Castiglione between about 1424 and 1427, and acknowledged help from visiting scholars such as Giovanni Aurispa and Leonardo Bruni.[86] In 1431 after failing to succeed his uncle as apostolic secretary he moved to Pavia, where he became lecturer in rhetoric at the university.

[80] Monfasani, *George of Trebizond*, 328–37 (with useful chart of edns., 335).
[81] Ibid. 38–9, 291–3.
[82] Monfasani, *Collectanea*, 463–4, lists five manuscripts and twelve editions.
[83] Ibid. 698–701.
[84] For Valla's life: Valla, *Epistolae*, ed. O. Besomi and M Regoliosi (Padua, 1984); R. Sabbadini, 'Cronologia documentata della vita di Lorenzo Valla', in L. Barozzi and R. Sabbadini, *Studi sul Panormita e sul Valla* (Florence, 1891), repr. in L. Valla, *Opera omnia*, ii (Turin, 1962); G. Mancini, *Vita di Lorenzo Valla* (Florence, 1891); M. Fois, *Il pensiero cristiano di Lorenzo Valla* (Rome, 1969). On his thought see esp. S. I. Camporeale, *Lorenzo Valla: umanesimo e teologia* (Florence, 1972) and O. Besomi and M. Regoliosi (eds.), *Lorenzo Valla e l'umanesimo italiano* (Padua, 1986).
[85] In later recensions he changed the setting and title (to *De vero bono*).
[86] Sabbadini, 'Cronologia documentata', 50–4; Fois, Il *pensiero cristiano*, 3–11.

Forced to move on in 1433 by the hostility he had provoked in the powerful law faculty, in 1434 he joined the court of Alfonso the Magnanimous, who was attempting to take possession of Naples.[87] During five years of continual movement and military campaigns (including eighteen months in exile after being captured by the Milanese) Valla conceived and began a series of major works. In 1439 he finished the first version of *Repastinatio dialecticae et philosophiae*, in which he attacks Aristotelian philosophy and attempts to construct a simplified logic. By 1440 he had written *De falso credita et ementita Constantini donatione*, which demonstrates that the document which was the basis of papal claims to temporal sovereignty was a forgery. He finished the first versions of *Elegantiae* in 1441 and of *De collatione Novi Testamenti* in 1443.[88] For the rest of his life he revised these works, taking advantage of his continually deepening knowledge of Greek and Latin literature, and defended himself against attacks. In 1447 he returned to Rome, to become an apostolic *scriptor*, and he taught rhetoric and translated Thucydides and Herodotus into Latin. In 1455 he became papal secretary. He was buried in San Giovanni in Laterano in 1457.

Repastinatio dialecticae et philosophiae was written out of his experience at the University of Pavia and as a response to the dominance of the arts faculty by logic-teaching and Aristotelianism.[89] The structure of the work corresponds to the first three treatises of Aristotle's *Organon*: *Categories*, *De interpretatione*, and *Prior Analytics*. In book 1 Valla examines the metaphysical foundations of Aristotelian logic, arguing that they are misconceived and attempting to simplify them. He adds a section on definition which he regards as the key foundation of logic. According to Valla the purpose of the categories and predicables is to make definition possible. In book 2 Valla criticizes Aristotle's teaching on the proposition and the square of contraries. He insists that logic should work with the full resources of classical Latin instead of with a single sentence form and a restricted group of signs of quantity and negation (e.g. 'All horses are white'; 'Some horses are not white'). At the end of the second book he adds a long section on the invention of arguments taken from Quintilian's *Institutio oratoria* 5.8–10. This provides a general account of proof, a discussion of the use of evidence, accounts of enthymeme, epicheireme,[90]

[87] 'Cronologia documentata', 58–67, 74; *Epistolae*, 115–24, 151, 157–60, 191.

[88] 'Cronologia documentata', 79, 83–8; *Epistolae*, 151–60, 171–90; Fois, *Il pensiero cristiano*, 170–4.

[89] The first and third recensions of the work are edited in L. Valla, *Repastinatio dialecticae et philosophiae*, ed. G. Zippel (Padua, 1982); C. Vasoli, *La dialettica e la retorica dell'Umanesimo* (Milan, 1968), 28–77; P. Mack, *Renaissance Argument* (Leiden, 1993), 22–116; L. Nauta, *In Defense of Common Sense* (Cambridge, Mass., 2009).

[90] J. Klein, 'Epicheirem', in G. Ueding (ed.), *Historisches Wörterbuch der Rhetorik*, ii (Tübingen, 1994), 1251–8.

and the four Stoic forms of argument, and a version of the topics of invention with advice on their use. Book 3 is devoted to the syllogism. Valla rejects the third figure of the syllogism and adds several new forms which Aristotle would have rejected. Then he describes alternative forms of argumentation, such as hypothetical syllogisms, extended syllogisms, sorites, dilemma, induction, enthymeme, and example. Valla emphasizes the range of ways in which arguments can be formulated and argues that the syllogism is one form in which arguments (found by the topics) can be expressed, among many others. Forms of argumentation, rather than being the guarantee of truthful inference (as the syllogism was for Aristotle) are ways of expressing arguments, almost analogous to the different stylistic choices open to the orator once the material of the speech has been devised.

Valla writes as an independent thinker not fully socialized within the Aristotelian tradition. He turns the tools of dialectic against the premisses of Aristotelian logic. Why should there be ten categories? And what sort of thing is a category in any case? Why should argument be restricted by the formulae of the proposition and the syllogism? He thinks in a new way in order to formulate his devastating criticisms and he backs up his thinking with painstaking philological analysis of the meaning of Latin expressions in context. He also enjoyed being provocative, taking a perverse pride in the number of Aristotelian ideas he was willing to overturn.[91]

In some ways *Repastinatio dialecticae et philosophiae* is a difficult and rather strange book. It makes a series of complicated philosophical arguments against metaphysics. In order to create space for practical arguing in classical Latin, Valla is forced to create a metaphysics which aims to show that everyday language makes the necessary distinctions about the world. Valla has written a dense controversial book in order to persuade people that logic should be clear and simple. His argument, which was a more thorough and philosophical expression of a discontent other humanists had expressed, prepared the way for a different understanding of the connections between rhetoric and dialectic, and for a group of textbooks of simplified dialectic, among them George Trapezuntius's *Isagoge dialectica*. Accounts of the philosophical implications of Valla's book are available elsewhere;[92] here I need to discuss its connections with rhetoric.

[91] *Epistolae*, 214–15 ; Mack, *Renaissance Argument*, 26–9.

[92] S. I. Camporeale, *Lorenzo Valla: Umanesimo e teologia* (Florence, 1972), 33–87, 149–71, 235–49; Mack, *Renaissance Argument*, 37–94; L. Nauta, In *Defense of Common Sense* (Cambridge, Mass., 2009).

Reading Quintilian was a formative experience for Valla. His first book was *De comparatione Ciceronis Quintilianique* (1428). The work is now lost but Panormita tells us that the comparison was greatly to Quintilian's advantage.[93] Valla learnt from Quintilian's approach to language, especially in the surveys of Latin authors' uses of individual words, which are so important in both *Elegantiae* and *Repastinatio*. He frequently cites Quintilian's observations on a range of subjects. For his description of the invention of arguments he borrowed three whole chapters from *Institutio oratoria*, as we have seen. Valla did not want or need to write a rhetoric textbook because Quintilian's *Institutio oratoria* gave him everything he looked for.

But he did want to alter the balance of power and time within the *trivium*. The cycle of liberal arts, on which the medieval university course was based, treated the three verbal arts (grammar, rhetoric, and dialectic) and the four mathematical arts (arithmetic, geometry, music, and astronomy) as essential preludes to the study of philosophy. In most universities, it was expected that students would have mastered Latin before attending university and rhetoric was taught briefly, if at all. Most of the time allocated to the BA course was given over to logic, which formed the basis for the study of physics, metaphysics, and ethics which followed. In the preface to book 2 of *Repastinatio* Valla argued that this distribution of time should be overturned. He insisted that learning grammar properly (that is to say, learning both Latin and Greek and reading the more important authors) would take a long time. Because dialectic, properly considered, was so short and simple it would take scarcely more months than grammar would take years. Where dialectic is simple and of use to everyone, Valla saw rhetoric as a highly demanding, specialized skill. Rhetoric requires exceptional skills but it needs to be learnt only by a few people.[94] The orator needs to know everything taught within dialectic and many other things as well.

Valla demands that logic concern itself with the practicalities of arguing in natural language. He rejects Aristotle's attempt to restrict argument to a few semi-formalized sentence-types. By the same token a thorough understanding of how language works in practice replaces many of the doctrines of logic. You study quantity and negation not by formulating rules but by observing the way in which a whole range of different expressions are used by the best writers. Potentially confusing implications of sentences, which the scholastics studied as *insolubilia* and in supposition

[93] Camporeale, *Lorenzo Valla*, 89–93, 126; *Valla, Opera omnia*, ii (Turin, 1962), 162–3.
[94] *Repastinatio*, 175–7; Mack, *Renaissance Argument*, 110–14.

theory, can be eliminated by considering the context in which words are uttered. In Valla investigation of sentences and texts from real language use (and especially from classical Latin literature) is the basis from which arguments about meaning and attempts to formulate rules must proceed.[95]

Valla developed a rhetoricized approach to logic. Logic aimed to teach ways of persuading people. Following Quintilian the first step was to use the topics of invention to discover arguments suited to the question at issue. These arguments then needed to be expressed in the way most likely to convince an audience. He employed the criterion of practical usefulness to determine what should be included within logic. At the same time the arguers must use their understanding of the implications of language to test drafted expressions and reject those which go beyond what they know or intend.

Sometimes Valla used rhetoric to investigate the rules of logic. Considering the dilemma and the conversion as a reply to it, Valla gives as an example a story from Aulus Gellius about the rhetoric teacher Protagoras and his pupil Evathlus. They had agreed that the second half of the fee for teaching Evathlus would only become due after he won his first case. But Evathlus refused to practise and Protagoras had to go to law to recover his fee. Protagoras made an argument in the form of a dilemma: 'if you lose the case, the court will require you to pay my fee; on the other hand if you win the case, you will have won your first case and so the fee will become due as a result of our agreement.' Evathlus replied with an argument in the form of conversion: 'if I lose the case I will not have to pay because of our agreement but if I win the case I will not have to pay because of the sentence of the judges'. Gellius commends Evathlus's reply, saying that the judges were unable to decide for either party. Valla considers Evathlus's reply ineffective and the judges' behaviour unjust. He supports this by writing a declamation rejecting Evathlus's argument and urging the judges to reach a decision.[96] He draws one series of arguments from a consideration of the judges' point of view. He urges them not to fear that if they make a decision against Protagoras their verdict will then be overturned: their decision will not be appealed, rather it will create the circumstances in which a new case can be made. Then he turns to Evathlus, first exposing the slipperiness of his argument (in the way

[95] There are some cases in which Valla relies on meanings of terms not intended by Boethius in order to make his examples seem ridiculous. *Repastinatio*, 232–3, 482–3; Mack, *Renaissance Argument*, 76–80, 100–4.

[96] *Repastinatio*, 312–14, 316–20, 562–4, 565–8; Aulus Gellius, *Noctes atticae* 5.10.5–16; Mack, *Renaissance Argument*, 105–8.

when faced with a sentence against him he appeals to the agreement and when faced with the agreement he relies instead on the judges' verdict) and then accusing him of ingratitude. By composing a speech for Protagoras Valla is in a sense imitating and going beyond what Quintilian did in outlining the arguments which the Thebans could make in order to recover their hundred talents from the Thessalians.[97] Valla made a point of arguing like an orator both in his defence of freedom of thought in the preface to *Repastinatio* book 1 and in his dialogue *De vero bono*. He believed that, whereas philosophy corrupts religion, rhetoric can serve it by urging people to do good. Where philosophical language obfuscates, rhetoric illuminates. Rhetoric is invaluable in understanding and preaching the scriptures.[98]

Repastinatio dialecticae et philosophiae did not enjoy great success. It was hard to find copies of the work in Valla's lifetime; the Aristotelians did not even feel that they had to reply to Valla's arguments against their hero. The work was printed a few times in northern Europe but, with the exception of Nizolio, later writers took more notice of Valla's comments on Latin usage than of his ideas about logic.[99] But Valla's emphasis on the importance of the topics of invention and on the need to understand argument as functioning in real language (and not simply in formal syllogisms) was important for the development of humanist logic, particularly through the work of Rudolph Agricola. Valla's empirical approach to understanding the meaning and usage of words and his quest to understand the distinctions observed in classical Latin underpinned his *Elegantiae,* which was one of the most important reference works of the sixteenth century both in Italy and in the North.[100] IJsewijn and Tournoy list forty-five manuscripts of *Elegantiae* and 152 editions before 1620. The peak of production was in the 1530s and 1540s, with twenty-four editions in each decade. Production declined quite rapidly after 1570. Paris produced thirty-eight editions (the last in 1547), Venice thirty-two, Lyon twenty-six, and Cologne eighteen.[101] In a sense Valla inspired and

[97] *Institutio oratoria* 5.10.109–18, part of the section Valla borrowed, *Repastinatio*, 272–4.

[98] Valla, *Opera omnia*, i. 117–20; *Repastinatio*, 7–8; Camporeale, *Lorenzo Valla: Umanesimo*, 211–33, 302–11.

[99] Mack, *Renaissance Argument*, 114–16.

[100] D. Marsh, 'Grammar, Method and Polemic in Valla's *Elegantiae*', *Rinascimento*, 19 (1979), 91–116; W. Ax, 'Lorenzo Valla (1407–1457), *Elegantiarum linguae latini*', in Ax (ed.), *Von Eleganz und Barbarei* (Wiesbaden, 2001), 29–57;Ann Moss, *Renaissance Truth and the Latin Language Turn* (Oxford, 2003), 35–43.

[101] J. IJsewijn and G. Tournoy, 'Un primo censimento dei manoscritti e delle edizioni degli *Elegantiae*' and 'Nuovi contributi per l'elenco', *Humanistica Lovaniensia*, 18 (1969), 25–52, and 20 (1971), 1–4.

supported the success of a whole series of guides to effective and elegant Latin expression.

Grammarians continued to contribute to the reform and the diffusion of rhetoric. In 1450 Gasparo Veronese's *Grammar*, though it followed the outlines of Guarino's *Regulae grammaticales*, added a comprehensive list of the figures of speech taken from the medieval *Graecismus*. This work was printed later in the century.[102] In 1468 Niccolò Perotti, a pupil of Guarino and Vittorino da Feltre, completed his highly influential *Rudimenta grammatices*. Besides the usual sections on accidence and syntax, Perotti added a brief listing of the figures of speech and a letter-writing manual, which bases its modifications of *ars dictaminis* practice on observation of classical letter-writing and especially of Cicero. According to Green and Murphy this work was printed 133 times between 1473 and 1535. Percival considers that the forty-four sixteenth-century editions he has so far identified must be an understatement of the true picture.[103] I shall consider this work in more detail in Chapter 11 below. These examples show the connections between the higher stages of teaching basic grammar and the beginnings of rhetoric. Grammar teaching necessarily leads on to (and is completed and reinforced by) composition and study of the authors, for which simplified aspects of rhetorical doctrine (here the figures of speech and the principles of letter-writing, elsewhere the doctrine of sentence composition) are helpful or even essential. The letter-writing and preaching manuals (both 1478) of Lorenzo Traversagni of Savona (1425–1503) will be discussed in Chapters 11 and 12 below. They remind us that fifteenth- and sixteenth-century Italians tended to contribute more to the so-called minor genres of tropes and figures, letter-writing, and preaching rather than writing new manuals of the whole of rhetoric.

Among the great achievements of Italian scholars in the second half of the fifteenth century was the printing of the first (and many subsequent) editions of the major texts of classical Latin rhetoric. For example Cicero's *De oratore* was first printed in Subiaco in 1465. There were a further nine Italian editions (and one Nuremberg edition) in the fifteenth century. *Rhetorica ad Herennium* was first printed in Venice in 1470, with nineteen further Italian (and six northern European) fifteenth-century editions.

[102] W. K. Percival, 'The Place of the *Rudimenta Grammatices* in the History of Grammar', *Res Publica Litterarum*, 4 (1981), 235–6, 260.

[103] See Percival's article in the previous note and his 'The Influence of Perotti's *Rudimenta* in the Cinquecento', in Sesto Prete (ed.), *Protrepticon* (Milan, 1989), 92, 98–9, both now collected in his *Studies in Renaissance Grammar* (Aldershot, 2004) with identical pagination. Pedro Martín Baños, El *arte epistolar en el Renacimiento europeo 1400–1600* (Bilbao, 2005), 262–3.

Quintilian's *Institutio oratoria* was first published in Rome in 1470, with eight further Italian fifteenth-century editions. These early Italian editions made it much easier for later northern printers to publish editions of classical Latin rhetorics. Altogether classical Latin rhetorics were printed in seventy-five editions between 1460 and 1500.[104]

One Italian whose work was much reprinted in northern Europe in the fifteenth century was Albertano da Brescia, a thirteenth-century *causidicus*. His *De arte loquendi et tacendi* advises his son on when and how to speak. The treatise is organized into six questions: who, what, to whom you speak, why, how, and when. Much of the advice given is moral and prudential (e.g. it is better to be silent than to speak; don't trust your enemies; don't reveal secrets), but under 'how' Albertano makes comments about delivery, appropriateness, and style. Under 'when' he gives brief outlines for sermons, letters, diplomatic salutations, and laws. Albertano gives as many reasons for remaining silent as for speaking but he advises his son to think carefully about speaker, audience, and occasion. Paola Navone listed 238 manuscripts of the work, mostly fifteenth-century. It was printed forty-three times from 1472, thirty-nine times before 1500, mainly from Cologne, Antwerp, Leipzig, Paris, and Lyon (with only two Italian editions, both sixteenth-century). A Dutch translation was printed seven times (1484–98).[105]

Only George Trapezuntius's *Isagoge dialectica* and Perotti's *Rudimenta grammatices* were much reprinted later; yet fifteenth-century Italians made innovative contributions to the development of renaissance rhetoric. They discovered new Latin texts, publicized and edited them, and made a start on absorbing the lessons of Greek rhetoric. They analysed Cicero's speeches in relation to the doctrines of rhetoric, showing that Cicero used rhetoric in practice and that practical situations sometimes required adaptation of the rules. By emphasizing the application of logic to argument in classical texts and in everyday debate they began to reform the teaching of dialectic in ways that would prove important to rhetoric. They composed new textbooks on letter-writing which were widely used and

[104] J. J. Murphy and M. Davies, 'Rhetorical Incunabula STC', *Rhetorica*, 15 (1997), 355–470.

[105] James M. Powell, *Albertanus of Brescia: The Pursuit of Happiness in the Early Thirteenth Century* (Philadelphia, 1992); P. Navone, 'La "Doctrina loquendi et tacendi" di Albertano da Brescia: Censimento dei manoscritti', *Studi Medievali*, 35 (1994), 895–930; Albertano, *Liber de doctrina dicendi et tacendi*, ed. P. Navone (Tavarnuzze, 1998); A. Graham, 'Albertanus of Brescia: A Supplementary Census of Latin Manuscripts', *Studi Medievali*, 41 (2000), 429–45; Witt, *Footsteps*, 58–62. More information with texts and an English tr. by William Askins at http://freespace.virgin.net/angus.graham/Albertano.htm.

copied throughout Europe. They wrote manuals and rules intended to help in the composition of elegant Latin prose and they began to argue about imitation of classical authors, especially Cicero. The rhetorical innovations of northerners like Agricola, Erasmus, and Latomus were in part prompted by what they learnt from Italy.

4

Rudolph Agricola

Rudolph Agricola (1444–85) wrote the most original textbook on writing of the fifteenth century and the first modern rhetoric which can be placed among the classics of the subject, alongside Aristotle, Cicero, and Quintilian. Agricola lived for ten years in Italy (1469–79), longer than any other early northern humanist, and his *De inventione dialectica*, completed in Dillingen, near Augsburg, on his homeward journey in 1479, was the fruit of his Italian experiences. But he went to Italy already thoroughly educated, and for much of his time in Pavia and Ferrara he lived among northern fellow students, acting as their unofficial tutor in humanistic studies. This experience of teaching writing to advanced students may have encouraged his book's critical approach and its familiarity with the best Latin writing. If he had been a more conventional schoolteacher or a tutor to a young aristocrat his work may have been less original.

Agricola's work is notable for the way he used Latin literary texts to show how dialectic contributes to all aspects of persuasion. He placed the topics of invention at the centre of his work but he analysed the nature of each topic in a new way and showed through analysis of examples how writers have used the arguments and other material the topics generate. He provided the theory for, and the first example of, the significant renaissance genre of dialectical analyses of literary works. He made an original exploration of the relationship between exposition (including narrative) and argument. He directed attention back to emotional persuasion, amplification, and disposition. Many of the innovations of Erasmus, Melanchthon, and Ramus develop from Agricola's contribution.

Agricola was born Roelof Huusman in Baflo near Groningen on 17 February 1444, the son of a priest, Hendrik Vries, who was elected abbot of the Benedictine convent at Selwerd on the day his son was born. He remained abbot until his death in 1480. Thanks to his father's influence Agricola's studies were supported from the income of a farm belonging to the bishop of Münster. He attended the school of St Martin in Groningen in 1454; in 1456 he matriculated at Erfurt and in 1465 'Rudolphus Agricola ex Baflo prope Groeningen' took first place in the Master of Arts degree at Louvain where he had probably studied for seven years, following a course in Aristotelian logic and natural philosophy. Soon after that he may have begun to study law. In any case by 1469 he was in Italy, studying law at the University of Pavia which attracted many northern students. Although he gave up his law studies he played a full part in the life of the university, giving Latin orations at the installation of three northern rectors (1472–4). At Pavia he lived with several other 'Germans', including Johannes Müller (Regiomontanus), Adolph Occo, Johann and Dietrich von Plieningen, and Johann von Dalberg. His letters show that he gave private tuition in Latin composition and literature to the last three. In 1475 Agricola moved to Ferrara in order to learn Greek. For a time he was employed by Count Ercole I d'Este as an organist. The von Plieningens and his half-brother Johann had joined him in Ferrara by 1476, when Agricola gave the *Oration in Praise of Philosophy* to inaugurate the university year. While in Ferrara he made several translations from Greek, worked on the texts of Tacitus and the younger Pliny, and made the acquaintance of Battista Guarini, Guarino's son, and Ermolao Barbaro. Presumably he used the fine library which Guarino and the d'Este family had built up, including Guarino's copies of Valla's works, among them *Repastinatio*. Agricola so much valued the progress of his Greek studies that in 1477 he refused the offer of the newly founded chair of poetics at Louvain in order to remain in Ferrara. After Dietrich von Plieningen took his law degree Agricola travelled back to Germany with him. They spent much of the summer in Dillingen where Agricola left the completed manuscript of *De inventione dialectica* so that Dietrich could make the fair copy for Adolph Occo.[1]

Agricola's plan for *De inventione dialectica* is straightforward but highly original.[2] Book 1 is concerned with the topics of invention; book 2 with the subject-matter of dialectic (the question), its instrument (exposition and argumentation), and training; book 3 with moving, pleasing, and disposition. Table 4.1 illustrates the scheme.

[1] The main sources for the life of Agricola are his letters and six early biographies: Agricola, *Letters*, ed. A. van der Laan and F. Akkerman (Assen, 2002); F. Akkerman and A. J. Vanderjagt (eds.), *Rodolphus Agricola Phrisius* (Leiden, 1988), 3–20, 79–95, 313–27. F. Akkerman is at present editing the early lives of Agricola for the series Bibliotheca Latinitatis Novae. All the events in this paragraph are documented in my *Renaissance Argument* (Leiden, 1993), 117–19, from which it is condensed.

[2] R. Agricola, *De inventione dialectica* (Cologne, 1539; repr. Nieuwkoop, 1967), also re-edited (with German tr.) by L. Mundt (Tubingen, 1992), selections tr. in J. R. McNally, 'Rudolph Agricola's *De inventione Libri Tres*: A Translation of Selected Chapters', *Speech Monographs*, 34 (1967), 393–422 (NB McNally was using a slightly different edn. with different chapter numberings to the Cologne 1539). Good French trs. of some chapters in Agricola, *Écrits sur la dialectique et l'humanisme*, ed. Marc van der Poel (Paris, 1997). Marc van der Poel and I intend to produce a complete English tr.

Table 4.1. Plan of Agricola, *De inventione dialectica*

Section		Chapter
	Book 1	
A	Introduction	1
B	The Topics	
	Introduction to the Topics	2–4
	The Topics	5–19, 21–7
	Discussion of other treatments of them	20, 28, 29
	Book 2	
A	Introductory	
	The deficiency of contemporary dialectic	1
	What is dialectic?	2–3
	Teaching, moving, and pleasing	4–5
B	Matter	
	The nature of the question	6–8
	Divisions of the question	8–11
	The chief question and its dependents	12–14
C	Instrument	
	Kinds of language use	15–17
	Argumentation	18–21
	Exposition	22–23
	The parts of the oration	24
	The topics belong to dialectic	25
D	Training	
	Knowing the topics and using them	26–30
	Book 3	
A	Moving	
	The handling of emotions	1–3
B	Pleasing	
	Pleasing and digression	4
	Copia and brevity	5–7
C	Disposition	
	Overall disposition	8–11
	Arranging questions and arguments	12–15
	Exercises, reading, and conclusion	16

Even on the basis of this short summary it is clear that the organization of *De inventione dialectica* is very different from the traditional textbook of rhetoric. Agricola has combined elements from rhetoric and dialectic to produce an original account of the process of composition. So, for example, the section on the topics (1B in the table) is developed from the versions of the topics in Cicero, Quintilian, and Boethius; the discussion of the question (2B) draws on Boethius, Aristotle, the rhetoric manuals, and original material; the discussion of emotion (3A) draws on Aristotle's

Rhetoric, Cicero's *De oratore,* and Quintilian; and the treatment of disposition (3C) is developed from materials in Aristotle's *Categories*, *Posterior Analytics*, Quintilian's *Institutio oratoria,* and *Rhetorica ad Herennium.* Agricola knew both Aristotelian logic and the rhetorical tradition very well when he wrote his book. In addition, as we shall see, much of the argument is driven by close analysis of Latin literature, especially Virgil, Cicero's *Orations,* and the *Declamations* attributed to Quintilian. Reading Valla may have prompted Agricola to emphasize the topics (and suggested some details of the treatment of three topics) but the actual overlap between the *De inventione dialectica* and *Repastinatio* is rather small, and there are numerous specific issues on which Valla and Agricola take different views.[3]

In Table 4.2 I try to demonstrate Agricola's originality and his wide-ranging use of his source-traditions by listing the main contents of the manuals of rhetoric and dialectic in the usual order in which they occur (in textbooks like *Rhetorica ad Herennium* and Peter of Spain's *Tractatus*). The cross-references aim to show which elements from the traditional syllabuses of both subjects are found in *De inventione dialectica* and where Agricola puts them. So, for example, in Table 4.2, the letters 2C and 3C against *exordium* indicate that the issue of the *exordium* is discussed both in section C of book 2 (specifically in chapter 24 on the parts of the oration) and in section C of book 3 (in Agricola's account of disposition).

A comparison of the two tables shows, first, that most of Agricola's teachings draw on the traditional contents of the manuals of rhetoric and dialectic but, second, that he chooses selectively among the materials in both subjects and combines them in an original framework. The work is unified around the topics and the Ciceronian tasks of the orator (teaching, moving, and pleasing). Book 1 describes the topics; book 2 shows how material is prepared for dialectical invention (chapters 1–14), how material found using the topics can be presented to an audience (chapters 15–24), and how pupils can be trained to make use of the topics (chapters 26–30). While these two books are devoted to teaching, which Agricola declares to be the most important of the orator's tasks,[4] book 3 considers the place of the topics in moving and pleasing, and the ways in which the different types of material found through topical invention should be organized into a literary composition. Several of the key ideas of the whole work (teaching, moving, and pleasing; exposition and argumentation; and the rationale underlying the topics)

[3] Mack, *Renaissance Argument*, 244–50.
[4] Agricola, *De inventione dialectica*, 1.

Table 4.2 Courses in Rhetoric and Dialectic Compared with *De inventione dialectica* (*DID*)

Rhetoric	*DID*	Dialectic	*DID*
Invention		**Predicables** (genus, species,	1B
Exordium	2C, 3C	differentia, properties)	
Narration	2C	**Categories**	
Status-theory	2B	Substance	1B
Special topics		Quantity	
General topics	1B	Relatives	
Forms of argumentation	2C	Quality	1B
(includes syllogism, induction,		Post-predicaments (contraries,	3C
enthymeme)		meanings of prior, kinds of	
Refutation	2C	change)	
Amplification	3AB	**Proposition**	
Emotional appeals	3A	Quantity	2B
Humour		Quality	2B
Disposition:		Contraries	1B
Varying four-part form	3C	Modals	2B
Argument order	3C	**Syllogism**	
Deliberative speech		Figures and moods (list of valid	2C
Epideictic speech	2B	forms of syllogism and	
Style		conversions between them)	
Three kinds		Advice on use of forms	2C
Qualities		**Topics**	
Tropes		Forms of argumentation	2C
Figures		(syllogism, induction,	
Memory		enthymeme, example)	
Delivery		Maxims and differences	
		List of topics	1B
		Definition	1B
		Division	1B
		Sophisms (i.e. how to deal with	
		deceptive arguments):	
		Kinds	
		Strategy	

are presented in the first chapter and returned to at key moments throughout the book.

Agricola offers both restrictive and expansive definitions of his task. On one view dialectical invention is dialectic (i.e. not rhetoric, and especially not the tropes and figures) with the judgement section (the predicables to the syllogism) left out. But he also defines dialectic as concerned with teaching, which he regards as the most important of the three duties of the orator. After he has defended dialectic's right to be considered an art, he opens his main discussion of the nature of dialectic by considering the purpose of language.

> At the beginning we said that all language has the object that someone should make someone else share in his or her thoughts. Therefore it is apparent that there should be three things in every speech: the speaker, the hearer, and the subject-matter. Consequently there are three points to be observed in speaking: that what the speaker intends should be understood, that the person addressed should listen avidly, and that what is said should be plausible and should be believed. Grammar, which passes on the method of speaking correctly, clearly teaches the first. The second is taught by rhetoric, which provides embellishments and elegance of language, and all the bait for capturing ears. Dialectic consequently seems to claim for itself what is left, that is, to speak convincingly on whatever matter is included in a speech.[5]

Agricola presents the *trivium* as a whole as a study of the resources of language. Where grammar is concerned with correctness and rhetoric is preoccupied with attracting attention, dialectic's task is to teach the way of speaking convincingly. In book 3 he shows that the topics assist the speaker in moving and pleasing his audience and argues that it would be pointless to know how to invent material if one did not also learn how to organize it (and he shows that logical principles apply here too). So tasks which would ordinarily (and even on his own definition) belong to rhetoric are here added to dialectical invention. If one thinks about the sequence of the writer's tasks dialectical invention is concerned with the whole process of thinking through the question, finding the arguments, expressing them as argumentation or exposition, working out ways to move and please the audience, and arranging all the materials assembled into a structure suited to the task and the audience. What is left to rhetoric is style and in particular the tropes and figures; what is left to dialectic is the detailed working out of the syllogism and other ways of arranging arguments. The main task of thinking about what to say belongs to dialectical invention and will be taught by Agricola. Taking this approach both prompts Agricola to reconsider issues which the textbooks of rhetoric had taken for granted and asserts the primacy of the topics of invention.

[5] Ibid. 192: 'Orationem omnem initio diximus in id paratam esse, ut animi sui participem quisque faceret alium. Tria ergo constat in omni oratione posse oportere, eum qui dicit, eum qui audit, et rem de qua habetur oratio, tresque proinde in dicendo observationes: ut percipi possit quid sibi velit qui dicit; ut cupide audiat cui dicitur; ut probabile sit, habeaturque fides ei, quod dicitur. Primum grammatice docet, quae emendate et aperte loquendi viam tradit. Proximum rhetorice, quae ornatum orationis cultumque et omnes capiendarum aurium illecebras invenit. Quod reliquum igitur est videbitur sibi dialectice vendicare, probabiliter dicere de qualibet re, quae deducitur in orationem.'

Agricola's original contribution to the topics consisted first in his clear and explicit explanation of the rationale of the topics and the practical method of using them, second in his additions to the list of topics he inherited from Cicero and Boethius, and third in his original investigations of several of the topics.[6] Agricola explains that the topics work because they help people find the specific connections between things which are needed in order to construct arguments. Both the things in the world and the connections between them are too numerous for anyone to remember them all, so dialecticians have listed the kinds of connections which exist between things. When we need to think about a particular thing (or two things joined in a proposition or a question) we can find out a great deal about it by thinking of it in relation to all the different types of connection. These kinds of connections are the topics. Because they lead us to think of arguments we can say that the arguments are within the topics, like precious objects in a treasury.[7] In order to train his readers in using the topics Agricola describes the exercise of topical description (thinking of connections from one particular thing through all the topics in turn).[8]

So, for example, if we need to make arguments about 'a philosopher', we may examine the definition of philosopher, and its genus, species, causes, effects, and other topics. Arguments suited to proving a proposition may be found by comparing topical descriptions of the two main terms of the proposition. Agricola takes the example of the question whether the philosopher should marry and finds that the philosopher's final cause of promoting virtue can be linked with the effects of marriage. The exercise of making topical descriptions trains the student to look into all aspects of both terms of a proposition in order to find possible supporting arguments.

Agricola takes Cicero's and Boethius's lists of topics as the starting point for his own list but he consciously aims to remove redundancy and to achieve coherence and completeness.[9] His earliest commentator Phrissemius translated Agricola's description of the organization of his topics into a diagram (see Table 4.3), which shows how the system works and which may have inspired Ramus's later graphic representations of his textbooks.

Topics are divided into internal and external. Internal topics are either within or around the thing. External topics are either necessarily joined or joined without necessity. In broad terms Agricola's topics are organized

[6] Mack, *Renaissance Argument*, 130–67.
[7] *De inventione dialectica*, 9.
[8] Ibid. 362–72.
[9] Ibid. 14–18, 170–4. Mack, *Renaissance Argument*, 142–50.

Table 4.3. Scheme of Agricola's Topics, by Phrissemius

		Within the substance of the thing, from which the thing receives what it is	Species Property/difference Whole Parts Conjugates
	Internal		
		Around the substance. Although they inhere to the thing, they bring a certain manner or disposition to it	Adjacents Actions Subject
Topics		Causes	Efficient
		Cognates, which share their origin	Final
		Results	Effects
		Necessarily joined	*Destinata*
		Applicita which added to the thing from outside provide it	Time
		with a certain disposition and name	Place *Connexa*
	External		
		Accidents which can exist with or without a thing	Contingents Name of a thing Opinions Comparisons Similars/dissimilars
		Joined without necessity	
		Repugnants (the same thing cannot participate in both)	Opposites *Distantia*[a]

[a] *De inventione dialectica, 22–5*

into groups corresponding to their distance from the thing itself, starting with elements which are part of the identity of the thing and ending with opposites. Organizing the topics in this way is an attempt to instil some order and logic into the list of headings. While this has some explanatory power it is not entirely successful. The list of topics is not logically exhaustive. The topics remain an arbitrary list of headings but Agricola has done more than earlier writers to introduce order into the list.

In his handling of the individual topics Agricola adapts and enlarges what Quintilian had done and breaks decisively with Boethius. Where Cicero concentrates on the kinds of argument that can be made from each topic and Boethius adds maxims supposedly guaranteeing the inferences made under each topic Agricola takes the view that the reader needs to understand the nature of each topic relationship in order to make the best use of arguments from each topic and to appreciate their relative strengths. So while earlier writers concentrate on the arguments which can be drawn from the definition of something, Agricola discusses the ways in which definitions are constructed, giving worked examples of definitions of law and state, and providing rules for checking well-formed definitions. He regards definition as something which a writer constructs to express his knowledge of some object rather than as something which is given in advance. The person who knows how to construct definitions will be able to use the topic in more instances and will have a better understanding of the types of argument from definition which will be effective.[10]

In his analysis of causes Agricola tries to understand how will, necessity, purpose, and action combine in order to make things happen. He shows that from different points of view the same aspect of a linked chain of cause and effect may be final cause, assisting effect, or efficient cause. Thus for the ship-builder the ship is the effect and the final cause is making money from its construction; but for the merchant the ship is an efficient cause enabling him to trade. By investigating the different kinds of cause and the viewpoints of different people Agricola hopes to understand how events can be described as being achieved and what types of responsibility can be inferred from them. Thinking about examples of different kinds of event helps the reader to a richer comprehension of the topic of causes, which can in turn be applied to new situations she or he wants to investigate. By learning how to adapt the topic to different cases one fashions an understanding of the topic which is more flexible and better able to generate ideas.[11]

Agricola is particularly illuminating on the generally neglected topic of similitudes.

> Of all the topics from which arguments are drawn almost none has less strength against a resistant reader than similitude. On the other hand there is none more suitable for the hearer who follows willingly and shows himself apt to be taught. For if it is correctly applied, it opens up a thing and places a sort of picture of it before the mind so that although it does not bring with it the necessity of agreeing, it does cause an implicit reluctance to disagree. Therefore it is not so frequently used for proving things but it is often used by orators for exploring and illuminating things, and is even more often used by poets. In spite of this similitude often has an appearance of proving by the

[10] *De inventione dialectica*, 26–9. Mack, *Renaissance Argument*, 150–6.

[11] *De inventione dialectica*, 78–89. Mack, Renaissance Argument, 156–9. M. Baxandall, 'Rudolph Agricola on Art and on Patrons', in his *Words for Pictures* (New Haven, Conn., 2003), 69–82.

> very fact that it shows how something is. Thus when you read that similitude of Quintilian: 'just as a vase with a narrow mouth rejects an excess of liquid but is filled by flowing or pouring gradually', it does not therefore follow that, on account of this, the delicate minds of boys must be taught according to their own strengths, but nonetheless, once someone has conceived the matter in his mind according to this image, he persuades himself that it cannot be otherwise.[12]

Agricola's comment here is extremely subtle and perceptive, registering the power of arguments from similitude as well as their limitations. Similitude is not proof but it can be very powerful in conditioning a mind to think in a particular way. Agricola then analyses a simile from Lucan, first to show how similes function logically and then to show how they may be discovered. He tries to find alternative comparators for the point Lucan makes, discussing the implications and advantages of each.[13]

Agricola's approach to the topics is detailed and practical. He analyses factual instances and literary examples to explore the nature of the connection and the types of effect that can be achieved by using it. Although there is a logical aspect to his investigation much of it involves thinking about the different ways words are used and reflecting on the practice of the best writers. He rejects Boethius's maxims because they miss the potential and the complexity of actual arguing by trying to reduce all arguments to maxims which are either entirely obvious (e.g. 'whatever is present to the genus is present to the species') or rather questionable (e.g. 'if whatever appears more likely to belong does not belong, nor will what seems less likely to belong').[14]

Near the beginning of *De inventione dialectica* Agricola proposes that there are two ways of using language to teach an audience. If the audience

[12] *De inventione dialectica*, 142: 'Omnium locorum e quibus ducuntur argumenta, nulli fere minus est virium contra renitentem auditorem, quam similitudini. Ad eum vero qui sponte sequitur, docendumque se praebet, accommodatior nullus est. Aperit enim rem (si recte adhibeatur) et quandam eius imaginem subiicit animo, ut cum assentiendi necessitatem non afferat, afferat tacitum dissentiendi pudorem. Quapropter ad probandum non ita crebro, ad explanandum illustrandumque saepe ab oratoribus, a poetis saepius adhibetur. Habet tamen persaepe probantis speciem similitudo, eo ipso, quod rem qualis sit indicat. Itaque cum legis Quintiliani illud: Vascula oris angusti superfusam humoris copiam respuunt, sensim autem influentibus vel instillantibus etiam replentur, non conficitur utique, debere propter hoc tenera puerorum ingenia pro modo virium suarum doceri. Sed tamen concipiendo quisque rem apud animum suum sub hac imagine, persuadet sibi, aliter fieri non posse.' Quintilian, *Institutio oratoria* 1.2.28.

[13] Lucan, *De bello civile*, 5.335–9. *De inventione dialectica*, 142–5. Mack, *Renaissance Argument*, 163–5.

[14] *De inventione dialectica*, 175–6. Boethius, *Opera*, PL 64, 1188B: 'quae generi adsunt speciei adsunt' 1191A: 'si id quod magis videtur inesse non inest, nec id quod minus videtur inesse inerit.'

is willing to believe what we say we can use exposition, that is, stating our view as clearly as possible. But if the audience is likely to resist our ideas we will need to use argumentation in order to force them to believe what we say.[15]

This is a rhetorical distinction because it has to do with the speaker's estimate of the audience's reaction and because it affects the choices the speaker will make about the verbal expression of particular sections of the speech. Characteristically Agricola makes his point about the difference between exposition and argumentation by analysing two passages from Virgil's *Aeneid.*[16] For Agricola the argumentative and emotional force of Juno's soliloquy makes it argumentation rather than exposition. He shows that the same material could be expressed in either form depending on the kinds of connections made, the elaboration of the material, and the writer or character's intention. Argumentation here is a matter of density of texture, of the way material is presented. We would also think of this passage from Juno, argumentative though it is, as emotional. As Agricola says, Juno uses arguments to stoke up her anger.

A little later Agricola discusses Sinon's speech to the Trojans from book 2 of the *Aeneid*, in which he explains the value of the wooden horse and in effect persuades them to take it within their walls, to illustrate the ways in which exposition can contribute to persuasion. His analysis of this speech shows that Sinon sets out a series of propositions (some true, some so connected to the true ones as to be plausible, some not unlikely) which the Trojans then gather together into arguments to persuade themselves that taking the horse inside the walls will give them an advantage.[17] The psychological insight that people are more likely to believe what their own reasoning has persuaded them of is linked to an argument about the way in which an exposition can be organized in order to create belief. Agricola suggests that when we wish to write a convincing exposition the logical connections between the propositions must be there in our minds but should not be stated explicitly. Argumentation, by contrast, is a matter of setting out logical connections and of repeating important points.

Now Agricola's distinction between exposition and argumentation is, as he admits, related to the classical distinction in the plan of the oration between narration and confirmation.[18] But Agricola insists that his way of putting it is more useful, first because it is of more general application

[15] *De inventione dialectica*, 1–2.
[16] *Aeneid* 1.12–33, 37–49. *De inventione dialectica*, 258–9.
[17] *De inventione dialectica*, 262–3. Analysed in Mack, 'Rudolph Agricola's Reading of Literature', *Journal of the Warburg and Courtauld Institutes*, 48 (1985), 23–41.
[18] *De inventione dialectica*, 258.

outside the oration, second because it recognizes the fact that you may need exposition within your confirmation or arguments in your narration, and third because it makes the link between features of linguistic form and decisions which the speaker makes about his or her audience. These features of linguistic form can be syllogisms or enthymemes but they can also be figures of emphasis and repetition.

Agricola's main treatment of argumentation falls into four sections. First he outlines the traditional four forms of argumentation (syllogism, enthymeme, induction, and example), giving some examples and discussing connections between the forms. Then he considers the ways in which forms of argumentation are used in orations. Analysing examples from Cicero's speeches he shows that orators can use the full forms but that generally they omit parts of the proof, since the missing elements can always be added if they are challenged. He argues that rhetorical commonplaces function as if they were major propositions of syllogisms. In the third section he outlines ways of buttressing incomplete arguments and using subordinate arguments to establish points one needs to prove a case. Finally he describes ways of rebutting arguments both on logical grounds and by exploiting the persona of one's opponent, giving examples of each of these approaches from Cicero.[19]

Agricola outlines his theory of exposition in book 2, chapters 22 and 23. There are three types of exposition: exposition which aims at delighting the audience, which is associated with poetry and which need have no connection with plausibility but may be more effective if it resembles truth; exposition of things which happened in the past, associated with history, in which the writer aims to relate what really happened but does not need to prove that something is true; and exposition intended to create belief, which belongs to oratory, philosophy, and pedagogy.

In expositions intended to create belief it is not enough that what you say should be true; you need to make it firm and self-evident because your opponent will be on the alert for any mistake. Every exposition of this kind will need to be both convincing and suited to the argument which follows. An exposition needs three qualities to be convincing: it must be *argumentosa*, which Agricola explains to mean 'including the causes or reasons for things, minor as well as major'; it must be *consentanea*, that is to say it must fit in with persons, places, times, and facts: the way the story is told must suit the nature of the story. Finally, the exposition must be *consequens*, meaning that later events must follow naturally and almost inevitably from earlier ones. All these references to times, places,

[19] Ibid. 265–93.

characters, and ends coming from beginnings show that, although Agricola writes here about *expositio*, the prime case he has in mind is in fact narrative.[20]

Agricola begins chapter 23 by stating that it is much harder (and more crucial to winning our case) to make an exposition 'suited to what we are trying to prove'. First of all we need to focus on the point we are aiming to prove and to compare it with the material of the exposition so that we can see which parts of the story help our case and which are more difficult for us. Then we must try to make the things which are favourable help us as much as possible, not by connecting them with the main headings of our argument, but by fixing them in the audience's minds so that they realize for themselves what weight these aspects carry. When the audience think these things over the points made will help us all the more because they did not seem like part of the argument.

Ambiguous aspects must be related in such a way as to benefit us and negative aspects must be minimized so that they do us the least possible damage. We may relate points which apparently favour our opponents in ways which make them seem ridiculous or of little value as the basis for proof.

Then Agricola makes a series of practical points on the basis of examples from Terence, Cicero, and the *Declamations* then attributed to Quintilian. We should always begin our narrative with something favourable. It may be advantageous to begin far back in the history of the case with something which establishes the characters and relationships of the main protagonists. We must always look at the narrative from the opponents' point of view, doing our best to work out which parts are most helpful to them. This will help us to work out how to discuss things which might seem to go against us. Some things which are of real benefit to our opponents we will have to omit.[21]

Agricola's treatment of exposition incorporates most of Quintilian's ideas, but the overall structure and much of the content is very different. Close analysis of poetic and rhetorical texts helps Agricola develop and present his ideas. Agricola rethinks the relationship between narrative and argument. They involve different styles of expression and different approaches to teaching but they often share content. Exposition needs to be shaped according to what we are trying to argue; exposition ought to be *argumentosa*, based on causes, *consentanea*, fitting in with characters, times, and places, and *consequens*, moving effectively from beginning to end. The topics of invention will be important for exposition as well as for

[20] Ibid. 296–9.
[21] Ibid. 302–6.

argumentation. By the same token the significance of argument will be clarified by exposition, and argument will be more successful if it proves conclusions which suit the subjects, characters, and circumstances set out in the exposition. Agricola's ideas about narrative and argument are driven by considering the audience's attitudes and responses. Agricola regards imagining an opponent's point of view as helpful in thinking about how to construct an effective speech.

Turning to the second of the orator's tasks Agricola argues that the topics of invention can help in arousing emotions in an audience. He shows how Virgil and Cicero achieve emotional effects by repeating and amplifying arguments encouraging an emotional reaction.[22] In book 3 he sets out a general theory of emotion. He defines emotion as an impetus of mind by which we are impelled to desire or reject something more vehemently than we would in a relaxed state of mind.[23] We desire the good or the apparent good and we reject what we believe to be harmful. Therefore in arousing emotion the orator needs to consider two elements: the thing which happens and the person to whom it happens. If the person deserves the thing which happens (whether it is good or bad) the audience is pleased. If the person does not deserve what happens, the audience is moved—to anger if the thing undeserved is good, to pity if it is bad. To arouse the emotion of pity, for example, the orator will need to establish both the harshness of the fate and the degree to which it is undeserved. The particular circumstances of the case (or the previous opinions of the audience) may lead the orator to emphasize one or other of these arguments in the speech. Agricola refers to the second book of Aristotle's *Rhetoric* for a comprehensive treatment of the different emotions.[24]

Agricola's main point is that arousing emotions involves a logical calculation based on the way in which an audience can be made to regard a person and a past or future event. In this logical approach to arousing emotion he is generalizing and simplifying Aristotle's view. But Aristotle's account of emotion had not really featured in the most widely used rhetoric textbooks of the fifteenth century, Cicero's *De inventione* and the pseudo-Ciceronian *Rhetorica ad Herennium*. So Agricola was directing attention back to Aristotle, presenting Aristotle's views in a form that could be used by students and analysing Latin texts to show the effectiveness of his theory. Within this framework Agricola describes three ways to

[22] *Aeneid* 4.314–16. *Pro Milone* 34.93–35.98. *De inventione dialectica*, 199–200.

[23] *De inventione dialectica*, 378: 'Affectus autem mihi non aliud videtur esse quam impetus quidam animi, quo ad appetendum aversandumve aliquid vehementius quam pro quietu statu mentis impellimur.'

[24] Ibid. 380.

convey emotions in compositions. First, emotion may be a matter of style, in particular of the choice of vocabulary and of the tone of a passage. Agricola illustrates this by comparing the tone of the three famous Latin satirists, and the very different emotional impacts of Horace and Juvenal. Second, the writer may describe someone in the grip of an emotion. Agricola gives examples from tragedy and epic. Finally an author may wish to arouse a particular emotion in the audience. In this case it will be necessary to focus on the person involved and the thing which happens.[25]

Agricola linked the theory of emotional manipulation to the technique of amplification. If emotions are aroused too quickly they also pass quickly. Orators use amplification to build up emotion gradually. By making the subject they talk about seem great they prepare their audience to expend great emotion on it. You can make something seem important to an audience by linking it to things which are important to everyone or to the deepest interests of a particular audience. More generally things can be made to seem great by comparisons, by dividing a topic into sections and considering each section, and by descriptions.[26] In this section Agricola relies on Quintilian's account of amplification.

But he adds to this a little later in his discussion of *copia* and brevity. Agricola links *copia* to the aim of pleasing an audience. Pleasing can be brought about either by the intrinsic interest and delight of the subject-matter or from the skilfulness of the language in which something is expressed. By thinking about the audience and using the topics one can make comparisons or arguments which appeal to their interests. The doctrine of *copia* teaches writers to add detail to descriptions and fullness of incident to narratives. It encourages writers to multiply questions, to add further arguments and propositions.[27] Although *copia* is presented as an ideal of style, many of the techniques which Agricola recommends for achieving *copia* are derived from dialectic. Taken together Agricola's accounts of amplification and *copia* constitute a major source for Erasmus's *De copia* (1512), perhaps the most influential rhetoric textbook of the sixteenth century.

At the end of the book Agricola turns to disposition. In the rhetoric textbook disposition could become a rather empty category since the treatise on invention was usually organized according to the contents of the oration, beginning with the exordium, continuing with narration and confirmation, and ending with the peroration. This left disposition to discuss occasions when one of the four parts might be omitted or when

[25] Ibid. 382–4.
[26] Ibid. 386–91.
[27] Ibid. 400–3.

their order might be altered. Disposition could not really be discussed because the textbook assumed that there was only one practical system of organization for a speech.

Agricola, by contrast, starts his account with a general theory: disposition is defined as 'the ordering and distribution of things which shows what belongs and what should be positioned in which places'.[28] He distinguishes three kinds of order: natural order (broadly temporal), arbitrary order (when there is no natural order or we choose not to follow it), and artificial order (when we deliberately place later things first, as when the account of Aeneas's voyage precedes the account of the fall of Troy). These three orders are then connected with four kinds of natural order (or four senses of the word *prius*).[29] Then Agricola describes the organization of a number of texts: Virgil's *Aeneid*, Terence's *Andria*, the histories of Tacitus, Livy, and Valerius Maximus, and Ovid's *Metamorphoses*.[30] He aims to show that the best authors have provided models of a large number of different forms of organization. This enables him to reject the traditional rhetorical assumption that the four-part oration is the only acceptable form for a work. From such questions of overall organization (and still working with examples) Agricola descends to consider the order in which one might discuss a series of questions, the order in which a series of arguments might be placed, the ordering of propositions within an argument and the tactical ordering of arguments in a disputation. He shows that in all these cases the ordering of points will depend on the position one wishes to uphold and the audience for whom one is writing. He concludes this section of the work with a broad summary.

> Let us now bring all that pertains to disposition into some sort of summary. The first requirement for anyone who wishes to do well at disposition is that he should lay out in front of him the whole raw material of his invention, that is everything he is thinking of saying. Then he should decide carefully what he wishes to bring about in the mind of the hearer. Then he should compare the things themselves, the parts of the things, the force and nature of them singly and together, first among themselves and then all together with the precepts. Then he will see without difficulty when the order of time should be followed, when things should be separated into their species and single things should be distinguished as if by certain boundaries: when one should be derived from another, depending on whichever is nearest or most suitable. Then he should determine how to please the audience, how to make his point and win it, and what order of questions, argumentations, and

[28] Ibid. 413: 'ordo et distributio rerum, quae demonstrat, quid quibus locis conveniat et collocandum sit.'

[29] Ibid. 413–15.

[30] Ibid. 416–23.

propositions to observe. Disposition is to be treated thoroughly and with great care, since skill in this part is rightly praised.[31]

For Agricola each composition needs to be planned on the basis of full information about subject-matter, speaker's intention, and audience. The writer needs to have an understanding of the principles of ordering and a knowledge of a range of structural forms which have been created by previous writers. Only at the point when all the material for the work has been gathered together should the writer attempt to determine the organization of the particular work. We need to see this perhaps rather utopian position as a strong and practical response to the rather empty role assigned to disposition by the rhetoric textbook. At the same time we should see it as consonant with one of the abiding principles of rhetoric, which is that rhetoric concerns itself with a very wide range of different skills in the use of language. Where the traditional rhetoric textbook makes this range of skills comprehensible to the student by separating issues and simplifying them, Agricola insists that the most effective way to intervene in practice is to gather all the relevant information together and to apply general principles to each particular case.

Agricola's conclusions are always based on a knowledge of the textbook tradition tempered by critical reflection and analysis of literary examples. This intellectual strength of the text could also cause problems for its audience. As Agricola himself recognized, it has the approach and some of the contents of a textbook, yet its discussions of Latin literature are best appreciated by people who are already quite well read.[32] Characteristically he clings to a small number of central doctrines (the topics, exposition and argumentation, reflecting on the audience, notions of priority, the idea of emotion being linked to what is undeserved) but shows that each of these principles must be adapted to the complexities of the particular assignment. As a system this contrasts, for example, with developed theories of status, in which a complicated taxonomy of possibilities is outlined in order that the procedure in each sub-case should be presented as a simple

[31] 'Ut ergo quae ad dispositionem pertinent, in summam quandam redigamus: opus est in primis, quisquis bene disponere volet, ut totam inventionis suae sylvam, hoc est, omnia quaecunque dicturus est, velut conspectui suo subiiciat. Tum quid in animo auditoris efficere velit, diligenter expendat. Deinde res ipsas, rerumque partes, et vim naturamque singularum, omniumque, et inter se conferat, et cum praeceptis omnia. Tum non difficulter videbit ubi temporum sequenda ratio, ubi per species res digerenda, et quibusdam velut limitibus singula discernenda, ubi aliud ex alio, et quicque proximum aptissimumve fuerit, ducendum. Tum quid tribuendum voluptati, quomodo victoriae certaminique serviendum, quis quaestionum ordo, quis argumentationum, quis propositionum servandus. Est autem diligenti multaque cura tractanda dispositio, quando veram haec pars ingenii laudem meretur.' *De inventione dialectica*, 449–50.

[32] Ibid., sig. b1^{v} (bound after p. 16).

choice. Agricola achieves both an original synthesis of rhetoric and dialectic and a redirection of interest within each field, for example throwing attention back to disposition and techniques of emotional persuasion, within rhetoric, and developing a new approach to the topics of invention, within dialectic.

Among the techniques designed to increase his readers' familiarity with the topics Agricola outlined the technique of dialectical reading. He illustrated this technique with his rhetorical and dialectical analysis of Cicero's *Pro lege Manilia*, which exercised considerable influence on later humanist commentaries. Dialectical reading involves both identifying the topics from which an author has derived a particular argument and reconstructing chains of argument underlying a passage from a text. To uncover the argumentative structure of a text it is always necessary to identify the main question being addressed and investigate the way in which a particular passage of argument contributes to that, often via a subsidiary question.[33]

Alongside this form of reading which focuses on the structures unifying a text, Agricola also describes (in his letter *De formando studio*) the technique for compiling a commonplace book, which will enable the fruits of one's reading always to be ready for reuse in one's own compositions. Each page of this notebook would be headed by the name of a subject, such as Friendship, Justice, Mercy. As the student read his Latin texts he would copy especially striking sentences or stories related to this topic on to the appropriate page. As students read they continually asked themselves, whether a particular story, comparison, or maxim merited being recorded, and, if so, which heading it should go under. Here Agricola was probably drawing on Guarino's methods of teaching. Agricola's description of the commonplace book was later elaborated by Erasmus and Melanchthon.[34]

De inventione dialectica at first circulated only among Agricola's friends. Agricola himself was without a copy for several years. He once wrote of sending it to the printer but took no steps to do so, and nor did the friends who carefully compiled manuscript collections of his works.[35] It took more than thirty years before the first edition appeared, at Louvain in 1515.

[33] Ibid. 354–60, 461–71. M. van der Poel, 'The Scholia in Orationem Pro Lege Manilia' of Rudolph Agricola', *Lias,* 24 (1997), 1–35. K. Meerhoff, *Entre logique et littérature* (Orleans, 2001), 25–62, 171–90. Mack, Renaissance Argument, 227–33.

[34] Agricola, *Lucubrationes* (1593), 198–200. Erasmus, *De copia* (1988), 258–63. Melanchthon, *De locis communibus ratio*, *Opera omnia*, xx, cols. 695–8. Ann Moss, *Printed Commonplace-Books and the Structuring of Renaissance Thought* (Oxford, 1996), 107–13, 119–26.

[35] Agricola, *Letters*, 117, 141, 155.

The second edition was printed in Cologne in 1520. Thereafter the work enjoyed great success in northern Europe, with many favourable comments, much use of its ideas, commentaries, epitomes, and eventually forty-four editions of the text (usually accompanied by a substantial commentary) and thirty-two of various epitomes. Agricola's work probably succeeded better with a wide audience in the 1520s than it could have in the 1480s because of the reforms which Erasmus and his followers had brought about in grammar schools and in rhetoric teaching, and because of the enthusiastic support of a group of influential teachers who regarded Agricola as an heroic pioneer of northern humanism. People like Sturm, Latomus, and Melanchthon, as well as learning from *De inventione dialectica*, created a climate in which its originality could be appreciated and could to some extent be absorbed within an educational programme.[36]

De inventione dialectica was most regularly printed at Cologne, where generally four items a decade were produced between 1520 and 1580, with a peak production of eight editions and seven epitomes between 1530 and 1544. In all Cologne produced eighteen editions and thirteen epitomes. Paris produced a similar number of items (twenty editions and twelve epitomes) over a shorter period (1529–61) and with a much higher peak. Seventeen editions and nine epitomes were produced between 1529 and 1543. At the same time, and for some years after, many other versions of the topics were also produced in Paris and Cologne. Agricola's text may have helped create the vogue for the topics but some teachers seem to have preferred a more traditional version of the work. It looks as though the teaching of Agricola was brought from Louvain to Paris by a group of university teachers including Sturm and Latomus,[37] and that it became a University of Paris intellectual fashion of the 1530s and early 1540s, which was eclipsed by the rise of Ramism. Thereafter there was a reduced but regular demand for the text until the more general decline of the humanist version of dialectic (and indeed of publication of Latin rhetoric) around 1580.[38] *De inventione dialectica*'s original synthesis of elements from rhetoric and dialectic caused some problems for teachers. It plays

[36] L. Jardine, *Erasmus, Man of Letters* (Princeton,1993), 83–128, has some interesting comments on Erasmus's role in promoting Agricola. Her contention that the text of *De inventione dialectica* was somehow constructed by Alardus and others is incorrect, since manuscripts in Stuttgart and Uppsala which date from the 1490s contain almost the same text as the early edns.

[37] K. Meerhoff, 'Logique et éloquence: Une révolution ramusienne?', in Meerhoff and Moisan (eds.), *Autour de Ramus* (Montreal, 1997), 97–101.

[38] G. C. Huisman, *Rudolph Agricola: A Bibliography* (Nieuwkoop, 1985). Mack, *Renaissance Argument*, 257–79.

several different roles in the university syllabuses which include it. Sometimes it functions as a humanist introduction to the whole Aristotelian logic syllabus, sometimes it replaces or introduces Aristotle's *Topica*, sometimes it seems to be the dialectic element within a training which is primarily literary, and sometimes it acts as a rhetoric textbook. Some teachers preferred to recommend it as supplementary reading for advanced pupils rather than trying to find a place for it within the syllabus.[39]

Agricola's originality is founded on a deep understanding of rhetoric, logic, and Latin literature. It displays a new understanding of the process of composition, based in a thoughtful approach to the topics of invention. Through logical analysis of Latin literature his work develops a new understanding of the relationship between rhetoric and dialectic and new approaches to central doctrines of rhetoric. Following Erasmus's lead several sixteenth-century rhetoricians recognized Agricola as a pioneering figure and his works were widely circulated, but many of his innovations were not taken up before Keckermann in the early seventeenth century. In some respects the originality of his contribution to rhetoric and dialectic is only now being understood.

[39] Mack, *Renaissance Argument*, 280–302.

5

Erasmus

Erasmus of Rotterdam (?1469–1536) rose from unpromising beginnings to become the most publicly prominent European intellectual of the early sixteenth century. From the first decade of the sixteenth century he worked closely with printers, frequently correcting copy for his own works and ensuring their availability in good (and often expanded) editions. He may have been the first northern humanist to exploit the possibilities of printing to ensure wide circulation of new works and editions. While traditional theologians accused his new Latin version of the text of the New Testament (1516) of preparing the way for Luther's heresies, reformers chided him for lacking the courage of what they took to be his convictions.[1] Alongside his scholarly editions of Seneca (1515) and St Jerome (1516) and his authorship of *The Praise of Folly* (1509) and numerous collections of letters, he was enormously successful as a writer of textbooks and reference works. Among these are: *De copia*, the most often printed rhetoric textbook written in the renaissance, with 168 editions between 1512 and 1580; *De conscribendis epistolis*, a letter-writing manual which went through ninety editions (six of them after 1620); the *Colloquia*, a best-selling collection of Latin dialogues for schoolboys; and the *Adagia*, a much-used collection of proverbs.

Erasmus contributed to the development of renaissance rhetoric over an astonishingly wide range of doctrines. His *De copia*, which combined an understanding of the tropes and figures with knowledge of a wide range of authors and an acute adaptation of dialectical techniques, defined and established the centrality of amplification for the next eighty years. He gave a new importance to many of the components of writing, such as proverbs, axioms, descriptions, examples, and comparisons, and provided a new kind of training in their construction, selection, and use. Particularly in his work on letter-writing he directed the attention of students of

[1] C. Augustijn, *Erasmus: His Life, Works and Influence* (Toronto, 1991), 109, 118–54. R. Schoeck, *Erasmus of Europe: 1501–36* (Edinburgh, 1993). J. C. Margolin, *Erasme: Précepteur de l'Europe* (Paris, 1995). James D. Tracy, *Erasmus of the Low Countries* (Berkeley, Calif., 1996).

rhetoric back to the crucial question of the audience. He enabled a new capability to write in a dense metaphorical and argumentative style, and he played a crucial role in debates about imitation and reading. The materials for these works were developed over a lifetime of reading and editing, both in the phrases he chose to include and in the ethical orientation. Writers and thinkers of the later sixteenth century probably owed more to Erasmus than to any other immediate predecessor.

Erasmus, the son of a priest, was born in Rotterdam probably in 1469. He went to school at first in Gouda and then in Deventer, at the school of Alexander Hegius, where he once met Rudolph Agricola (probably in 1484). After his father's death, under pressure from his guardians (as he tells us), he entered the Augustinian monastery of Steyn, near Gouda, in 1487. At school and in the monastery he seems to have read widely in Latin literature, in humanist writers (particularly Filelfo, Dati, Poggio, and Valla), and in St Augustine and St Jerome. He was ordained in 1492 and left the monastery in 1493, never to return.[2] At first he worked as secretary to the bishop of Cambrai, then from 1495 to 1499 he went to the University of Paris to study theology, but he never took the doctorate. In Paris in 1497–8 his tutoring of the Englishman Robert Fisher prompted him to compose the *Brevissima... conficiendarum epistolarum formula*, the first version of the *De conscribendis epistolis*, which he projected and revised for many years prior to its publication in 1520. This brief manual, discussed in Chapter 11 below, was printed fifty-nine times in the sixteenth century, most often as part of collections of letter-writing manuals. At about this time Erasmus also made a preliminary version of *De copia* and an epitome of Valla's *Elegantiae*, presumably for the use of his pupils. His experience of tutoring in the late 1490s was formative for all his rhetorical works. Another English pupil William Blount, Lord Mountjoy, brought him back to England in 1499–1500 where he met Prince Henry (the future Henry VIII, then aged 8), More, Colet, Grocyn, and Linacre.[3]

In 1500 in Paris he published the *Adagiorum collectanea*, a collection of 818 Latin proverbs, probably another fruit of his work as a tutor in Latin grammar and literature. As with Erasmus's other rhetorical works the *Adagia* grew through reading and revision to become a collection of 4,151 proverbs. At about this time he began learning Greek. In 1504 he discovered the manuscript of Valla's *Annotations on the New Testament*, which he published in 1505 and which, in conveying to him the part

[2] Augustijn, *Erasmus*, 21–4.

[3] Ibid. 27, 31–2. J. Chomarat, *Grammaire et rhétorique chez Erasme*, 2 vols. (Paris, 1981), 242–52, 712–13, 1003–5.

which philology could play in theology, in a sense inspired his life's work.[4] He spent the years 1506–9 in Italy, publishing the expanded *Adagiorum chiliades*, perhaps the first true edition of the work (with 3,260 proverbs), with Aldus Manutius in Venice in 1508.[5] Under the proverb 'canis in balneo' (a dog in a bath) in that edition he expressed the hope that Agricola's *dialectic*, hiding in someone's collection of manuscripts, would be published.[6] In 1509–14 he was in England, where he composed the *Praise of Folly* (first printed in 1511) and lectured at Cambridge. For Colet's newly founded school of St Paul's he composed *De copia* (1512).[7] The second edition of *De copia* (1514) also included the first publication of his collection of similes, *Parabola*.

In Basel he published a new edition of *Adagia* (1515), the first to include the long reflective essays, an edition of St Jerome (1516), and the first edition of his Latin translation of the New Testament, accompanied by the Greek text (1516).[8] At first Erasmus appears to have sympathized with Luther's complaints against the Church and attempts at reform. He was urged to condemn Luther and was initially reluctant to do so. Later he found Luther's positions too radical and engaged in controversy with him over the freedom of the will.[9] Erasmus's last years were divided between Basel (1521–9, 1535–6), which he left when it became Protestant, and Freiburg (1529–35). He completed his contribution to rhetoric by publishing *De conscribendis epistolis* (1522), *Ciceronianus* (1528), and his long-awaited guide to preaching, *Ecclesiastes* (1535), along with revised editions of his earlier works.

In the *Adagia* Erasmus collects proverbs from his reading in classical literature so that his pupils can embellish their writings. But he insists that proverbs are also useful in guiding one's life, for persuasion, and in enabling one to understand what earlier writers have written. Erasmus's introduction to the work (first published in 1508) is a minor masterpiece. After reviewing previous definitions of the proverb and noting that their emphasis on allegory and moral teaching does not fit all examples, he fixes

4 Augustijn, *Erasmus*, 37–9.

5 Ibid. 34, 40.

6 From *c.*1505 he had been urging printers to collect and publish Agricola's works. *Opus epistolarum Erasmi*, ed. P. S. Allen, 12 vols. (Oxford, 1906–58), i. 414, ii. 32, iii. 19, 30, 55; L. Jardine, *Erasmus, Man of Letters* (Princeton, 1993), 86–7, 90.

7 Erasmus, *Collected Works of Erasmus*, xxiv (Toronto, 1978), 280, 284–8. Chomarat, *Grammaire*, 712–14.

8 Augustijn, *Erasmus*, 90–6. M. Mann Phillips, *The Adages of Erasmus: A Study with Translations* (Cambridge, 1964), 41–168. Chomarat, *Grammaire*, 761–82. K. Eden, *Friends Hold All Things in Common: Tradition, Intellectual Property and the* Adages *of Erasmus* (New Haven, Conn., 2001).

9 Augustijn, *Erasmus*, 119–32.

on the pragmatic definition 'a saying in popular use, remarkable for some shrewd and novel turn',[10] which he then analyses in detail. Proverbs must be well known and current. They can be taken from the sayings of gods, wise men, or poets, from the theatre, from legend, fable, or history, from the qualities of objects or animals, or from apophthegms (witty replies). He shows that collections of proverbs have a long and respectable ancestry and that great authors, both pagan and Christian, frequently use them. He draws on Aristotle's *Rhetoric* and Quintilian to emphasize the role which proverbs can play in winning an argument; he discusses their usefulness in enriching style and introducing humour. At the same time he warns of the jumpy effect caused by excessive use of proverbs, since proverbs have a conclusiveness which requires the writer to make a new beginning.[11]

Within the entries for individual proverbs (some of which are very short) Erasmus always names the proverb and gives some explanation of its meaning. Usually he adds several examples from classical literature showing where and how the proverb has been used. Sometimes he supports his explanation of the meaning of the proverb with quotations. In more developed entries he draws moral and political lessons from the proverb or outlines its history and gives suggestions for ways in which it could be used. Sometimes he adds instances of expressions which involve similarities of language or idea. In particular he has an eye for witty uses of proverbs and for jokes.

In a few instances the entry for the proverb develops into a full-blown essay illustrating some of the major themes of Erasmus's thought. He uses 'A Dung-beetle hunts an Eagle' (3.7.1) to elaborate an Aesopian fable with a contemporary allegory against war. From 'One ought to be born a king or a fool' (1.3.1) he draws conclusions about his favourite topic of the education of princes. 'Man is a bubble' (2.3.48) provides the occasion for a collection of quotations on the shortness and frailty of life and for a lament on the death in 1506 of Philip, Archduke of Austria.

The most powerful of all the *Adagia*, *Dulce bellum inexpertis*, 'War is sweet to those who have not experienced it' (4.1.1),[12] can be analysed as an exercise in copious speech. After praising and exemplifying the adage Erasmus supports it from an argument from generality (all things seem sweet to those who have not tasted them). Then he makes a comparison between war and man, the creature who promotes war. Since in comparison with other animals the human body is unarmed and defenceless, gifted

[10] Paroemia est celebre dictum, scita quapiam novitate insigne. Erasmus, *Opera omnia*, ii/1 (Amsterdam, 1993), 46. W. Barker, *The Adages of Erasmus* (Toronto, 2001), 5.

[11] Erasmus, *Opera omnia*, ii/1. 46–68. Barker, *Adages*, 4–20.

[12] Erasmus, *Opera omnia*, ii/7 (Amsterdam, 1999), 11–44; tr. Barker, *Adages*, 317–56.

chiefly with speech which promotes collaboration, it is unnatural that man should be so addicted to war. He describes in detail the sights, sounds, occurrences, and consequences of war, later contrasting this description with a commonplace in praise of peace. He collects quotations from scripture in favour of peace and examples from classical poetry of the monstrous savagery and madness of war. Comparisons between men and beasts and between pagan and Christian kings are used to belittle the Christian enthusiasm for war. Personification is used both to answer opponents' arguments and to set out the case for solving disputes by discussion and sharing rather than fighting over things which would be destroyed many times over by battle. The deeply rhetorical combination of argument, description, and figurative language creates an eloquent moral denunciation of war, which must certainly be ranked among Erasmus's finest writings. Its success derives from its employment of rhetorical principles, copiously elaborating a moral theme to which Erasmus felt the strongest commitment

In the *Adagia* Erasmus adapts the minor classical genre of the annotated list of proverbs to make it do more. *Adagia* is primarily a reference book, a resource which helps readers to understand their texts and writers to convince and dazzle their audiences, but the longer entries also serve as models of committed and elegant writing and as guides to ethical behaviour. Where *Adagia* offered comprehensive assistance with a small aspect of the orator's armoury, *De copia* proclaims itself as providing a new method of enriching all types of writing.[13]

De copia is concerned with supercharging, taking a sentence or an idea and making it more impressive. Literally *copia* means abundance. In Cicero and Quintilian *copia* had been an incidental term denoting success in inventing material,[14] but the idea there seems to be 'a broad range of ideas and arguments' more than 'a style which is highly amplified', though *Rhetorica ad Herennium* speaks of *copia dicendi*, abundance of style. Quintilian mentions two different kinds of *copia*, one rich, the other joyful in flowers.[15] Agricola devoted three chapters to describing *copia* and brevity in different genres and giving advice on when to use each. For Agricola *copia* mainly involves going into details about causes and attendant circumstances, deducing additional questions, arguments, and proofs, and saying the same thing in different ways.[16]

[13] Terence Cave, *The Cornucopian Text* (Oxford, 1979), 18–34. Chomarat, *Grammaire*, 736–61. V. Wels, *Triviale Künste* (Berlin, 2000), 71–82, 170–83.

[14] Cicero, *De oratore* 1.19.85, 2.14.58; Quintilian, *Institutio oratoria* 5.10.100, 7.pr.1, 10.1.69, 10.5.3; *Rhetorica ad Herennium* 1.1.1.

[15] Alia copia locuples, alia floribus laeta . *Institutio oratoria* 8.3.87.

[16] *De inventione dialectica*, 400–3. Mack, *Renaissance Argument* (Leiden, 1993), 216–17.

Erasmus was the first to devote an entire book to the subject. He divides *copia* into two parts, *copia* of words and *copia* of things. Under *copia* of words he sets out twenty different methods for varying the way in which a sentence is expressed. Many of these methods involve varying one of the words of the sentence. At the end of this list Erasmus provides examples of hundreds of ways of varying two sentences and then offers alternative phrasings for many concepts which frequently occur. *Copia* of things involves discovering additional material implied in a phrase or situation. Here Erasmus gives eleven methods and several additional suggestions. Table 5.1 aims to specify the methods and to indicate the other types of material included.

De copia is extremely focused and practical, providing a range of well-explained methods of varying a pre-existing text, together with examples of the practice of variation and collections of alternative expressions for many much-used phrases. Erasmus draws on different aspects of the traditions of rhetoric and dialectic. In general terms book 1 is more rhetorical, with its advice on style and diction, the tropes (Erasmus adapts around half of the methods of book 1 from Quintilian's account of the tropes[17]) and the figures, while book 2 is more related to topical invention and dialectic; but book 2 also includes material from the *progymnasmata* and from the parts of the oration. It has the great merit too of emphasizing some important aspects of writing which had been relatively neglected by both traditions: description, examples, comparisons, maxims. At least some of Erasmus's approach appears to be indebted to ideas on varying and expansion which were part of the medieval tradition of the arts of poetry.[18]

Erasmus sets out four main advantages of *copia*. Exercise in varying phrases will assist pupils to acquire a good style. It will help them avoid repetition. It will enable them to express themselves with a variety which will delight their audience. It will be of great assistance in commenting on authors, translating, and writing poetry.[19] He emphasizes the training function of this book by describing at the outset exercises for practising *copia*. Once the theory has been memorized pupils should regularly take phrases and express them in as many ways as possible. Groups of pupils should compete in doing this so as to learn from each other. Then they should go on to treat a whole argument in different ways. Students will

[17] *Institutio oratoria* 8.6.

[18] G. Engelhardt, 'Medieval Vestiges in the Rhetoric of Erasmus', *PMLA* 63 (1948), 739–44. M. C. Woods, *Classroom Commentaries: Teaching the Poetria nova across Medieval and Renaissance Europe* (Columbus, Ohio, 2010), 17–19, 23, 258–65.

[19] Erasmus, *De copia*, *Opera omnia*, i/6 (Amsterdam, 1988), 32–4; tr. B. Knott, *Collected Works of Erasmus*, xxxii (Toronto, 1978), 302.

Table 5.1. Plan of Erasmus, *De copia*

Meth.		Page
	BOOK 1: *COPIA OF WORDS*	
	Advantages and dangers of *copia*	26
	Exercises in *copia*	32
	Issues of correctness and diction	34
1	Synonyms	38
2	Enallage (same word, different form)	54
3	Antonomasia (change of name)	60
4	Periphrasis (descriptive phrase instead of a specifying noun)	61
5	Metaphor and reciprocal metaphor	62
6	Allegory (extended metaphor)	66
7	Catachresis (misapplied word, extension of meaning)	66
8	Onomatopoeia (formation of a new word based on sound of thing denoted)	67
9	Metalepsis (related meaning)	68
10	Metonymy (use the name of something related)	68
11	Synecdoche (part for whole, instance for type)	70
12	Equivalents (negation of opposites)	72
13	Comparatives (more and less with opposites)	72
14	Related expressions (e.g. husband/wife, pupil/teacher)	72
15	Amplification (choosing more forceful words)	73
16	Hyperbole	74
17	Meiosis (diminution)	74
18	Compositio (sentence construction)	74
19	Syntax	75
20	Various changes of figure	76
	Practical demonstration of 195 variations on 'your letter pleased me greatly' and 200 variations on 'as long as I live I shall always remember you'	76
	Ways of combining phrases	90
	Comparison and emphasis	94
	Variations of quantity and negation	108
	Connectives and transitions	117
	Alternative phrasings for many ideas, e.g. custom, purpose, appropriate, hinder, usefulness, dying	119–96
	BOOK 2: *COPIA* OF THINGS	
1	Explain something expressed concisely at more length, by describing its separate parts	197
2	Antecedents (describe what leads up to an event)	200
3	Causes	201
4	Consequences	201
5	Enargeia: Vivid description (things, persons, places, times)	202
6	Digression	215
7	Epithet (descriptive phrases)	216
8	Circumstances	218
9	Amplification: augmentation, comparison, inference, accumulation	218

10	Invent many propositions	220
11	Accumulate proofs and arguments: the topics	230
	Examples (three subdivisions)	232
	Comparisons	244
	Judgments and maxims	248
	Chreia (which he calls *expolitio*)	252
	Fable	254
	Making a commonplace book	258
	How to use different types of material from reading: different uses, different sources	259
	Expanding the different parts of the oration	270
	Brevity, and faults to avoid	279–81

add to their store of eloquence by translating or paraphrasing from Greek into Latin. They should convert poetry to prose and vice versa. Finally they will be helped by imitation, especially of Cicero, Aulus Gellius, and Apuleius.[20] Erasmus makes pupils aware of the dangers of pursuing *copia*, prefacing his methods with remarks on correctness, elegance, and appropriateness (drawing on Quintilian and the rhetoric textbooks), and including comments on the disadvantages of certain types of diction in his account of synonyms.[21]

The first fourteen methods involve substitutions of individual words within a phrase. Erasmus is careful to note that no synonym is an exact equivalent and to advise pupils to exercise judgement in view of the particular flavours which words taken from different registers can bring with them.[22] He gives special attention to metaphor as a source of variation, following Quintilian in analysing the different kinds of transition involved (e.g. related concepts, transfer from irrational to rational, from inanimate to animate). He advises students to make lists of metaphors from their reading and from their observation of ordinary expressions.[23] The next three methods involve ideas of greater and lesser, heightening an expression by alterations of diction or phrasing, or diminishing it. Erasmus here combines material from Quintilian's comments on amplification and on the trope of hyperbole.[24]

[20] Erasmus, *De copia*, 34; tr. Knott, 303.
[21] Erasmus, *De copia*, 26, 40–52; tr. Knott, 295, 309–20.
[22] Erasmus, *De copia*, 40; tr. Knott, 307–8.
[23] Erasmus, *De copia*, 62–6; tr. Knott, 333–6.
[24] *Institutio oratoria* 8.4.1–3, 8.6.67–9.

The final three methods involve alterations in the phrasing. Under these headings Erasmus draws in a number of the figures (e.g. asyntedon, polysyntedon, epanalepsis, interrogatio, dubitatio, exclamatio, occupatio, subiectio) and irony, omitted from the tropes above.[25] Weltkirchius's commentary, which was frequently reprinted with *De copia,* here adds definitions of many of the figures of speech which Erasmus had not otherwise included,[26] with the consequence that many pupils would have had access to a quite extensive list of the figures and tropes within their textbook on *copia*.

Erasmus begins his demonstration of varying by commenting on alternative expressions for each of the words in his model sentence ('your letter pleased me greatly'), at first avoiding metaphor. Then he starts to combine variations, at the outset commenting on what he has done in each group of cases. Once he has shown how fifty or so phrases can be made through these combinations, he then starts to add metaphors, later leaving it to the reader to reconstruct the different kinds of varying he has combined.[27] This first model sentence copies and extends an example which Perotti had already developed in the letter-writing section of his *Rudimenta grammatices* (1468) and which other authors of letter-writing manuals had used.[28] His second example ('as long as I live, I shall always remember you') is deliberately chosen for the lack of synonyms for the key words and the difficulty in finding equivalents.[29] This section of the work links back to the exercises in acquiring style which were listed at the beginning. Erasmus here exhibits a pride in his own virtuosity but also a delight in the play of expression inherent in language.

The remaining 173 chapters of book 1 comprise lists of alternative expressions. He begins with techniques of sentence construction: ways of linking predicates, contrasting expressions and negations; ways of comparing clauses and achieving emphasis within longer sentences; ways of signifying negation or quantity (universal or particular) in a sentence; different types of connectives and ways of making transitions.[30] But most of this section of the work consists of a sort of thesaurus, providing many different phrases and expressions for ideas which writers often need to express. We all need different ways of saying that something is important, useful, or appropriate and Erasmus here provides many possibilities,

[25] Erasmus, *De copia*, 74–6 ; tr. Knott, 345–7.
[26] Erasmus, *De copia*, with commentary of Weltkirchius (London, 1569), STC 10472, sigs. E4^r–6^v.
[27] Erasmus, *De copia*, 76–82 ; tr. Knott, 348–54.
[28] See Ch. 11 below.
[29] Erasmus, *De copia*, 82–3; tr. Knott, 354–5.
[30] Erasmus, *De copia*, 90–118 ; tr. Knott, 365–410.

partly taken from his reading and partly generated using his methods of varying. Towards the end of the book he discusses different ways of talking about dying, while the last section of all comprises different phrases meaning 'no further'.[31]

Book 2 begins with a series of ways of generating additional material from the thing being discussed rather than by variations of words. The first four involve looking into what is implied in some event. One may break up something which is expressed in a summary into its parts, or one may investigate what happened before an event, what caused it, or what its consequences are. These are all logical manoeuvres related to the topics of invention.[32] The fifth method, vivid description, is more literary and more rhetorical. Erasmus gives examples of different types of description and shows how they can be made vivid and affecting. Description is a construction in language and its effectiveness depends both on the elements the writer chooses (or invents) to depict and on the choice of expressions. Although recipes for descriptions can be helpful, one learns most from the examples of descriptions in poems, histories, and speeches.[33] Erasmus's account of digressions which make a contribution to the argument (method 6) is based on Quintilian, as are his accounts of elaboration of circumstances (8) and amplification (9).[34] Erasmus's methods of building up the importance of something and of making something seem greater through comparisons are carefully compressed from his source. The section on epithet seems to overlap a little with methods 3 and 4 from the first book.[35]

The final two methods of amplification rely on dialectical methods. Invention of additional propositions can be drawn either from the general issues involved in a case or from the specific circumstances. Erasmus illustrates the point by proposing his own arguments for the case of the Theban talents (taken from Quintilian[36]), which George Trapezuntius and Agricola had also discussed. Then he gives more advice wrapped up in further worked examples ('Should Cicero destroy the *Philippics* to save his life?', 'Should the Pope make war on the Venetians?', 'Should some king attack the King of France?'). The accumulation of arguments and proofs (method 11) relies on evidence of various kinds and on the topics of person (family, nation, country, sex, age, education, actions, etc.) and

[31] Erasmus, *De copia*, 191–2, 196 ; tr. Knott, 560–4, 570–1.
[32] Erasmus, *De copia*, 197–202 ; tr. Knott, 572–7.
[33] Erasmus, *De copia*, 202–15 ; tr. Knott, 577–89.
[34] Erasmus, *De copia*, 215–16, 218–20 ; tr. Knott, 589–95. *Institutio oratoria* 4.3.12–17, 5.10.104, 8.4.
[35] Erasmus, *De copia*, 216–18, 60–2; tr. Knott, 590–1, 331–2.
[36] *Institutio oratoria* 5.10.109–18.

things (cause, place, time, opportunity, means, instrument, etc.).[37] This material is taken from the headings of Quintilian's account of arguments.[38] In his brief listing of the topics of invention, Erasmus refers to the fuller discussions in Aristotle, Boethius, Cicero, and Quintilian.[39]

After the eleven methods Erasmus discusses a number of other elements which can be used to strengthen a composition. The commentator Weltkirchius numbers these as further methods of producing *copia* of things but there is no evidence that Erasmus did this.[40] An effective way of making a piece of writing convincing and pleasing is to back one's points up with illustrative examples. Erasmus explains the necessity of having a wide range of examples to hand and of being able to handle examples in a variety of ways. He provides three methods of expanding examples and discusses the use of fictional examples, basing his own comments on passages from classical literature, and referring the reader to Aristotle and Quintilian for an account of the part examples play in dialectic. Further sections discuss and illustrate the use of parallels, likenesses, comparisons, judgements, maxims, and fables. Erasmus's instructions for and example of *chreia* are taken directly from *Rhetorica ad Herennium* (where it is called *expolitio*, as in Erasmus).[41]

Erasmus's section on the way of accumulating and using such material begins with a description of the method of composing commonplace books. Any type of reading may provide material which can be reused as example or comparison. Then he shows (taking the example of the death of Socrates) that particular examples (and later, similes) can be used to support many different types of argument, even arguments which oppose each other. This means that the same example may have to be entered in different places in the commonplace book. He illustrates the process of gathering material from different places by taking the heading of changeableness and finding examples in Greek and Roman poetry, science, history, comedy, tragedy, and fables.[42] Maxims can be invented as well as discovered in one's reading. Erasmus suggests ways of adapting one maxim to fit a different topic or of using material which is critical of inconstancy to praise adaptability.[43]

[37] Erasmus, *De copia*, 220–30 ; tr. Knott, 595–605.

[38] *Institutio oratoria* 5.1.1–2, 5.8.7, 5.9.1–3 (treatment of signs is slightly different), 5.10.23–52.

[39] Erasmus, *De copia*, 230 ; tr. Knott, 606.

[40] So he labels examples as the thirteenth method, parallels as the fourteenth, and so on. Erasmus, *De copia* (1569), sigs. Q8^{r}, R7^{v}.

[41] *Rhetorica ad Herennium* 4.44.57.

[42] Erasmus, *De copia*, 258–68; tr. Knott, 635–46.

[43] Erasmus, *De copia*, 268–9 ; tr. Knott, 646–7.

He considers ways of making speeches longer, by including all six parts of the oration and by finding additional ways of achieving the aims of each part. The sections on proof and refutation, for example, can be enriched with additional arguments and strengthened with summaries and recapitulations of points made. Exposition can be developed by using the figure of dialogue and by imitating the historians. The speaker who aims at brevity must avoid all introductory and emotional material and stick to the point of argument. Both expansive and laconic speakers must avoid excessive straining of the material and must ensure that what they say is clear to the audience.[44]

As Table 2.2 indicates, *De copia* was astonishingly successful from its first publication, with sixty editions in the first eighteen years from publication and 165 editions between 1512 and 1569, an average of more than three each year. Almost equally striking, though, is the decline in printing after 1569, with only four editions produced in the rest of the century.

De copia is an exceptionally rich textbook, deserving of its great success and influence. Although most of the material is derived either from the rhetorical handbooks or from Erasmus's reflections on his reading, he manages to create an original and helpful overall structure. He adds something new to the tradition in a way that is well calculated to fit in to the grammar-school syllabus, rather than cutting across established discipline boundaries, as Agricola's *De inventione dialectica* had. By pitching his material at a fairly simple level and linking it to the earliest composition exercises Erasmus enabled his book to be used as an introduction to the full classical course in rhetoric, allowing a place of honour for Cicero and Quintilian later in the programme of study. Terence Cave has shown how Erasmus's teaching on *copia* transformed sixteenth-century ideas about writing and reading and stimulated the literary experiments of Rabelais, Ronsard, and Montaigne.[45]

Some publishers and teachers believed that a shortened version of *De copia* would be more useful to schoolboys. An anonymous forty-page abridgement of the first book, *Epitome libri de copia verborum Erasmi Roterodami* (1527), was printed seven times up to 1578, in Antwerp, Paris, and Strasbourg. It concentrated on the nineteen methods outlined at the start of the book, defining each method, giving examples, and then quoting other rhetorical authorities (for example, *Rhetorica ad Herennium*, Quintilian, Mancinelli, and Melanchthon).[46] The page is laid out so that

[44] Erasmus, *De copia*, 270–9 ; tr. Knott, 648–58.

[45] Cave, *Cornucopian Text.*

[46] *Epitome libri de copia verborum Erasmi Roterodami* (Antwerp, 1527), RRSTC 1550, sigs. A1^{v}, B4^{v}, B5^{r}, C2^{r}.

the main points and examples appear as lists. The Wittenberg theology professor Georg Major wrote a brief epitome of both books in eight pages to accompany his epitome of Melanchthon's *Institutiones rhetoricae*. His *In Erasmi Roterodami libellum de duplicia copia*, first published around 1525, treats synonyms (method 1) as a separate type, *copia* of diction. Then he lists the other nineteen methods of *copia* of words, defining each method and giving brief examples, before identifying another nineteen methods of *copia* of things. The first nine of these correspond to the eleven methods listed by Erasmus (see Table 5.1). To cover the rest of the book, Major adds the following methods: treatment of commonplaces, commonplaces, examples, treatment of examples, imagined examples, chreia, fable, dreams, fictional narratives, and multiplying parts of the oration. He sets out the main subheadings of each type in tabular form, but there are no examples. This work accompanied later editions of Schade's very popular treatise on the tropes and figures and was probably printed fifty-five times in the sixteenth century.[47]

Parabolae, first published with Schürer's 1514 Strasburg edition of *De copia*, was an off-shoot of Erasmus's work for the 1515 revision of *Adagia* and his edition of Seneca. We know of more than fifty sixteenth-century editions.[48] It is a collection of material which Erasmus found during his rereading of Plutarch's *Moralia*, Pliny's *Natural History,* and works by Seneca, Aristotle, and others which were not exactly proverbs (and so were unsuitable for *Adagia*) but which conveyed moral teaching so effectively as to be useful in composition. The *Parabolae* are comparisons, mostly in the form of metaphors but in some cases involving contrast or other types of comparison. Erasmus presents them as a list sorted according to the works from which they are taken without further comment from him. The following examples are all taken from the Plutarch section, the longest part of the book, which must have been an important means of transmitting Plutarch's ideas to the Latin renaissance.

> Like an actor who comes on stage all made up for his part is he who enters public life not to improve the lot of his fellow-citizens but to win reputation for himself. (799A)
>
> As wine is at first the obedient servant of the man who drinks it, but as it gradually creeps into his veins carries him away and makes him behave in its own fashion, so does the ruler of a polity adapt himself at the outset to the

[47] See RRSTC 3223 and 3230.

[48] Erasmus, *Parabolae*, ed. J.-C. Margolin, *Opera omnia*, i/5 (Amsterdam, 1965), 3–85. Tr. R. Mynors in *Collected Works of Erasmus*, xxiii (Toronto, 1978), 124–7. Chomarat, *Grammaire*, 782–803.

traditions of his people, and then by degrees bring it over to his own way of thinking. (799B–C)
The overstrung bow snaps; the spirit that relaxes is broken. (792C)[49]

Whereas these examples from Plutarch are quoted directly, with occasional omissions, in the following examples taken from Pliny, Erasmus has added the moral application to Pliny's observation.

Like the chameleon, which lives on nothing but air and so has its mouth always open, some men live on public applause, and have no object but empty praise and glory. (8.122)
The she-bear produces her whelps half-formed and licks them into shape; and the unfinished offspring of the mind needs prolonged care to polish it. (8.151)[50]

Erasmus's introductory letter asserts the usefulness of metaphor to writers.

Of the other ornaments of style, each brings its own particular charm and flexibility to style; metaphor taken alone adds everything in fuller measure, while all the other kinds of ornament add one each. Do you wish to delight? Nothing adds more sparkle. Are you concerned to teach? Nothing else makes your point so convincingly, so clearly. Do you intend to persuade? Nothing gives you greater penetration. Are you trying for *copia*? Nowhere is material readier to your hand.... Have you a fancy for the sublime? Metaphor can exalt anything, and to any height you please... Do you want to achieve *enargeia* and illumination? Nothing else brings something before the eyes better.[51]

Parabolae is like a notebook of Erasmus's reading before the quotations have been transferred to a commonplace book. It makes available to

[49] 'Ut qui personatus in theatrum procedit histrio, sic qui ad rempublicam administrandum accedit, non ut civibus prosit, sed sibi gloriam comparet... Ut vinum primum servit ac paret bibenti, at paulatim admixtum venis, rapit hominem ac traducit in suos mores, ita qui rempublicam administret, initio se populi moribus accommodat, post sensim eum ad sua trahit instituta... Ut arcus tensus rumpitur, sic animus remissus frangitur.' Erasmus, *Parabolae*, 96, 108, tr. in *Collected Works of Erasmus*, xxiii. 135, 142. References in parentheses are to Plutarch, *Moralia*.

[50] 'Uti chameleon non alio pascitur alimento quam aeris, et idcirco ore est semper hiante, ita quosdam aura popularis alit, neque quicquam captat praeter inanes laudes et gloriam... Ursus informos gignit catulos, eos lambendo format, ita rudem ingenii foetum diutina cura expoliri convenit.' Erasmus, *Parabolae*, 284, tr. 252. References in parentheses are to Pliny, *Natural History*.

[51] 'Caeterorum ornamentorum singula suam quandam ac peculiarem adferunt gratiam et commoditatem dictioni; metaphora sola cumulatius praestat universa, quam exornationes reliquae singula. Delectare vis? Nulla plus habet festivitatis. Docere studes? Non alia probat vel efficatius, vel apertius. Flectere paras? Nulla plus addit acrimoniae. Studes copiae? Nusquam supellex locupletior... Sublimitatem affectas? Haec quidvis quantimvis attollit... Ἐνάργειαν captas ac lucem? Nulla melius rem ob oculos ponit.' Erasmus, *Parabolae*, 90, tr. 130–1 (with changes).

readers both models and formulae of expression with which to enrich their original compositions. Its usefulness is confirmed by the number of editions it went through.

De conscribendis epistolis was Erasmus's second most successful rhetoric textbook, appearing in ninety editions. Erasmus had worked on a letter-writing manual sporadically over many years. In Paris in 1497–8 he gave a manuscript of a short treatise on letter writing to his English pupil Robert Fisher. This was subsequently published as *Brevissima... conficiendarum epistolarum formula* (Leipzig, 1520), a text which was printed fifty-nine times in the sixteenth century. In 1511 from Cambridge he wrote of completing his *De conscribendis epistolis* at the same time as correcting *De copia*; though some of the new chapters must have been finished before 1509.[52] In 1521 a *Libellus de conscribendis epistolis* was published over Erasmus's name but without his assistance by John Siberch in Cambridge. The appearance of this unauthorized edition, which must have been based on manuscripts which Erasmus had left with English friends, prompted Erasmus to publish his own full edition with Froben in Basel in 1522.[53] Comparing this new edition with the *Libellus* Judith Rice Henderson notes that Erasmus's later version represents a compromise between medieval and classical approaches, particularly on the issue of the salutation.[54]

De conscribendis epistolis was a great and immediate success. There were twenty-four editions in the first decade of publication and a total of seventy-four editions between 1521 and 1559. It also continued to be available, in much reduced quantities, for a long time, with a further sixteen editions 1560–1692. It is a very full textbook, combining materials drawn from the rhetoric textbooks with description and exemplification of twenty-five kinds of letter. The treatise has five main elements: (1) an introduction to the letter and its possible styles; (2) instructions on the teaching of letter-writing; (3) advice on forms of salutation and farewell; (4) advice on writing twenty-five types of letter, interspersed with (5) observations on audiences, beginnings, amplification, and argument applicable more generally to different types of letter. For each of the types of letter, Erasmus usually provides the following: a discussion of the aims of the letter, advice on what to include, constructed examples of the type

[52] J. R. Henderson, 'Despauterius's *Syntaxis* (1509): The Earliest Publication of Erasmus's *De conscribendis epistolis*', *Humanistica Lovaniensia,* 37 (1988), 175–210.

[53] J.-C. Margolin, 'Introduction', in Erasmus, *De conscribendis epistolis, Opera omnia,* i/2 (Amsterdam, 1971), 157–73, Erasmus, Letter 241.

[54] Chomarat, *Grammaire*, 1003–38. J. R. Henderson, 'Erasmus on the Art of Letter-Writing', in J. J. Murphy (ed.), *Renaissance Eloquence* (Berkeley, Calif., 1983), 331–55. And on its influence, J. R. Henderson, 'Humanism and the Humanities', in C. Poster and L. Mitchell (eds.), *Letter-Writing Manuals and Instruction* (Columbia, SC, 2007), 141–77.

(with in some cases references to classical and modern letters of that kind), and phrases which may be helpful in composing that type of letter. Table 5.2 summarizes the structure of the work. Types of letter are given in Latin in italics. The different elements (as above) are indicated by bold numerals.

De conscribendis epistolis is not a full classical rhetoric applied to letter-writing. It is not organized in relation to the three key tasks of invention, disposition, and style. Rather it combines a listing of types of letters (less extensive than some of its renaissance predecessors) with advice on points of particular importance for letter-writing (such as salutations and valedictions) and résumés of some rhetorical and dialectical doctrines (such as amplification and the forms of proof). The work assumes that the teacher will have briefly summed up the principles of rhetoric before beginning on letter-writing.[55]

For Erasmus the principal characteristic of the letter is its variety. In opposition to what is often claimed, he points out that letters are not necessarily brief, that they are not all written in the conversational style, that they do not have to avoid figures of speech, and that the criterion of clarity depends on the audience being addressed.[56] The best kind of letters are those which are furthest removed from vulgar and uneducated usage, which consist of refined thoughts and carefully chosen words suited to their subject-matter, which are best suited to the subject, place, time, and people involved.[57] Even if one excludes certain types of letter as being more like declamations or books there is still a great variety. The style should be like that of friends conversing together.[58] It is impossible to sum up briefly the requirements of the letter so that the pupil can master the skill quickly. What is required is wide knowledge, vigilance, and assiduous practice.

After summarizing the precepts of rhetoric for his pupils the teacher must set them practice letters on subjects taken from poetry or history or made up by the teacher. Rather than merely outlining the situation and aim of the letter, the teacher should explain the genre to which the proposed letter belongs and make suggestions about how the ideas and expression should be developed, while leaving considerable freedom to the pupil.[59] The teacher should correct faults and provide a model answer. He

[55] 'posteaquam suis tradiderit compendio artis rhetoricae praecepta', *De conscribendis epistolis*, 231. Tr. C. Fantazzi, *Collected Works*, xxv (Toronto, 1985), 24.

[56] Ibid. 212–21. trs. 13–18.

[57] Ibid. 222. trs. 19.

[58] Ibid. 224–5. trs. 19–20.

[59] Ibid. 237–53, trs. 28–38.

Table 5.2. Plan of Erasmus, *De conscribendis epistolis*

Chs.		Pages
1–4	1 Defining the letter	209–15
5–8	Style of the letter	215–27
9–11	2 Teaching letter-writing: presenting subjects and correcting work	227–66
12–25	3 Salutations and names	266–95
26–8	Saying farewell at the end of the letter	295–300
29	The order of a letter	301–2
30	Example of a mixed letter	303–9
31–2	4 The kinds of letters: the three genres of rhetoric	309–15
33	Difference between *exhortatio* and *suasio*	315–16
34–5	5 Beginning the letter	316–24
36	4 *Exhortatio* (encouragement)	324–29
37	5 Using and ordering examples	330–40
38–9	4 Concluding and moderating *exhortatio*	340–41
40–2	5 Style; amplification; figures; example of *exhortatio*	341–53
43–4	4 *Dehortatio* (discouragement); answering letters of encouragement	353–65
45	*Suasoria* (persuasion)	365–70
46	5 Forms of argumentation; topics of invention	370–400
47	4 Example: persuasion to marriage	400–29
48	*Dissuasorio* (persuading against something)	429–32
49–50	*Consolatoria* (consolation)	432–65
51	*Petitoria* (request)	465–76
52	*Commendatitia* (recommendation)	476–88
53–4	*Monitoria* (giving advice); advice on study and life at court	488–509
55	*Amatoria* (friendship)	509–13
56	Letters of the demonstrative class	513–16
57	Judicial class: *criminatoria* (accusatory)	516–20
58	*Expostulatoria* (complaint)	520–5
59–60	*Purgatoria* (apology)	525–31
61	*Exprobratio* (reproof)	532–5
62	*Invectiva* (invective)	535–7
63–4	*Deprecatoria* (entreaty)	537–41
65	Unusual types of letter: *Nunciatio* (information)	541–7
66–7	*Mandatoria* (instruction) and *Collaudatoria* (commendation)	547–9
68	*Actio Gratiarum* (giving thanks)	549–54
69	*Lamentatoria* (lamentation)	555–61
70	*Gratulatoria* (congratulation)	561–6
71	*Iocosa* (humorous)	566–8
72	*Conciliatoria* (seeking goodwill) and praise	568–72
73	*Officiosa* (offering help)	572–8
74	*Disputatoria* (debate): references to previous letters only	578–9

should ensure that there is progression between the exercises, enabling the pupil to grow in skill.[60]

Erasmus urges pupils to begin by thinking about the purpose of the letter and the person to whom they are writing.

> I shall give this one preliminary piece of general advice to young students, that when they are going to write a letter they should not at once have recourse to rules nor take refuge in books from which they may borrow elegant little words and sententious expressions. Rather, they should first consider very carefully the topics on which they have decided to write, then be well acquainted with the nature, character, and moods of the person to whom the letter is being written and their own standing with him in favour, influence, or services rendered. From the careful examination of all these things they should derive, so to speak, the living model of the letter. After that has been determined I shall allow them to search out passages in the authors from which they can borrow a plentiful supply of the best words and sentiments.[61]

Although imitation of existing models and repetition of appropriate phrases have their place, Erasmus insists that they are subsidiary to thinking through the subject-matter and the relationship between writer and addressee. Having emphasized the importance of thinking about the person addressed, Erasmus makes detailed suggestions for ways in which one might seek to make a favourable impression on a remote acquaintance, attempt to renew a lapsed friendship, or prepare to make an awkward request.[62] Erasmus's advice on obtaining goodwill is based on sections on *exordia* from rhetoric manuals,[63] but it is always carefully adapted both to the genre of the letter and to the social situation of the people involved. His reflections on his own experience of reassuring friends or winning over the uncommitted inform the ideas and phrases he suggests. As well as teaching letter-writing, Erasmus is giving advice on prudent ways of addressing other people.

[60] Ibid. 254, 261–4. trs. 39, 42–4.

[61] 'Sed illud unum prius in genere studiosis adolescentibus praecipiemus, ut epistolam scripturi, non statim praecepta respiciant; aut ad libros, unde voculas, sententiolasve aliquot mutuentur, confugiant, sed prius res, de quibus scribere constituerunt, solertissima cogitatione dispiciant; tum eius ad quem scribitur, naturam, mores, affectusque omnes perspectos habeant: quantum etiam ipsi apud eum vel gratia, vel autoritate, vel meritis denique valeant. Eque his omnibus diligenter pensiculatis, epistolae tanquam vivum exemplar ducant. Quo constituto, tum demum nihil equidem morabor, quo minus locos aliquot ex autoribus petant, unde tum verborum optimorum, tum sententiarum copiosam supellictilem possint mutuari.' *De conscribendis epistolis*, 316; tr. Fantazzi, 74.

[62] *De conscribendis epistolis*, 317–23; tr. Fantazzi, 74–8.

[63] *Ad Herennium* 1.3.5–7.11; Cicero, *De inventione* 1.15.20–18.26; Quintilian, *Institutio oratoria* 4.1.

Within his treatment of the persuasive letter Erasmus inserts a section on the forms of argumentation and the topics of invention. He prefaces this with a note suggesting that this material was not in his own manuscript of *De conscribendis epistolis* but had been added in Siberch's unauthorized edition, using notes which Erasmus had written for another purpose. Nevertheless he decides not to remove it from the text, since, even though it could have been expressed better, it remains useful.[64] Erasmus's list of forms of argumentation seems to be based on Cicero's *De inventione* but the ordering of the forms (complexio, enumeratio, simplex conclusio, subiectio, oppositio, violatio, inductio, collectio, ratiocinatio) copies George Trapezuntius's *Rhetoricorum libri V*, which was itself based on Cicero and Hermogenes.[65] Erasmus goes on to list the topics of person and thing,[66] and the topics of invention.[67] The latter section again looks very similar to George Trapezuntius, who was here basing himself on Peter of Spain and Boethius, though Erasmus shortens the text and alters some of the examples.[68] Finally Erasmus returns to listing topics associated with deliberative oratory. It is very striking both that Erasmus included so much technical material on the discovery and presentation of arguments in a treatise on letter-writing and that he chose George Trapezuntius as a source, emphasizing types of proof which are likely to be effective in rhetorical argument.

Erasmus initially proposes that the three main types of letter should correspond to the traditional rhetorical doctrine of the three kinds of case: judicial, deliberative, and demonstrative. He groups many of his types of letter under these headings. So, for example he claims that the judicial class of letters includes *accusatio*, *querela*, *defensio*, *expostulatio*, *expurgatio*, *exprobratio*, *comminatio*, *invectiva,* and *deprecatio*.[69] We notice that three of these types (*querela*, *defensio,* and *comminatio*) are not in fact discussed in the manual. Then we see that the demonstrative class lists only a series of descriptions. Erasmus later explains that the demonstrative letter is rarely found on its own (and he gives no examples) but is often a part of other genres.[70] Finally he adds a fourth genre, which he at first calls 'familiar' and later 'unusual genres'.[71] This class contains more types of

[64] *De conscribendis epistolis*, 370. trs. 110. Chomarat, *Grammaire*, 1006–7.

[65] *De conscribendis epistolis*, 370–83. trs. 110–18. George Trapezuntius, *Rhetoricorum libri V*, 207–35. John Monfasani, *George of Trebizond* (Leiden, 1976), 275. George includes *summissio*, between *subiectio* and *oppositio*. Cf Margolin, in *De conscribendis epistolis*, 188–9.

[66] *De conscribendis epistolis*, 383–7. trs. 119–21. Compare George, *Rhetoricorum libri V*, 278–89.

[67] *De conscribendis epistolis*, 390–9. trs. 122–8.

[68] George, *Rhetoricorum libri V*, 256–77. Monfasani, *George*, 276–7.

[69] *De conscribendis epistolis*, 311. trs, 71.

[70] Ibid. 311, 513. trs. 71, 205.

[71] Ibid. 311, 541. trs. 71, 225.

letter than any of the other three. The crude criterion of the space allocated to each subgenre suggests that there are five principal motivations for letters: encouragement, persuasion, consolation, request, and advice. Less prominent than these five but still occupying a considerable amount of space are six further purposes: recommendation, providing information (*narratoria*), giving thanks, lamenting sorrows, congratulation, and offering assistance. These headings seem like a more realistic account of the reasons to write a letter in the sixteenth century (and probably for that matter in the first century BC) than the three types of classical oration. Erasmus appears to be honouring the tradition enshrined in the classical textbooks while at the same time adapting his teaching to the practicalities of writing letters.

Most of the richness of Erasmus's book lies in the accounts of the individual types of letter, which critical commentary has tended to pass over. While many of the later letter types receive only a brief definition, one or two examples, and a collection of useful phrases, some types of letter, especially from the deliberative kind, are dealt with at considerable length. So, for example, he explains that the letter of encouragement originates in the emotions, and he examines a list of sources of persuasion which will bring about the desired emotional response: praise, hope, fear, hatred, love, pity, rivalry, expectation, example, and entreaty. He discusses ways of presenting praise so that it will inspire the recipient. Under the rubric of encouragement Erasmus provides an original account of emotional persuasion tailored to this particular type of letter. Later in the same sequence he discusses the question of amplification. Under persuasion he writes out a declamation in praise of marriage and then discusses ways in which the material could be adapted into an argument against marriage. Here the exercise of letter-writing resembles a preparation for declamation.

His discussion of the letter of consolation emphasizes the importance of the task and the care with which it must be handled. Under the straightforward method one may produce philosophical arguments against grief but more often an indirect approach will be required. In writing to a very proud person we may need to speak as if it is our own grief we are trying to assuage rather than theirs. We need to show that we share the recipient's grief before we can start finding arguments to diminish it. We must take great care not to give any suggestions that we are more fortunate than the person being consoled. If it cannot be argued that the misfortune will be short-lived, the letter-writer must show that it is not so serious as it appears, that some good will come of it, or that it is part of the human condition.[72] Erasmus's second model letter consoles a father for the loss of

[72] Ibid. 432–5 ; tr. 148–51.

his son. After showing his respect for the father's grief, Erasmus urges him that as a philosopher he ought at least to moderate it. Since bereavement at the death of children is a common experience, reason and law urge that mourning should be kept within bounds. Excessive sorrow will become an evil in itself, useless to the person mourned, and harmful to the mourner. Erasmus combines pagan and Christian arguments for the immortality of the soul before making specifically Christian arguments for resignation, for death as the gateway to eternal life, and for the happiness of the son living in heaven.[73]

The specially composed model-letters, the collections of phrases to use, and the references to examples for imitation, from the works of Cicero, Pliny, and Poliziano, are crucial helps to the pupil. Erasmus treats the letter as important in itself but also as an exercise which can teach useful writing skills. He attacks his renaissance predecessors for being too rigid. Instead he wishes to promote a flexibility based on a consideration of the nature of the task and the relationships between writer and recipient (and in some cases also the person being recommended). So the letter is a preparation for other types of writing but also an exercise in thinking about how we relate to other people and what our duties are in relation to them. Much of Erasmus's advice about what to put in a letter is also guidance about how to conduct oneself more generally.

It might have been expected that, with the publication of *De conscribendis epistolis*, Erasmus's shorter *Formula*, whose authorship he often did not acknowledge, would have been ignored. This did not happen, partly because the *Formula* already included some of Erasmus's most important guiding principles, about flexibility of content and style, but mainly because its brevity made it suitable for classroom use and for inclusion in the popular omnibus editions of letter-writing treatises.[74]

Erasmus composed his dialogue *Ciceronianus or on the best kind of style* in 1527 and 1528 in Basel.[75] It was first published by Froben in 1528 and was printed 11 times in the sixteenth century, alongside either *Colloquia* or *De recta pronuntiatione*. In the seventeenth century there were three editions of the text on its own. The dialogue is lively and biting, mocking a caricature of Ciceronian obsessions and arguing for a more moderate approach to imitation. True Ciceronianism would involve imitating Cicero's real practice rather than trying to copy every detail of

[73] Ibid. 441–55; tr. 156–64.

[74] e.g. Green and Murphy, *Renaissance Rhetoric Short-Title Catalogue* (Aldershot, 2006), RR 603, 1540, 2269, 3692.

[75] Erasmus, *Ciceronianus*, ed. P. Merdard, *Opera Ounia* i/2 (Amsterdam, 1971). B. I. Knott, in *Collected Works of Erasmus*, xxviii (Toronto, 1986), 327. Cave, *Cornucopian Text*, 35–48. Chomarat, *Grammaire*, 815–40.

his phraseology and not permitting oneself to use words which do not appear in Cicero. Erasmus argues that Cicero always informed himself about the case and worked out his own line of argument before he began to write. While reading widely in previous authors he always tried to write in his own way.[76] The key to style is always appropriateness to situation. Cicero's style would not always be appropriate to Christian writers now. Cicero himself wrote in several different ways, and so should we. Within this necessary variety we must always try to remain true to our own natural inclination.[77]

At the end of the dialogue Erasmus sums up his conclusions. True imitation of Cicero depends on a firm grasp of the principles of rhetoric. Then the student needs someone who can show him how Cicero uses the techniques of rhetoric. Here Erasmus seems to envisage something like the rhetorical commentaries which would become so familiar in the 1530s. Even though Cicero should occupy the first place, the student must read other authors, for style as well as matter, following them where it seems appropriate. Imitation must be critical, not slavish. It must aim at writing something equally good, not something superficially similar.[78]

Erasmus was prompted to write the work partly by the example of Christophe de Longueil (1488–1522), who he believed had wasted his real talent as a result of becoming obsessed with Ciceronianism during his stay in Italy, and partly by Italian criticisms of his own style. His review of the Ciceronian credentials of contemporary writers enabled him to show his admiration for Valla and Poliziano in particular, whom he admired for being good writers who were not particularly Ciceronian, but also for Sadoleto, Bembo, Pontano, and Sannazaro.[79] Several of his contemporaries took offence at the judgements of their styles made by the semi-reformed Ciceronian Nosoponus in the latter part of the dialogue, even though Erasmus was careful to include criticisms of himself.[80]

He highly praised Rudolph Agricola—'a man of superhuman mentality, of deep learning, with a style far from commonplace, solid, vigorous, polished, controlled, but he has a touch of Quintilian in expression and of Isocrates in word arrangement, though he rises to greater heights than either of them'—in terms which suggest the limitations of being purely Ciceronian.[81] Earlier he had claimed that Quintilian was a more thorough

[76] *Ciceronianus*, 651–2; tr. Knott, 402.
[77] *Ciceronianus*, 654–6; tr. Knott, 405–7.
[78] *Ciceronianus*, 707–8; tr. Knott, 445–6.
[79] *Ciceronianus*, 697–701, 705; tr. Knott, 435–7, 443.
[80] *Ciceronianus*, 680–1; tr. Knott, 425.
[81] 'Agnosco virum divini pectoris, eruditionis reconditae, stilo minime vulgari, solidum, nervosum, elaboratum, compositum, sed qui nonnihil resipiat et Quintilianum in eloquendo,

teacher of rhetoric, including important material which Cicero had omitted or merely touched on: arousing of emotion, the use of the different types of maxims, the methods of amplification, and the invention of propositions.[82] Some of these aspects correspond to the areas where Agricola and Erasmus had done their major work. He praises the talent and ease of expression of his younger contemporary Philipp Melanchthon, while suggesting that he had more important goals in view than studied eloquence.[83] Although Erasmus was careful to praise Valla and agree with Poliziano,[84] *Ciceronianus* implied that northern scholars were taking the study of rhetoric forward while the Italians had become obsessed with the self-defeating minutiae of strict Ciceronianism.

Erasmus found it difficult to compose *Ecclesiastes*. He first agreed to write a textbook on preaching in response to a request from Jean Bekker de Borsselen in 1519. In the 1520s he was further encouraged by Bekker and by John Fisher, but he only really began work in 1533 when he finished the first book and made good progress with books 2 and 3. In 1535, aware of his deteriorating health he gave the work to the printers unfinished, rather than allow someone else to publish it posthumously.[85] Its ten editions (1535–54), mostly from Basel and Antwerp, pale in comparison with Erasmus's other major rhetorical texts but look more respectable in relation to the generally small numbers of editions of preaching manuals. Possibly the inclusion of Erasmus's works in the *Index librorum prohibitorum* promulgated in Rome in 1557 made it impractical to continue to reprint his preaching manual intended for Catholic clergy.

Ecclesiastes offers a defiantly classical model for preaching, criticizing the medieval 'thematic' sermon,[86] and proposing instead a model based on the six-part oration proposed by Cicero and Quintilian. Although he adopts a few of St Augustine's ideas in his discussion of the importance and difficulty of preaching in book 1, his major treatments of invention, organization, and style, in books 2 and 3, are firmly based on classical models.

et Isocratem in orationis structura, utroque tamen sublimior.' *Ciceronianus*, 682–3; tr. Knott, 427–8.

[82] *Ciceronianus*, 653; tr. Knott, 403–4.

[83] *Ciceronianus*, 686; tr. Knott, 427.

[84] *Ciceronianus*, 706–7; tr. Knott, 443–5; G. W. Pigman III, 'Imitation and the Renaissance Sense of the Past: The Reception of Erasmus' *Ciceronianus*', *Journal of Medieval and Renaissance Studies*, 9 (1979), 155–77.

[85] Chomarat, *Grammaire*, 1053–5. Erasmus, *Opera omnia*, v/4, ed. Chomarat (Amsterdam, 1991), 3–5. Debora Shuger, *Sacred Rhetoric* (Princeton, 1988), 63–4. Judith T. Wozniak, *A Time for Peace: The Ecclesiastes of Erasmus* (New Orleans, 1996).

[86] Chomarat, *Grammaire*, 1074–92.

Table 5.3. Plan of Erasmus, *Ecclesiastes*

1	Definition of preaching	v/4. 35–44
	Qualities required in a preacher	44–76
	Dignity and difficulty of preaching	76–246
2	Importance of holiness and practice	247–51
	Preliminary study of dialectic and grammar, reading	251–68
	3 genres, 3 aims, 5 skills, 6 parts of oration (*exordium*, narration, division, confirmation, refutation, conclusion)	268–80
	Exordium and division	280–310
	Invention of arguments: arguments suited to the three genres	311–44
	Advice on arguing against an adversary	344–50
	Types of proof and topics of person	350–400
	Topics	400–62
	Forms of argumentation	463–8
	Epilogue	468–70
3	Disposition	v/5. 8–14
	Memory	14–16
	Delivery	16–44
	Amplification	44–66
	Emotion	66–98
	Figures (including example of man sick of the palsy)	98–176
	Tropes and interpretation of scripture	176–288
	Adapting the sermon to its audience (decorum)	288–308
4	Outline of subjects most commonly found in sermons	311–58
	Collections of material for each subject (covering only the first few subjects, including Nature of God, Son, Angels)	358–84
	Example of discussion of concord	384–91

This table is indebted to the analyses by Chomarat, *Grammaire et rhétorique*, 1061–71; Erasmus, *Opera omnia*, v/4 (Amsterdam, 1991), 8–16.

In the first part of book 4 Erasmus provides definitions and explanations of the subjects for sermons which amount almost to a summary of the theology most suitable for saving souls. He lists a large number of subjects but then explains that it would take several volumes to collect arguments, confirmations, comparisons, *sententiae*, examples, and amplifications for all of them.[87] The few examples he provides give an idea of how the larger project might work.

Erasmus's discussion of the preacher in book 1 focuses on his moral obligations, the importance and dignity of the task of preaching, and its difficulty. In order to succeed in this difficult and crucial task the preacher must be aware of its significance and must exhibit a blameless life. His

[87] Erasmus, *Opera omnia*, v/5, ed. Chomarat (Amsterdam, 1994), 346–58, 378.

success with his audience will depend on their respect for his office and for the person who occupies it.[88] The preacher's piety, ability to project his beliefs, and practical experience will be more important to his success than the rules of rhetoric.[89] From time to time Erasmus interjects strong criticism of current preaching practices into his instructions for good preaching.[90]

Where books 1 and 4 provide materials and guidance devoted specifically to preaching, books 2 and 3 represent an adaptation of the general course in the whole of rhetoric to the needs of the preacher. Although the text discusses the five skills of the orator and four of the parts of the oration in some detail, most attention is given to invention, style, amplification, emotion, and decorum, as Table 5.3 shows. This could be seen as enriching the basic outline of *Rhetorica ad Herennium* with further material from Quintilian, Aristotle, and Erasmus's own rhetorical works. Erasmus's account of invention begins by discussing arguments suited to the three genres of rhetoric: demonstrative, deliberative (which includes exhortation, consolation, and admonition), and judicial (in which he shows that ideas connected with status theory can be applied to scripture).[91] Then he discusses types of proof and the topics of person before reaching the general topics. Erasmus praises Agricola's account of the topics,[92] but his version relies more on Cicero's *Topica*. In this section, as in Erasmus's treatment of the figures of rhetoric, teaching from classical sources is illustrated with literary and biblical examples.[93]

Amplification may be achieved through employment of the commonplaces and through amplification of words (using certain tropes and figures, comparisons, and accumulations of materials). The aim of amplification is to touch the emotions of the audience, the most important aspect of the preacher's task.[94] Erasmus places considerable stress on the importance of emotion in preaching, quoting John the Baptist and Jesus as well as Aristotle.[95] Following Aristotle and Quintilian he shows how emotion can be drawn from people's circumstances and what happens to them. Where classical accounts of emotion had focused on methods of arousing anger he gives more attention to the Christian virtues of pity and

88 Erasmus, *Opera omnia*, v/4. 54–8, 68–76, 222–35.
89 Ibid. 222–35, 247–51.
90 Ibid. 112–40, v/5. 10–14, 204–6, 224–6, 230–42.
91 Ibid. v/4. 311–44.
92 Ibid. 402.
93 e.g. v/4. 402, 406–8, 414–16; v/5. 100–6, 158, 162.
94 Ibid. v/5. 44–66.
95 Ibid. 66–8.

charity.[96] Like Quintilian, Agricola, and Vives he emphasizes the role of vivid description and imagination in conveying emotion.[97]

Erasmus divides his account of the figures into those which give bitterness and vehemence, and those which give pleasure, clarity, and brilliance. In both halves he begins by following the terminology and order of *Rhetorica ad Herennium*, with appropriate omissions in each half and some interpolations from Quintilian. To the generally classical definitions of the figures Erasmus adds examples from classical literature, the Bible, and the Church Fathers. He gives particular attention to prosopopeia, hypotyposis (vivid description), epitheta (added from Quintilian), sententia, metaphors, and similitudes.[98] The section on the figures closes with a worked example in which he suggests commonplaces and figures to develop the teaching of the gospel story of Christ healing the man sick of the palsy (Matthew 9: 1–8).[99]

His discussion of the tropes begins by showing that the Bible employs tropes, that an understanding of how the tropes work is essential to understanding the Bible, and that the Fathers of the Church employed their understanding of the tropes in order to interpret the Bible.[100] He moves on to an extensive discussion of the necessity but also the possible excesses of allegorical interpretation of the Bible. Although he prefers literal interpretations (and shows that many problems in interpretation can be resolved using grammatical knowledge and understanding of the context), he acknowledges that on occasion allegorical interpretations are required in order to understand a passage or teach an audience.[101] He gives reasons for the obscurity of some passages in scripture and mocks certain scholastic interpretations of scripture. This section, which almost forms a separate treatise on the interpretation of the Bible, concludes with a critical discussion of the Tychonian rules for interpretation and St Augustine's observations on exegesis.[102]

Erasmus ends his third book with a discussion of decorum. From all the things which could be said about a biblical text, the preacher will need to choose what is most useful in teaching and what is most effective in arousing emotions in a particular audience. He gives examples of speakers adapting their message to their audience from Demosthenes, St Peter, and St Paul. He suggests a number of different considerations which might

[96] Ibid. 72–82.
[97] Ibid. 88–98.
[98] Ibid. 124–32, 148–64.
[99] Ibid. 164–76.
[100] Ibid. 176–82.
[101] Ibid. 200–56.
[102] Ibid. 280–8.

affect ideas of decorum but insists that there are no firm rules and that everything depends on the judgement of the speaker.[103] This strong emphasis on decorum is also found in the work of Vives (to be discussed in the next chapter) and it is quite possible that his work influenced Erasmus here.

Erasmus contributed to renaissance rhetoric over a broader range of textbooks than any other author. The origins of most of his rhetoric textbooks can be found in his experience of private tutoring in Paris in the late 1490s; his textbooks always pay attention to pupils' needs: phrases to employ, practical advice, suggestions of models, and reading. But he always employed his deep scholarship to improve the books and he directed them towards practical and ethical aims: advice on how to write and how to behave, and persuasions towards good conduct. He was a crucial model of educated writing for contemporary and later readers. His textbooks were more successful than those of any other author, partly because, even when they founded new genres of textbook, he carefully designed them to fit into places in the grammar-school syllabus, and partly because they were so practical and useful, providing students with so much material for practice and for reuse in their own writing. The practical elements in his textbooks, such as the lists of phrases, often convey a strong sense of playful virtuosity, showing one's skill in the use of language by going to extremes and making jokes.

He directed thorough attention to many important elements of writing which had been neglected by the classical rhetorical tradition: proverbs, maxims, descriptions, examples, comparisons. Some of these elements had been cultivated by medieval rhetoricians, such as Geoffrey de Vinsauf, whose work Erasmus knew. He promoted the letter as a way of practising skills which would be needed for other rhetorical tasks: argumentation, handling the emotions, thinking about the audience. He found new ways of thinking about style. First he insisted that style must flow from knowledge of subject-matter and audience. Then he proposed ways of varying and supercharging one's first formulations. Synonyms and alternative phrasings are never exactly the same. They bring different flavours and implications which we may want to try out, before deciding which expression best suits what we are trying to convey to a particular audience.

Erasmus made his original contribution by utilizing the work of earlier rhetoricians. Like Valla and Agricola he sought to combine rhetoric and dialectic, though he used dialectical methods to produce new material for rhetoric. In common with Agricola and many other exponents of the

[103] Ibid. 288–308.

humanist tradition he emphasized the connection between reading and writing, arguing that students needed to study the technical achievements of earlier writers. Like Valla he admired Quintilian more than any other rhetorician. Like Valla he employed surveys of usage to discover established alternative expressions which students could then select among or vary in their own ways, using the methods he outlined. He gave many indications of texts which could be imitated but, in conscious rejection of Italian Ciceronianism, he insisted that writers must follow their own natural bent in absorbing lessons from their reading. He always emphasized the need to adapt one's arguing and writing to the circumstances and audience of a particular assignment. Appropriateness was his key concern but he also believed in experiment and play. Once you think you know what you want to say you can try out different ways of expressing an idea which may in turn lead your thought in new directions.

Erasmus never wrote the comprehensive handbook of rhetoric which would introduce (or perhaps substitute for) the classical manuals, nor did he attempt a new presentation of rhetoric's most enduring feature, the list of the tropes and figures. Both those tasks were to be attempted by the next generation, led by Philipp Melanchthon. Erasmus's work was enormously influential throughout northern Europe and in Spain and Portugal, though the diffusion of his rhetorical works was affected by the listing of his name on the Index in 1557 and 1559.[104] In Italy his influence peaked in the period 1518–30, when several of his works were printed there. After 1525 Italians increasingly attacked him as a crypto-Lutheran.[105]

[104] M. Bataillon, *Erasme et l'Espagne* (Paris, 1937), repr. and enlarged (Geneva, 1991). Henderson, 'Humanism and the Humanities', 162–4.

[105] S. Seidel Menchi, *Erasmo in Italia* (Turin, 1987).

6

Northern Europe 1519–1545

The Age of Melanchthon

The first half of the sixteenth century was the heroic period of northern humanism, both for innovation and for growing influence over the universities. Erasmus was publishing and revising his rhetorical works; Agricola's *De inventione dialectica* appeared in 1515; Melanchthon began his series of textbooks on rhetoric and dialectic, based on his teaching in Wittenberg, in 1519; Sturm, Latomus, and others brought the new logical approach to commenting on Cicero from Louvain to Paris, where it completed the eclipse of scholastic logic. Melanchthon was the dominant figure of this period. Unlike Agricola and Erasmus he took a personal role in the reform of universities and attracted many direct followers.

Melanchthon built his work around the connections between rhetoric and dialectic, insisting that effective writing required a thorough and coordinated knowledge of both subjects. Reading and commenting on Latin literature in the light of rhetorical teaching was at the heart of his project. He always explained and illuminated his theoretical teaching with literary examples. He devoted many teaching hours each week to commenting on Cicero, Virgil, and the Bible. While recognizing the complexity of rhetoric he tried to begin with simplified procedures in order to get his pupils started on the practice in writing and speaking which would develop their rhetorical skills. The combination of teaching, dialectic, and simplification led him to introduce the didascalic genre which remains the strongest marker of a Melanchthonian approach to rhetoric.

JOHANN CAESARIUS OF JULICH (*C.* 1468–1550)

Around the beginning of the sixteenth century northern European writers composed manuals of dialectic which covered the traditional Aristotelian logic syllabus, omitting some of the medieval accretions, in a language closer to humanist requirements. Jacques Lefèvre d'Étaples (*c*1460–1536) wrote Latin paraphrases of Aristotle's works on logic and natural philosophy in the 1490s.[1] Johann Caesarius, who studied with Lefèvre in Paris, wrote his *Dialectica* in 1520. This work was published (both in the original text and in a catechism-style version prepared by Caspar Rodolphus) fifty-one times before 1577, mostly in Cologne and Mainz. Production was regular, with some concentration of editions in the 1540s and 1550s. Much later, in 1534, Caesarius composed a summary of rhetoric for those who had used his dialectic. This work was printed fourteen times up to 1565, mostly in Cologne and Leipzig.

Caesarius's *Dialectica* summarizes the teaching of the whole *Organon* in ten treatises, starting with the predicables and ending with the sophisms. He includes sections on hypothetical propositions (4), hypothetical syllogism (6), demonstration (7), and definition and division (8), as well as the expected subjects. In comparison with Peter of Spain's *Tractactus*, the most popular medieval introduction to logic, which was still required by some university statutes, Caesarius returns to the Aristotelian order (rather than beginning with the proposition) and omits all the material relating to supposition, to disputation (the treatise on obligations), and to medieval techniques for analysing certain types of fallacy (e.g. the treatise on composition and division). Although Caesarius's preface parades his humanist credentials and makes reference to Valla, Agricola, and Trapezuntius among others, he generally restricts himself to summarizing Aristotelian doctrine.[2] He follows Boethius's account of the topics (treatise 9), including the topical maxims, even though he introduces his account by praising Agricola.[3] In comparison with George Trapezuntius's *Isagoge*, which was much printed in northern Europe at this time, Caesarius is more thorough where George summarizes briefly, includes the topics of invention which George omits, excludes the rules of debate which George summarizes so briefly as to be scarcely intelligible, and avoids George's use of some scholastic logical terms, such as *terminus*. Both Caesarius's and George's introductions to dialectic were often printed at the same places and times as Agricola's *De inventione dialectica*. Both provided the traditional account of the categories and the forms of argumentation (in particular the valid forms of the syllogism), which Agricola omits.

[1] C. Vasoli, *La dialettica e la retorica dell'Umanesimo* (Milan, 1968), 183–213. Ann Moss, *Renaissance Truth and the Latin Language Turn* (Oxford, 2003), 91–4.

[2] Caesarius, *Dialectica* (Cologne, ?1520), British Library 520d6, sig. Bb1^{v}. Vasoli, *La dialettica*, 260–77.

[3] Caesarius, *Dialectica*, M2^{v}, 3^{r}.

Caesarius's *Rhetorica* (1534) is an inclusive summary in seven tractates. It is based mainly on a reorganization of material from Cicero and Quintilian but also includes teaching from Aristotle (occasionally), Victorinus, Martianus Capella, and Melanchthon. It insists on the close connections between rhetoric and dialectic, but explains the difference by saying that dialectic is concerned with general issues (theses) while rhetoric deals with particular cases (hypotheses), that dialectic uses the syllogism, while rhetoric prefers the enthymeme, and that rhetoric aims to persuade a judge, while dialectic strives to force an admission of defeat from an adversary.[4] Caesarius's third tractate, on invention, includes both an account of status theory taken from Cicero and a version of the topics of invention taken from Quintilian 5.10. Tractate 4, on skills of rhetoric other than invention, includes sections on memory taken from Cicero and on delivery from Quintilian. Unusually the fifth tractate describes the six-part oration (exordium, narration, division, confirmation, refutation, conclusion) after the five skills of the orator have been described (rather than within the section on invention). The seventh treatise on the figures of speech uses Melanchthon's three-fold division of the figures and a slightly enlarged version of his list, but takes the descriptions from *Rhetorica ad Herennium*. Caesarius is truthful in his claim that he has excerpted his rhetoric from the writings of the best authors[5] but his original structure enables him to present all the main doctrines of classical Latin rhetoric in a clear and easily intelligible form. Caesarius's works are useful but traditional summaries, whereas Melanchthon presents the whole of rhetoric and dialectic through an original response to the discoveries of Agricola and Erasmus.

PHILIPP MELANCHTHON (1497–1560)

Philipp Melanchthon was one of Martin Luther's closest associates, long-term rector of the University of Wittenberg and a very prominent Protestant reformer of schools and universities. He was the author of the Augsburg confession (1530), which became the broad doctrinal standard of the Lutheran churches, and the *Loci communes* (1521–43), a systematic account of Protestant theology. He studied at Heidelberg (1509–11), where he read widely in classical and humanistic literature as well as following the Aristotelian arts course, and Tübingen (1512–14), where he began to teach. In 1516 his Tübingen friend Oecolampadius presented

[4] Caesarius, *Rhetorica* (Cologne, 1565), sigs. a7^{v}–8^{r}.
[5] Ibid., sig. a6^{r}.

him with a copy of the 1515 first edition of Agricola's *De inventione dialectica*. In 1518 he was appointed to the new chair of Greek at the University of Wittenberg, where he also taught rhetoric and dialectic, New Testament, and, in the absence of the Hebrew lecturer, the Psalms. Alongside his commentaries on scripture and classical literature, he wrote six textbooks of rhetoric and dialectic, which were among the most successful of the sixteenth century. *De rhetorica libri tres* (1519), which concentrated on invention, insisted on the close relationship between rhetoric and dialectic and on the necessity of studying both together. This work was printed fourteen times between 1519 and 1537. His friends urged him to produce a concise textbook of dialectic, *Compendiaria dialectices ratio* (1520), which was printed twenty-two times, all but one before 1527. This in turn necessitated a simplified but complete account of rhetoric, *Institutiones rhetoricae* (1521), which appeared thirty times up to 1535, twenty-five of them before 1529.[6] This work includes an original and influential account of style, which I discuss in more detail in Chapter 10 below.

Melanchthon was much occupied with Bible commentaries, theology, educational reform, and attempts to unite the Protestant churches in the 1520s, but late in the decade he decided to write more comprehensive introductions to dialectic and rhetoric. *Dialectices libri quatuor* (1528) is a considerably enlarged survey of dialectic, intended to prepare students to read fuller textbooks, such as those by Caesarius, Agricola, and Aristotle.[7] It was printed fifty-five times, all but one before 1547. This work was significantly revised and added to by Paul Eberus in 1544.[8] Its companion *Elementa rhetorices libri duo* (1529) is a thorough and original treatment and one of the most influential rhetoric texts of the century. It was printed seventy-one times up to 1610, with large numbers of editions in the 1530s (twenty) and 1540s (fourteen) but also many in the 1550s (nine) and 1560s (fifteen). The work was printed roughly five times a decade up to 1595. Up to 1560 it was printed widely across northern Europe; after that it appeared mainly in Wittenberg, Leipzig, and Basel. *Erotemata dialectices* (1547) is a comprehensive textbook, which could be used as a self-sufficient course in dialectic. It was printed forty-seven times until 1603, mostly in Wittenberg, Frankfurt, and Leipzig, especially between

[6] Biographical material is taken from Heinz Scheible's article in *Contemporaries of Erasmus*, ii (Toronto, 1986), 424–9. See also K. Hartfelder, *Philipp Melanchthon als praeceptor Germaniae* (Berlin, 1889).

[7] Melanchthon, *Dialectices libri quatuor* (Lyon, 1534), sig. A2^{v}.

[8] P. Melanchthon, *Opera omnia*, ed. C. Bretschneider, *Corpus Reformatorum*, 28 vols. (Brunswick, 1834–60), hereafter *CR*, xiii. 509–10. The Eberus edn. (Strasbourg, 1545) is available through the internet.

1547 and 1579 (thirty-nine editions). Some of the medieval additions to logic (such as the consequences and the theory of supposition), which had been dropped from other humanist dialectics, reappeared in this book, which may reflect the beginning of the gradual revival of scholastic logic, described in Chapter 8 below.

From the beginning Melanchthon emphasized the connections between rhetoric and dialectic. In 1520–1 and 1528–9 he wrote paired manuals of the two subjects coordinated with each other. In 1519 he began with a rhetoric which asserted the centrality of dialectic.

> In my view all the things which are needed at the beginning of one's studies, and which therefore shape whatever follows, depend on dialectic. Letters flourished when this was observed. I mean when dialectic and rhetoric educated young people with equal benefit. For once rhetoric was expelled from the schools, look how thin, how deprived, how useless dialectic became.
>
> Rhetoric and dialectic have a common purpose. The latter travels within the confines of the matter with its sails reefed, the former spreads itself more freely. The discourse of dialectic is suited to teaching, the language of rhetoric to moving an audience.[9]

Melanchthon insists on the two subjects' mutual need and assistance. Dialectic is an essential foundation for rhetoric, and shows rhetoric how to investigate a subject and inform an audience. Rhetoric teaches the technique of persuading and moving the audience. Without the direction provided by rhetoric, dialectic becomes inward-looking and overtechnical.

De rhetorica libri tres concentrates on invention. Of sixty-eight pages in the first edition, fifty-five are devoted to invention (book 1), four to disposition (book 2), and nine to style (book 3).[10] Melanchthon organizes

[9] Melanchthon, *De rhetorica libri tres* (Wittenberg, 1519), sig. A2^r: 'Ac nisi fallit opinio mea, ex dialectica pendent omnia, quae ut sint initia studiorum, reliqua ex suo modo temperant. Vigebant literae quondam cum et illa esset salva, hoc est cum paribus officiis dialectica et rhetorica iuventutem erudirent. Iam explosa ex scholis rhetorica vide quam sit exigua, quam sit manca, quam sit inutilis dialectica . . . commune argumentum est et rhetori et dialectico. Hic intra fines propositi negotii velis paulum contractioribus navigat, ille evagatur liberius: huius ad docendum, illius ad movendum est accommodata oratio.' This metaphor from sailing suggests that Melanchthon may have read Valla's *Repastinatio*, which makes a similar comparison (ed. Zippel, 176, 448).

[10] See K. Meerhoff, 'Mélanchthon, lecteur d'Agricola', in his *Entre logique et littérature* (Orleans, 2003), 25–38. J. Classen, 'Neue Elemente in einer alten Disziplin: Zu Melanchthons *De rhetorica libri tres*', in his *Antike Rhetorik im Zeitalter des Humanismus* (Munich, 2003), 254–309. On Melanchthon's rhetoric more generally see Meerhoff, 'The Significance of Philip Melanchthon's Rhetoric in the Renaissance', in P. Mack (ed.), *Renaissance Rhetoric* (Basingstoke, 1994), 46–62. J. Knape, *Philipp Melanchthons Rhetorik* (Tübingen, 1993). P. Mack, *Renaissance Argument* (Leiden, 1993), 320–33. O. Berwald, *Philipp*

his treatment of invention according to the three genres of classical oratory. Unusually he begins with demonstrative oratory, which he subdivides into the genre which describes the technique of teaching and the genre concerned with praise and blame. Under the method of teaching he describes eight questions for investigating simple subjects (named by a single word, A4^{v}) and ten questions for analysing complex subjects (propositions, B4^{r}). Under praise and blame he sets out the topics of person and thing; then he describes three topics of deliberative oratory (honourable, useful, and easy). For judicial oratory he summarizes three headings of status theory (conjectural, definition, and quality). He also gives advice about allegorical interpretation (C2^{v}–3^{v}), emotional manipulation (E4^{r-v}), the commonplaces (E3^{r}–4^{r}), and preaching (G4^{v}–H1^{v}), subjects which he will develop in later rhetorics. The book contains an innovative discussion of techniques for writing commentaries (B4^{v}–C2^{r}), treated as a subdivision of the demonstrative genre, which does not appear in his later rhetorics.[11] In book 2 he discusses occasions on which one might omit one of the five parts of the oration (exordium, narration, confirmation, refutation, conclusion) or change their normal order, and the ordering of arguments within the confirmation. In book 3 he describes amplification before giving brief definitions of thirteen tropes and twenty-five figures of thought, which he says are derived from the topics of invention (I2^{v}). He makes several references to Erasmus, particularly recommending *De copia* and *Adagia* (A2^{v}, C3^{v}, E3^{r}).

In *Compendiaria dialectices ratio* Melanchthon defines dialectic in terms of its methodical approach to general issues.

> Dialectic is the technique of discussing any general issue in a relevant and suitable way. It shows the nature and parts of any subject simply and describes the proposed subject in such clear words that the audience cannot fail to understand what it contains, whether it is true or false.[12]

Dialectic helps students to understand the nature of any subject, through definition and division, and it helps teachers to set out their material in the way best suited to enable their students to understand it.

Melanchthons Sicht der Rhetorik (Weisbaden, 1994). V. Wels, *Triviale Künste* (Berlin, 2000). Moss, *Renaissance Truth*, 153–69, 174–6, 247–52.

[11] Moss, *Renaissance Truth*, 162–3. This section does not appear in either of Melanchthon's subsequent rhetorics. *Elementa rhetorices* has a longer and different discussion of the four senses of the holy scriptures, placed under the trope of allegory: *CR* xiii, cols. 466–72.

[12] *CR* xx. 711–12: 'Dialectica est artificium apposite ac proprie de quocunque themate disserendi. Simpliciter enim cuiusque thematis naturam et partes ostendit, et quod proponitur, adeo certis verbis praescribit, ut non possit non deprehendi, quicquid inest, sive veri, sive falsi.'

The first book is focused on definition, which is taken to embrace the predicables and the categories, and division. The book ends with five questions for investigating a simple subject. (What does the name mean? What is it? What are the causes? What are the parts? What is the function?[13]) This connects back to the technique of simple invention described in *De rhetorica libri tres*. The second book describes the proposition, and the third argumentation, giving a full account of the valid modes of the syllogism but including enthymeme, example, induction, and sorites. The fourth book is devoted to the topics. Melanchthon describes the topics as the sources of argument, but he implies that they are used to amplify and support what some people will have thought of automatically.[14]

Later versions of the dialectic maintain the same basic plan but expand the material considerably. *De Dialectica libri quatuor* (1528), which presents itself as an introduction to Caesarius and Agricola, before the students read Aristotle, strongly emphasizes the use of dialectic.[15] Melanchthon says that the examples he gives will throw light on the instructions and show how helpful dialectic is in understanding arguments between learned men. Dialectic is concerned above all with teaching, which consists of defining, dividing, and arguing. Dialectic provides the argumentative basis for speeches and texts, which rhetoric then makes more forceful by choosing expressions which will move and please an audience.[16] Where earlier Melanchthon had used a distinction of subject-matter, between general issues (theses) and particular cases (hypotheses), to differentiate dialectic from rhetoric, here he emphasizes differences in the way two subjects treat their material. In *De dialectica libri quatuor* Melanchthon covers the whole Aristotelian logic syllabus, devoting most attention to categories, syllogisms, topics, and fallacies.

Within the categories Melanchthon concentrates on outlining and dividing the contents of each, because this will be helpful in constructing definitions. He links definition with the four questions which develop simple themes. (What is the thing? What are its causes? What are the parts? What are the functions or effects?[17]) Propositions are needed for debates, literary compositions, and conducting business. Formulating the proposition is the basis for topical invention.[18] The study of argumenta-

[13] *CR* xx. 724–6: 'Quid nomen significet, quid res sit, quae caussae, quae partes, quid officium.'

[14] *CR* xx. 749.

[15] Melanchthon, *De dialectica libri quatuor* (Strasburg, 1545), sig. A8^{v}.

[16] Ibid., sigs. A8^{v}, B1^{r}.

[17] Ibid., sig. F6^{r-v}.

[18] Ibid., sigs. G3^{r}–4^{r}, L7^{v}.

Table 6.1. Plan of Melanchthon, *De dialectica libri quatuor*

BOOK 1: INTRODUCTORY DEFINITIONS	1
Predicables	8
Categories	13
Definition and division	59
How to explain simple themes (nature, causes, parts, effects)	74
BOOK 2: THE PROPOSITION (INCLUDING SQUARE OF CONTRARIES)	83
BOOK 3: ARGUMENTATION	98
The syllogism	106
Other forms of argumentation (enthymeme, induction, example, sorites)	133
Rules of consequence	147
BOOK 4: INVENTION OF ARGUMENTS	156
Questions, complex themes, method, demonstration	160
Topics	170
Hypothetical syllogisms	195
Refuting faulty arguments	197
Fallacies	208
How to make distinctions	234–6

tion shows the practical usefulness of dialectic in reducing a text which one reads to a syllogism, which can then be judged according to the rules for well-formulated arguments. Melanchthon explains that his version of the topics can be briefer because he assumes that his pupils will go on to read Agricola's account, but in this version he also includes maxims and a substantial discussion of the fallacies.

Throughout the book Melanchthon adds worked examples on theological themes, alongside literary examples, primarily from Cicero and the Roman poets, but including some taken from Greek literature. Some of his additions emphasize the connection between dialectic and the practice of reading and writing while others summarize sections of Aristotelian logic (such as the fallacies and the rules of consequence) often omitted by humanist dialecticians.

Erotemata dialectices (1547) increases the questions used in developing a simple theme to ten (What does the word mean? Does the thing exist? What is the thing? What are its parts? What are its species? What are its causes? What are its effects? What are its adjacents? What are its cognates? What are its contraries?) and names these as method.[19] It adds a new

[19] Melanchthon, *Erotemata dialectices*, *CR* xiii. 573–8. Wels, *Triviale Künste*, 120–3, 135–41, 145–8.

section on different degrees of likelihood and the sources of certainty.[20] The topics (now a list of twenty-five) are reserved for invention of arguments related to propositions (which preserves the distinction first outlined in *De rhetorica libri tres*). *Erotemata dialectices* also includes more material taken from scholastic logic, such as future contingents, and consequences.[21] The account of the fallacies is longer, with more explanation of how to defeat each false argument.

Elementa rhetorices libri duo (1531) begins by warning pupils of the limitations of the rhetoric textbook. Reading the textbook on its own will not make you eloquent; that will require both talent and practice in addition to an understanding of the art. At first the art of rhetoric helps not to make orators, but to teach students how to read the speeches of outstanding orators. The art of rhetoric is required to help people understand complicated debates and to show them how to imitate the great orators in their own writing.[22] Rhetorical training needs to be part of a programme of general education and it needs to include reading and composition exercises.

> Eloquence is the faculty of speaking wisely and elegantly. For the first requirement of speaking well is a perfect knowledge of the thing you are going to speak about . . . Since knowledge of things is necessary in order to speak, it befits orators not to be ignorant of those arts which contain knowledge of things. What can anyone say about religion, about the nature of things, about law, and lastly about any part of life if they are not informed about the subjects which embrace those things. Truly rhetoric is the art which teaches the method and the rationale of speaking correctly and elegantly.[23]

Rhetoric and dialectic are so closely related that they can scarcely be separated, not just because invention and disposition belong to both arts, but also because the orator will often need to teach, using the techniques of dialectic. Dialectic teaches things as it were nakedly, while rhetoric adds style as a sort of clothing. The aim of dialectic is to teach, while rhetoric aims also to move and almost compel the mind. Dialectic

[20] *CR* xiii. 641–52.
[21] Ibid. 592–4, 626–36.
[22] Ibid. 417–18.
[23] *CR* xiii. 418–19: 'Eloquentia facultas est sapienter et ornate dicendi. Nam ad bene dicendum in primis requiritur perfecta earum rerum cognitio, de quibus oratio instituitur . . . Cum autem rerum cognitio ad dicendum necessaria sit, oportebit oratorem harum artium, quae rerum scientiam continent, non esse rudem. Quid enim de religione, de natura rerum, de iure, denique de ulla vitae parte dicit is, qui doctrina illa non instructus est, quae eas ars continet? Rhetorica vero est ars, quae docet viam et rationem recte et ornate dicendi.'

Table 6.2. Plan of Melanchthon, *Elementa rhetorices*

	Cols.
1 Introduction	417
Tasks of the orator	419
Difference between rhetoric and dialectic	419
Three kinds of case	421
The use of knowing the genus of the case	422
Didascalic genre and topics of the simple question	423
Topics of the complex question	428
Judicial genre and status-theory	429
Six parts of the oration (*exordium*, narration, proposition,[a] confirmation, refutation and conclusion)	431
Conjectural status	433
Juridical status	436
Legal status	440
Deliberative genre	445
Demonstrative genre	448
Commonplaces	451
Emotions	454
Disposition	455
2 *Elocutio*	459
Three parts of *elocutio*: grammatical expression, figures, amplification	461
Tropes	464
Allegory and four-level interpretation of scripture	466
Other forms of allegory	472
Figures:	474
1. Grammatical figures	475
2. Figures of thought	476
3. Figures of amplification (divided into definition, division, causes, contraries, similars, genus, circumstances and signs)	479
On imitation	492
Composition of sentences and periodic style	498
Choice of models	502
Three types of style: high, middle, and low	504–6

Col. nos. refer to the Corpus Reformatorum edn., which reprints the 1542 Wittenberg edn., *CR* xiii, cols. 417–506. Minor textual changes are analysed in P. Melanchthon, *Elementa rhetorices*, ed. V. Wels (Berlin, 2001), 465–9. Wels surveys this work's teaching, *Triviale Künste*, 189–244.

[a] 'Hanc [narratio] sequi debet propositio, quae contineat summam rei.' *CR* xiii. 432. This one sentence is the addition Melanchthon makes to his textbook, to accommodate a sixth section, in contrast to the five sections of his earlier rhetoric textbooks. The proposition is also recommended in deliberative oratory, but not in the demonstrative genre (*CR* xiii. 445, 449). The emphasis on the proposition of the speech, rather than the division, connects with the procedures of dialectic.

can show you what virtue is, its causes, parts, and effects, while rhetoric can exhort you to uphold virtue.[24] *Elementa rhetorices* is arranged in two books: the second is concerned with style, considering the subject at greater length than in *Institutiones rhetoricae* and with a few changes of emphasis, adding important sections on imitation and composition of sentences. The first book discusses invention, centred on the four kinds of oration, commonplaces, emotions, and disposition.

Melanchthon follows tradition in stating that there are three types of case, but he then immediately adds the didascalic genre, which he calls the method of teaching and which is related to the demonstrative genus. Both use definition but the demonstrative genre decorates it with all the amplifications of the orators in order to elicit an appropriate emotional response. Psalms of praise belong to the demonstrative genre, as does the giving of thanks. Petitions, commendations, and advice fall into the deliberative class.[25]

Deliberative orations aim to persuade people to undertake a course of action, while demonstrative orations want the audience to know about and admire someone's actions. Knowing the aim of the speech affects our understanding of everything the orator does, but pupils need to be warned that some orations mix different genres, including elements of demonstrative in judicial, as in Cicero's *Pro Archia*, or demonstrative with deliberative, as in Demosthenes's invectives against Philip of Macedon.[26] While Melanchthon makes reference both to classical orations and to biblical examples, many of his worked examples refer to Christian themes, as if he wants to embed a treatise on sermon writing within his more general study of rhetoric.

The didascalic genre asks five questions of simple subjects. What is it? What are its parts or species? What are the causes? What are the effects? What things are similar and opposed? Melanchthon then gives worked examples of short didactic speeches on virtue, penitence, and faith, organized as answers to these questions. Complex questions are analysed in relation to five topics of invention (closely related to the questions above): from definition, from causes, from effects, from parts, and from things opposed. He explains that he has already described these techniques in his dialectic books and that he wishes only to remind readers of these principles here.[27]

[24] Ibid. 419–20.
[25] Ibid. 421–2, 448.
[26] Ibid. 422–3.
[27] Ibid. 424–8.

After discussing demonstrative oratory Melanchthon explains his view that invention should be taught quite briefly, 'because once the principles are known matter for speaking should not be sought in rhetoric textbooks but should be taken both from common wisdom and from the other arts and sciences'.[28] The principles of rhetoric will help you choose the most suitable material from what the other arts offer. They will also assist the imitation which creates eloquence, helping pupils understand complex cases by recognizing the argumentative bases on which speeches are built. He wants to add to the received precepts of invention one which has very great force in all arguments, that is to say moving from the particular question at issue (hypothesis) to the underlying general question (thesis). So beneath the detailed question, hedged in with particular circumstances 'should we make war on the Turks?', lies the general question 'is it permitted to Christians to wage war?' (451). Melanchthon then gives examples of general issues being brought to bear on particular cases, from Cicero, a putative sermon on the life of David, and Christ's own words.

This is Melanchthon's way of introducing the commonplaces (*loci communes*).[29] Commonplaces can be used both to prove a case and for the sake of amplification. They include not just the virtues and vices but also the principal headings of all the arts, which form the basis for and summarize their teaching. At the moment of introducing the idea of the commonplace book he points out its limitations.

> Some people think that they are in possession of the commonplaces, when they have collections of quotations on various subjects, which they have excerpted indiscriminately from the poets and orators. And because they think that this heap of famous sayings is perfect learning they have no plan in reading authors apart from excerpting from them certain *sententiae*, as if cutting flowers. As a result they learn no art perfectly, they understand no book as a whole, they take no account of the whole genus of a speech. This kind of study has very little use and causes much harm through the name, because among foolish people it produces the illusion of learning, and nothing is more harmful than that. Therefore it is important to realize that the commonplaces are truly understood when the arts which contain them are perfectly known. So we need to have perfect knowledge of the arts in order to be able to interweave the commonplaces properly into our speeches. Because in public affairs we often have arguments about virtues and vices, about fortune and laws and habits, for that reason the teachers of rhetoric

[28] Ibid. 451: 'Nam via quadam cognita, postea res non in libellis rhetoricis quaerendae erunt, sed tum a communi prudentia, tum ex aliis artibus sumendae.'

[29] For the *locus communis* as a key to understanding Melanchthon see K. Meerhoff, 'Logique et création selon Melanchthon', in his *Entre logique et littérature*, 63–82.

> mainly mention these topics. But these topics cannot be fully understood nor can they be discussed copiously and elegantly without knowledge of the arts in which they are taught. Therefore in order to speak well it is necessary to add a study of all the most important arts, of philosophy, of religious teaching, of law, and of histories.[30]

Perhaps influenced by his study of Cicero's *De oratore*, Melanchthon here requires the orator to master an almost encyclopedic knowledge in order to handle general issues authoritatively. The commonplace book is a useful interim measure on the road to a fuller understanding. Pupils should collect and arrange impressive and instructive sentences from their reading. Quotations can bring gravity and moral teaching into a composition, but a proper understanding of them requires full knowledge of the arts and sciences to which they belong. Melanchthon refers the reader to Agricola's letter *De formando studio* for a full description of the method of compiling commonplace books.

Also somewhat Agricolan is Melanchthon's short account of emotional manipulation. The principal emotions used by the orator are those which involve things to be sought and avoided, which are discussed also in deliberative speeches. Melanchthon gives examples of milder expressions of ordinary human emotions (*ethos*), from Virgil and Cicero, contrasting this with stronger emotions (*pathos*), which will require more brutal and tragic language. Amplifications which will move minds by exaggerating either the worthiness of a person or the disgracefulness of an action performed or suffered can be derived from all the topics of dialectical invention. The strongest and most effective will involve lifelike descriptions which create a sort of image in the eyes, as in Virgil's portrayal of Mezentius. The poets and orators provide many examples of how this is done.[31]

[30] *CR* xiii. 452–3: 'Quidam putant se locos communes tenere, cum de variis rebus coacervatas sententias habent, quas passim ex poetis et oratoribus excerpserunt. Et quia iudicant hanc coacervationem insignium dictorum perfectam esse doctrinam, nihil habent consilii in legendis autoribus, nisi ut inde tanquam flores, dicta quaedam decerpant. Interim nullam artem perfecte discunt, nullum scriptum totum intelligunt, nusquam totum orationis genus considerant. Hoc studium exiguam habet utilitatem, et hoc nomine plurimum nocet, quia in stultis doctrinae persuasionem parit, qua nihil est perniciosius. Sciendum est igitur, ita locos communes recte cognosci, si artes illae, in quibus versantur, perfecte cognitae fuerint. Et ut locos communes apte in causis intertexere possimus, opus erit perfecta eorum cognitione. Verum quia in civilibus negociis saepe existunt disputationes de virtutibus, de vitiis, de fortuna, de legibus, de consuetudine. Ideo rhetores horum locorum precipue mentionem faciunt, qui tamen neque perfecte intelligi, neque copiose ac varie tractari possunt, nisi cognitis illis artibus, in quibus versantur. Quare necesse est ad bene dicendum addere studium omnium maximarum artium, philosophiae, doctrinae religionis, iuris et historiarum.'

[31] Ibid. 454–5. Melanchthon cites the example of Pleminius from Livy 29.20–2.

Melanchthon explains the great importance of disposition, both in winning cases and in understanding texts. In Paul's Epistle to the Romans, for example, unless the reader grasps the organization of the text and works out when Paul proposes something, when he argues, when he concedes, it will not be possible to interpret the text without going wrong. At the same time there are only quite simple precepts for disposition and even these tend to be varied according to the circumstances of the case. No one writing a textbook can anticipate all the different circumstances which might arise so here again students need to study the great orations, to observe how they adapt to their situation, and to reflect carefully on the situations and subject-matters of their own writing. Melanchthon provides two major pieces of advice, which he then illustrates with examples. First, the reader (and the writer) must always bear in mind the purpose for which a certain text has been (has to be) composed. Secondly, the reader should remember that texts make arguments and that these arguments have different parts which we learn about in dialectic. So, if we find a proposition, in an *exordium*, for example, we need to look for ideas which support or amplify it, or which draw conclusions from it. Melanchthon briefly examines the openings of *Pro Archia*, *Pro Marcello,* and Romans to uncover their argumentative structure.[32]

The key to understanding and performing disposition is the technique of dialectical reading, which Agricola outlined in *De inventione dialectica* and which Melanchthon and others practised in their commentaries on Cicero.

The second book, which was in some ways anticipated by the style section of his *Institutiones rhetoricae* (1521), offers the first substantial renaissance rethinking of the classical doctrine of style, all the more effective for being an adaptation of classical principles and doctrines. In Chapter 10 we shall see that Melanchthon's rethinking of the approach to style in these two works had an important influence on the development of the separate manuals of style in the sixteenth century. His first task is to re-emphasize the necessity of the study of style.

> Therefore style (*elocutio*) is what expresses subject-matter (*res*) in clear and comprehensible language. Nor should one spend less time on this part of rhetoric than on the others. For things (*res*) cannot be understood without the light of language. For this reason at the start of this work I criticized those who despise the teachings of style and falsely think that the method of

[32] *CR* xiii. 458.

eloquence is not a necessity but has been thought up for the sake of empty ostentation.[33]

Melanchthon insists that, far from being a decoration, style is a necessity and a virtue. Without clarity of expression, without accurate use of language, without discreet exaggeration and appropriate comparison, nothing worthwhile can be communicated to another person. Sweetness of speech is a greater advantage to a person than any other human accomplishment. It should be cultivated even more than music or painting (460).

Melanchthon reduces the whole method of speaking eloquently to three aspects: grammatical language, the figures of speech, and amplification. He develops the idea by analysing Crassus's requirement in *De oratore* 3, that the orator speak good Latin, clearly, elegantly, and suitably.[34] Grammar teaches the way of speaking good Latin and clearly. To speak elegantly involves the figures and amplification. To speak suitably requires that one keep decorum. Following Quintilian, Melanchthon pronounces that speaking grammatically requires the use of words which are familiar, appropriate, and meaningful, joined together observing the rules of grammar.

Turning to figurative language Melanchthon organizes the received material in a new way. He describes seven ordinary tropes (metaphor, metalepsis, synecdoche, metonymy, antonomasia, onomatopoeia, and catachresis), then discusses allegory at some length, including a criticism of the scholastic four-level allegorical interpretation of scripture, before describing six species of allegory (enigma, irony, sarcasm, mikesis, proverb, and fable). He divides the figures into twelve grammatical figures (including repetition, which includes anaphora and anadiplosis), nine figures of thought (including interrogatio, communicatio, and licentia, which he discusses at some length) and thirty-four figures of amplification, which he subdivides according to the dialectical topics from which they are derived (definition, division, cause, contrary, similars, genus, circumstances, and signs). These subdivisions have the effect of making the long list more easily comprehensible and memorable, by organizing these sixty-nine figures into groups with a maximum size of twelve. They also help

[33] Ibid. 459: 'Est itaque elocutio, quae dilucida et perspicua oratione res exponit. Neque vero minus in hac parte, quam in caeteris elaborandum est. Nam res sine lumine verborum intelligi nequeunt, quare initio huius operis error illorum reprehendendus est, qui contemnunt elocutionis praecepta, et falso arbitrantur eloquendi rationem non necessitatis causa, sed inanem ostentationem excogitatam esse.'

[34] Ibid. 461: 'ut latine, ut dilucide, ut ornate, ut apte', *De oratore* 3.37, 48–54, 149–72, 206–8.

link the figures in with Erasmus's doctrine of *copia* and force home the original point which Melanchthon first made in *De rhetorica libri tres* about the connection between the dialectical topics and the figures of speech.[35]

Melanchthon rejects the universal application of four levels of interpretation because he believes that it opens the way to many foolish and unjustified interpretations. By contrast he believes that sentences of scripture always yield a single interpretation which we can reach using the principles of grammar, dialectic, and rhetoric. Melanchthon insists on the literal meaning of scripture. Allegory can follow when things which are similar to what the literal sense proposes are compared with it. But the application of allegory to scripture can only be carried out successfully by someone with a perfect understanding of Christian doctrine. He offers as an example Luther's interpretations of Deuteronomy, in which the literal sense is compared with the commonplaces of faith and works in order to generate allegorical interpretations (466–72).

Because he said at the outset that acquiring eloquence requires imitation of models as well as understanding of the principles Melanchthon concludes his rhetoric with a discussion of imitation. He begins by insisting that imitation involves subject-matter as well as words and requires the study of invention and disposition as much as style. Although Cicero excelled others in argument, arrangement, and emotional manipulation, nevertheless other authors must also be studied. In order to write good Latin students must immerse themselves in the vocabulary and sentence structure of the best Latin writing, which for Melanchthon as for Quintilian was the Latin of Cicero's age, represented by Cicero, Caesar, Terence, Plautus, Livy, and Sallust. Cicero's composition of sentences is especially recommended for imitation. Melanchthon insists on the practical usefulness of well-composed sentences, arguing that it is worthwhile to set out the rules for composing the kinds of sentence Cicero composed since they represent the best achievement of the greatest era of Latin prose. But again he rejects purely verbal imitation and insists that other authors have similar or equally valuable virtues. Melanchthon closes his account of style where *Ad Herennium* began it, with a description of the three levels of style. This can be understood better now that the techniques for forming style have all been described. He adds examples of writings in the different levels of style which his pupils may have already

[35] Melanchthon, *De rhetorica libri tres*, sig. I2^{v}, where he makes the point in relation to the figures of thought. His 1533 commentary on Cicero's *Topica* connects the topics of invention with figures used in amplification, referring to Erasmus's *De copia* and examples from the Psalms, *CR* xvi. 807–8.

read: Terence and Erasmus's *Colloquies* for the low style, Cicero's letters for the middle and sections from Virgil and Cicero's orations for the high.

Elementa rhetorices libri duo is a clear and comprehensive guide to rhetoric which fully deserved its great success. It presents much of the material in a new way, insisting on the connections between rhetoric and dialectic, the importance of logical analysis of the authors, and the usefulness of Erasmus's ideas about *copia*. It supports the techniques it proposes with analysis of existing texts and worked examples, which often show the necessity of adapting the rules to the circumstances of speaking. Dilwyn Knox has shown that Melanchthon's manuals of rhetoric and dialectic (taught together) were staples of the higher forms of Protestant grammar schools in the sixteenth century. They were read alongside Cicero's orations, which were analysed to illustrate the principles of rhetoric and dialectic in practice.[36]

Throughout the period in which he composed textbooks of rhetoric and dialectic Melanchthon's primary teaching duty was lecturing on classical and biblical texts.[37] In the 1520s, alongside his famous commentaries on Matthew (1522, sixteen printings), Proverbs (1525, twenty-two printings), and Romans (1529, twenty printings),[38] Melanchthon published a series of successful commentaries on Cicero's rhetorical works. His commentary on *De oratore* which first appeared in 1525 was published a total of thirty-seven times before 1620. His commentary on *Topica* first appeared as student notes in 1524. In the version Melanchthon prepared in 1535 it was printed eighteen times.

Melanchthon's commentary promotes *De oratore* as a work which encourages reflection on the effectiveness of textbook rhetoric, and which emphasizes the orator's need of wide-ranging knowledge and the connection between rhetoric and philosophy, and as a model of urbane writing suitable for imitation.[39] Most of his comments explain historical background and vocabulary. Melanchthon responded to the wide-ranging discussion of *De oratore* by supplementing its teaching with issues of importance to sixteenth-century orators, such as imitation and the stages of building up a stylistic effect. Taking his cue from Cicero

[36] D. Knox, 'Order, Reason and Oratory: Rhetoric in Protestant Latin Schools', in P. Mack (ed.), *Renaissance Rhetoric* (Basingstoke, 1994), 63–80. J. Matthaeus, *Scholae Cremsensis in Austria descripta formula* (Wittenberg, 1581), sigs. b1^{r-v}, b4^{v}–5^{r}.

[37] Meerhoff, 'Significance of Philip Melanchthon's Rhetoric', 49–50, citing Hartfelder, *Philipp Melanchthon*, 555–9.

[38] S. Wiedenhofer, *Formalstrukturen humanistischer und reformatorischer Theologie bei Philipp Melanchthon*, 2 vols. (Munich, 1976). T. Wengert and P. Graham (eds.), *Melanchthon and the Commentary* (Sheffield, 1997).

[39] Melanchthon, *Scholia in Ciceronis de oratore, Opera omnia*, *CR* xvi. 689–91.

he emphasizes that successful amplification, far from being simply ornament, requires knowledge of the topic under consideration.[40] Thinking of the arousal of emotion in a slightly different way from Cicero prompts him to analyse another text.

The method of handling emotions is largely taken from the topics of deliberative oratory, that is from the honourable and the useful. For we love honourable and useful things and we hold in hatred and flee from disgraceful and harmful ones. But this same argument of rational and useful things needs to be clothed with circumstantial details, in which pictures, which rush into our eyes, and as Quintilian says, carry force to the eyes, have great effect. For example this passage from Virgil on the slaughter of Priam:

> He dragged him quivering to that same altar,
> Slipping in the pool of blood of his child, (*Aeneid* 2.550–1)

Here each individual word has an associated emotion. First he amplifies the savageness of the killing because it happened 'at the altar', later the pathos invades the eyes with 'quivering'. Likewise 'he dragged'; likewise 'falling' and rolling about 'in blood': but the most appalling of all is that he rolls about in the blood 'of his child'. In this way he held back the highest point of emotion for the last place.[41]

Melanchthon here combines a new idea about the theory of arousing emotion with a close analysis of the impact of Virgil's word-order on his audience. Explaining Cicero's point makes him want to add to it through his own close reading of Virgil. Reading a major rhetorical text and reflecting on a well-known passage of poetry prompts him to refine his ideas about how language evokes emotion.

The 1530s also saw publication of Melanchthon's commentaries on Cicero's orations: in 1533, *Pro Marcello* and *Pro Archia Poeta*, which eventually went through twenty-seven and thirty editions respectively (including publications in omnibus volumes) and *Pro Milone* (1535) of which there were nineteen printings. Melanchthon's approach in these commentaries was to begin by analysing the structure of the oration and the main arguments, then to provide a paraphrase of the main argumentative

[40] *CR* xvi. 714–15, 722–7.

[41] 'Ratio tractandorum affectuum magna ex parte sumitur ex locis generis deliberativi, scilicet ex honesto et utili. Honesta enim et utilia amamus, turpia et damnosa odio habemus ac fugimus. Sed haec ipsa ratio honestorum utilium vestienda est circumstantiis, in quibus plurimum valent picturae, quae incurrunt in oculos, et ut Fabius ait, vim oculis afferunt: quale est Virgilii de caede Priami. Altaria ad ipsa trementem/ Traxit et in multo lapsantem sanguine gnati. Hic enim in singulis verbis singuli affectus sunt. Primum auget atrocitatem caedis, quod ad aras fit. Postea πάθος est in oculos incurrens, Trementem. Item Traxit, item Lapsantem ac volutantem in sanguine, sed atrocissimum est, quod in gnati sanguine volutatur. Itaque quod summum erat, in postremum locum distulit.' *CR* xvi. 734.

drift of the whole speech and finally to give a sentence-by-sentence commentary.[42]

In order to estimate the impact of Melanchthon's ideas on his contemporaries and to register the originality of their own contributions, it may be helpful to summarize his main innovations in rhetoric.[43] He regarded rhetoric and dialectic as closely connected. Dialectic is concerned with teaching, which for Melanchthon always remains the most important function of language. Rhetoric adds the skills of pleasing and moving, which make teaching more effective. Both are essential to good writing and can best be understood through analysis of classical and biblical texts. Melanchthon organized his treatment of rhetorical invention according to the genres of rhetoric rather than the parts of the oration. He added a fourth genre, the didascalic, which he linked to invention of simple themes through a short series of questions. Complex questions should be explored using the topics of invention, which are analysed more carefully in his dialectic books. The topics are also useful for amplification. Melanchthon's rhetoric included new sections on employing the general case (thesis), commonplaces, and emotional persuasion, together with a new approach to disposition, based on dialectical analysis of texts. He emphasized the importance of style, adding a new presentation of seven ordinary tropes and six types of allegory. He divided the figures of rhetoric into three types (grammatical, thought, amplification; the latter section was subdivided according to the topics of invention) and added a new section on imitation. Melanchthon treats the three levels of style at the end of the style treatise (the second book) rather than at the beginning.

BARTHOLOMAEUS LATOMUS (1485–1570)

Bartholomaeus Latomus studied and taught in Freiburg (from 1516), Cologne (from 1526), where he probably met Phrissemius (d. 1532), who edited and commented on Agricola, and Louvain, where he matriculated in 1530. In the gymnasium at Cologne he taught his pupils rhetoric and dialectic before embarking on a series of rhetorical commentaries on Cicero. In 1527 he published his teaching materials as *Summa totius rationis disserendi*, in which he teaches the essential elements of both subjects in a unified and original structure based on the ideas of Agricola.

[42] P. Mack, 'Melanchthon's Commentaries on Latin Literature', in G. Frank and K. Meerhoff (eds.), *Melanchthon und Europa*, ii (Stuttgart, 2002), 29–52.

[43] On Melanchthon's followers in dialectic see W. Risse, *Die Logik der Neuzeit*, i. *1500–1640* (Stuttgart, 1964), 107–19.

So he first divides rhetoric into aims, subject-matter, and tasks. Under aims he considers teaching (which consists of definition, division, and argumentation), moving, and pleasing.[44] He includes the predicables and the categories under definition, as Melanchthon had. Argumentation includes the topics (Agricola's list, with brief definitions and advice on how to use each, with examples) and the forms of argumentation. His discussion of arousing emotion relies heavily on Agricola.[45] The section on tasks focuses on disposition, which uses some of the same examples as Agricola, and style, which includes *illustratio* (images, emphasis, and comparisons), amplification (following Quintilian and Agricola), and figures.[46] This work was printed four times in Cologne up to 1554. In 1528 Latomus published his commentary on *Pro Milone*, which was later reprinted seven times in Paris and in 1530 his epitome of Agricola's *De inventione dialectica*, which was reprinted twenty-eight times, including eleven Paris printings 1534–61.

Melanchthon's commitment to the connections between rhetoric and a humanistically rewritten dialectic, reinforced by the use of both arts together in analysing classical texts, can usefully be connected with one of the great changes in sixteenth-century rhetorical pedagogy which reached Paris in 1529 and 1530, at more or less the time that Melanchthon was writing his *Elementa rhetorices*.[47] This was the moment at which scholastic logic, which had enjoyed a revival in Paris in the early sixteenth century and which underpinned much medieval philosophy and theology, was largely superseded by humanist dialectic.[48] In 1529 the 21-year-old Johann Sturm (1507–89) left Louvain for the University of Paris, where he lectured on Cicero's orations. In 1529 Colines printed the first Parisian edition of Agricola's *De inventione dialectica*. In 1531 Sturm's Louvain friend Latomus was appointed lecturer at the Collège de Ste-Barbe, where he too specialized in rhetorical and dialectical commentary on Cicero's speeches. Both men began to publish Cicero commentaries with Gryphius

44 B. Latomus, *Summa totius rationis disserendi* (Cologne, 1527), sigs. 3^r–8^r.

45 Ibid., sigs. $D6^v$–7^v.

46 Ibid., sigs. $E5^r$, $I7^r$, $K1^r$, $K3^r$.

47 This story is told in two articles by Kees Meerhoff, 'Jean Sturm et l'introduction de l'humanisme du Nord à Paris', in Matthieu Arnold (ed.), *Johannes Sturm (1507–1589): Rhetor, Pädagoge und Diplomat* (Tübingen, 2009), 109–29, and 'Logique et éloquence: Une révolution ramiste', in Meerhoff and J.-C. Moisan (eds.), *Autour de Ramus* (Quebec, 1997), 87–132.

48 E. J. Ashworth, 'The Eclipse of Medieval Logic', in N. Kretzmann, A. Kenny, J. Pinborg, and E. Stump (eds.), *The Cambridge History of Later Medieval Philosophy* (Cambridge, 1982), 787–96. A. Broadie, *The Circle of John Mair* (Oxford, 1985). A. Tuilier, *Histoire de l'université de Paris et de la Sorbonne*, i (Paris, 1994).

in 1531.[49] The first Paris edition of Latomus's epitome of Agricola appeared from Gryphius in 1534, when Latomus was appointed lecturer in classical Latin at the Collège Royale.[50] To accompany his commentaries on the orations he published commentaries on Cicero's *Topica* (1538) and *Partitiones oratoriae* (1539). For fifteen years from 1530 an extraordinary series of editions of rhetorical commentaries on Cicero's orations and editions of Agricola's text and epitomes flowed from Parisian printers associated with the University. Students of Sturm, Latomus, and Omphalius (1500–67) spread this reformed programme of the *trivium* through France, Spain, and Portugal. Ramus and Talon followed the lectures on Cicero by Latomus and Sturm.

JOACHIM VAN RINGELBERG (1499–1531?)

By the time of his presumed death Joachim van Ringelberg of Antwerp had published four books on rhetoric and dialectic, which were reprinted together eleven times up to 1556. His *Dialectica* (1529), which had six separate printings, follows the same four-part structure as Melanchthon's. He outlines a form of definition (genus, differentia, four causes, effects or functions, parts, accidents) which resembles Melanchthon's teachings on the invention of simple themes but then adds eight similar questions for simple themes (Etymology? Does it exist? What is it? Causes? One or many? What and how many species? Parts? Functions or effects?).[51] At first his list of topics follows Melanchthon's *Compendiaria Dialectices Ratio*, but he then adds further topics. His section on the use of the topics owes something to Agricola. *De rhetorica* (1531), which had twelve separate printings up to 1561, is a brief summary focused on invention. Its comments on the relationship between rhetoric and dialectic are heavily dependent on Melanchthon.[52]

Like Melanchthon Ringelberg subdivides the demonstrative genre into teaching and praise and blame. Unlike him he organizes most of his discussion of invention around the six parts of the oration. Ringelberg

[49] Cicero, *Philippicae*, with Sturm's commentary (Paris: Gryphius, 1531); Cicero, *Pro Plancio*, with Latomus's commentary (Paris: Gryphius, 1531). Illustrations of title-pages in Meerhoff, 'Jean Sturm'.

[50] K. Meerhoff, 'L'Enseignement des lecteurs royaux pour l'éloquence et la philosophie. De Latomus à Ramus', in A. Tuilier (ed.), *Histoire du Collège de France*, i. *La Création 1530–1560* (Paris, 2006), 293–352.

[51] Ringelbergius, *Opera* (Lyon, 1556), sigs. n1^r–2^r, 3^r.

[52] Ibid., sig. q3^r.

quotes Ulysses's speech from Ovid's *Metamorphoses* to illustrate ways to construct an *exordium*.[53] His very brief account of *elocutio* is replaced by two short treatises: *De figuris* (1531) which subdivides the figures but in a different way from Melanchthon and *De formis dicendi* (1529) which discusses three kinds of style (Attic, Asiatic, Rhodian) and the virtues and vices of three levels of style. Ringelberg has similar views to Melanchthon but he copies him more closely in dialectic than in rhetoric.

JOHANN RIVIUS (1500–1553)

In 1531 Johann Rivius of Attendorn, who studied with Phrissemius in Cologne, published *De rhetorica libri duo* which went through fifteen editions (including some editions as part of a combined grammar, rhetoric, and dialectic), mostly from Leipzig and Louvain. Set out in question and answer format, the work takes a broad, inclusive view of rhetoric, as exemplified by this opening definition:

> What then is rhetoric? It is a liberal art which teaches the method and rationale of speaking elegantly and ornately, or, it is the science of speaking well. For the task of rhetoric seems to be to speak in a way suited to persuade, as Cicero says.[54]

The first part of the answer, which resembles Melanchthon, is completed with direct quotations from Quintilian and Cicero. The basic organization of the work resembles Melanchthon's (devoting the second book to style and the first book to everything else; using the three genres as the main structuring device for invention; the three types of figures) but Rivius omits some of Melanchthon's distinctive features (such as the didascalic genre and the questions for developing simple themes). At times there are quite close verbal similarities.[55] In his treatise on the figures Rivius tends to follow Melanchthon's order, adding in additional figures from time to time. Rivius adds a section on types of description, which may owe something to Erasmus, *De copia*.[56]

[53] Ibid., sig. q6^{r}.

[54] J. Rivius, *De rhetorica libri duo* (Louvain, 1550), sig. A2^{v}: 'Quid igitur est rhetorica? Est ars liberalis, quae viam et rationem eleganter et ornate dicendi tradit, vel, Est bene dicendi scientia. Officium enim rhetoricae esse videtur, dicere apposite ad persuasionem, ut Cicero inquit.'

[55] e.g. definition of status: Rivius, a8^{r}, *Elementa rhetorices*, 429; *potestas*: Rivius, b1^{v}, *Elementa*, 433–4; legal status: Rivius, b4^{v}, *Elementa*, 440.

[56] Rivius, *De rhetorica*, f1^{r}.

GEORG MAJOR (1502–1574)

Georg Major of Nuremberg, who studied with Melanchthon in Wittenberg, and in the 1520s wrote an epitome of Melanchthon's *Institutiones rhetoricae*,[57] published his *Quaestiones rhetoricae ex libris Ciceronis, Quintiliani et Melanthonis* at Magdeburg in 1535. It went through sixteen editions, mainly from Tübingen, up to 1600. His work follows *Elementa rhetorices* very closely, organizing the book as a series of questions. He adds examples of each of the genres, including Cicero's *Pro Archia* and *Pro Marcello*, with Melanchthon's comments. He teaches a longer list of figures of speech, which is more like Rivius's than Melanchthon's. Major also made a collection of quotations from the poets organized as a commonplace book, *Sententiae veterum poetarum per locos communes digestae* (1534), which was printed fourteen times.

ERASMUS SARCERIUS (1501–1559)

After studying in Leipzig, in 1524 Erasmus Sarcerius went to Wittenberg where he became closely associated with Melanchthon and Luther. He taught in Lübeck, Rostock, Siegen, and Leipzig, and was active as a Protestant theologian and supervisor of schools and parishes.[58] His *Rhetorica plena ac referta exemplis* (1537), which was printed ten times up to 1583, was more a supplement to Melanchthon's rhetoric than an introduction to it. The book provides a brief diagrammatic summary of Melanchthon's teaching about each type of speech, followed by one or two short speeches divided into paragraphs with headings indicating the topic used in that section. The book takes seriously Melanchthon's injunction that the precepts of rhetoric need to be supplemented by study of examples. Sarcerius focuses on the invention side of Melanchthon's teaching, giving many examples of demonstrative and didascalic speeches (e.g. Exhortation to the Study of Theology, Praise of Lübeck) and, within the judicial genre, examples for the most important types of status (e.g. conjectural, definition, contrary laws, letter and spirit). For one of the examples of a deliberative speech (Persuasion against Undertaking a

[57] This was usually published with Schade's *Tabulae de schematibus et tropibus*, though obviously not in the earliest edns., and as such enjoyed a wide diffusion, see RRSTC 3223 and Ch. 10 below.

[58] S. Rhein and G. Wartenberg (eds.), *Reformatoren im Mansfelder Land: Erasmus Sarcerius und Cyriakus Spangenberg* (Leipzig, 2006).

War Against the Turks) Sarcerius notes that Melanchthon had spoken on the same subject.[59] The full title of Sarcerius's work suggests that he was making a connection between Melanchthon's rhetorical teaching and the practice of declamation. According to Risse, Sarcerius's *Dialectica multis ac variis exemplis illustrata* (Marburg, 1536) was a pure Melanchthonian textbook, though the title suggests that it may have included constructed examples like those in his rhetoric.[60]

JOHANN SPANGENBERG (1484–1550)

The *Trivii erotemata* (1542) of schoolmaster, Protestant minister, and hymn-writer Johann Spangenberg surveys the principal doctrines of grammar, dialectic, and rhetoric in a question and answer format, with a strong basis in Melanchthon's teaching. The work was printed six times complete; the separate sections on dialectic and rhetoric were printed a further five times each. Of the book's 350 pages, roughly 150 are devoted to grammar, 125 to dialectic and 75 to rhetoric (which includes twenty pages on memory and ten on letter-writing). Within dialectic Spangenberg gives considerable space to the predicables, the categories, and the fallacies. The major definitions and rules are taken from Melanchthon's *De dialectica libri quattuor*, and George Trapezuntius's *Isagoge dialectica*, with some phrases resembling Melanchthon's later *Erotemata dialectices*, perhaps on the basis of notes on his oral teaching.

In rhetoric the main definitions are taken from *Rhetorica ad Herennium* and *De inventione*, with some phrases from Melanchthon. Spangenberg follows Melanchthon in including a section on commonplaces, before a very brief account of emotion.[61] In describing the tropes and figures, he follows the order and many of the definitions and examples from Melanchthon's *Institutiones rhetoricae*, supplementing it with concisely summarized material from *Elementa rhetorices* and from Susenbrotus.[62] The

[59] Sarcerius, *Rhetorica plena ac referta exemplis, quae succinctorum declamationum loco esse possunt* (Marburg, 1537), sigs. i1^{r}, i6^{r}–7^{r}.

[60] Risse, *Die Logik der Neuzeit*, 107. I have not seen Sarcerius's dialectic, which was printed nine times up to 1566.

[61] J. Spangenberg, *Erotemata Trivii* (Mainz, 1549), fos. 145^{v}–146^{r}. Compare *Institutiones rhetoricae*, sigs. B4^{v}–C1^{v}.

[62] Spangenberg, *Erotemata Trivii*, fos. 147^{r}–155^{v}; Melanchthon, *Institutiones rhetoricae*, sigs. C3^{v}–E3^{v}; *Elementa rhetorices*, 459, 461, 464; Susenbrotus, *Epitome troporum*, cited in Ch. 10 below, A5^{r}–6^{v}.

section on style ends by quoting Geoffrey de Vinsauf's Lament of the Cross, from the *Poetria nova*, as an example of amplification.[63]

LUCAS LOSSIUS (1508–1582)

Lucas Lossius studied with Melanchthon in Wittenberg in the 1530s. From 1533 until his death he taught at the gymnasium at Luneberg. He is well-known for his work in Protestant church music, for his hymns and his psalm-settings.[64] His *Erotemata Dialecticae et rhetoricae Philippi Melanchthonis* (1550), which was printed thirty-five times up to 1620, presents the major doctrines of Melanchthon's *Erotemata dialectices* and *Elementa rhetorices*, and Erasmus's *De copia*, in the framework of brief catechism-style questions suited to rote-learning by schoolboys. For example:

> What is the difference between rhetoric and dialectic?
> Dialectic is concerned with all subject-matters and sets out the headings of things in bare words, but rhetoric adds ornament to the subject-matter, which can be illuminated with splendour and copia of language and painted in different ways.[65]
> What is rhetoric?
> Rhetoric is the art which teaches the method and rationale of speaking correctly and ornately, which is called the power of eloquence.[66]

Lossius summarizes the main points of Melanchthon's teaching, usually by abbreviating his words. He gives most attention to dialectic (three-quarters of the book). In rhetoric he follows Melanchthon's order closely. Under style he adds lists of grammatical and syntactical figures, which Melanchthon alluded to but did not list, and he slightly extends the list of figures, while retaining Melanchthon's three-fold division and the allocation of figures of amplification to particular topics of invention. He gives an interesting original summary of the general imitation of subject-matter

[63] 'Querela Crucis Christi, ex Ganifredo de Prosopopeia', Spangenberg, *Erotemata Trivii*, fos. 155^{v}–6^{v}. I am grateful to Marjorie Woods for this point.

[64] F. Onkelbach, *Lucas Lossius und seine Musiklehre* (Regensburg, 1960).

[65] Lossius, *Erotemata Dialecticae et rhetoricae* (Leipzig, 1624), sig. B1^{v}: 'Quid differunt Dialectica et Rhetorica? Dialectica circa omnes materias versatur et rerum summas verbis nudis proponit, sed rhetorica addit ornatum in materiis, quae orationis copia et splendore illustrari et varie depingi possunt.' All the words are taken from Melanchthon, *Erotemata dialectices*, *CR* xiii. 515, but with considerable shortening.

[66] Lossius, *Erotemata*, sig. N5^{v}: 'Quid est rhetorica? Rhetorica est ars quae docet viam et rationem recte et ornate dicendi, quae facultas eloquentiae vocatur.' The words are taken from *Elementa rhetorices*, *CR* xiii. 419.

and treats the section on composition as special imitation of Cicero's sentence structure.[67] At the end of the work, he summarizes Erasmus's *De copia*.[68] The great success of this work shows that Melanchthon's teachings continued to be seen as effective ways of introducing rhetoric and dialectic together in the highest forms of German gymnasia until the first quarter of the seventeenth century.

MARTIN CRUSIUS (1526–1607)

In 1563 the historian Martin Crusius, Professor of Greek and Latin at Tübingen from 1559, published his *Quaestiones* as an extensive commentary on Melanchthon's *Elementa rhetorices*. It was printed seven times in Basel up to 1589 and three editions of an epitome appeared in Tübingen between 1581 and 1611. Crusius's commentary makes a few additions to Melanchthon's text, supplementing it with a great deal of comparative material, especially from Greek rhetoric, some additional figures of speech, and a very long list of headings for a commonplace book.[69] It shows the careful attention and intense study which Melanchthon's rhetoric continued to inspire.

JUAN LUIS VIVES (1492–1540)

While most early sixteenth-century rhetoricians were indebted to Melanchthon, some took a more independent approach. Juan Luis Vives attacked the foundational assumptions of classical rhetoric (such as the five skills and the three genres). He regarded style as the central concern of rhetoric. He gave new attention to decorum and described ten genres of sixteenth-century writing, which included history, commentary, and translation.

Vives, one of the foremost intellectuals of the early sixteenth century, famous today for his works on social theory and psychology, and for his commentary on St Augustine's *City of God* (1522), published eleven works concerned with rhetoric and dialectic, mostly in the last decade of his life, while he was living in Bruges after losing the patronage of Henry VIII and Catherine of Aragon during the royal divorce. His main intellectual debts

67 Lossius, *Erotemata*, sigs. R1^{v}–2^{v}.

68 Ibid., sigs. V3^{v}–4^{r}.

69 Melanchthon, *Elementa Rhetorices libri duo, Martini Crusii quaestionibus et scholiis explicati* (Basel, 1589), sigs. s1^{r}–4^{r}.

were to Valla, Agricola, and Erasmus. His only really successful rhetoric was his contribution to the genre of letter-writing manuals, *De conscribendis epistolis* (1534), discussed in Chapter 11 below.

His *De causis corruptarum artium* (1531), published as part of the twenty-book work *De disciplinis* (1531) and printed seven times up to 1612, attacked several of the foundational assumptions of classical rhetoric. Rhetoric should not be regarded as comprising five skills since, for example, invention belongs to the activity of the mind in general and memory to psychology. Rather, the special domain of rhetoric is the doctrine of style. The restriction of rhetoric to three genres is mistaken since there are many more occasions for speaking. The analysis of style into three levels greatly underestimates the varieties of style available to a writer.[70]

De ratione dicendi (1533), printed three times, provides an original synthesis of rhetorical teaching based around style.[71] Book 1 focuses on the resources of language, showing how diction and sentence structure contribute to stylistic effects and including discussion of prose rhythm, amplification, the periodic sentence, and selected figures and tropes. Book 2 begins by characterizing around thirty different qualities of style (replacing the three levels) before analysing ways of achieving the four aims of rhetoric: to explain, to persuade, to move, and to keep the attention (*detinere*, here taking the traditional place of *delectare*, to please). The division of *docere* into explaining and persuading reflects Agricola's division of language into exposition and argumentation. The third section of book 2 is concerned with decorum, suiting one's expression to subject, speaker, and audience, before a discussion of the composition of opening sections and of disposition more generally. The third book describes the composition of ten genres in which a sixteenth-century writer might write: description, history, persuasive narration, fable, poetic fiction, precepts of an art, paraphrase, epitome, commentary, and translation. Here Vives decisively replaces the traditional three genres with forms which he and his contemporaries regularly practised. His approach is to define the form, to describe the main types of each form, to discuss the purpose and effect of the genre, to give examples, to suggest structures, and to advise on issues of language and style.[72] This work was printed with Vives's *De*

[70] Vives, *Opera omnia* (Valencia, 1782–90), vi. 152–80. See E. George, 'Rhetoric in Vives', in *Ioannis Lodovici Vivis Valentini Opera omnia*, i (Valencia, 1992), 113–77. P. Mack, 'Vives's Contributions to Rhetoric and Dialectic', in C. Fantazzi (ed.), A *Companion to Juan Luis Vives* (Leiden, 2008), 227–76.

[71] There is a good modern edn., with introduction and tr., J. L. Vives, *Del arte de hablar*, ed. J. M. Rodríguez Peregrina (Granada, 2000).

[72] Mack, 'Vives's Contributions', 238–9.

consultatione, a treatise on deliberative oratory and the giving of counsel, which Vives wrote in Oxford in 1523. The treatise focuses on invention, showing that the speaker must craft a self-presentation and arguments suited to the people being advised, the other advisers, the subject-matter, the place, the time, and the state of affairs.[73] Vives's attacks on the assumptions of classical rhetoric struck a chord with later writers, among them John Rainolds, Ben Jonson, Nicolas Caussin, and perhaps also Peter Ramus.[74]

GERARD BUCOLDIANUS (FL. 1520–1555)

The German humanist and medical authority Gerard Bucoldianus, known today for the first description of a case of anorexia in 1542, followed the humanist approach of basing the teaching of rhetoric on topical invention and literary examples, without referring to Erasmus or Melanchthon. His *De inventione et amplificatione oratoria; seu de usu locorum libri tres* (1534) was printed eight times up to 1551, mainly in Lyon. Bucoldianus builds a complete course in rhetoric around the topics of invention, for which he follows Cicero's *Topica*.[75] He cites Cicero, Quintilian (whose work he edited), and Menander Rhetor (in Greek) on the usefulness of the topics in all types of oratory.[76] He refers to Agricola's disagreements with Cicero.[77] For each of the topics of invention he gives literary examples, including an interesting discussion of poetic definitions using metaphor.[78] Once he has outlined the topics he shows how they can be used for amplification, giving examples from Cicero and Livy.[79] Book 2 shows how the topics can be used in epideictic rhetoric, for praises of persons, cities, and examples. Then Bucoldianus briefly describes the parts of the oration, the figures, and tropes (basing his list on Cicero's *De oratore* and Aquila Romanus), the commonplaces (working from Aphthonius and *Rhetorica ad Herennium*), and the emotions, which he connects with style and for which he gives examples from Virgil. The third book shows how the topics can be used in deliberative oratory, with examples from Cicero's

73 Vives, *Opera omnia*, ii. 245–7.

74 L. Green, *John Rainolds's Oxford Lectures on Aristotle's Rhetoric* (Newark, NJ, 1986), 74–6 and index; Jonson, *Works*, xi (Oxford, 1952), 214–18, 265–6, 268–72; for Caussin, see Ch. 9 below.

75 G. Bucoldianus, *De inventione et amplificatione oratoria* (Lyons, 1551), sigs. a6^{r-v}, b2^{v}.

76 Ibid., sig. b1^{r}.

77 Ibid., sigs. b6^{v}, b7^{r}, c7^{r}. Under similitudes he uses Agricola's 'vascula oris' example (*De inventione dialectica*, 142) from Quintilian but without referring to either authority.

78 Bucoldianus, *De inventione*, sig. b7^{v}.

79 Ibid., sigs. g3^{v}–6^{r}.

Pro lege Manilia, Ovid, and Livy. He tells us that his medical studies (the book is dedicated from Bologna) prevented him from adding a fourth book on the use of the topics in judicial oratory.[80]

JOHANN STURM (1507–1589)

Johann Sturm shared Melanchthon's commitment to bringing out the connections between dialectic and rhetoric and to using both subjects to analyse classical texts. This was the basis of his influential teaching in Louvain and Paris. His publications from Strasbourg reinforced this position, adding a focus on Greek rhetoric, especially Hermogenes, on the periodic sentence, on the characteristics of style, and on method.

In 1536, as prospects worsened for Protestants in France, Sturm left Paris for Strasbourg, where in 1538 he became rector of the newly established school which became a model of humanist schooling for the rest of Europe.[81] His school syllabus gives great importance to Greek and keeps returning to four key authors: Cicero, Virgil, Homer, and Demosthenes. This selection reflects his emphasis on Latin writers' imitation of Greek. Rhetoric is introduced early in the programme, starting with the tropes and figures, but is then maintained through classical works giving an overview of the subject (*Rhetorica ad Herennium* 1 and *Partitiones oratoriae*) and more specialized handling of particular aspects (Hermogenes and Cicero's *Topica* and *Orator*). Like Agricola Sturm regards the topics as the key to invention. The practical use of the rules of rhetoric and dialectic is explored by reading orations and dialogues alongside the textbooks. Perhaps surprisingly the programme makes no reference to letter-writing.[82]

Sturm's two most successful books both appeared first in two-book versions, with two further books being added in 1543 (dialectic) and 1545 (rhetoric). The two-book *In partitiones oratorias Ciceronis* was printed seven times up to 1547 in Strasbourg and Paris; the four-book version seventeen times up to 1565, with more Paris than Strasbourg printings

[80] Ibid., sig. m2^{v}.

[81] C. Schmidt, *La vie et les travaux de Jean Sturm* (Strasbourg, 1855). A. Schindling, *Humanistische Hochschule und freie Reichsstadt: Gymnasium und Akademie in Strassburg 1538–1621* (Wiesbaden, 1977). J. Rott, *Investigationes Historicae*, ii (Strasbourg, 1986), 471–559 (bibliography of Sturm). J. Classen, *Antike Rhetorik*, 310–31.

[82] J. Sturm, *De literarum ludis recte aperiendis* (Strasbourg, 1538 ; repr. Strasbourg, 2007), sigs. E1^{v}–F4^{v}, H1^{v}–2^{r}. L. W. Spitz and B. Sher Tinsley, *Johann Sturm on Education* (St Louis, 1995), 47, 69–118.

prior to 1556.[83] The four-book version was printed another seven times as part of an omnibus commentary assembled by Sturm's pupil and colleague Erythraeus.[84] The two-book version comments on Cicero's text up to 7.26, allowing Sturm to discuss the five tasks of the orator, with particular attention to topical invention and style. The later books are concerned with the contents of the five-part oration (book 3) and the topics appropriate to the three kinds of case, including the theory of status in judicial orations (book 4, corresponding to Cicero, *Partitiones* 18.61 to the end). While Sturm follows Cicero's order he adds quite lengthy sections on subjects which Cicero had mentioned sketchily (such as the topics of invention[85]) or not at all (such as theories of method and Hermogenes's ideas of style[86]). In the later books he continues to bring in Greek material, particularly from Hermogenes, on *exordia*, on the seven circumstances as a contribution to narration, on status theory, on amplification, and on the useful as a topic in deliberative oratory.[87]

Partitiones dialecticae, which was printed four times up to 1546 in the two-book version, and eleven times up to 1591 in the four-book version, summarizes most of Aristotelian logic in an original four-part structure. The first part is devoted to the topics (including the topical maxims), which absorb the predicables and the categories. His advice on the use of the topics resembles Agricola.[88] Part two covers the proposition, the syllogism and other forms of argumentation. Part three is devoted to demonstration, which includes definition, division, and different types of method (including discussion of Plato, Euclid, and Galen), and part four to the sophisms.

Sturm showed his interest in questions of method from as early as the first book of *In partitiones oratorias* (1539). There he argued that in order to secure reliable, brief, and comprehensive teaching of the numerous doctrines which make up each art, arts need to be organized methodically.[89] He mentioned three methods, which he later connected with observations of Galen, Aristotle, and Plato: the method of discovery (or the analytic method) moving from perceived individual objects in the world to the

[83] These and the figures for the dialectic in the next paragraph are taken from Rott, *Investigationes Historicae*, ii. 487–91, which is much fuller than Green and Murphy for these texts.

[84] Green and Murphy, *Renaissance Rhetoric STC*, 190–1. V. Montagne, 'Jean Sturm et Valentin Erythraeus', *BHR* 63 (2001), 477–509.

[85] Sturm, *In partitiones oratorias Ciceronis dialogi quatuor* (Strasbourg, 1549), sigs. B6^r–C8^r.

[86] Ibid., sigs. A1^v–2^v, G7^{r-v}, H6^r–I3^v.

[87] Ibid., second listing of signatures, sigs. a3^r, f6^r–g3^v, l6^r–m4^r.

[88] Sturm, *Partitionum dialecticarum libri IV* (Strasbourg, 1571), sigs. H4^r–5^r.

[89] Sturm, *In partitiones oratorias 4*, sigs. A1^v–2^v.

principles governing a particular art; the synthetic method of expounding an art, moving from general principles to specific instances; and the method of definition and division, summarizing the teaching of an art by defining the art, dividing into parts, defining each part, subdividing what has been defined, and so on.[90] Sturm saw Cicero's *Partitiones oratoriae* as a model of this type of presentation, which he also tried to follow in his own *Partitiones dialecticae*.

De imitatione oratoria (1574), which appeared three times up to 1617, with a commentary by Erythraeus more than twice as long as the original text, sets out a method of reading, analysing, and imitating classical texts, primarily Cicero and Demosthenes. Sturm uses some of Hermogenes's categories of style to analyse the stylistic virtues of both authors. Hermogenes's categories are also among the foundations of Sturm's *De universa ratione elocutionis rhetoricae* (1575), printed only once, which also absorbs Sturm's work on the periodic sentence.[91] Sturm also published translations of and commentaries on Hermogenes's *On invention* (1570), *On ideas of style* (1570), *On the method of seriousness* (1571), and *On status* (1570). Sturm wrote a preface for the 1539 Strasbourg edition of Melanchthon's *De dialectica libri quatuor*.[92]

VALENTINUS ERYTHRAEUS (1521–1576)

Sturm's colleague Valentinus Erythraeus published tables and epitomes on dialectic and works on style and letter-writing. This latter teaches pupils to imitate Cicero's letters, taking examples and teachings from Erasmus. These works were mostly printed only in Strasbourg and in one or two editions each. The most successful was his tables of Cicero's *Partitiones oratoriae*, which was published seven times alongside Sturm's four-book commentary.[93]

In the years 1519–45 the humanist renewal of dialectic, the Agricolan combination of rhetoric with dialectic, and the logically informed reading of classical oratory and poetry spread across northern Europe and the

90 Sturm, *Partitionum dialecticarum libri IV*, sigs. T7^r–Z1^r. N. W. Gilbert, *Renaissance Concepts of Method* (New York, 1960), 122–4. Vasoli, *La dialettica*, 319–25.

91 V. Montagne, 'Le *De suavi dicendi forma* de Jean Sturm: Notes sur la douceur du style à la Renaissance', *BHR* 66 (2004), 541–64.

92 Rott, *Investigationes Historicae,* ii. 486.

93 Green and Murphy, *Renaissance Rhetoric STC*, 190–2. J. R. Henderson, 'Erasmian Ciceronians: Reformation Teachers of Letterwriting', *Rhetorica*, 10 (1992), 295–300. Spitz and Sher Tinsley, *Johann Sturm*, 300–1, 329–31, 337–9.

Iberian peninsula. Melanchthon was the key figure in this period, insisting on the connections between rhetoric and dialectic by writing paired manuals of the two subjects. He founded his rhetorical teaching on analysis of classical texts. Rhetoric showed him ways of understanding what he read, while points he noticed in his reading enabled him to refine his understanding of the way in which the rules of rhetoric should be adapted and applied. Melanchthon always emphasized the importance of rhetoric in approaching other subjects and the contribution which knowledge in other fields made to one's competence in speaking and writing. His grasp of Cicero's *De oratore* and his knowledge of Greek were crucial to his rhetorical thinking. He can be regarded as the originator of the encyclopedic programmes of knowledge which Ramus and seventeenth-century educators developed.

7

Northern Europe 1545–1580

Ramus and Company

Peter Ramus and his colleague Omer Talon revolutionized the study of logic and rhetoric by linking the two subjects together and reducing the core teaching of both to a very small number of doctrines. Ramist dialectic comprised a short version of the topics, the proposition, the syllogism, and method, while rhetoric was reduced to four tropes, prose rhythm and poetic metre, twenty figures, and delivery. Ramus and Talon illustrated every aspect of their teaching with practical examples from the great writers. By reducing the number of doctrines Ramus ensured that pupils would move rapidly on from studying the textbook to observing the way in which Cicero and Virgil used the principles. His teaching was based on an alliance between rhetoric and dialectic, on reading classical literature, and on focusing on what was practical for students. In these three respects Ramus can be thought of as inspired by Melanchthon's programme, but Ramus took simplification much further than Melanchthon had, and lacked his interest in Greek rhetoric, amplification, and emotion. After an initial success in Paris in the mid-sixteenth century Ramus and Talon's doctrines spread throughout northern Europe and into Spain. Their works were printed and taught into the seventeenth century, especially in Protestant Germany, Britain, Scandinavia, and North America.

Peter Ramus (Pierre de la Ramée) was born in the tiny village of Cuts in Picardy in 1515.[1] Because of his humble origin he struggled to obtain an education, entering the Collège de Navarre in 1527 as the servant of a fellow student. He studied in Paris at the moment when Sturm and

[1] For the biography which follows, see C. Waddington, *Ramus: Sa vie, ses écrits et ses opinions* (Paris, 1855); W. Ong, *Ramus: Method and the Decay of Dialogue* (Cambridge, Mass., 1958), 17–35; P. Sharratt, 'Nicolaus Nancelius, *Petri Rami Vita*', *Humanistica Lovaniensia*, 24 (1975), 161–278; K. Meerhoff, 'Les Lecteurs royaux pour l'éloquence latine et la philosophie', in A. Tuilier (ed.), *Histoire du Collège de France*, i. *La Création 1530–1560* (Paris, 2006), 328–52. Ramus admitted that his father was a charcoal-burner, *Collectanae praefationes, epistolae, orationes* (Marburg, 1599; repr. Hildesheim), 339–40.

Latomus were reading Cicero dialectically and when new editions of Agricola were changing the way in which dialectic was taught. After taking his MA in 1537, allegedly defending the thesis that everything that Aristotle wrote was mistaken, Ramus began teaching at the Collège du Mans, moving to the Collège de l'Ave Maria, where he worked with his lifelong associate Omer Talon (*c.*1510–62). In spring 1543 he published *Dialecticae partitiones*, in which, after a preface attacking Aristotle's logic for poor organization and for straying outside the bounds of the subject, he presents a simplified form of logic in three parts: invention, judgement, and practice. This work probably represented the teaching he had been giving in the previous few years. In the autumn he published two separate volumes, *Dialecticae institutiones*, which elaborates the three parts of the earlier book, notably by dealing with invention in much more detail, and *Aristotelicae animadversiones*, which advances the ideas of the previous work's preface into a broader attack on the traditional Aristotelian teaching of logic. For example, Ramus attacks Aristotle and his followers for failing to divide dialectic into invention and judgement, for the inclusion of material which belongs to metaphysics in *Categories,* and Porphyry's *Isagoge*, for the confusion of *Topica*, and for the inclusion of much unnecessary material in *Prior Analytics* and *Sophistical Refutations*, as well as making the familiar humanist attack on the language of scholastic logic.[2] Publication of these works provoked protests from other teachers in the arts faculty, including Antonio de Gouveia, brother of the principal of the Collège de Ste-Barbe, Pierre Danès, royal lecturer in Greek, and François Vicomercato, who later became royal lecturer in natural philosophy. These men saw the basis of their syllabus being called into question in public and they believed that Ramus's interpretation simplified logic to the point where it no longer prepared students for their higher studies in Aristotelian philosophy and in theology.

After a public debate François I condemned Ramus's position in the *Sentence donnée par le Roy contre maistre Pierre Ramus* of 26 March 1544, which forbade Ramus from teaching philosophy. In the autumn of 1544 Ramus announced his teaching plans for the academic year in response to this ban. His colleague Barthélemy Alexandre would teach Greek at the Collège de l'Ave Maria, while Talon would lecture on Aristotle's *Ethics,* and Ramus would teach mathematics. In 1545 he was invited to teach at the more prestigious Collège de Presles, where he soon became principal, organizing the curriculum according to his humanist principles.

[2] C. Vasoli, 'La prima polemica antiaristotelica di Pietro Ramo', in K. Meerhoff and J.-C. Moisan (eds.), *Autour de Ramus: Le Combat* (Paris, 2005), 47–105.

As principal he always ensured that a number of poor students would be taught by him free of charge. Talon moved with him and in the same year published the first version of his textbook on rhetoric, *Institutiones oratoriae*, which was to become his share of their collaboration. In 1546 Ramus published a revised version of his dialectic over the name of Talon. Ramus's *Brutinae quaestiones*, the first version of the controversial work attacking traditional teaching in rhetoric, as exemplified by Cicero's *Orator*, followed in 1547, backed up by *Rhetoricae distinctiones in Quintilianum*, in which he attacks Quintilian's teaching of rhetoric, in 1549. Ramus attacks the orators for their absence of method, their failure to provide definitions of key terms, and their errors in delimiting the subject-matter of rhetoric. He also attacks Quintilian's views on sentence composition.[3] These works were in turn attacked by Joachim Périon and Pierre Galland.[4]

In 1547 Henri II succeeded François I and, at the intercession of Ramus's schoolfellow Charles, Cardinal de Lorraine, lifted the ban on Ramus teaching or publishing in philosophy. In 1551 Ramus was appointed royal lecturer in eloquence and philosophy. He began to publish commentaries on Cicero's *Orations* and on Virgil and continued to revise and republish his and Talon's works on rhetoric and dialectic, notably giving greater importance to method. In 1555 he extended his teaching of dialectic and rhetoric into the vernacular with his *Dialectique*, whose examples from Latin poetry were translated into French by the Pléïade poets, and Antoine Fouquelin's *Rhétorique française*, which is an adapted translation of Talon's *Rhetorica* with French-language illustrative examples taken from the poems of the Pléïade.[5] Ramus further argued in favour of the vernacular languages in his *Ciceronianus* (1557).[6] He underlined his nationalist credentials with a publication on the glories of ancient France, *Traité des façons et coutumes des anciens Gaulois* (1559). He applied his universal method to other subjects in his lectures on physics and metaphysics and in the continuation of his work in mathematics.

After Talon's death in 1562, Ramus continued to publish new versions of Talon's rhetoric and commentaries on dialectic. In the mid-1560s he began to embrace Protestantism. In 1568–70 he made an extensive but

[3] K. Meerhoff, *Rhétorique et poétique au XVIe siècle en France: Du Bellay, Ramus et les autres* (Leiden, 1986), 199–220.

[4] K. Meerhoff, 'Pierre Galland: Un mélanchthonien masqué', in Meerhoff and Moisan, *Autour de Ramus*, 237–322.

[5] Meerhoff, *Rhétorique et poétique*, 236. See also Ch. 13 below, for Ramus's *Ciceronianus*.

[6] K. Meerhoff, 'Ramus and the Vernacular', in S. Reid and E. Wilson (eds.), *Ramus, Pedagogy and the Liberal Arts* (Ashgate, forthcoming).

not especially successful tour of German and Swiss universities.[7] The culmination of his attacks on the traditional teaching of university arts subjects, the enormous *Scholae in liberales artes,* appeared in Basel in 1569. At this time too he must have been preparing the posthumously published *Commentariorum de religione Christiana libri quatuor* (1576). On 26 August 1572 he was murdered in his rooms in the Collège de Presles in the course of the St Bartholomew's Day Massacre of the Protestants in Paris, even though, according to Nancel, orders that he should be spared had been given by the king. Subsequent publication of Ramus's work was concentrated in Germany, especially Frankfurt to where his Paris printer Andreas Wechel moved, but also in Cologne, and in Protestant countries of northern Europe.

Ramus elaborated his teaching in rhetoric and dialectic in stages.[8] At each stage the new textbook of each, which was sometimes accompanied by an extensive commentary, was paired with one or more controversial works, attacking the classical sources (Aristotle for logic; Cicero and Quintilian for rhetoric) which underpinned traditional teaching. The bibliographical labours of Ong, Bruyère, and Meerhoff have given us an idea of the complexity of this development, which can be understood as having five stages.[9]

1. Early 1543. The earliest versions of the dialectic: *Partitiones dialecticae* in the manuscript Bibliothèque Nationale Ms. Latin 6659 and in the printed edition of spring 1543.[10]
2. 1543–7. The second version of the dialectic and Talon's first rhetoric, together with the supporting controversial works: Ramus, *Dialecticae institutiones* (Paris, 1543), *Aristotelicae animadversiones* (Paris, 1543), *Brutinae quaestiones* (Paris, 1547), Talon, *Institutiones oratoriae* (Paris, 1545).

[7] K. Meerhoff, 'De Paris à Heidelberg', in Meerhoff and Magnien (eds.), *Ramus et l'université* (Paris, 2004), 89–120. W. Rother, 'Ramus and Ramism in Switzerland', in M. Feingold *et al.* (eds.), *The Influence of Peter Ramus* (Basel, 2001), 9–14.

[8] Peter Sharratt surveys studies of Ramus, 'The Present State of Studies on Ramus', *Studi francesi*, 47–8 (1972), 201–13; 'Recent Work on Peter Ramus', *Rhetorica*, 5 (1987), 7–58; 'Ramus 2000', *Rhetorica*, 18 (2000), 399–455. M. Hinz, 'Ramismus', in G. Ueding (ed.), *Historisches Wörterbuch der Rhetorik*, vii (Tübingen, 2005), 567–95.

[9] W. Ong, *Ramus and Talon Inventory* (Cambridge, Mass., 1958). N. Bruyère, *Méthode et dialectique dans l'œuvre de La Ramée* (Paris, 1984), 7–40. Meerhoff, *Rhétorique et poétique*, 173–330. Meerhoff's book has a valuable stage-by-stage plan of the rhetoric textbook. His detailed exposition focuses mainly on doctrines connected with prose rhythm.

[10] P. Mack, 'Agricola and the Early Versions of Ramus's Dialectic', in Meerhoff and Moisan, *Autour de Ramus*, 17–35.

3. 1547–9. The third version of the dialectic, which drops the section on practice; new, extended version of the controversies in dialectic; Talon's new rhetoric organized to fit in with Ramus's dialectic; completion of the controversial works in rhetoric: Ramus, *Institutionum dialecticarum libri III* (Paris, 1547), *Animadversionum Aristotelicarum libri XX* (Paris, 1548), *Rhetoricae distinctiones in Quintilianum* (Paris, 1549), Talon, *Rhetorica* (Paris, 1548)
4. 1555–7. The French dialectic and rhetoric which prompt new Latin versions, with commentary. Ramus, *Dialectique* (Paris, 1555), *Dialecticae libri duo Audomari Talaei praelectionibus illustrati* (Paris, 1556), Fouquelin, *Rhétorique française* (Paris, 1555), Talon, *Rhetorica* (Lyon, 1557). Talon's last version of the rhetoric adopts the changes in definitions of figures made in Fouquelin's French rhetoric and incorporates many quotations in Greek from Aristotle's *Rhetoric*, *Poetics,* and the *Rhetoric to Alexander*. Talon had come across many of these passages while composing his commentary on Cicero's *De oratore* (1553).[11]
5. 1565–74. New versions of the textbooks with brief instructions and fairly lengthy commentary, published around 1565–9, with a new version of the controversial work, followed by very short, text-only, versions of the textbook from 1572. These texts were very widely diffused after Ramus's death and formed the basis of his later reputation: Ramus, *Dialecticae libri duo Audomari Talaei praelectionibus illustrati* (Paris, 1565), Talon, *Rhetorica, Petri Rami praelectionibus illustrata* (Paris, 1567), Ramus, *Scholae in liberales artes* (Basel, 1569); Ramus, *Dialecticae libri duo* (Paris, 1572), Talon, *Rhetorica* (Paris, 1572). At this period Ramus rewrote all Talon's contributions. In the rhetoric he omitted most of the Greek quotations but retained Talon's order of presentation, many of his definitions, and most of his examples. He rewrote the sections on rhythm to emphasize the importance of pre-classical (including Gaulish) poetic rhythm and rhyme.[12]

While the shortened textbooks formed the basis for the intense republication of Ramus's works after his death, individual editors, such as MacIlmaine (1576), Piscator (1580), Beurhaus (1581), Temple and Wasserleider (both 1584) also added further material to assist students

[11] Meerhoff, *Rhétorique et poétique*, 262–75.
[12] Ibid. 289–316, esp. 289–92.

and to supplement what was taught.[13] We need more studies of the different materials which these later editors added.

Of the enormous numbers of editions of Ramist textbooks of rhetoric and dialectic, the great majority reprinted the later versions. So, for the Latin-language dialectic, using the lists in Green and Murphy there were seven editions from 1543–9, ten in the 1550s, nine in the 1560s, twenty in the 1570s, thirty-two in the 1580s, twenty-four in the 1590s, twelve in the 1600s, and ten between 1610 and 1620. Since few other dialectic books ever achieved ten editions in a decade, we must treat all these figures as large, as is the total of 124 editions, but the peak is between 1570 and 1599, with seventy-six editions in thirty years, at a time when other humanist logical works were in decline. While the majority of editions prior to 1570 are from Paris, Paris editions stop in 1572, when Wechel moved to Frankfurt, and later production is overwhelmingly from Frankfurt, with Cologne, London, and Hanau also producing significant numbers of editions.[14]

For the Latin rhetoric the overall total is smaller, though still very large, at 101 editions, and the spread is broadly similar, though perhaps more even and with a lower, but still very high, peak (fifty editions between 1570 and 1599). There were seven editions 1545–9, thirteen editions in the 1550s, six in the 1560s, sixteen in the 1570s, fifteen in the 1580s, nineteen in the 1590s, eleven in the 1600s, and fourteen between 1610 and 1620. Prior to 1560 and after 1600 the rhetoric was printed more frequently than the dialectic. Paris dominated early production of the rhetoric and continued sporadically until 1599, but the main centres of printing after 1575 were Frankfurt, far ahead of the others, London and Hanau.

The pattern of publication of Ramus's manuals is related to the success of Cicero's *Topica* and Agricola's *De inventione dialectica*. While the latter were highly successful in Paris in the late 1530s and early 1540s, Ramist manuals at first took over from them, with many Paris publications in the late 1540s. From Paris publication spread to other centres such as Lyon, Cologne, and Basel. In the 1550s Ramus's publications shared the European market with Agricola, Melanchthon, and Cicero, but in the 1560s production of Agricola declined and after 1570 both Melanchthon's

[13] e.g. MacIlmaine as editor adds references, parallels, and examples from scripture which considerably lengthen the basic 1572 text, P. Ramus, *Dialecticae libri duo* (London, 1576).

[14] On production in Frankfurt and in Germany more generally see I. Maclean, 'Philosophical Books in European Markets 1570–1630: The Case of Ramus', in J. Henry and S. Hutton (eds.), *New Perspectives in Renaissance Thought: Essays in Memory of Charles B. Schmitt* (London, 1990), 253–63; and H. Hotson, *Commonplace Learning: Ramism and its German Ramifications 1543–1630* (Oxford, 2007), 5.

works and Cicero's *Topica* were printed less frequently, while Ramus's works enjoyed extraordinary success, especially in Frankfurt and Cologne.[15] Production of other humanist textbooks slowed down after the point around 1580 when printing of Ciceronian rhetoric declined, but Ramus's manuals reached their highest peak of publication, continuing to be printed in large numbers of editions in Protestant Europe well into the seventeenth century. Hotson has documented the immense demand for Ramist manuals in Germany and in academies at the fringes of Europe where the full Aristotelian training may have been impossible to support.[16]

The structure of the classic Ramist manuals, which can best be appreciated in the beautiful diagram summaries which Freigius made in 1576 (reproduced on pp. 143–4), is deliberately simple. Dialectic is divided into invention and judgement.[17] Invention equates to the topics of invention; judgement involves traditional logical teaching on the proposition, a simplified version of the syllogism, and method. Rhetoric is divided into style and delivery. Style is divided into tropes (concerned with alterations to the meaning of individual words) and figures which apply to words joined together in phrases or sentences. There are only four tropes (metaphor, synecdoche, metonymy, and irony). Poetic metre and rhythmical prose form a section of the figures of words founded on the dimension of sound. Nine other figures of words are connected with repetition of sound (e.g. anaphora, gradatio). The eleven figures of meaning describe attitudes a speaker might take to an audience. Delivery discusses use of the voice and gestures appropriate to hand, face, and body. Meerhoff comments on Ramus's rigorous logical dichotomization of rhetoric in the final version of the textbook.[18]

At the core of Ramus's system is the requirement that rhetoric and dialectic be studied together. It is important to insist on this because, following on from Ong and Howell, some sketches of renaissance rhetoric, particularly from students of English literature, still claim that Ramus reduced rhetoric to style and delivery.[19] The element of truth in this view is that Ramist rhetoric textbooks contain only sections on style and

[15] Ong, *Ramus and Talon Inventory*. J. Freedman, 'The Diffusion of the Writings of Petrus Ramus in Central Europe *c.*1570–*c.*1630', *Renaissance Quarterly*, 46 (1993), 98–152.

[16] Hotson, *Commonplace Learning*, 25–37, 68–98.

[17] See C. Vasoli, *La dialettica e la retorica dell'Umanesimo* (Milan, 1968), 333–601. P. Mack, *Renaissance Argument*, 334–55.

[18] Meerhoff, *Rhétorique et poétique*, 290.

[19] W. S. Howell, *Logic and Rhetoric in England 1500–1700* (Princeton, 1956), 148, 152, 254. E. Armstrong, *A Ciceronian Sunburn* (Columbia, SC, 2006), 18–19.

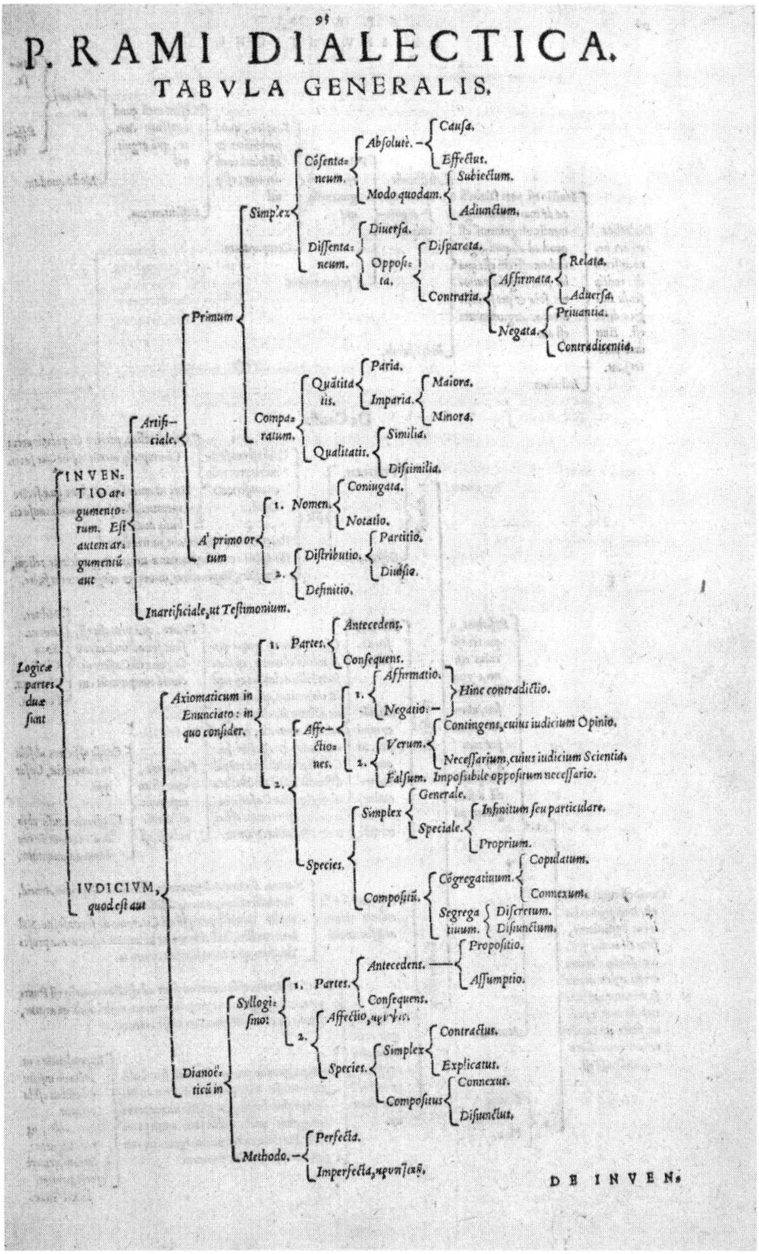

Figure 1 Scheme of Ramus's dialectic from P. Ramus, *Professio Regia*, ed. J. T. Freigius (Basel, 1576), p. 95, reproduced by permission of the British Library

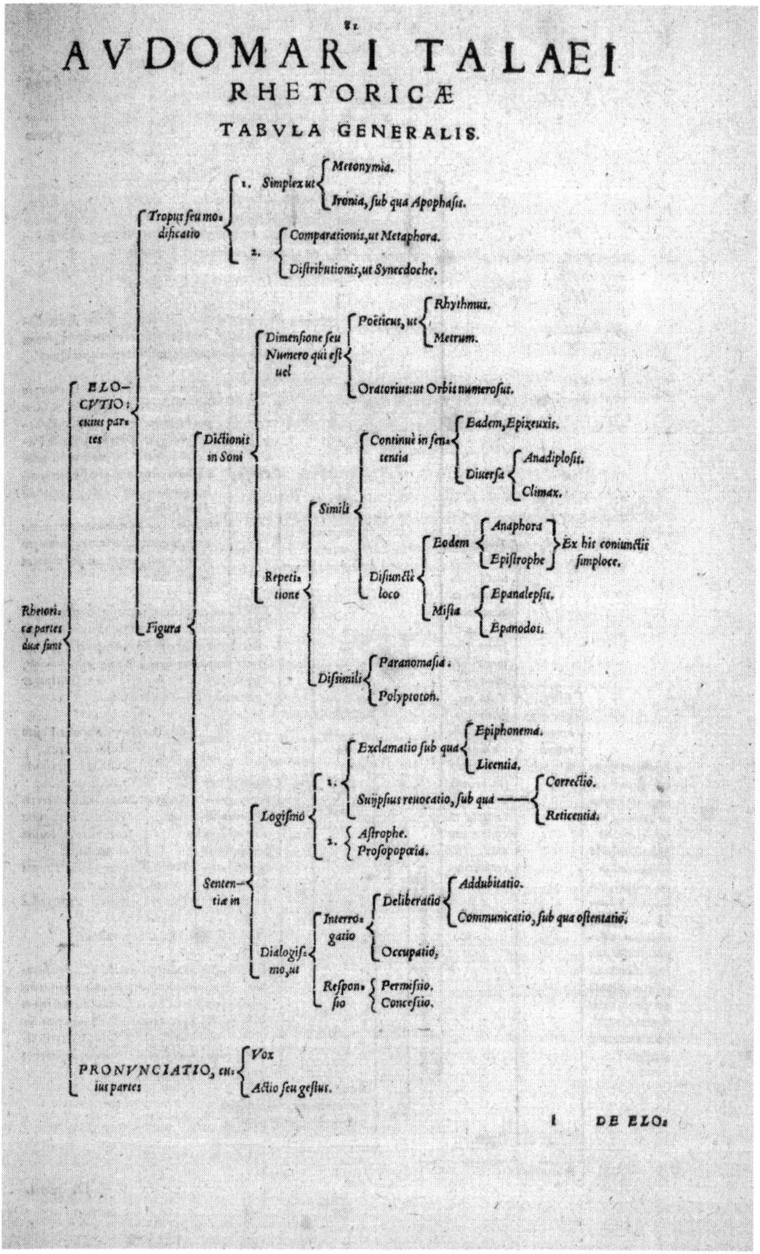

Figure 2 Scheme of Talon's rhetoric from P. Ramus, *Professio Regia*, ed. J. T. Freigius (Basel, 1576), p. 81, reproduced by permission of the British Library

delivery; but nevertheless the view is false because Ramus always insists that rhetoric and dialectic have to be studied together. In a properly Ramist scheme of teaching, everyone who studies Ramus's rhetoric will also learn about invention and organization from the dialectic text which is studied alongside the rhetoric. So whereas a traditional rhetoric course teaches five skills: invention, disposition, style, delivery, and memory; Ramus's students learn invention and disposition in the dialectic manual, style and delivery in the rhetoric manual. Ramus regarded the study of memory as part of psychology rather than as a section of rhetoric and he believed that an effective logical organization, such as that used in his textbooks, offers the best possible help to memory.

For a pedagogically oriented reformer like Ramus the textbooks have to be interpreted in the light of the audience and syllabus the writer had in mind. Thanks to the publications of Peter Sharratt we have some strong indications, both from Nancel's description of Ramus's teaching in the Collège des Presles and from Ramus's projects for the reform of the University.[20] The scheme he had in mind was that the rhetoric and dialectic textbooks should be studied in the mornings, with the afternoons given over to learning about the impact of their teaching in practice by reading through speeches by Cicero and classical Latin poetry, especially the work of Virgil. The point of the textbooks was that they should be brief and clear in their organization so that pupils would be sure to finish the book and to know the doctrines thoroughly, leaving them plenty of time to understand how logic and rhetoric work in practice through their study of literary texts. The quotations from Cicero and Latin poetry in Ramus's textbooks are intended to prepare for and reinforce that afternoon reading. Reading through the textbooks the precepts would be illustrated from Latin literature, while reading Latin literature would enable the teacher to show the impact of the skills taught in the textbook. The commentaries which Ramus published on Cicero's speeches and on Virgil's *Eclogues* and *Georgics* give us a taste of what that teaching was like. Meerhoff has shown that other renaissance literature teachers copied the approach of Ramus's commentaries.[21]

Ramus focuses on the most famous and distinctive elements of both subjects, that is to say the syllogism and the tropes and figures, but overall

[20] P. Ramus, *Scholae in liberales artes* (Basel, 1569), cols. 1010–17. Sharratt, 'Nicolaus Nancelius'. Idem, 'Ramus and the Reform of the University', in Sharratt (ed.), *French Renaissance Studies 1540–1740* (Edinburgh, 1976), 4–20.

[21] P. Mack, 'Ramus Reading: The Commentaries on Cicero's *Consular orations* and Vergil's *Eclogues* and *Georgics*', *Journal of the Warburg and Courtauld Institutes,* 61 (1998), 111–41. K. Meerhoff and J.-C. Moisan, 'Précepte et usage: Un commentaire Ramiste de la 4e Philippique', in their *Autour de Ramus*, 305–70.

his selection of material better represents the long-lasting preoccupations of rhetoric. His main focus is on teaching people to argue effectively using the full resources of the Latin language and on showing them how to recognize and analyse argument in the classical texts they read. He is not interested in the quasi-formalized language described in Aristotelian and scholastic logic. To put it more simply and provocatively, Ramus is strongly committed to the broad syllabus of rhetoric: invention, organization, style, and delivery. This needs to be qualified a little. The method and approach of Ramus's textbooks is primarily dialectical. His treatment of both subjects is articulated through definition and division. He uses logical criteria to determine both the content and the organization of his textbooks. So it might be fairer to say that Ramus's rhetoric and dialectic textbooks take a strongly dialectical approach to a syllabus which is primarily rhetorical.

For Ramus, dialectic is the art which teaches discussing well (*bene disserendi*).[22] This depends on finding appropriate arguments and arranging them effectively, so invention is about finding arguments, that is to say, about the topics. Ramus sets out a shortened, rationally organized list of the most important topics: causes, effects, subject, adjunct, contraries, from equals, greater and lesser, similars, dissimilars, conjugates, etymology, division, definition, and testimony. Genus and species are discussed under division; the concept behind differentia as part of definition.[23] Ramus does not explain how to use the topics but gives some subdivisions and literary examples of arguments derived from each topic, sometimes with explanation of how a particular argument works. The implication is that the topics are a classification of the arguments, the genera or classes into which the particular arguments are grouped. The discussion is not as thorough as in Agricola (who also placed the topics first) but the examples show how the arguments derived from the individual topics work in practice and the subdivisions indicate the richness of some topics (particularly cause, contrariety, division, and testimony) more thoroughly than accounts based on Cicero or Boethius.

There is no overt reference to Erasmus in Ramus's dialectic but he does point out that certain topics (such as adjuncts, similars, and descriptions) are particularly suited to amplification and his examples bear this out.[24] Ramus does not make a distinction between arguments which are certain and those which are persuasive but not reliable. The implication of his

[22] 'Dialectica est ars bene disserendi; eodemque sensu Logica dicta est.' P. Ramus, *Dialecticae libri duo*, 1.1 (London, 1576), sig. A7^{r}.

[23] Ibid. 1.26, 29, sigs F4^{r-v}, F7^{v}–8^{r} (without using the word *differentia*).

[24] Ibid. 1.10, 20, 30, sigs. C5^{r}–6^{r}, E5^{r-v}, F8^{v}–G1^{v}.

laws of method is that he is only concerned with arguments which are true, but several of his examples contain arguments which are merely probable.

From the topics Ramus moves directly to judgement, the way of constructing valid arguments, which involves material which was traditionally taught: the proposition and the syllogism. This means that he omits both the predicables and the categories, which are usually taught before the proposition, on the ground that they belong to metaphysics rather than logic. He gives a brief but thorough account of the different types of proposition, with examples, some constructed, some taken from classical texts. Then he sets out the valid forms of the syllogism, providing specially devised examples in simplified form, followed by literary examples for some of the types. He shows that writers often use shortened forms of the syllogism which are nevertheless valid.[25] He follows this with an account of the hypothetical syllogism ('If there are gods, then divination exists; but there are gods, therefore divination exists').[26] There is no description of the other forms of argumentation which are usually found in dialectic manuals (enthymeme, induction, example) and none of the additional forms sometimes described in humanist manuals (such as sorites and dilemma).

The third kind of judgement is correct organization at a higher level than the syllogism, which Ramus calls method. Method is regulated by three laws which state: (1) that only things which are true and necessary may be included; (2) that all and only things which belong to each particular art must be included in that art; and (3) that general things must be dealt with in a general way. While the first two laws provide the basis for much of Ramus's criticism of Aristotle, Cicero, and Quintilian, the third law sets out the perfect method, which moves from the most general axioms by definition and division to particular instances. The perfect method must be observed in organizing arts and sciences. Ramus acknowledges that this method owes something to Sturm's teachings on method, as well as to Aristotle's *Posterior Analytics*.[27] In addition to his single method Ramus also allows the need for the method of prudence, when we adapt the order of presentation to the knowledge and attitudes of the audience. This method of prudence is usually employed by poets and orators. Earlier versions of the dialectic go into some detail on different

[25] Ibid., 2.10, sig. H4$^{r–v}$.

[26] Ibid., 2.13, sig. H7^{v}.

[27] Ibid. 2.17, 18, sigs I2^{r}–3^{r}. P. Ramus, *Scholae dialecticae*, 31, 154, in *Scholae in liberales artes* (Basel, 1569). Sturm, *Praefatio*, ibid., sig. α2^{v}. N. W. Gilbert, *Renaissance Concepts of Method* (New York, 1960), 129–63.

examples of the method of prudence; later versions leave it in place but say less about it.

For Talon, rhetoric is the art (or science) of speaking well.[28] This means that it is concerned with style and delivery. Style is the adornment of language (*exornatio orationis*) and it consists of the tropes and the figures. A trope is an aspect of style through which a word is changed from its natural signification to another meaning.[29] He finds that there are only four tropes, which he links to the topics of invention. So metonymy shifts meaning from cause to effect or vice versa, or from subject to adjunct and vice versa, while irony shifts meaning between contraries and metaphor moves from one thing to something similar to it. Synecdoche transfers meaning between part and whole or genus and species. Talon gives literary examples for all these types. In the earlier versions Talon bases his discussion of the tropes on a logical schematization of the accounts in *Rhetorica ad Herennium* and Quintilian, enriching his version of metaphor from *De oratore*.[30] Around 1557 he adds references to and quotations from Aristotle's *Rhetoric* and *Poetics*.[31]

A figure changes the shape of a segment of language from its correct and simple custom.[32] It achieves its effect by elaborating the form of language. Figures are divided into figures of words and figures of meaning. Figures of words operate either through sound or repetition. The former describe poetic metre and prose rhythm, the latter figures like epizeuxis when the same sound is repeated in one sentence, anadiplosis when the sound at the end of one sentence is repeated to start the next, climax which is a succession of anadiploses, anaphora in which the same sound begins a succession of sentences, and epistrophe where the same sound closes a series. This short list of figures of speech reliant on repetition includes paronomasia, when there is a play on the meaning of a word that sounds similar, and polyptoton, where the same word appears in the sentence in different cases. For figures of words Talon gives his own definitions, which change a little over phases 3 to 5 in the numbered points set out earlier in

[28] 'Rhetorica est doctrina bene dicendi.' A. Talon, *Rhetorica* (Lyon, 1557), sig. A3^{r}; 'Rhetorica est ars bene dicendi.' A. Talon, *Rhetorica* (Frankfurt, 1581). sig. a4^{r}. Although the manual is attributed to Talon and much of his material is retained, the manual was entirely rewritten by Ramus after Talon's death. Ramus's versions were far more widely diffused than the rhetorics Talon himself published.

[29] Talon, *Rhetorica* (Cambridge, 1631), A3^{v}: 'Tropus est elocutio, qua verbum a nativa significatione in aliam immutatur.'

[30] Talon, *Rhetorica* (Paris, 1549), sigs. a4^{r}–b2^{r}. *Rhetorica ad Herennium* 4.32.43, 33. 44–34.46. Quintilian, *Institutio oratoria* 8.6.4–29.

[31] Talon, *Rhetorica* (Lyon, 1557), sigs. A3^{v}–B3^{v}.

[32] Talon, *Rhetorica* (Cambridge, 1631), B3^{v}: 'Figura est elocutio, qua orationis habitus a recta et simplici consuetudine mutatur.'

this chapter (pp. 139–40); some of the illustrative quotations are identical to those in Mosellanus and Susenbrotus, which suggests that he had their handbooks before him as he wrote.[33] The majority of the rest are taken from Virgil or from speeches of Cicero which Ramus commented on.

Talon defines a figure of thought as a figure which alters the whole meaning through a certain motion of the mind. Figures of thought are divided into monologue figures (exclamation, correction, *aposiopesis*, apostrophe, and *prosopopeia*) and dialogue figures (*addubitatio*, *communicatio*, *occupatio*, *permissio*, and *concessio*). Talon gives several examples of all of these figures, mainly from Cicero, but also from Virgil, Terence, and Martial. Some of the figures are explained through subdivision. It is hard to find parallels either for Talon's definitions of these figures or for his choice of examples, but the majority of them appear in Susenbrotus under the same Latin names, so perhaps that was the main source.[34] In the early editions the figures of thought appear immediately after the tropes and before the discussions of metre, prose rhythm, and the figures of speech. The later editions are ordered: tropes, metre and rhythm, figures of speech, figures of thought.[35]

Talon has succeeded in producing a clearly organized and easily memorable list of tropes and figures, and his numerous examples give a good idea of how these techniques can be employed. Most rhetoricians, however, would probably feel that he omits much useful material and that the clarity is bought at the cost of impoverishing rhetoric's description of the resources of expressive language.

In the second part of the book Talon recovers delivery, which Melanchthon and others had omitted from rhetoric. Delivery is divided into voice and gesture. Talon begins with general advice on the use of the voice (the voice should not be too deep nor too high; one should not raise phrases of lower pitch too suddenly), and then borrows a section where Quintilian, discussing the pronunciation of individual words, comments on the delivery of a passage from Cicero's *Pro Milone*.[36] Then he quotes the

[33] e.g. Talon, *Rhetorica* (Lyon, 1557), sig. B8^{v}: 'Occidi, occidi etc, Vivis etc' (= Susenbrotus, sig. D2^{r}), 'Pierides etc' (= Susenbrotus, D2^{v}) 'Me, me etc' (= Mosellanus, *Tabulae*, sig. A5^{v}); Talon, C1^{r}: 'Nate meae etc.' (= Susenbrotus, D1^{v}); Talon, C4^{r}: 'Littora littoribus etc' (= Mosellanus, A6^{r}, Susenbrotus, D3^{v}). For Mosellanus and Susenbrotus see Ch. 10 below.

[34] Susenbrotus, *Epitome troporum*, sigs. D6^{r}–E2^{v}. Mosellanus does not describe the figures of thought; see Ch. 10 below.

[35] So far as I know there is as yet no detailed account of the evolution of the different sections of the Ramist rhetoric textbook, though Meerhoff, *Rhétorique et poétique*, gives many helpful indications.

[36] Talon, *Rhetorica* (Cambridge, 1631), D8^{r}–E1^{r}. Quintilian, *Institutio oratoria* 11.3.47–51.

views of Cicero and Quintilian on the delivery of whole sentences before giving examples of passages which should be delivered in different tones of voice.[37] Finally he quotes passages from poets and orators in which the voice must convey emotions: wretchedness, anger, fear. After explaining the forcefulness of gesture, he provides literary examples showing the use of heads, eyes, arms, hands, and feet in conveying emotions. The chief rules, he says, are that the gestures you employ must be suited to the whole meaning that you wish to convey and that they must not be overdone in the manner of actors.[38] Almost all of the observations in this section are quoted directly from Quintilian 11.3, and Cicero's *De oratore* 3.213–17 and *Orator* 55–60, but the numerous examples are generally chosen by Talon, largely from Cicero's *Orations*.

Ramus and Talon provide a clear, carefully organized and coordinated account of the key doctrines of rhetoric and dialectic but they also omit several of the traditional doctrines. From dialectic they leave out the predicables, the categories, several of the forms of argumentation, observations on arguments which are convincing rather than certain, the sophisms, teaching on disputation, and all the medieval accretions. Ramus believed that these doctrines were either unreliable or fell outside the limits of the subject. From rhetoric they omit the three genres of speeches, detailed teaching about the four parts of the oration, the topics of deliberative and demonstrative speeches, status-theory, amplification, the qualities and levels of style, and memory. Crucially there is no theory of emotional manipulation, though the examples of the figures and the discussion of delivery both touch on the emotional impact of oratory.[39]

Some of these aspects of the traditional syllabus were contested by other renaissance rhetoricians. For example Melanchthon and Sturm sought ways to integrate the predicables and categories with definition and/or invention. Erasmus, Melanchthon, Vives, and others correctly believed that the three classical genres of oratory did not reflect the occasions and audiences of sixteenth-century writing. Agricola, Erasmus, Melanchthon, and Vives showed the importance of structures of writing outside rhetoric's traditional focus on the four- or six-part oration. But Agricola and Melanchthon at least would not have been happy to omit the emotions, amplification, and levels of style.

[37] Talon, *Rhetorica* (Cambridge, 1631), E1$^{r–v}$. Cicero, *Orator* 57. Quintilian, *Institutio oratoria* 11.3.168.

[38] Talon, *Rhetorica* (Cambridge, 1631), E4^{v}.

[39] e.g. *Rhetorica* 1.8, 14, 18, 28–9, 2.3 (Cambridge, 1631), sigs. A8^{r}–B1^{r}, B4^{r}, B7^{v}, C5^{v}–7^{r}, D8^{v}–E1^{r}.

Ramus and Talon's simplification of rhetoric and dialectic has the advantage that it ensures that pupils will finish the course of instruction quickly and will rapidly move on to what they, with Melanchthon, think of as the real training in eloquence, reading poems and speeches in order to understand how writers have used and adapted the precepts. The idea that the rules are relatively simple and that what counts is understanding the complexity of their use in practice is in fact central to the rhetorical tradition, particularly in the way Cicero in *De oratore* magnifies the importance of experience and adaptation to the actual circumstances of speaking, while treating the rules as a necessary preliminary, a way of preparing schoolboys for the apprenticeship in which they will learn the true complexity of the art. So where some of Ramus's contemporaries (and later historians) would argue that Ramus has thrown away too much, others could reply that he was developing the logical implications of the humanist approach to rhetoric.

Ramus's published commentaries, representing his public teaching in the first few years as royal lecturer, tend to support the image of Ramus as a continuer of the humanist tradition, teaching the rules quickly and simply so that he can get on to the texts, knowing that refinements can be added later. These commentaries certainly provide evidence of Ramus going beyond the syllabus laid out in his manuals. The commentary on *De lege agraria* and its successors refer to about six figures of speech outside the list given in the rhetoric manuals and also admit some of Ramus's generic divisions (such as *exclamatio* and *dialogismus*) as figures in their own right.[40] It is worth noting too that, whereas Ramus's manuals tend to prefer Greek names for the figures, some of the figures listed in the commentary appear under their Latin names. More significant examples of Ramus's commentaries going outside his manuals would include discussion of tactics for the *exordium* in his accounts of Cicero's speeches and references to amplification in his analysis of Virgil.[41] Most of the time Ramus attends very closely to the arguments implied in the speeches and poems and this enables him both to uncover main lines of argument in the speeches and to provide thoughtful and innovative accounts of the structure of the individual *Eclogues* and *Georgics*. At times too his logical approach forces him to worry about connections between the ideas in the poems and to work out their implications in ways that seem new to the commentary tradition.[42] In fairness one should add that Servius's

[40] Ramus, *In Ciceronis orationes* (Frankfurt, 1582), sigs. N4^{v}–6^{v}, O8^{r}.

[41] Ibid., sigs. A3^{v}–6^{r}, F3$^{r–v}$, Q1^{v}. Virgil, *Bucolica P. Rami . . . praelectionibus exposita* (Paris, 1555), sigs. A5^{r}–8^{r}.

[42] Mack, 'Ramus Reading', 111–41; Meerhoff and Moisan, 'Précepte et usage', 305–70.

commentary in particular suggests to Ramus several ways to develop his own work on Virgil beyond what he had done with Cicero. Ramus's attention to the texts often takes precedence over his logical teaching, as when he allows that Cicero's second Catalinarian is highly effective despite its neglect of the principles of method.[43]

Ramus's commentaries are very thorough in reconstructing chains of argument, in noticing Cicero and Virgil's use of the topics of invention, and in labelling tropes and figures of speech. In some of the commentaries Ramus concludes with an analysis of the preponderant figures and topics. But he is less good at reacting to poetic or emotional effects. Here the examples of the commentaries of Melanchthon and Latomus ought to have suggested to him more than they apparently did. Ramus reconstructs the arguments of Cicero's second Catalinarian but he has nothing to say about the extremity and inventiveness of the vituperation. He picks out the structure and implications of Virgil's teaching in the *Georgics* but he has nothing to say about the dramatically visualized narratives, such as the fire in the vineyard, or the storm. He makes very few references to the audience but one of them at least shows both his flexibility of approach and the potential of his analysis.

> Everything by which the minds of a crowd can be moved and persuaded was employed in this speech: elegance of discourse, argument of fact, and maxim (*sententia*) disposed methodically. Once you have imagined that consular majesty of such a popular face, that voice which, when it was raised a little (as Plutarch says), inspired fear deep in the hearts of his audience, and the whole eloquence of Cicero's body, how much more will you understand the more important reasons for its success?[44]

But however discriminating Ramus could be as a commentator on classical texts, his aim, his fatal flaw his detractors would say, was to achieve more than that. He wanted to teach a system of thinking and arguing which would be valid for all subjects and he himself wrote introductions to, and controversial works in, many of the other arts. Where other humanist authors were generally content to reform the *trivium* and to argue that rhetoric should have a larger place in the university syllabus, Ramus wanted to extend his dialectical approach to the teaching of the whole

[43] Ramus, *In Ciceronis orationes*, sig. T5^{r}.

[44] 'Ea quibus animi multitudinis oblectari et confirmari poterant, hic esse adhibita: orationis ornatum, rei sententiaeque argumentum via et ordine positum. Quid si consularem illam vultus tam popularis majestatem, quid si vocis, quae paulo altius elata intimis audientium praecordiis (ut Plutarchus ait) timebatur, quid si totam illius Ciceroniani corporis eloquentiam animo conceperis, quanto maiores eventus huius causas concipies?' Ramus, *In Ciceronis orationes*, sig. T5^{v}. Mack, 'Ramus Reading', 122–3.

university syllabus, dethroning Aristotle in philosophy as well. In the previous chapter we saw Melanchthon opening up an aspiration to encyclopedic knowledge and at times Ramus professed the same ambition.[45]

RAMUS'S OPPONENETS: GALLAND AND CHARPENTIER

As his biography indicates, Ramus was strongly criticized by other Parisian professors. The earliest attacks, which succeeded in getting Ramus suspended from teaching philosophy, were made in response to the first printing of his *Aristotelicae animadversiones* in 1543 and were motivated by the desire to maintain the traditional Aristotelian syllabus in logic, physics, and philosophy.[46] In 1547 on the publication of the *Brutinae quaestiones* Pierre Galland (1510–59), royal lecturer in Latin eloquence, attacked Ramus from the point of view of a Christian humanist and editor of Quintilian. Meerhoff picks out four salient points of attack: Ramus's lack of coherence and inconsistency of doctrine; the folly of linking eloquence and philosophy; the injustice of Ramus's attacks on Aristotle's *Ethics*; and the dangers of scepticism. While Galland favoured the Erasmian view that theologians needed an excellent knowledge of grammar and rhetoric, he attacked the idea of studying literature and philosophy at the same time, or of studying philosophy through literary texts. He believed that by choosing to teach easy texts in a simple way Ramus did not prepare students for the reading of difficult philosophical texts. Thanks to the death of Francis I and the support of the Cardinal of Lorraine, Ramus answered this criticism by getting the ban on teaching philosophy lifted. When he was appointed royal lecturer in eloquence and philosophy, he replied by insisting that, contrary to Galland's views, Cicero's orations were full of dialectic.[47]

More intellectually provocative were three attacks by Jacques Charpentier (1524–74). In 1551 as rector of the University Charpentier ruled that because Ramus did not teach the Aristotelian logic required by the statutes, his pupils could not enjoy the privileges of Paris university students. Ramus appealed first to the assembly of regents of philosophy

[45] Meerhoff, 'Les Lecteurs royaux', 340–4, 347–8. Ramus, 'Oratio de sua professione', in *Scholae in liberales artes* (Basel, 1569), cols. 1103–16 (second numeration).

[46] Ong, *Ramus, Method*, 215–19. Meerhoff, 'L'Enseignement des lecteurs', 332–3.

[47] Meerhoff, 'Pierre Galland: Un Mélanchthonien masqué', in *Autour de Ramus*, 290, 293, 307. For other controversies see the articles in the same volume by van der Poel and Henderson, pp. 323–89.

and later to the Parliament of Paris. Before the parliament Ramus outlined a programme of study in which grammar, rhetoric, and dialectic led first to natural and moral philosophy and later to theology or law. He argued that his method of teaching avoided wasting time on scholastic technicalities and produced graduates who were better prepared for practical life. The effectiveness of this speech and the support of his patron helped him to avoid censure and obtain a royal lectureship. In order to defend his hard-won academic position Ramus was forced to seek support in the wider political world.[48] Charpentier's second attack in 1554 focused on the detail of Ramus's teaching. He showed that Aristotle, whom Ramus now cited in support of his doctrines, believed in a double method (from universals to individuals for organizing a science, but also from particular instances to general principles in order to found a science) rather than Ramus's single method (which ran from the most general questions gradually down to specifics); he rejected Ramus's division of dialectic into invention and disposition; he held that the subject which provided the basis for other disciplines was not dialectic but metaphysics; and he pointed out that Ramus's belief in imitation of classical authors was inconsistent with his assertion that all their texts were badly organized. According to Vasoli Ramus replied to these criticisms with the new formulation of *Dialectique* (1555).[49] In 1564 Charpentier again attacked Ramus's doctrine of method, arguing that he had omitted the method of discovery, that his use of the term analysis was inexact, and that his use of poets and orators in teaching was a mistake. Behind Ramus he saw the impact of Lorenzo Valla's criticism of Aristotle. He thought that with Ramus the true idea of knowledge was in danger of eclipse.[50]

While many recent scholars have argued that Ramus's opponents were better-trained as philologists and philosophers than he was, many of their critiques seem to be motivated by the desire to maintain the ascendancy of Aristotelian logic and philosophy and by an idea of knowledge that was primarily contemplative. In conflict with this Ramus wanted to teach a dialectic which would be useful in the world and which would help students understand other texts and subjects rather than devoting the majority of the arts course to logical technicalities. Although Ramus differed from other humanists on many important points, quite a number

[48] P. Ramus, *De philosophica parisiensis academiae disciplina* (Paris, 1551). Vasoli, *La dialettica*, 438–55.

[49] J. Carpentarius, *Animadversiones in libros tres Dialecticarum institutionum Petri Rami* (Paris, 1554). Vasoli, *La dialettica*, 469–73.

[50] J. Carpentarius, *De analytica methodo,* in idem, *Platonis cum Aristotele . . . comparatio* (Paris, 1573), 56–60, 62, 72. Vasoli, *La dialettica*, 530–5.

of these criticisms levelled mainly at him were attacks on positions (for example, about the use of dialectic in literary texts) which he shared with the other humanists. He also had critics among the humanists who believed that he had gone too far in developing to their logical extremes ideas that were basically worthwhile. Even though Ramus was far more severely criticized in his own time than any of the other authors we shall discuss, his work was more frequently printed and widely diffused than anyone else's.

Apart from the numerous editors of his later works mentioned above, and those who translated and adapted them for the vernaculars, Ramus also inspired new manuals developed on the lines he had established. These manuals illustrate a choice which Ramus presented to teachers. One could use his textbooks to teach the principles of dialectic very rapidly, allowing time for the students to move on to analyse the use of the principles in classical texts. This is the position of Ramus's own earlier teaching. Alternatively one could move on from dialectic to other subjects. Hotson argues that both these ways of using Ramus were important for the spread of his doctrines in Germany. Where some gymnasia used Ramus and Talon mainly as a quick introduction to rhetoric and dialectic, others formulated a wide-ranging course, involving Ramist approaches to many other subjects.[51] A third possibility, which we find in some commented editions, was to use Ramus's somewhat spare, gnomic text as the basis on which to present a much more comprehensive account, noting the views of other authorities and explaining why Ramus disagreed with them. In this way the forty or so octavo pages of one of Ramus's late manuals can be expanded to fill a volume of 800 pages.

RAMUS'S FOLLOWERS

The tendency to brevity is most marked in those who incorporate Talon's rhetoric and Ramus's dialectic in a textbook designed to provide pupils with an encyclopedic programme of learning. Joannes Freigius (1543–83) prepared shortened textbooks of rhetoric, poetics, and dialectic in question-and-answer format, *Rhetorica, Poetica, Logica ad usum rudiorum* (Nuremberg, 1580), which was printed four times up to 1594, and a fifth time as a logic alone. In rhetoric Freigius begins with traditional material taken from Melanchthon (the five duties of the orator, status-theory,

[51] Hotson, *Commonplace Learning*, 72–82, 97–8, 114–15.

commonplaces, emotions, but not the didascalic genre)[52] before following Ramus's account of the tropes and figures and of delivery. The section on poetics is a selection from Horace's *Ars poetica*, reorganized so as to answer Ramus-style questions about the nature and types of poetry. In dialectic, the initial definitions are Cicero's but almost all the treatment of topics, proposition, syllogism, and method comes from Ramus, with the addition of sections on topical invention, the principles of knowledge, and the sophisms.[53] Freigius also includes simplified outlines of Ramist rhetoric and dialectic in his *Paedagogus* (Basel, 1582), a once printed school course stretching from Latin, Greek, and Hebrew grammar to music, geometry, architecture, ethics, law, and medicine. His *Ciceronianus* (Basel, 1575), which was printed in three editions, is a commonplace book gathering the opinions of classical authors on subjects such as god, man, nature, the arts, the emotions, and the virtues.[54] Joannes Bilsten's *Syntagma Philippo-Rameum artium liberalium* (Basel, 1592), printed twice, includes a shortened pure Ramist rhetoric in a course which runs from German, Latin, and Greek grammar through physics, ethics, and history to law, with the main emphasis on grammar, logic, and law. To a mainly Ramist dialectic he adds a definition of argument, the predicables and categories, the scholastic mnemonics for the valid forms of the syllogism, examples of the fallacies, and (under method of prudence) summaries of the kinds and parts of the oration, the didascalic genre and the simple question, and status-theory, taken from Melanchthon.[55]

Among those who devote longer works to rhetoric, dialectic, or both we find a spectrum of opinions from pure Ramism to different degrees of adaptation.[56] Joannes Piscator (1546–1625), professor of theology in Herborn, supplemented his successful editions of Ramus's dialectic (Frankfurt, 1580) and Talon's rhetoric (Frankfurt, 1588),[57] with excerpts from their work and Ramist commentaries on Cicero's orations and books of the Bible. Most of these works were printed only once or twice, mainly

[52] Freigius, *Rhetorica, Poetica* (Nuremberg, 1594), sigs. A4^{r}, A6^{r}–B2^{v}; compare Melanchthon, *Elementa Rhetorices*, *CR* xiii. 429–54. Rother, 'Ramus in Switzerland', 14–21.

[53] Freigius, *Rhetorica, Poetica*, sigs. H6^{r}–7^{v}, I1^{v}–2^{v}, K5^{r}–7^{v}.

[54] Ann Moss, *Printed Commonplace-Books and the Structuring of Renaissance Thought* (Oxford, 1996), 158–60.

[55] J. Bilsten, *Syntagma Philippo-Rameum artium liberalium* (Basel, 1596), sigs. s4^{r}, u1^{v}, u2^{v}–5^{r}, u7^{r}–x2^{v}. Hotson, *Commonplace Learning*, 114–26. I have not seen Bilsten's *Rhetorica* (Herborn, 1591), one edn., or his *Dialectica* (Hanau, 1592), three edns., but the full titles suggest the same sort of mixture of Ramism and Melanchthon as in the *Syntagma*.

[56] See the studies collected in Feingold *et al.*, *Influence of Peter Ramus*.

[57] Green and Murphy, *Renaissance Rhetoric STC* (Aldershot, 2006), 366, 426. Piscator could also be critical of Ramus, as in his *Animadversiones* (1580).

at Herborn.[58] Friedrich Beurhaus (1536–1609), rector of the gymnasium at Dortmund and a writer on music, published lengthy question-and-answer commentaries on Ramus's dialectic, starting in 1581, which went through a total of twelve editions up to 1603. The commentaries provided information on the views of other writers and made small additions to Ramus's teaching, for example on the sources of knowledge and on the sophisms.[59] Another purist follower of Ramus was Rudolph Snell (1546–1613) who published enormous dialogue commentaries on Ramus's dialectic (Herborn, 1587) and Talon's rhetoric (Frankfurt, 1596), which went through six and five editions respectively. Occasionally he reports a doctrine (e.g. enthymeme, induction and example, simple invention) which Melanchthon includes but explains that Ramus was correct to omit it.[60]

Those who mainly followed Ramus while making some additions include Francisco Sánchez de las Brozas, 'El Brocense' (1523–1601), who taught logic and rhetoric at Salamanca for many years. While the first edition of his *De arte dicendi* (Salamanca, 1556) is a brief survey of the whole of rhetoric, based on Cicero and Quintilian, and with examples from classical literature, editions from 1558 onwards demonstrate his conversion to Ramism.[61] His *Organum dialecticum et rhetoricorum* (Lyon, 1579), which was printed five times in the sixteenth century, mostly in Salamanca, provides a Ramist dialectic with some additions, followed by a strictly Ramist rhetoric. In introducing the dialectic he adds some comments on status, on the distinction between thesis and hypothesis based on Melanchthon, and a definition of argument based on Cicero.[62] After the topic of testimonia (at the end of book 1 of the Ramist dialectic) he adds a quite lengthy section ('On rhetors' invention') on status-theory taken from Hermogenes.[63] He omits Ramus's account of the proposition and includes the scholastic mnemonics for the

[58] Green and Murphy, *Renaissance Rhetoric STC*, 342. On the importance of Herborn in the diffusion of Ramus's work in Germany, Hotson, *Commonplace Learning*, 30–3, 82–90, 93–4, 103–5.

[59] See Green and Murphy, *Renaissance Rhetoric STC*, 68–9. Beurhaus, *Dialecticæ P. Rami . . . libri duo, prælectionum et repetitionum quæstionibus illustrati* (Cologne, 1587), sigs. A8^r–B3^v; Beurhaus, *Ad P. Rami dialecticae praxin generalis* (Cologne, 1596), sigs. Fff1^v–Ggg6^v.

[60] Snellius, *De ratione discendi et exercendi logicam* (Herborn, 1599), sigs. h7^r, k1^r. I am grateful to Russell Edwards for fetching Snell's books from inaccessible shelves in the Bodleian.

[61] F. Sánchez de las Brozas, *El arte de hablar (1556)*, ed. L. Merino Jerez (Alcañiz, 2007), pp. xxix–lxxi.

[62] F. Sanctius Brocensis, *Organum dialecticum et rhetoricorum* (Lyon, 1579), sigs. B1^r–2^r. A. Martín Jiménez, *Retórica y literatura en el siglo XVI: El Brocense* (Valladolid, 1997).

[63] Sanctius, *Organum dialecticum*, sigs. D8^v–F2^v.

syllogism.[64] At the end of the dialectic under method of prudence he describes the parts of the oration and the art of memory.[65] He makes two references to Rudolph Agricola's topics and discusses the usefulness of concealed forms of syllogism, with an example from Terence.[66]

Harmoniae logicae Philipporameae libri duo (Lemgo, 1595), by Heizo Buscher (1564–98), which went through five editions up to 1599, provides a thorough explication of Ramus's 1572 dialectic with a few additions, such as the scholastic mnemonic for the syllogism.[67] Generally he shows that either Melanchthon supports Ramus's view or that he is wrong in opposing it.[68] From Melanchthon's *Erotemata dialectices* Buscher adds maxims for the topics, an account of the predicables and why Ramus has left them out (under *distributio*), other forms of argumentation (enthymeme, induction, example, sorites, and dilemma), the didascalic genre, and Melanchthon's ten-question method.[69] Andreas Libavius (d. 1616) in *Dialecticae emendatae libri duo* (Frankfurt, 1595) follows an essentially Ramist structure while making some additions and expressing some reservations. Before beginning on Ramus's dialectic he gives a short account of the categories; after the syllogism he surveys the sophisms, and at the end he sets out the six parts of the oration, summarizes status theory and the didascalic genre, and adds comments on the methods of different types of writers (poets, disputers, letter-writers, historians, and preachers).[70] At the end of the work he criticizes some of Ramus's views and attacks his opponents before showing that Ramus had misrepresented Aristotle's views on method.[71] Libavius's *Dialectica Philippo-Ramaea* (Frankfurt, 1608), which includes a version of Talon's rhetoric, is essentially a Ramist textbook with parallels and occasional supplements from Melanchthon and some references to Agricola. Both Libavius's books were printed once only. Conrad Dieterich, in a series of moderately successful manuals discussed in Chapter 9 below, supplemented a Ramist structure with some of the traditional contents of dialectic and rhetoric, including the categories, the sophisms, and several tropes and figures which Talon had omitted. After his 1597 edition of Talon's *Rhetorica*, Charles Butler (1560–1647) published *Rhetoricae libri duo* (London,

64 Ibid., sigs. F8^{r}–G2^{r}.
65 Ibid., sigs. G6^{v}–H3^{v}.
66 Ibid., sigs. ¶2^{r}, C4^{r}, F6^{r-v}.
67 Buscher, *Harmoniae logicae PhilippoRamaeae libri duo* (Lemgo, 1595), sig. T5^{v}.
68 e.g. ibid., sigs. A1^{r}, A4^{v}–6^{r}, B6^{v}.
69 Ibid., sigs. D4^{v}–7^{r}, E8^{v}–F2^{r}, N1^{r}–5^{r}, X2^{v}–3^{v}, Y2^{r}, Y3^{v}.
70 Libavius, *Dialecticae emendatae libri duo* (Frankfurt, 1595), sigs. B3^{r}–8^{r}, R8^{r}–S7^{v}, T3^{v}–V2^{r}.
71 Ibid., sigs. Bb6^{r}–Ll8^{v}.

1598), a commented edition of Talon, which was printed four times before 1620 (and another twelve times up to 1684). In 1629 he supplemented this with his *Oratoriae libri duo* (printed eight times up to 1684) which teaches schoolchildren aspects of rhetoric which Talon omitted: the parts of the oration, status-theory, topical invention, disposition, and memory.[72]

One indicator of Ramus's success is that in the 1580s and 1590s even writers who are critical of central elements of his teaching set their manuals out as versions of his, with additions and reservations. Protestant dialecticians present the possibilities of the subject as a choice between Ramus and Melanchthon, and even those who claim to combine or harmonize the views of these two masters in practice copy Ramus's outline, with relatively minor additions. But other approaches to dialectic and rhetoric were available in the second half of the sixteenth century. Valerius and Dresser were on the whole orthodox Melanchthonians, while Junius and Bersman wrote rhetorics which were more dependent on classical sources. In the wake of the Council of Trent Ramist and Melanchthonian dialectic were both threatened by a revival of scholastic logic, which we can associate with the names of Fonseca and Case.

NON-RAMISTS

Between 1545 and 1580 textbooks of rhetoric and dialectic continued to be produced which did not follow Ramus's innovations. Cornelius Valerius (1512–78), professor of Latin at Louvain composed *Tabulae totius dialectices* (1545), which went through eighteen editions up to 1591, mainly from Louvain, Cologne, and Antwerp, and *In universam bene dicendi rationem tabula* (1557), which was printed seventeen times up to 1620 (and twice afterwards), mostly in Antwerp and Cologne. Valerius aims to cover the traditional syllabus of both subjects in full. In dialectic his major debt is to Melanchthon, whom he does not name, presumably on religious grounds. He follows Melanchthon's order of presentation in *Dialecticae libri quatuor* (though not the four-book division). Agricola's influence is apparent in the definition of dialectic, the list of topics, the section on the use of the topics, and some of the topics entries.[73]

Valerius's rhetoric does not follow Melanchthon's structure but absorbs some of the sections which he had introduced (e.g. didascalic genre treated

72 Butler, *Oratoriae libri duo* (Oxford, 1633).
73 Valerius, *Tabulae totius dialectices* (Louvain, 1549), sigs. A5^r, H1^r, H2^r, I1^v, I6^v–7^v.

Table 7.1. Plan of Valerius, *In universam bene dicendi rationem*

		Page
1	Definitions, rhetoric and dialectic, thesis and hypothesis	5
2	Invention: five parts of the oration	11
	Types of case: demonstrative, including didascalic	26
	deliberative	38
	judicial (including status-theory)	41
3	Disposition	57
4	Style	60
	Composition	67
	Tropes and figures	74
	Descriptions	118
5	Memory	122
6	Delivery	124
7	Imitation	125–8

as part of demonstrative oratory, commonplaces, imitation).[74] The large section on *elocutio* begins with discussion of levels and qualities of style and of named faults to avoid, which resembles *Rhetorica ad Herennium*, before a discussion of sentence composition, based on Quintilian and Cicero's *Orator*.[75] The organization of tropes and figures, with figures divided into figures of words (grammatical and rhetorical) and figures of thought (subdivided into those that adorn and those that amplify) resembles Melanchthon,[76] but Valerius includes many figures which Melanchthon omitted. Each figure is treated very concisely, with a name, an explanation, one or two examples (mainly from Cicero), and sometimes an explanation of a difference in terminology in Quintilian or *Rhetorica ad Herennium*. Valerius's book gives a great deal of information very concisely, usually through definition and explanation of the terms. It provides a good basis for a comprehensive course in rhetoric but a teacher would probably need to add further explanations and examples.

Matthaeus Dresser (1536–1607), humanist and doctor, professor at Erfurt and Leipzig, published two versions of his *Rhetorica inventionis, dispositionis et elocutionis* (Basel, 1567). Together the different versions of the work went through fourteen editions mainly in the 1570s and 1580s and mostly from Basel and Leipzig. The later version, first published in 1578, included books 2 and 4, entirely devoted to commented examples

[74] Valerius, *In universam bene dicendi rationem tabula* (London, 1580), sigs. B6^r, C1^r, H7^r–8^v.
[75] Ibid., sigs. E2^r–5^v.
[76] Ibid., sig. E6^r.

of different types of speech. Dresser's teaching was mostly based on Melanchthon, but with a new introductory section and with an emphasis throughout all four books on connecting the precepts of rhetoric with examples of classical and modern writing which showed how the rules should be used. In the four-book version, book 1 is devoted to invention; book 2 to commented examples of the different genres of writing described in book 1, giving background information and showing the structure and argumentative technique of the texts through footnotes and marginal notes; book 3 to style; and book 4 to examples of speeches, introducing each speech's situation, organization, genus, status, and type of style, then breaking the speech up into its parts and providing detailed commentary on all aspects of language, figures, and sentence structure. In books 1 and 3 Dresser intersperses his teaching with examples (for instance showing that Cicero's *De amicitia* and Paul's Epistle to the Romans can be considered as examples of simple invention).[77]

Dresser's *Prolegomena* shares Melanchthon's emphasis on the need to speak wisely and elegantly:

> The high point of this art and its greatest glory is to be able to judge wisely and truly about things, and to explain them eloquently, clearly, and elegantly.[78]

Like Melanchthon Dresser puts *res* first and *verba* afterwards. There are six foundations of knowledge: heavenly teaching, ethics, physics, mathematics, history, and poetry.[79] The study of eloquence helps you understand other sciences and pass them on clearly. It teaches the way to read other people's works, by attending to the structure, the arguments, and the ornaments of expression and, through that, the way of expressing yourself.[80] Dresser sets out a six-level process for reading: first you need to know the kind of case, the status, the chief proposition, and the main syllogism of the case; secondly you must consider the order of the parts; thirdly from which topics the *exordium* and the arguments of confirmation and refutation are taken; fourthly you should observe the figures, similitudes, examples, and proverbs; fifthly the best and most choice words and phrases; and sixthly the organization of sentences and use of prose-rhythm.[81] After describing suitable writing exercises he lists three aspects which make a speech most clear, strong, and effective: the relationship

[77] M. Dresser, *Rhetoricae inventionis, dispositionis et elocutionis libri quatuor* (Leipzig, 1588), sigs. K2^{v}–4^{v}.

[78] 'Summa ars est, et decus eximium, posse sapienter et vere de rebus judicare, easdemque diserte, ornate et perspicue explicare.' Ibid., sig. A8^{r}.

[79] Ibid., sig. B1^{r}.

[80] Ibid., sigs. B2^{v}–3^{r}.

[81] Ibid., sigs. C5$^{r–v}$.

between general and particular arguments (thesis and hypothesis), amplification, and the techniques for arousing emotions.[82]

Under invention, Dresser adapts Melanchthon's order of proceeding, including the topics of invention while describing the parts of the oration, before discussing the genus didascalicon and the invention of simple themes. Dresser's examples show the importance of analysing the structures of different kinds of texts. As in Melanchthon the principal structuring element is the types of case, with a thorough presentation of status-theory within the section on judicial oratory.

Within style (book 3) Dresser begins with considerations about the types of words to be employed and the dangers of archaic vocabulary[83] before proceeding through the tropes and figures in an order and using a list which resembles Melanchthon's. Dresser includes some of Melanchthon's most notable additions in *Elementa rhetorices*: the discussion of the use of allegory in the reading of scripture, the organization of the figures of amplification according to the topics, and the method of imitation.[84] Dresser supplements Melanchthon with other elements from the tradition: the use of proverbs and similars, the grammatical figures, a few additional figures in Melanchthon's groups, the vices and virtues of the different styles.[85]

A few late-century northern rhetoricians are neither Ramists nor Philippists. The *Artis dicendi praecepta* (Strasbourg, 1589), by Strasbourg professor of rhetoric Melchior Junius (1545–1604), which was printed five times up to 1607, collects observations from ancient orators (including Aristotle, Cicero, Hermogenes, and Quintilian) on a range of rhetorical subjects, such as the usefulness of eloquence, the definition of rhetoric, the kinds of cases, jokes, the virtues of style and decorum. It is almost a commonplace book of rhetoric. Junius's *Methodus eloquentiae comparandae* (1585) which was printed nine times, describes the technique of acquiring eloquence, which requires natural gifts, a firm grasp of the rules of the art, wider knowledge of other subjects, imitation, and practice in writing.[86] Junius urges pupils to begin with *Rhetorica ad Herennium* and *Partitiones oratoriae* before moving on to *De oratore*, Quintilian, Aristotle, and Hermogenes.[87] Gregor Bersman (1538–1611) in *Erotemata Rhetorices* (Leipzig, 1601), which was printed twice, sets out the subject-

82 Ibid., sig. D1^{v}.
83 Ibid., sigs. Aaa6^{r}–8^{r}.
84 Ibid., sigs. Ddd3^{r}–6^{v}, Ggg5^{v}–Lll6^{r}, Nnn1^{v}–7^{r}.
85 Ibid., sigs. Eee2^{r}–3^{v}, Eee4^{v}–5^{v}, Mmm4^{v}–Nnn1^{r}.
86 M. Junius, *Methodus eloquentiae comparandae* (Strasbourg, 1585), sig. A3^{r-v}.
87 Ibid., sigs. B8^{r}–C5^{v}.

matter of *Rhetorica ad Herennium* in a series of questions and answers, adding supporting material from other classical authorities.

Between 1580 and 1600, at a time when the production of Cicero's rhetorics had declined sharply, three traditions dominated the teaching of rhetoric and dialectic in northern Europe. Ramism was the most successful, particularly in Germany and at smaller universities at the fringes of Europe, where Ramus was often taught in versions supplemented with more traditional material. The school of Melanchthon, while definitely in a minority, continued to be productive of new ideas about teaching rhetoric and logic in the humanist tradition. The third tradition involved a revival of Aristotelian dialectic and a revival of rhetoric in the service of the Catholic Church. This third tradition, which originated in southern Europe, will be the subject of the next chapter.

8

Southern Europe in the Sixteenth Century

After around 1470 no Italian rhetoric textbook was printed or much used outside Italy. Few new rhetorical works were written, and those that were written were not printed often. But Italians raised issues which later became important throughout Europe. So Italy saw the beginnings and much of the development of the controversy about Ciceronianism; Italians were much concerned with the use of rhetoric in the *volgare* and wrote the most innovative vernacular rhetorics, most notably Bartolomeo Cavalcanti's *La retorica* (1559); Italians played the major role in working out how to use Aristotle's *Rhetoric* within a mainly Ciceronian rhetorical syllabus; they were also the first to use newly discovered texts, especially in the field of poetics, which they made their own. There is a striking contrast between the large number of influential Italian writings on poetics in the sixteenth century, by writers such as Trissino, Robortello, Vettori, Castelvetro, Piccolomini, Riccoboni, Vida, Fracastoro, Capriano, Minturno, Scaliger, and Patrizi,[1] and the lack of an important new Latin textbook on rhetoric. In the wake of the Council of Trent, Italy produced a number of deliberately restrained preaching manuals, which I shall discuss in Chapter 12, but the most successful general rhetoric textbook of the Counter-Reformation came from the Iberian peninsula, Cyprian Soarez's *De arte rhetorica libri tres* (Coimbra, 1562). The revival of scholastic logic, and the breaking up of the humanist rapprochement between rhetoric and dialectic, can also be associated with Portugal and Pedro da Fonseca's *Institutionum dialecticarum libri octo* (Lisbon, 1564).

The lack of new Italian textbooks of the whole of rhetoric may partly be explained by the position of rhetoric in Italian education. At the school level rhetoric was taught through letter-writing (in which Italian manuals continued to be printed) and through study of one of the classical Latin

[1] For bibliography on 16th-cent. Italian poetic theory see n. 51 below.

summae of rhetoric.[2] Italian schoolteachers may not have seen any need to compose new manuals of the whole subject. The new manuals which were written in the North were not printed much in Italy. In most Italian universities the arts faculty was relatively unimportant in comparison with the higher faculties. Teaching in classical literature and rhetoric was usually in the hands of one or two professors who were not required to cover a particular syllabus of texts with any frequency (as their colleagues in other subjects were, in relation to Aristotle's works) but could choose which texts to lecture on each year. The result was that key rhetoric texts were taught scarcely more often than other works of Greek and Latin literature.[3] So Italian masters tended to compose commentaries on classical texts and were more likely than their northern colleagues to lecture on unusual or newly recovered texts, such as Aristotle's *Rhetoric* and *Poetics*, Tacitus's *Dialogue on Orators* or pseudo-Longinus's *On the Sublime*. Perhaps Italian scholars felt that there was more interesting and more urgent work to do in the field of poetics.

When he lectured on Quintilian's *Institutio oratoria* in 1480, the great Florentine humanist and poet Angelo Poliziano (1454–94) used his inaugural lecture to make a strong case for the importance of studying rhetoric, though the implication of his remarks must be that such study was far from usual in fifteenth-century Italian universities.

> What, I ask, could be more outstanding than solely or greatly to excel other men, in that in which men themselves are superior to the other animals? What could be more admirable than for you, speaking to a multitude of people, so to thrust into the hearts and minds of men that you direct their wills where you want, draw them back from whence you want, that you mould their emotions either to those milder ones or to these fiercer ones, and in summary that you exercise control in the desires and wills of men's minds?... What moreover could be more useful and beneficial than to persuade them through words to those things which you find most useful and helpful to your country and to the people dearest to you, and dissuade them with reason from bad or unprofitable things?[4]

[2] P. Grendler, *Schooling in Renaissance Italy* (Baltimore, 1989), 172–229. R. Black, *Humanism and Education in Medieval and Renaissance Italy* (Cambridge, 2001), 339–41, 352–65.

[3] P. Grendler, *The Universities of the Italian Renaissance* (Baltimore, 2002), 35, 214–21, 229–39.

[4] 'Quid est, quaeso, praestabilius quam in eo te unum vel maxime praestare hominibus, in quo homines ipsi ceteris animalibus antecellant? Quid admirabilius quam te in maxima hominum multitudine dicentem, ita in hominum pectora mentesque irrumpere, ut et voluntates impellas quo velis atque unde velis retrahas, et affectus omnes vel hos mitiores, vel concitatiores illos emodereris, et in hominum denique animis volentibus cupientibusque domineris?... Quid autem tam utile tamque fructuosum est, quam quae tuae reipublicae

GIORGIO VALLA (1447–1500)

The translator, commentator and university teacher Giorgio Valla spent much of the Venetian period of his life (1485–1500) preparing his encyclopedic work *De rebus expetendis et fugiendis* (1501), which was printed only once. The section on rhetoric was printed twice separately and the section on the invention of arguments eight times, mainly in northern Europe. Valla's fourth book of grammar (book xxxiv of the whole work) includes a treatment of the tropes and the figures of speech.[5] The three books on dialectic discuss in turn the predicables and categories (book xxxv), the invention of convincing arguments, which discusses sophisms and definition but not the topics of invention (book xxxvi) and the proposition and the syllogism (book xxxvii). The first book on rhetoric (xxxix) is devoted to the five skills and the three genres. The section on style deals with the qualities of style, amplification, the three levels of style, and prose-rhythm.[6] Book xl, on the instrument of rhetoric describes the five parts of the oration (including a short account of eleven topics of invention), the writing of history, dialogues, the kinds of letters, imitation, and practice.[7] So Valla's encyclopedia organizes its rhetorical material in some new ways, but the treatment of each doctrine is too brief for a pupil to learn much without considerable help from a teacher.

IMITATION AND CICERONIANISM

Italian writers made highly influential contributions to debates about imitation and Ciceronianism.[8] In the preface to his letters Angelo Poliziano defends their eclectic style, arguing that different subjects and different recipients call for the employment of different styles.[9] In an exchange of letters with Paolo Cortesi (?1465–1510), which probably

carissimisque tibi hominibus utilia conducibiliaque inveneris, posse illa dicendo persuadere eosque ipsos a malis inutilibusque rationibus absterrere?' E. Garin (ed.), *Prosatori latini del Quattrocento* (Milan, 1952), 882.

[5] G. Valla, *De rebus expetendis et fugiendis* (Venice, 1501), ii, sigs. Aa1^r–8^r. C. Vasoli, *La dialettica e la retorica dell'Umanesimo* (Milan, 1968), 132–44.

[6] Valla, *De rebus expetendis*, ii, sigs. Hh7^v–Ii3^v. Bk xxxviii is given over to poetics.

[7] Ibid.. ii, sigs. Ii4^r–Kk3^r.

[8] In addition to the works cited below, see R. Sabbadini, *Storia di Ciceronianismo* (Turin, 1885). I. Scott, *Controversies over the Imitation of Cicero* (New York, 1910; repr. Davis, Calif., 1991).

[9] Poliziano, *Opera* (Basel, 1553), 1. G. W. Pigman III, 'Versions of Imitation in the Renaissance', *Renaissance Quarterly*, 33 (1980), 1–32.

took place in 1485, he compares those who imitate Cicero's vocabulary and sentence structure to parrots, finding their work lifeless. Style should be a way of expressing oneself.

> Someone might say, 'you do not write like Cicero'. What of that? I am not Cicero. I think I express myself.[10]

Writers should imitate any model that helps them find their own voices rather than restricting themselves to copying Cicero's words.[11] Like Erasmus, Poliziano saw Seneca as a stylistic model to pose against Cicero. Cortesi took the view that imitation was a universal principle in the arts and that Cicero, although not the only model, was the best one to choose.[12]

The question was taken up in the sixteenth century by the philosopher Gian-Francesco Pico (1470–1533) and the cardinal and writer Pietro Bembo (1470–1547). In the introduction to his collection of letters Pico defends an eclectic approach. Many different Latin styles are available to the letter-writer. For that reason it is better to read many different authors and to learn from them their particular excellences. But one should do this without losing hold of one's own natural virtues as a writer.[13] In his first letter to Bembo of 1512, Pico restates both the variety of the models available and the need to develop one's own style by imitating a range of them. He now sees this in Neoplatonic terms: the writer's innate instinct will guide him to an idea of eloquence by which he will judge all writing. This means that invention is the most important aspect of writing, the place where the writer can show originality. Arrangement and style must be suited to invention through the law of decorum. Then, like Poliziano, he attacks those who copy Cicero's words and sentence structures, pointing out the absurdity of their attempts to rewrite Cicero.[14]

[10] 'Non exprimis, inquit aliquis, Ciceronem. Quid tum? non enim sum Cicero; me tamen, ut opinor, exprimo.' Poliziano, in Garin (ed.), *Prosatori latini*, 902. J. Dellaneva (ed.), *Ciceronian Controversies* (Cambridge, Mass., 2007), 2. M. L. McLaughlin, *Literary Imitation in the Italian Renaissance* (Oxford, 1995), 187–204.

[11] *Prosatori latini*, 902–6. Dellaneva, *Ciceronian Controversies*, 4. M. Fumaroli, *L'Age de l'éloquence* (Geneva, 1980), 81–3. McLaughlin, *Literary Imitation*, 187–204.

[12] *Prosatori latini*, 906–10. Dellaneva, *Ciceronian Controversies*, 6–12. McLaughlin, *Literary Imitation*, 204–6.

[13] G. F. Pico, *Opera omnia* (Basel, 1557), 1266–7. McLaughlin, *Literary Imitation*, 253–6.

[14] G. Santangelo, *Le epistole 'De imitatione' di Giovanfrancesco Pico della Mirandola e di Pietro Bembo* (Florence, 1954), 24–38. Dellaneva, *Ciceronian Controversies*, 16–41. McLaughlin, *Literary Imitation*, 253–61.

Replying in 1513, Bembo regarded imitation as central to all forms of human activity; one cannot obtain ideas about writing except by reading and one cannot write except by modelling oneself on earlier writers. Where earlier in his career he had tried to imitate a range of writers or had tried to eschew models and write originally, he now finds that following Cicero alone is the practical way to write all types of prose. He is assisted in this by the variety within Cicero's prose, with different works offering suitable models for different types of writing.[15] As we have seen, Erasmus attacked the extreme Italian imitators of Cicero in his *Ciceronianus*. This, however, did not prevent the expansion of the project of verbal imitation of Cicero in works like *Thesaurus Ciceronianus* by Mario Nizolio (1498–1566), first published as *Observationes in M. T. Ciceronem* (Brescia, 1535), which grew into an immense concordance and lexicon of Ciceronian usage. Green and Murphy list a total of forty-three editions up to 1620, mostly produced in Venice (twenty-two editions), Basel, and Lyon. The fashion for Ciceronianism also extended to Spain.[16]

Prompted to defend his advocacy of Cicero against the critique of his friend Maioragius, Nizolio also composed a defence of rhetoric, which took up and extended many of Lorenzo Valla's criticisms of Aristotelian logic.[17] *De veris principiis* (1553) was printed only once in the sixteenth century, but it was edited by Leibniz in 1670 and printed twice in the late seventeenth century. Nizolio argues that orators employ a considerable range of logical arguments, which are in fact superior to the arguments of the dialecticians. After criticizing scholastic and Aristotelian ideas about knowledge he sets out four principles for arriving at truth: (1) a thorough knowledge of Greek and Latin; (2) a knowledge of the rules of grammar and rhetoric; (3) a careful reading of the principal authors which results in an understanding of the common meaning of words (since philosophy is inseparable from speaking well); and (4) liberty of thought and judgement in order to determine the truth of things as they are.[18] The work goes on to attack the contents of each of the books of the *Organon*, including Porphyry's *Isagoge*. Nizolio asserts the primacy of the humanistic method in its strongest possible form but, in contrast to his *Thesaurus Ciceronianus*, his attack on Aristotelian dialectic and assertion of the primacy of rhetoric had very little influence on a university system dominated by Aristotelianism.

[15] Santangelo, *Le epistole*, 39–61 (esp. 55–8). Dellaneva, *Ciceronian Controversies*, 45–89 (esp. 66–75). McLaughlin, *Literary Imitation*, 262–5.

[16] J. M. Núñez González, *El ciceronianismo en España* (Valladolid, 1993).

[17] E. Garin, *Italian Humanism* (Oxford, 1965), 157–8. Vasoli, *La dialettica*, 605–32.

[18] M. Nizolio, *De veris principiis*, ed. Q. Breen, 2 vols. (Rome, 1956), i. 22–7. Vasoli, *La dialettica*, 613–16.

Latin arguments about Ciceronianism became linked with theories about styles and appropriate models in the vernacular. The French Protestant martyr Etienne Dolet (1509–46), who composed a violent reply to Erasmus, *De imitatione Ciceroniana* (Lyon, 1535), also wrote a French treatise on translation, *La Manière de bien traduire d'une langue en autre* (1540).[19] Pietro Bembo was one of the first great stylists of sixteenth-century Tuscan prose, in his *Gli Asolani* (Venice, 1505) and *Prose della volgar lingua* (Venice, 1525).[20] In describing the ideal courtier Baldassare Castiglione (1478–1529) consciously modelled *Il libro del Cortigiano* (Venice, 1528) on Cicero's *De oratore.* He discussed the appropriate way for the courtier to express himself, adapting contemporary debates about imitation and Latin usage to the case of the vernacular. So the courtier should speak and write Tuscan, according to the standards of great writers like Petrarch and Boccaccio, but recognizing that it is a language in progress, discarding old words and coining or borrowing new where they could best aid understanding.[21] Such men defended the cultivation of Ciceronianism in Latin prose at the same time as trying to enrich the expressive potential of the vernacular. Just as fifteenth-century writers had laboured to recover the distinctions of classical Latin, now writers hoped to establish a vernacular literature as thoughtful and pointed as the classics. This connection between Ciceronianism, imitation and campaigns to promote the vernacular will be discussed in more detail in Chapter 13 below.

COMMENTARIES ON ARISTOTLE'S *RHETORIC*

Many sixteenth-century Italian scholars dedicated themselves to translating and interpreting Aristotle's *Rhetoric*. In the early years of printing the Latin translations by William of Moerbeke and especially George Trapezuntius of Crete dominated the market, with three and twenty-seven editions respectively. New Latin translations were made by Ermolao Barbaro (completed in 1479, but first printed in 1544; six editions before 1620), Marcus Antonius Maioragius (1550; eleven editions), Carlo Sigonio (1557; ten editions), Antonio Riccoboni (1577: thirteen editions), Marc Antoine Muret (who was working in Rome, 1577; four

[19] Fumaroli, *L'Age de l'éloquence,* 110–14. E. V. Telle, *L'Erasmianus sive Ciceronianus d'Etienne Dolet (1535)* (Geneva, 1974). T. Cave, *The Cornucopian Text* (Oxford, 1979), 48–55.

[20] P. Bembo, *Prose e rime,* ed. C. Dionisotti (Turin, 1966).

[21] Castiglione, *Il libro del Cortegiano,* ed. V. Cian (Florence, 1947), 1.25–39.

editions), Pietro Vettori (1592), and Emilio Porto (1598). There were also four translations into Italian, by Felice Figliucci (1548), Bernardo Segni (1549), Alessandro Piccolomini (1565), and Annibal Caro (1570). Piccolomini's translation was printed four times.[22] (In contrast, the work was not translated into French or English until the seventeenth century.) These translators and other Italians also composed a total of thirteen printed commentaries on the text. The most often printed commentaries were those by Riccoboni (eight editions) and Maioragius (five).

We must await Lawrence Green's study of renaissance commentaries on Aristotle's *Rhetoric* before we can draw firm conclusions, but his preliminary articles show that during the second half of the sixteenth century scholars exercised great ingenuity in interpreting this difficult text in the light of current understandings of the rhetorical tradition and of Aristotelian philosophy. Daniele Barbaro (1514–70) published his commentary with his uncle's Latin translation in 1544. According to Green, Barbaro thought that the main interest of Aristotle's work lay in its teaching about the passions and how to manipulate men's souls. Barbaro begins his commentary by dividing the human soul (in what looks like an adaptation of St Thomas Aquinas's view) into natural, appetitive, and mental parts. 'Rhetoric operates in the middle ground between the appetitive and mental faculties'. He tries to analyse all the fourteen emotions Aristotle describes, in terms of Aquinas's shorter list. Green calls this approach a reconceiving of Aristotle's *Rhetoric* in terms which make sense to the Italian renaissance.[23] The manuscript commentary by the Jesuit Francesco Benci (1542–94) goes even further in reorganizing Aristotle's text so that it yields a systematic account of the different kinds of audience and of the emotions appropriate to them.[24]

By contrast, Green sees Antonio Riccoboni (1541–99), whose 1587 commentary was intended to defend his 1579 edition of the Greek text with Latin translation, as attempting to reconstruct a classical model of the soul, as a basis on which to interpret Aristotle's *Rhetoric*. Riccoboni struggles to separate traditional Latin philosophical language infused with Stoic ideas from appropriate Latin equivalents for Aristotelian

[22] At first the individual books were printed separately. It appears that there were two editions in that form and two more of the work as a whole.

[23] L. Green, 'Aristotle's *Rhetoric* and Renaissance Views of the Emotions', in P. Mack (ed.), *Renaissance Rhetoric* (Basingstoke, 1994), 7–11; Green, 'Aristotle's *Rhetoric* and Renaissance Conceptions of the Soul', in G. Dahan and I. Rosier-Catach (eds.), *La Rhétorique d'Aristote: Traditions et commentaires* (Paris, 1998), 286–90.

[24] Green, 'Emotions', 13–15; Green, 'The Reception of Aristotle's *Rhetoric* in the Renaissance', in W. Fortenbaugh and D. Mirhady (eds.), *Peripatetic Rhetoric after Aristotle* (New Brunswick, NJ, 1994), 336.

ideas. To interpret Aristotle's view of the emotions he first has to explain how it differs from Stoic conceptions. He sees rhetoric as working between the sensations and the intellect. Emotion aroused in the sensitive faculty may be transferred through the *fantasia* to the intellect. Riccoboni then connects this with ideas from the *Ethics* about how dispositions and habits are formed in the senses and the intellect.[25] Green shows how Maioragius, Riccoboni, and Zabarella became involved in controversies about the meaning of the words that Aristotle had used to describe the relationship between rhetoric and dialectic and the nature of the enthymeme.[26] This effort of interpretation was not exclusively the work of Italian scholars (for example, Melanchthon, Lambinus, Sturm, and Chytraeus also produced commentaries) but the principal contributions were from Italians.

ITALIAN VERNACULAR RHETORIC

Rhetorical questions became the subject of treatises in the *volgare*. In opposition to Plato the *Dialogo della retorica* (1542) by Sperone Speroni (1500–88) upholds a place for rhetoric, as a distinctively human and civil art, persuading ordinary people and maintaining harmony in the state.[27] For him demonstrative oratory, which depicts virtue for honest purposes, is the most important type.[28] Speroni's *Dialogo* is discussed in more detail in Chapter 13 below. The Venetian nobleman and commentator on Aristotle and Vitruvius, Daniele Barbaro (1514–70) is said to have written his *Della eloquenza* (Venice, 1557), which was only printed once, when aged about 20. The dialogue between Art, Nature and the Soul begins by explaining how nature, art, and the powers of the mind can be combined in order to achieve good conduct and eloquence. This includes a discussion of the powers of the mind, the imagination, and the emotions.[29] Then, after explaining that meaning comes before expression and that an oration should be proportioned like the human body, Barbaro provides a summary of Hermogenes's *On Ideas of Style*, with examples of each of the types of style taken from Dante, Boccaccio, and Petrarch, and including

[25] Green, 'Soul', 291–3.

[26] Green, 'Aristotelian Rhetoric, Dialectic and the Traditions of Antistrophos', *Rhetorica*, 8 (1990), 5–27; Green, 'Reception', 337–45; Green, 'Emotions', 17–19.

[27] S. Speroni, *Dialogo delle lingue e dialogo della rettorica*, ed. G. De Robertis (Lanciano, 1912), 134–7. Fumaroli, *L'Age de l'éloquence*, 118–19.

[28] Speroni, *Dialogo*, 107. Meerhoff, *Rhétorique et poétique*, 82–102.

[29] Barbaro, *Della eloquenza*, in B. Weinberg (ed.), *Trattati di poetica e retorica del cinquecento*, 3 vols. (Bari, 1970), ii. 350–61.

detailed discussion of their expression.[30] The person who aims at eloquence should imitate the best writers in each style.[31]

BARTOLOMEO CAVALCANTI (1503–1562)

In 1559 Bartolomeo Cavalcanti published *La retorica*, a large-scale textbook of the whole of rhetoric in seven books in Italian. Cavalcanti was a scholar-diplomat. Exiled from Florence from 1537 for his republican opposition to the return of Medici rule, he served Pope Paul III, the Farnese family, and Siena. He began work on *La retorica* in the early 1540s, when the cardinal of Ferrara asked him to provide an Italian rhetoric, either a translation of Aristotle or a new work. He discussed problems of interpreting Aristotle's *Rhetoric* in letters to Pietro Vettori, who was preparing a Latin commentary on the text. Cavalcanti returned to his work and completed it in Padua in the late 1550s.[32] Depending neither on the five skills of the orator, nor on the parts of the oration, Cavalcanti's structure owes little to Roman models. The progression from initial definitions (book 1) through invention (books 2–4) to style and the parts of the oration (books 5–7) resembles Aristotle, but Cavalcanti treats proof before the emotions, adds an account of status theory and subdivides Aristotle's three genres. He builds an original account of rhetoric by adding Ciceronian and Hermogenean material to an Aristotelian base.

After discussing Quintilian's criticism of Aristotle's definition of rhetoric, Cavalcanti arrives at a definition which aims to preserve the most significant elements of both: 'La retorica è facoltà di parlare accommodatamente per persuadere.'[33] The first book is given over to definitions and divisions and to an explanation of the types and subtypes of rhetoric and the theory of status. Cavalcanti uses these subtypes, which reappear in books 6 and 7, to adapt the traditional three genres to modern conditions, as Erasmus had in *De conscribendis epistolis*. Thus deliberative oratory, which he calls *consultativo*, includes requests, recommendations, warnings, consolation, reconciliation, and exhortation; demonstrative oratory includes thanks, congratulation, description, and invective; while judicial includes accusation, justification, severe reprehension, and

30 Ibid. 379, 381, 382–449.
31 Ibid. 450.
32 Christine Roaf, 'Bartolomeo Cavalcanti, 1503–62: A Critical and Biographical Study', D.Phil. dissertation, Oxford, 1959, pp. i–x, 313–17, 364–78. B. Cavalcanti, *La retorica* (Pesaro, 1559), sigs +2^{r}–3^{v}. See also B. Cavalcanti, *Lettere edite e inedite*, ed. C. Roaf (Bologna, 1967).
33 Cavalcanti, *La retorica*, 11–12.

criticism (*rimproveratione*).[34] By subdividing the three classical genres into subgenres concerned with types of persuasion a sixteenth-century person might use, Cavalcanti aims to present the contemporary practical usefulness of rhetoric.

Book 2 describes the subject-matter and main headings of the three genres. He begins his account of deliberative oratory by locating it firmly in political reality, discussing eight topics on which governments consult (including war, peace, alliances, food, and laws) and the classical three types of good and bad government.[35] Cavalcanti's account of status theory here is based on Cicero and Quintilian.[36] The book ends with an analysis of the arguments made in five speeches, including Cicero's *Pro lege Manilia* and Quintilian's discussion of the declamation theme of the Theban talents.[37] Book 3 is concerned with proof, including the syllogism, the topics of invention, and the sophisms. In the absence of a vernacular treatise on logic, Cavalcanti finds it important to teach as much of the subject as is relevant here.[38] This emphasis on logic as a part of rhetoric links him with one of the main preoccupations of renaissance rhetoric. He gives the same list of topics as Boethius but his treatment is generally fresh, showing an awareness of Cicero, Boethius, and Quintilian but adding many observations and examples of his own.[39] Book 4 discusses emotions in general, particular emotions, and inartificial proofs. Cavalcanti accurately describes his approach to discussing emotions as not merely to follow the second book of Aristotle's *Rhetoric*, but to repeat what he says as clearly as possible, adding further explanations at each stage.[40]

Book 5 discusses *elocutio*, including prose-rhythm, tropes, figures of words, figures of thought, and Hermogenes's ideas of style. Cavalcanti uses Aristotle and Cicero as the basis for his remarks on sentence construction, also citing Demetrius, *On Style*. He gives examples from Cicero to illustrate the principles. He further comments that rhythm in Italian is different from that in Latin and Greek and gives some analysis of prose-rhythm and sentence composition in passages from Boccaccio.[41] He describes only seven tropes, forty-three figures of thought, and eleven figures of words. His accounts of the figures of thought and speech rely

34 Ibid. 17–24.
35 Ibid. 28–34.
36 Ibid. 59–71. Roaf, 'Cavalcanti', 330.
37 Cavalcanti, *La retorica*, 71–6.
38 Ibid. 9–10, 79–91, 110–13. Roaf, 'Cavalcanti', 367.
39 Cavalcanti, *La retorica*, 122–55.
40 Ibid. 175, 175–208.
41 Ibid. 267–8, 270, 276, 278.

heavily on Quintilian.[42] His comments on the urbane style and jokes rely on Vincenzo Maggi's treatise *De ridiculis* (1550), published with Maggi's commentary on Aristotle's *Poetics*.[43] Cavalcanti's account of ideas of style is based very closely on Hermogenes, translating the precepts, including some of the examples from Demosthenes, while adding new examples from Cicero.[44] Book 6 is concerned with *exordia* and narrative for all the different types and subtypes of oration, while book 7 discusses confirmation and confutation in these same genres and, briefly, the peroration, ending with an original section on decorum.[45] In these two books, which amount to about a third of the whole work, Cavalcanti shows how the general principles underlying, for example, the structure and aims of the *exordium*, can be applied to the speakers and audiences of the different types of oration in order to produce arguments suited to each case. He then quotes or refers to *exordia* in Livy, Demosthenes, Cicero, and other writers which show how the principles have been applied in practice to produce effective writing.[46] This section of the work, by treating each of the five parts of the oration (*exordium*, proposition or division, narrative, confirmation and confutation, conclusion) in relation to all the various subtypes makes rhetorical theory relevant to the assignments which contemporary orators are likely to face. The examples illustrate the theories in practice and provide materials which can be imitated.

In spite of being written in Italian, *La retorica* is very much a summary of classical rhetoric, with a strong basis in Aristotle but adding in doctrines from the Ciceronian tradition, Hermogenes, and renaissance rhetoric. It was printed ten times in the sixteenth century, mostly in Venice. Cavalcanti's book may be considered as parallel to the work of Segni and Piccolomini in making Aristotelian logic and rhetoric available in the vernacular.[47] He translated many passages from Cicero and other classical orators to provide examples of rhetoric in use. He took a smaller number of examples directly from Italian works by Petrarch, Boccaccio, Machiavelli, and others.[48]

[42] Roaf, 'Cavalcanti', 388, 659–63.
[43] Cavalcanti, *La retorica*, 314–29. Roaf, 'Cavalcanti', 383–6.
[44] Cavalcanti, *La retorica*, 329–58.
[45] Ibid. 550–63.
[46] e.g. ibid. 363–8.
[47] Roaf, 'Cavalcanti', 367, 398.
[48] Ibid. 347–55, 664–81.

The use of Aristotle and Hermogenes in these vernacular works shows that Greek rhetoric was becoming more widely available in the sixteenth century. The work of Hermogenes was also taken up by Spanish rhetoricians.[49] Sixteenth-century Italian works on poetry, which drew on the Latin commentaries being written on Aristotle's *Poetics* and Horace's *Ars poetica*, began to make an impression on rhetorical works, especially in areas of shared interest, such as imitation, decorum, character and style. The first edition of pseudo-Longinus's *On the Sublime* was edited in 1552 by Francesco Robortello (1516–67), who had commented on Aristotle's *Poetics* a few years earlier. Demetrius, *On Style,* was first printed in Florence in 1542, edited by Piero Vettori (1499–1585), who also edited and commented on Aristotle's *Rhetoric.*[50] The field of sixteenth-century Italian renaissance literary criticism is too vast to be surveyed here but it is clear that issues in poetics began to influence commentators and authors of textbooks on rhetoric.[51]

With *On the Sublime*, for example, it is easy to see how the anonymous author's comments on amplification, imitation, *enargeia*, word-arrangement, and sentence composition could be absorbed into rhetoric teaching.[52] The book makes many fine observations on the effect of figures like interrogatio, asyntedon, anaphora, polysyntedon, hyperbaton, polyptoton, periphrasis, metaphor, and hyperbole, with excellent analysis of Greek examples.[53] Many of the remarks are addressed to the situation of the orator, and several of the examples are taken from Demosthenes.[54] If the observations of pseudo-Longinus were absorbed into rhetoric teaching in late sixteenth-century Italy, as seems likely, it must have been through commentaries and lectures on classical texts, as Italian scholars like Robortello and Vettori did not write new textbooks of the whole of rhetoric. In a similar way, comments from Dionysius of Halicarnassus, *On the Arrangement of Words,* could easily be drawn on or adapted in

[49] A. Lulio, *De oratione libri VII* (Basel, 1558).

[50] L. D. Reynolds and N. G. Wilson, *Scribes and Scholars*, 2nd edn. (Oxford, 1974), 149. Fumaroli, *L'Age de l'éloquence*, 164–8, 493–4, 496.

[51] D. Aguzzi-Barbagli, 'Humanism and Poetics', in A. Rabil (ed.), *Renaissance Humanism: Foundations, Forms and Legacy*, 3 vols. (Philadelphia, 1988), iii. 85–169. M. T. Herrick, *The Fusion of Horatian and Aristotelian Criticism 1531–1555* (Urbana, Ill., 1946). B. Weinberg, *A History of Literary Criticism in the Italian Renaissance*, 2 vols. (Chicago, 1961). B. Hathaway, *The Age of Criticism: The Late Renaissance in Italy* (Ithaca, NY, 1962). G. Norton (ed.), *The Cambridge History of Literary Criticism*, iii. *The Renaissance* (Cambridge, 1999).

[52] [Longinus], *On the Sublime* 11–15, 39–40.

[53] Ibid. 17–32, 38.

[54] e.g. ibid. 12.3, 15.1, 15.8, 16.

discussions of Latin sentence composition. By the early seventeenth century, we find references to all these works in the rhetoric textbooks by Keckermann, Vossius, and Caussin, discussed in the next chapter.

IBERIAN RHETORIC

The Catholic Church's response to the Reformation through the Council of Trent (1545–63) prompted changes in the teaching and practice of rhetoric, spreading out from Rome and the Hispanic peninsula. The Society of Jesus, recognized by Pope Paul III in 1540, gave an important place in the educational system which was its central institution to learning classical languages, rhetoric, and logic. St Ignatius Loyola was in Paris, together with many of his earliest followers, during the years 1528–35, when Sturm and Latomus brought logic and rhetoric together to make both subjects serve the analysis of texts. The Counter-Reformation generally promoted a revival of traditional Aristotelian philosophy as a preparation for reading St Thomas but the Jesuits maintained their interest in rhetoric, particularly in a rhetoric strengthened with logic.

The Council of Trent recognized the necessity of preaching and promoted a restrained Christian eloquence based on the example of the Church Fathers, and especially St Augustine, rather than on Cicero. Marc Fumaroli has shown how a group of preachers connected with St Carlo Borromeo (1538–84), cardinal-archbishop of Milan, developed a theory of preaching based more on inspiration than on rhetorical art, which called for a restrained style in keeping with Christian humility.[55] I shall examine some examples of their work in Chapter 12 below. In contrast to the Borromeans, Jesuit education remained more open to Ciceronian influences.

In the early and middle sixteenth century it was common for promising pupils from Spain and Portugal to be sent to Paris to complete their university education. Prominent Iberian humanists like Andrea de Gouveia worked in France. Spanish control of the Netherlands led some Spanish humanists to teach and publish in Louvain and Antwerp. The result was that the doctrines of Erasmus and the other northern humanists were more widely diffused in Spain and Portugal than in Italy.[56] Agricola's *De inventione dialectica* was printed in Burgos, while Ringelbergius's *Rhetorica*

[55] Fumaroli, *L'Age de l'éloquence*, 135–52.
[56] M. Bataillon, *Erasme et l'Espagne* (Paris, 1937), repr. and enlarged (Geneva, 1991).

appeared in Coimbra.[57] At least twelve Spanish and two Portuguese humanists published rhetoric textbooks in the sixteenth century, though most were printed only once. Among them we might notice Alonso García Matamoros's *De ratione dicendi* (1548), which was printed three times, Francisco Sánchez de las Brozas, *De arte dicendi* (1556), printed three times and *Organum dialecticum seu rhetoricum* (1579), printed four times (both discussed in Chapter 7 above), and Benito Arias Montano's *Rhetoricorum libri quatuor* (1569) composed in Latin hexameters.[58] Even Ramism made an impression on Spanish universities.[59] Belmiro Fernandes Pereira has described the impact on renaissance Portugal from Paris of both humanist approaches to rhetoric and dialectic, and scholastic logic.[60]

CYPRIAN SOAREZ (1524–1593)

Cyprian Soarez wrote *De arte rhetorica libri tres* (Coimbra, 1562) which was the most successful rhetoric textbook of the second half of the sixteenth century and the most published textbook of the whole of rhetoric produced in southern Europe during the renaissance. Soarez joined the Society of Jesus in 1549, teaching rhetoric at their schools in Lisbon (from 1553) and Coimbra (from 1555) for seven years before going on to teach scripture, having taken his theology degree. He was prefect of studies and rector of the college of Braga until his retirement in 1580. The second edition of his book (Venice, 1565) was revised by Peter Perpinian (1530–66) who was Soarez's colleague at Lisbon and Coimbra, teaching the humanities class which preceded Soarez's class in rhetoric,

[57] G. C. Huisman, *Rudolph Agricola: A Bibliography* (Nieuwkoop, 1985), no. 64. B. Fernandes Pereira, 'A edição conimbricense da *Rhetorica* de Joachim Ringelberg', *Peninsula,* 1 (2004), 201–13.

[58] A. Martí, *La preceptiva retórica española en el Siglo de Oro* (Madrid, 1972). J. Rico Verdú, *Le retórica española de los siglos XVI y XVII* (Madrid, 1973), 43–245. L. López Grigera, *La retórica en la España del Siglo de Oro* (Salamanca, 1994). L. Alburquerque García, *El arte de hablar en público: Seis retóricas famosas* (Madrid, 1995). J. Fernández López, 'Rhetorical Theory in Sixteenth-Century Spain: A Critical Survey', *Rhetorica,* 20 (2002), 133–48. B. Fernandes Pereira, *Retórica e Eloquência em Portugal na época do Renascimento* (Coimbra, 2005), 550–84 (António Pinheiro's commentary on Quintilian), 675–727 (Tomé Correia). The Spanish texts are edited on a CD-Rom, *Retóricas españolas del siglo XVI escritas en latín*, ed. M. Garrido Gallardo (Madrid, 2003), which unfortunately I have not seen.

[59] A. Martín Jiménez, 'Rhetoric, Dialectic, and Literature in the Work of Francisco Sánchez, *El Brocense*', *Rhetorica,* 13 (1995), 43–59. J.-C. Moisan, 'Les Rhétoriques de Francisco Sánchez de Las Brozas et le système Ramiste', in Meerhoff and Moisan (eds.), *Autour de Ramus* (Quebec, 1997), 195–216.

[60] B. Fernandes Pereira, *Retórica e Eloquência em Portugal na época do Renascimento* (Coimbra, 2005).

before being summoned to teach rhetoric at the Society's Roman College from 1561, eventually moving to Lyon (1565) and then Paris (1566).[61]

In its composition and its earliest circulation, *De arte rhetorica* was associated with the Jesuit schools, which were established throughout Europe and in many overseas missions. *De arte rhetorica* was intended for use as a summary of rhetoric in the humanities class (fourth year). The first three years provide a graded course in Latin and Greek grammar, working through the grammar of Emanuele Alvarez in sequence and a group of easier Latin texts (Cicero's letters, *De amicitia*, *De senectute*, the easier poems of Ovid, Ovid's *Heroides*, selections from Catullus, Tibullus, Virgil's *Eclogues*, *Aeneid* 5 and 7) with a little Greek literature (Aesop, Chrysostom, and Agapetus).[62] The fourth year, or humanities class, was intended to complete pupils' knowledge of the properties and richness of the Latin language and prepare for rhetoric. They read Cicero's moral philosophy, Caesar, Sallust, Livy, and Curtius, and, for poetry, Virgil's *Eclogues*, *Aeneid* 4, selections from Horace's *Odes* and from the epigrammatists. They read the summary of rhetoric in Soarez's *De arte rhetorica libri tres*, with particular attention to the tropes and figures and to prose-rhythm. They studied the application of rhetoric by analysing Cicero's *Pro lege Manilia*, *Pro Archia,* and *Pro Marcello*. The teacher was instructed to comment on the usage and etymology of individual words, to pick out elegant expressions and passages for imitations, and to show how the rules of rhetoric are observed in the speeches.[63]

The aim of the fifth year or rhetoric class was perfect eloquence in oratory and poetry. Pupils studied the rhetorical works of Cicero, Cicero's speeches, Aristotle's *Rhetoric* and, on occasion also his *Poetics*. For Latin style they were taught to imitate Cicero alone. The teacher was instructed to explain each of the rules of rhetoric, citing the opinions of other rhetoricians where appropriate. He had to give reasons for the rule and cite and explain examples from Latin literature illustrating the use of the rule in practice. Finally he was meant to show how the rule could be adapted to present-day circumstances, giving the most elegant examples possible. In commenting on the texts of the orators and poets the teacher is told to explain the meaning of the passage, issues of invention, disposition, and style, and the use of topics to persuade, embellish, and move. He had to pick out the tropes and figures of speech and give parallels from

[61] L. J. Flynn SJ, 'The *De arte rhetorica* (1568) of Cyprian Soarez S.J.: A Translation with Introduction and Notes', Ph.D. thesis, University of Florida, 1955, pp. 55–87.

[62] A. Bianchi (ed.), *Ratio atque institutio studiorum Societatis Iesu* (Milan, 2002), 302–6, 296–8, 288–90, 246, 102.

[63] Ibid. 278–88.

other authors both for the subject and the words employed. Finally he was supposed to discuss the propriety, elegance, harmony, and variety of the words chosen.[64]

De arte rhetorica served as an introduction to a very broad course on rhetoric, including the most important classical authorities and several examples of the classical precepts in use. It may well have conditioned the way in which Jesuit teachers and their pupils understood rhetoric as a whole, but particular doctrines omitted (such as a detailed account of emotional persuasion) would very likely have been made good later in the course. It only became an official part of the *Ratio Studiorum* in 1599 but it must have been tried out in many Jesuit schools in Spain, Italy, Germany, and France before that.[65] It was a requirement of the Jesuit schools that pupils had to study rhetoric before moving on to philosophy and theology.[66] Between 1562 and 1620 *De arte rhetorica* was printed a total of seventy-eight times, most often from Cologne, Venice, Paris, Lyon, Brescia, Rome, and Ingolstadt. Including abbreviated versions there were a further fifty-one editions between 1621 and 1700 and the work continued to be reprinted throughout the eighteenth century. There were seven editions in the 1560s, seventeen in the 1570s, seventeen in the 1580s, twelve in the 1590s, sixteen in the 1600s, and nine between 1610 and 1620.

De arte rhetorica aims to provide a survey of the whole of rhetoric, setting out all the major doctrines in a clear and simple way, using Cicero's own words where possible, and providing examples of the doctrines in use, mostly from Cicero's speeches. The shape of the work is original but some of the introductory material included suggests that Soarez absorbed some lessons from northern humanist rhetoric and dialectic, from Agricola, Erasmus, Melanchthon, and perhaps even Ramus. Certainly he attends to Cicero's *De oratore, Partitiones,* and *Orator*, Quintilian, and Aristotle's *Rhetoric*, as well as to *De inventione* and *Rhetorica ad Herennium*.

When one considers the clarity and naturalness of the structure Soarez has produced using the traditional divisions of the subject, it is a little surprising to reflect that no one had hit on this arrangement before. The impact of Aristotle is felt mainly in the opening sections, for example in the explanations that rhetoric is an art and that unlike the other arts rhetoric and dialectic have no subject-matter of their own, and in the way of distinguishing between the three types of oratory. Like Aristotle, Soarez divides the oration into four parts (*exordium*, narration, confirmation,

64 Ibid. 264–72.
65 Flynn, 'Soarez', 23–8, 44–5. Bianchi, *Ratio Studiorum*, 264–72, 278–88.
66 Bianchi, *Ratio Studiorum*, 92, 116–18.

Table 8.1. Plan of Soarez, *De arte rhetorica*

Bk/Ch.	Contents	Pages
1	INTRODUCTION, INVENTION, TOPICS, EPIDEICTIC, DELIBERATIVE	
1–4	Rhetoric, its usefulness and subject-matter (questions)	4^{r}–5^{v}
5	Three kinds of rhetoric	5^{v}–6^{r}
6	Employing the general issue (thesis) in specific cases	6
7	Five skills of rhetoric	6^{v}–7^{r}
8–11	Nature, art, practice, imitation	7^{r}–10^{r}
12–14	Invention	10^{r}–11^{r}
15–32	Topics of invention and their use in argument	11^{r}–18^{v}
33–41	Using the topics for amplification and emotions	18^{v}–22^{v}
42–49	Demonstrative oratory: praise of persons and cities	22^{v}–26^{v}
50–56	Topics of deliberative oratory	26^{v}–30^{v}
2	ARRANGEMENT, STATUS-THEORY, FORMS OF ARGUMENTATION	
1	On disposition	31
2–7	*Exordium*	31^{v}–34^{v}
8–9	Narration	35
10	Confirmation	35^{v}–36^{r}
11–15	Using status-theory	36^{r}–38^{v}
16–24	Syllogism, enthymeme, induction, example, epicheireme, sorites and dilemma	38^{v}–44^{v}
25–6	Confutation	44^{v}–45^{v}
27	Peroration	45^{v}–47^{r}
3	STYLE, MEMORY, DELIVERY	
1–7	Style and its components	47^{v}–50^{r}
8–21	Tropes	50^{r}–57^{r}
22–9	Figures of words: repetition, omission, similarity	57^{r}–65^{v}
30	Figures of thought	65^{v}–72^{v}
31–50	Sentence construction and prose-rhythm	72^{v}–85^{v}
51	Three levels of style	85^{v}–87^{r}
52–5	Memory	87^{r}–89^{r}
56–8	Delivery	89^{r}–90^{v}

conclusion).[67] Although Soarez mentions the emotions prominently, he does not give a full Aristotelian analysis of the different types of emotion and the way of arousing each. The emphasis on the limitations of art without talent and practice, the early discussion of thesis and hypothesis, the inclusion of imitation,[68] the interest in the role of the topics in amplification, and the post-positioning of the three levels of style all

[67] Soarez, *De arte rhetorica* (Venice, 1568), 31^{v}.

[68] The section on imitation was added by Perpinian; the first four sentences are based on Cicero's own words at *De oratore* 2.89, 90, 92, 95, and 96. Soarez, *De arte rhetorica*, 9^{v}–10^{r}.

resemble Melanchthon's rhetorics, but several of Melanchthon's characteristic doctrines (e.g. the didascalic genre, the simple form of invention, the figures of amplification) are missing and the treatment of status theory is quite different. Soarez resembles the northern humanists in the prominence he gives within rhetoric to the topics of invention and the forms of argumentation, in his understanding of the links between the topics and emotional persuasion (an Agricolan theme), and in his understanding of amplification as involving discovering subject-matter as much as words (Agricola and Erasmus). While he sees his rhetoric as part of the Jesuits' linguistic training and avoids Christian examples, in his preface he urges Christians to purify rhetoric by avoiding the deceitfulness, aggressiveness, and pride characteristic of pagan oratory. He praises the example of Christian orators, such as Sts Gregory, Basil, John Chrysosotom, Ambrose, Augustine, Jerome, and Cyprian.[69]

Soarez's informed selection of the clearest classical definitions for each doctrine reveals his breadth of knowledge of classical Latin rhetoric. While the first few definitions privilege *De inventione*, he also selects from Quintilian, *Partitiones oratoriae*, *De oratore,* and *Rhetorica ad Herennium.* Most of the definitions of tropes and figures are taken from Quintilian and *Ad Herennium*, while he prefers *Topica* for the sixteen topics and *Orator* for prose-rhythm. For each doctrine he chooses examples from Cicero's orations which show how the teaching can be used in practice. For example, there is an excellent selection of Cicero's openings to illustrate the different aspects of the *exordium.*[70]

Soarez shows his practicality by adding sections on the use of each major doctrine and by emphasizing the need for the writer to choose among the many possibilities which the teachings of rhetoric will provide. For example Soarez gives a very general outline of the theory of status, restricting himself to explaining how one discovers the principal question at stake, what the types of status are (conjectural, definitive, and qualitative, subdivided into absolute and assumptive, adding a small group of lines of argument related to written documents)[71] and explaining the meaning of the terms *ratio* (line of defence), *firmamentum* (supporting argument), and *iudicatio* (point for decision), but he justifies this inclusion by explaining the usefulness of the doctrine of status. Knowing the point at which all the arguments should be directed will enable the orator to choose from the arguments he has found through the topics, and to place

[69] Soarez, *De arte rhetorica*, 3^{r}.

[70] Ibid. 31^{r}–34^{v}.

[71] Ambiguity, difference between letter and spirit, conflicting documents, and *ratiocinatio* (analogous laws). Ibid. 37^{v}–38^{r}.

the arguments most likely to succeed at the beginning and end of the confirmation, leaving some of the less conclusive arguments for the middle.[72]

At the end of his discussion of argumentation Soarez points out the need to avoid presenting a speech with too many arguments expressed directly in the forms of argumentation. The orator will not want the speech to become overloaded with syllogisms and enthymemes but will try to break them up and to express some of the arguments in a more expansive and attractive way. Arguments which are effectively embellished are more likely to persuade an audience.[73] Soarez gives considerable attention to demonstrative oratory because of its usefulness in other kinds of writing, neglecting specialized aspects of classical judicial oratory because the rules for trials have changed so much.[74]

While Soarez is properly attentive to invention and organization, he devotes far more space to style, to a full account of fifteen tropes, nineteen figures of speech (subdivided into figures of addition, subtraction, and similarity), and twenty-five figures of thought. He notes that there is no agreement on the number of the figures, claiming he has steered a middle path between the expansive and the restrictive.[75] For each figure he generally gives a definition and a group of examples, avoiding the advice on the use of particular figures which is sometimes found in his main sources, Quintilian and *Rhetorica ad Herennium*. Soarez is especially full on sentence construction and on prose-rhythm. Throughout the work he focuses attention on emotional persuasion.[76] His teaching insists on the power and richness of Ciceronian oratory. While Christianity must purify morally questionable aspects of rhetoric, Soarez does not believe that Christian rhetoric should restrict itself to simple teaching in the plain style.

Soarez's *De arte rhetorica* is an excellent example of the clarity and thoroughness of teaching which Jesuit methods of organization could achieve. Although it aimed mainly to introduce concepts which would later be studied more thoroughly through analysis of the classical texts, it probably exerted a much greater long-term influence than that role implies, encouraging Jesuits to understand language both in terms of a logical underpinning and as offering opportunities for elaborate and emotionally forceful expression.

[72] Soarez, *De arte rhetorica*, II.15: 'Quomodo status tractetur', 38^{v}.
[73] Soarez, *De arte rhetorica*, II.26: 'Quomodo sint argumentationes oratoriae tractandae', 45^{r-v}.
[74] Soarez, *De arte rhetorica*, 22^{v}–23^{r}, 30^{r-v}.
[75] Ibid. 58^{r}.
[76] Ibid., e.g. 10^{r}, 18^{v}–22^{v}, 31^{v}–34^{v}, 45^{v}–47^{r}, 48^{r}.

REVIVAL OF SCHOLASTIC DIALECTIC: FONSECA

Under Jesuit influence new logic manuals of the later sixteenth century promoted a swing away from humanist dialectic and back towards scholasticism, which we find in some university syllabuses of the time, especially in Catholic countries. The *Institutionum dialecticarum libri octo* (Lisbon, 1564) by Portuguese Jesuit philosopher Pedro da Fonseca (1528–99) was printed twenty-nine times before 1620 throughout Catholic Europe. He presents a clear exposition of the whole syllabus of scholastic logic, leavened with occasional quotations from Cicero.

> Therefore Dialectic is most fittingly defined as the science of reasoning, for it is the art which teaches all forms of reasoning, that is of discovering the unknown from the known through language.[77]

Fonseca's eight books centre on the Aristotelian syllabus but include many of the medieval accretions which humanist Aristotelians had rejected.

The strictly scholastic material is mostly concentrated in books 1 and 8. The version of the topics provided in book 7 is taken from Boethius's *De differentiis topicis*. Fonseca makes a gesture towards humanist logic when he points out that the topics (especially definition, description, enumeration of parts, consequences, circumstances, and comparisons) are often used as much for amplification of material as for discovering persuasive arguments.[78] The list of topics suggests that he may have in mind

Table 8.2. Plan of Fonseca, *Institutionum dialecticarum libri VIII*

Bk	Contents
1	Definition, division, signification: sounds, words, concrete and abstract, transcendentals, first and second imposition
2	Universals, predicables, categories
3	Propositions, simple and modal, the square of oppositions
4	Division
5	Definition
6	Consequences, argumentation, syllogism, enthymeme, induction, example
7	Demonstration, the topics (including maxims), use of the topics
8	Sophisms, supposition, ampliation, restriction, appellation

[77] 'Aptissime igitur definitur Dialectica disserendi doctrina, quasi ars, quae docet omnes formulas disserendi, hoc est, incognita ex cognitis oratione patefaciendi.' Fonseca, *Institutionum dialecticarum libri octo* (Lisbon, 1564), sig. A2^{v}.

[78] Ibid., sigs Bb4^{v}–5^{r}.

Erasmus's *copia* of things, though he does not mention him. He also notes that the tropes of rhetoric are derived from the topics, which looks like an allusion to Ramus.[79] Furthermore Fonseca adds sections on the ordering of deliberative and demonstrative orations and praises dialectical analysis of authors as a way of practising dialectic.[80] These humanist touches are only a small part of a clearly written but resolutely traditional logic textbook, whose content resembles Peter of Spain's *Tractatus* more than any renaissance dialectic textbook.

In the late sixteenth century the impact of the revival of scholastic logic was felt throughout Europe, for example in Oxford. John Case's *Summa veterum interpretum in universam dialecticam Aristotelis* (London, 1584), based on his teaching at Oxford, went through seven editions (four from Frankfurt) prior to 1620.[81] Organizing his teaching as if it were a series of disputations, Case upholds the scholastic interpretation of Aristotle against Ramus, while acknowledging humanist interest in the use of arguing. He denies that logic is a speculative science (contrary to the scholastics) and agrees with the humanist dialecticians that it consists of invention and judgement.[82] He gives most attention to the predicables and categories, also including treatises on demonstration and the sophisms and a version of the topics based on Boethius which nonetheless praises Agricola.[83]

Criticism of the cult of Cicero, from Erasmians as well as from Counter-Reformation preachers, led in the second half of the sixteenth-century to the promotion of Senecanism (sometimes also known as Taciteanism) as an alternative ideal of Latin style. The theoreticians of this style were Justus Lipsius (1547–1606), Guillaume Du Vair (1556–1621), and, on some accounts, Marc-Antoine Muret (1526–85). Its major practitioners were Lipsius, Montaigne, Guez de Balzac, Quevedo, and Bacon.[84] According to Croll the major features of the style were: 'studied brevity of members; hovering, imaginative order,

[79] Ibid., sig. Bb5^{v}.

[80] Ibid., sigs. Bb8^{v}–Cc2^{v}, Cc7^{r-v}.

[81] J. W. Binns, *Intellectual Culture in Elizabethan and Jacobean England* (Leeds, 1990), 366–77.

[82] Case, *Summa veterum interpretum* (London, 1584), sigs. A3^{r}–b1^{r}.

[83] Ibid., sigs. Dd1^{v}, 2^{v}, Ee1^{r}, Ii4^{r}–Kk1^{v}, Ll3^{v}.

[84] M. W. Croll, *Style, Rhetoric and Rhythm*, ed. J. Patrick *et al.* (Princeton, 1966), 1–233, a collection of five essays originally publ. between 1914 and 1929. Fumaroli, *L'Age de l'éloquence*, 92–109, 152–76. C. Mouchel, *Cicéron et Sénèque dans la rhétorique de la Renaissance* (Marburg, 1990), 145–235, with special attention to Pasquali, J.-C. Scaliger, Lipsius, and Lipsius's followers. J. Kraye, 'Senecanismus', in G. Ueding (ed.), *Historisches Wörterbuch der Rhetorik*, viii (Tübingen, 2007), 826–41.

asymmetry and the omission of the ordinary syntactic ligatures'.[85] Fumaroli writes of an avoidance of ornament and prose-rhythm and a penchant for discontinuity, the low style, the spontaneous, and the incomplete.[86] Lipsius's letter-writing manual, *De conscribendis latine epistolis* (Frankfurt, 1591) will be discussed in Chapter 11 below.

Sixteenth-century Italians did not produce a Latin *summa* of rhetoric, though Cavalcanti wrote an excellent one in Italian. But they made important contributions in some parts of the subject: the debate about Ciceronianism, the understanding of Aristotle's *Rhetoric* and the absorption of the doctrines of Greek rhetoric more generally, poetics, and Senecanism. There is some evidence in the later sixteenth century of Ciceronian rhetoric losing ground within the educational system and of a revival of scholastic logic. Paul Grendler believes that humanism was in decline in Italian universities after 1575.[87] In contrast to this the Jesuits continued to emphasize the importance of Ciceronian rhetoric. Soarez's *De arte rhetorica* provided a clear and straightforward introduction to the reading of classical rhetoric texts which found a place for humanist innovations. By emphasizing the topics of invention and the forms of argumentation it recognized the link between rhetoric and dialectic. Its many illustrative examples responded to Melanchthon's stress on the practical application of the rules. It focused appropriately on the figures and tropes (and on prose-rhythm), while acknowledging the humanist emphasis on amplification and emotion. Soarez's intelligent adaptation of the traditional arrangement of the textbook enabled him to make appropriate use of the 'new' Latin rhetorics discovered in the fifteenth century and take some notice of Greek rhetoric.

While recognizing the impact of Borromeanism and Lipsius's version of Senecanism within late sixteenth-century Catholic culture, Marc Fumaroli has described a new Ciceronianism and a Christian sublime, promoted by Counter-Reformation writers and especially by the Jesuits. He convincingly associates this Christian grand style with baroque art and architecture.[88] His prime example is Nicholas Caussin's *Eloquentiae sacrae et humanae parallela libri XVI* (Paris, 1619), which I shall discuss in the next chapter as one of the large new syntheses of rhetoric published at the beginning of the seventeenth century. This group of new rhetoric textbooks, which also includes works by Keckermann and Vossius, absorbed the lessons of Greek rhetoric, and proposed a new role for rhetoric in the seventeenth century.

[85] Croll, 'The Baroque Style in Prose', *Style, Rhetoric and Rhythm*, 214.
[86] Fumaroli, *L'Age de l'éloquence*, 147–8, 155.
[87] Grendler, *Italian Universities*, 248.
[88] Fumaroli, *L'Age de l'éloquence*, 162–272.

9

New Syntheses 1600–1620

Keckermann, Vossius, and Caussin

Three large textbooks of the whole of rhetoric, which were produced in the first two decades of the new century, collected, summarized, and redirected the work in rhetoric of the previous two centuries. All three absorbed Aristotle's *Rhetoric* and other Greek rhetorical works, but in different ways. Keckermann used Greek rhetoric to enrich a Ciceronian framework and an approach based on the ideas of the major northern rhetoricians, Agricola, Erasmus, and Melanchthon. By contrast Vossius added an account of style which combined Latin and Greek authorities to three books based on Aristotle's *Rhetoric*. Caussin enriched an essentially Ciceronian structure and approach with lessons derived from his wide reading in the theory and practice of oratory before arguing that Chrysostom offers an appropriately magnificent model for a revival of Christian eloquence. All three gave great emphasis to style and emotion, and included additional types of deliberative and epideictic rhetoric. Only Vossius's doubly shortened *Elementa rhetoricae* (1626) was printed very often and even that had nowhere near the number of editions of Talon, Soarez, or Melanchthon.

BARTHOLOMAEUS KECKERMANN (1571–1609)

Bartholomaeus Keckermann was born into a Danzig Calvinist family and studied at the local gymnasium. He matriculated at Wittenberg in 1590, moving to Heidelberg around 1592, when non-Lutherans were expelled. In Heidelberg he followed an Aristotelian syllabus and was taught by pupils of the Paduan Aristotelian Zabarella (1533–89). After taking the MA in 1595 he taught logic in Heidelberg while pursuing his studies in theology, becoming professor of Hebrew in 1600 and publishing his *Rhetoricae ecclesiasticae* (1600). In 1602 he accepted a well-paid post in the *gymnasium illustre* at Danzig. There he taught and published a three-year course in philosophy (including separate works on mathematics, physics, astronomy, geography, metaphysics, politics, and ethics), alongside his theological studies, and also composed his immense *Systema Rhetoricae* (1606). Overwork drove him to an early death.[1]

Although he was a convinced Aristotelian he recognized that many students needed a more rapid philosophical grounding than the traditional survey of Aristotelian texts could provide. This led him to compose substantial textbooks to present subjects complete. His books were typically divided into *Praecognita*, which explained the nature and use of the subject and outlined its divisions, and *Systema*, which covered all the doctrines of the subject through rules (*Canones*) and commentary.[2] Logic is also subdivided into *Systema*, which sets out the rules, and *Gymnasium*, which shows how they work in practice.

Keckermann defines logic as the art of directing the mind to the knowledge of things.[3] He divides logic into three parts: the idea of simple thoughts (corresponding to the categories and definition), the idea of complex thought (the proposition), and discourse (syllogism and method).[4] The first book covers words, the predicables, the categories, the four causes, subject and accident, whole and part, and 'external terms', along with definition, division, identity, distinction, and opposition. This can be thought of as a version of the list of topics but Keckermann presents it in a strongly metaphysical way, investigating the nature of things and using a good deal of scholastic technical terminology. He makes frequent reference to Zabarella and occasional reference to Melanchthon and Vives, but there is no discussion of invention of arguments. The treatment of the proposition is very traditional. Keckermann is very thorough on the rules of the syllogism and the treatment of method is strictly Aristotelian.

Gymnasium logicum (1605), on the use and practice of logic, insists in a properly humanist way that, since logic is an art, understanding of it must come about through observation of examples. In no art is practice so necessary as in logic.[5] Book 1 provides principles of the use of logic and a history. Book 2 shows, with examples, how a range of logical forms can be composed: simple themes, complex themes, internal disputations (following

[1] H. Hotson, *Commonplace Learning* (Oxford, 2007), 136–42, 153–6. J. Freedman, 'The Career and Writings of Bartholomew Keckermann', *Proceedings of the American Philosophical Society*, 141 (1997), 305–64.

[2] Hotson, *Commonplace Learning*, 146–51.

[3] 'Logica est ars dirigendi mentem in cognitione rerum.' Keckermann, *Systema logicae* (Geneva, 1602), sig. A1^r.

[4] Ibid., sig. A2 ^{r}.

[5] Keckermann, *Gymnasium logicum* (London, 1606), sigs. A4^v, A8^r.

Vives), disputations with other people, methodically organized treatises, schemes of teaching, commonplaces. Book 3 describes textual analysis at different levels, working from biblical texts: analysing the way in which a simple theme has been developed, looking at ways in which arguments have been found to support a proposition, and showing how a longer work has been organized according to the principles of method. There were twenty editions of the *Systema logicae* up to 1620, twelve of them from Hanau, and four editions of the *Gymnasium logicum*.[6]

Keckermann's *Systema Rhetoricae* is divided into two three-book sections: general rhetoric and special rhetoric. General rhetoric covers the five skills of the orator, putting the emphasis on invention and style. Special rhetoric discusses the ways of writing for particular audiences. Books 2 and 3 provide advice on reading, practice, and imitation, and categories for judging texts. This work was printed four times up to 1620.

Keckermann defines rhetoric, which is the same as eloquence, as 'the art of composing and delivering an oration in order to inform people and move their souls'.[7] Where logic is mainly concerned with human knowledge and aims to teach things fully, clearly, and methodically, the orator must consider the circumstances of the people involved with practical understanding and must choose arguments to explain or prove something which can be understood by the audience and which can move and please their hearts.[8] Rhetoric is above all concerned with particular audiences and especially with their emotions.

> The main object of eloquence is the will and emotions of man. For the orator will be concerned mainly with the heart, with the aim of moving it and exciting it with different emotions.[9]

This focus on individual audiences and on emotion indicates that, however necessary it is pedagogically to understand the principles set out in the five skills, the most important concerns of rhetoric are included under special rhetoric and particularly in its first book.

[6] Freedman, 'Career and Writings', 340–3. Freedman lists two different versions of the *Systema logicae*.

[7] 'Rhetorica est ars orationis conformandae et habendae, ad popularem notitiam et commotionem animorum.' Keckermann, *Systema Rhetoricae* (Hanau, 1608), sig. A1^{r}.

[8] 'Nam Logica principaliter respicit mentem ac notitiam humanam, eamque vult plene, perspicue et methodice de rebus docere . . . Orator vero prudenter respicit ac considerat circumstantias personarum, atque ea argumenta solummodo ad explicandum aut probandum rem deligit, quae possint intelligi ac capi ab auditoribus, quaeque auditorum corda possint movere et delectare.' Ibid., sig. A2^{r}.

[9] 'Principale obiectum eloquentiae est hominis voluntas et affectus. Praecipue enim orator respicit ad cor, ut illud commoveat et vario affectu concitet.' Ibid., sig. A2^{v}.

Table 9.1. Plan of Keckermann, *Systema Rhetoricae*

Bk/chs,		Pages
	General Rhetoric	
1	ON HANDLING THE SUBJECTS OF RHETORIC	1–173
1	Nature, object, aim and parts of rhetoric	1
2–6	Invention of simple and complex themes	12
7–8	Amplification and exaggeration	75
9–11	Disposition: narration, argument, *exordium*, peroration	120
2	ON ORNAMENTING WHAT YOU HAVE FOUND	173–466
1	Ornamentation or eloquence in general	173
2–8	Tropes	185
9–10	Formulae and *sententiae*	237
11–19	Figures in nine classes	255
20–22	Sound, rhythm, periodic composition	339
23	Ornamentation through *copia*	437
3	ON DELIVERY	467–537
1–4	Memory, voice, gesture	467
	Special Rhetoric	
1	FIRST BOOK OF SPECIAL RHETORIC	538–872
1	Subject, audience and circumstances of practical rhetoric	538
2–9	Different types of subject: descriptions, comparisons, ecphrasis, fable, themes from history	556
10–13	On moving and pleasing: arousing particular emotions	619
14–25	Special types of oration (e.g. requests, complaints, consolations, ethical, political)	660
25–29	The three styles (including ideas of style)	768
30–2	Colloquies and letters	844
2	ON PRACTISING ORATORY	872–944
1	Reading and selection	872
2–4	Practice, declamation, letters	899
3	ON JUDGING ELOQUENCE	944–64
1	On judging complete speeches	944
2–3	On judging other types of speech and letters	952

Like the northern humanist rhetoricians of the early sixteenth century Keckermann emphasizes the dependence of rhetorical invention on logic. It is necessary to use logic to determine which type of theme one is dealing with. Knowledge of the topics is the assumed basis of invention; the canons of rhetoric explain which topics are likely to be useful for different kinds of theme.[10] Rhetoric supplements the topics of invention, taken over from logic, using the list from Cicero's *Topica*,[11] with the topics

[10] Ibid., sigs. B3^r–B7^v. [11] Ibid., sigs. D5^r–7^v.

of person.[12] Keckermann makes several references to Agricola in this section.[13]

He considers amplification, for which he relies on Agricola and Erasmus, both under invention and under style. Amplification is a key part of rhetoric because it contributes to arousing emotions in an audience.[14] Amplification can be achieved through certain topics, through moving from particular to general issues (as in Melanchthon), from causes, through descriptions and comparisons.[15] Keckermann regards exaggeration as a way of adding an additional level of emotional appeal to something.[16] Within style, he allocates certain figures to amplification and includes both a section from Agricola's discussion of *copia* and brevity and a summary of twenty-six kinds of verbal variation taken from the first book of Erasmus's *De copia*.[17]

His choice of four sections for the oration resembles Aristotle and Agricola. He bases his account of disposition on Aristotle, Quintilian, and Agricola. Effective disposition, which can be crucial in winning a case, needs to be based primarily on the aim of the oration, the attitude of the audience, and the location and time. Orators must ensure that logical connections are clear and that arguments which depend on other arguments are placed after them. Keckermann quotes Melanchthon on the importance of the principal syllogism of a work.[18] On *exordia* and perorations he mainly follows *Ad Herennium*, *De inventione,* and Quintilian, but the section concludes with citations of several of Agricola's general comments on disposition.[19]

He begins his account of style with references to the theories of Demetrius and Hermogenes. He sets out eight qualities of style (agreeing, pure, clear, suitable and appropriate, weighty, splendid and ornate, sonorous and appropriately rhythmical, and copious) and describes four principal tropes in detail (metonymy, synecdoche, metaphor, and irony—the same ones as Talon), referring frequently to Quintilian and Melanchthon.[20] He cites Erasmus (particularly the preface to *Adagia*) and Aphthonius (the section on the *chreia*) on the use of *sententiae* and proverbs for ornamentation, which he had previously mentioned as part of invention.[21] He divides the figures into eight classes according to their use: for explanation, for proof, for amplification, for expressing emotions, relating to others (e.g. *interrogatio*, apostrophe, *parrhesia*), for particular

[12] Ibid., sigs. B8^{v}–C2^{v}. [13] Ibid., sigs. A2^{v}–3^{r}, D4^{v}–5^{r}, E1^{v}.
[14] Ibid., sig. E6$^{r–v}$. [15] Ibid., sig. F5$^{r–v}$. [16] Ibid., sig. G6^{v}.
[17] Ibid., sigs. S1^{r}–5^{r}, Ee3^{r}–Gg2^{r}. [18] Ibid., sigs. K1^{v}–3^{r}.
[19] Ibid., sigs. K6^{r}–L6^{v}. [20] Ibid., sigs. L7^{r}–M1^{v}, M7^{v}–O5^{v}.
[21] Ibid., sigs. D8$^{r–v}$, P7^{r}–Q6^{v}.

emotions, common figures of words (figures shared with grammar and subdivided into defect and excess), and figures of repetition. He usually gives an original definition of each figure, followed by an example, rules for the use of the figure and further examples, frequently adding references to Quintilian, *Ad Herennium*, Melanchthon, and Sturm.[22] His account of rhythmic prose and the periodic style relies on Sturm and Rivius, while referring also to classical authorities. Under special rhetoric he gives an account of the three levels of style, which makes use of Sturm and Scaliger's *Poetices libri septem*, and which incorporates sections from Hermogenes's *On Ideas of Style* in its discussion of the grand style. This section concludes with a discussion of the laconic style in Seneca and in Lipsius.[23]

Keckermann introduces special rhetoric by discussing materials suited to different kinds of orator and different types of audience (based on the descriptions of different types of people in Aristotle's *Rhetoric* 2.12–17).[24] Much of the rest of the book is concerned with describing the invention, disposition, and style required for different types of composition (e.g. comparisons, descriptions of virtues or of states, fable, *ethopoeia*, historical themes),[25] or different purposes in writing (e.g. commendations, consolations, thanks),[26] which seem to be partly based on letter-writing manuals.

Keckermann regards persuasion through the arousing of emotions as the most important part of rhetoric. To move an audience effectively you must find an emotion which suits the particular audience and the case you are making, and you must ensure that you yourself feel the emotion you wish to transfer to others. He recognizes the usefulness of arguments in arousing emotions. Vivid depiction and amplification play an important role. Keckermann cites Quintilian, Cicero, and Aristotle here but his main source, which he quotes at length, is the third book of Agricola's *De inventione dialectica*.[27] Once he turns to individual emotions his rules tend to summarize ideas from Aristotle's *Rhetoric* 2.2–11. The section ends with lengthy quotations from Agricola on assuaging emotions and on Aristotle's treatment of emotions.[28]

The suggestions for reading focus on Aristotle, Cicero, and Quintilian among rhetoricians, adding Hermogenes, Longinus, and Demetrius, and Cicero, Demosthenes, and Aeschines among orators, before quoting Agricola's remarks on reading from *De inventione dialectica*, 3.16.[29] Keckermann wants his pupils to absorb the teachings of Greek rhetoric

22 Ibid., sigs. R2^{r}–Y2^{r}.
23 Ibid., sigs. Ccc1^{r}–Fff4^{r}.
24 Ibid., sigs. Ll5^{v}–Mm6^{v}.
25 Ibid., sigs. Nn3^{r}–Qq5^{r}.
26 Ibid., sigs. Vv8^{r}–Bbb2^{v}.
27 Ibid., sigs. Qq6^{r}–Rr4^{r}.
28 Ibid., sigs. Rr5^{v}–Tt2^{v}.
29 Ibid., sigs. Iii5^{r}–6^{r}.

and poetics. There follows an index of commonplaces of the rhetoricians divided into various classes.[30] Then Keckermann opens up the question of imitation, referring to the letters by Poliziano, Cortesi, Gianfrancesco Pico, and Bembo. Keckermann believes that up to the age of 15 pupils must strive above all for correctness in Latin. From 15 to 18 pupils should imitate Cicero only. After that they should extend their reading and imitation to other authors.[31]

In logic Keckermann is one of the northern European Protestants who has turned away from Ramus towards a full reinstatement of Aristotle. In rhetoric he follows many of the teachings of Aristotle's *Rhetoric*, especially in his comments on the individual emotions. But he follows Agricola and Melanchthon on rhetoric's dependence on topical invention and Agricola and Erasmus on amplification. He was the most acute reader of Agricola of all the later northern humanists, consistently quoting the sections where Agricola is most original. In his lengthy account of style he supplements Quintilian and *Rhetorica ad Herennium*, with Greek rhetoricians and recent writers who used them, such as Sturm and Scaliger. He is also aware of sixteenth-century debates about imitation.

GERARDUS VOSSIUS (1577–1649)

Gerardus Vossius studied at the Latin school in Dordrecht from 1587 and at Leiden University from 1595. In 1600 he returned to Dordrecht as rector of his old school, publishing his *Institutiones oratoriae* (1606) and presumably doing the groundwork for his later grammars of Latin and Greek while he worked there. In 1615 he became regent of the States College at Leiden, losing that job in 1619 when his religious opinions came under scrutiny, but resuming teaching at Leiden in 1620, where he became professor of eloquence and history in 1622 and professor of Greek in 1625. In 1631 he moved to the *Athenaeum Illustre* in Amsterdam. He also composed works on the Pelagian heresy, the Latin and Greek historians, grammar, imitation, and poetics. His scholarly works were widely appreciated throughout northern Europe.[32]

Vossius's major work on rhetoric is *Institutiones oratoriae* in six books, which he revised in 1609, and with additions to the commentary and examples in 1630, and again in 1643. There were four editions before

[30] Ibid., sigs. Kkk4^{v}–Lll2^{r}.
[31] Ibid., sig. Lll4^{v}.
[32] C. S. M. Rademaker, *Life and Work of G. J. Vossius (1577–1649)* (Assen, 1981), pp. xxv–xxvi, 74–5.

1620 and eleven in all in the seventeenth century. In 1621 he prepared a shortened version *Rhetorices contracta*.[33] The *Rhetorices contracta* was printed thirty-one times in the seventeenth century in Holland, Germany, and England. Vossius also composed in 1626 a very short rhetoric, *Elementa Rhetorica* (43 pages), which concentrates on *elocutio* (34 pages) and appears to be intended for grammar-school pupils. This was the most successful of all his rhetorics, with thirty-six seventeenth-century editions, from Holland, Germany, Britain, and Scandinavia.

Institutiones oratoriae begins with a succinct view of the aim, functioning, and definition of rhetoric.

> Since the aim of rhetoric is persuasion, its duty will be to speak well, or to speak in a way suited to persuade; its subject-matter will be any question, and above all civil questions, rhetoric will be correctly defined as the skill of speaking well on any matter so as to persuade, or, as Aristotle defines it, the skill of discovering in any subject-matter, what in it is suitable for persuading.[34]

This definition exemplifies the Aristotelian basis of Vossius's entire work but also acknowledges Quintilian and shows Vossius supplementing Aristotle with other authorities and with his own opinions, for example (adapting the Latin tradition) that the orator has four duties: invention, disposition, style, and delivery. The 1630 edition, which I shall be using as the basis of this discussion, was originally printed as two volumes, with separate pagination, signatures, and indexes.[35]

The first three books of *Institutiones oratoriae* cover largely the same subject-matter as Aristotle's three books of *Rhetoric*; the last three books add a very extensive treatment of style, focusing on the tropes and figures (taken from the Latin tradition, since Aristotle scarcely mentioned them) and on theories of style from later Greek rhetoricians.

One could think of Vossius as reversing the procedure of some sixteenth-century rhetoricians. Where they tried to fit Aristotle's *Rhetoric* within a mainly Ciceronian framework, he uses later orators to fill out and supplement Aristotle. He almost entirely avoids the innovations of northern

[33] Ibid. 79, 193–5. T. Conley, *Rhetoric in the European Tradition* (New York, 1990), 159–61, 185–6.

[34] 'Cum rhetorices finis sit persuasio, officium eius sit bene dicere, sive dicere ad persuadendum accommodate; materia sit quaelibet quaestio, ac praecipue civilis; recte difinitur Rhetorice, facultas de unaquaque re bene dicendi ad persuadendum; sive, ut definit Aristoteles, facultas perspiciendi in unaquaque re, quod in ea est ad persuadendum idoneum.' G. Vossius, *Commentariorum Rhetoricorum sive Oratoriarum Institutionum libri sex* (Leiden, 1630), sig. A1ʳ.

[35] Although most surviving copies are bound as one vol., my references will sometimes treat it as a 2-vol. work in order to reduce confusion.

Table 9.2 Plan of Vossius, *Oratoriarum Institutionum libri VI*

Bk/chs.		Pages
1	INTRODUCTION AND INVENTION	
1	On the nature of rhetoric	1
2	On invention	7
3	On the types of case	16
4	The deliberative genre	27
5	The demonstrative genre	42
6–11	The judicial genre and status-theory	111
12	Untechnical arguments (witnesses, documents, etc.)	183
2	INVENTION OF *PATHOS* AND *ETHOS*	
1	On emotions in general	193
2–13	On particular emotions (anger, love, hate, fear, pity, etc.)	199
14	Arguments supporting *ethos*	285
15	Commonplaces, argumentation, and amplification	310
3	DISPOSITION	
1	On disposition	321
2	On the *exordium*	326
3–4	On narration and proposition	354
5	On argument	368
6	On the epilogue	385
7	On invention and disposition of special forms, such as consolation, commendation, thanks, exhortation, etc.	389–431
4	STYLE	
1	On style and *elegantia*	1
2–4	Composition, period, rhythm	40
5	On tropes in general	80
6–9	Metaphor, metonymy, synecdoche, irony	83
10–13	On other tropes and pseudo-tropes	160
5	ON THE FIGURES (SCHEMES)	
1	On the schemes in general	257
2–5	Four classes of schemes of words	266
6–13	Eight classes of schemes of thought	335
6	ON KINDS AND IDEAS OF STYLE AND ON DELIVERY	
1	On kinds of style in general	425
2–4	On composition, sentences and words of the high style	431
5	On the middle and low styles	457
6–7	Attic and Asiatic and Hermogenes's Ideas of Style	465
8–10	Delivery in general and voice	498
11	Gesture	511
	Epilogue to the whole work	524–7

rhetoricians and rarely mentions recent writers. Vossius's chapters usually begin with a few paragraphs defining terms, dividing the material and stating his main teaching. These are followed by numbered sections of commentary, in which he explains in more detail, considers other views, and gives examples from classical literature. Sometimes a chapter will contain as many as thirty of these numbered sections.

Like Aristotle Vossius organizes his account of invention around the three forms of persuasion (*logos*, *pathos*, and *ethos*) and the three genres of rhetoric. He distinguishes between dialectical topics and rhetorical topics and insists that his book is concerned with the rhetorical kind only. Like Aristotle Vossius begins by considering the topics of deliberative oration, primarily the honourable and the useful, supplementing Aristotle's account with materials from Dionysius of Halicarnassus and Hermogenes, and discussion of the different types of political system.[36] Within demonstrative oratory he distinguishes different approaches for praises of people, deeds, and things. Much of his teaching here is based on analysis of examples but he often makes reference to Menander Rhetor and Dionysius of Halicarnassus.[37] Vossius's discussion of invention in judicial oratory focuses on the theory of status which he presents in Hermogenes's version.[38] In book 3 he gives instructions for the composition of twenty-two special kinds of composition.[39] These special types (e.g. warning, consolation, request, commendation, nuptial oration) resemble some of the sections of letter-writing manuals.[40]

Vossius's treatment of emotion is thoroughly Aristotelian, both in his understanding of how emotions function and in his teaching about how to arouse particular emotions. He also cites the opinions of Cicero, Quintilian, Galen, and St Thomas Aquinas.[41] Vossius follows Aristotle's list of thirteen emotions in full and in the same order. When it comes to individual emotions, for example, wrath, he goes through Aristotle's definition carefully explaining the implications of each of the phrases. He converts some of Aristotle's observations into lists, for example of fifteen things which make people angry.[42]

Vossius regards disposition as comprising simply the four parts of the classical oration, as outlined by Aristotle, though he adds a few comments on proposition, as part of the narration. His general remarks refer to Cicero, Quintilian, and Trapezuntius.[43] The aims of the *exordium* are taken from *Rhetorica ad Herennium*, the kinds from Aristotle, and the topics from Hermogenes. Vossius gives an analysis of the structure of the *exordium* of Cicero's *Pro Milone*.[44] On narration he uses Aristotle and Hermogenes, again showing how Cicero's practice in *Pro Milone* corresponds to their

36 Ibid., sigs. D2^{r}–E2^{v}.
37 e.g. ibid., sigs. F3^{r}, G2^{r}, M1^{r}, N3^{v}, N4^{r-v}.
38 Ibid., sig. Z1^{v}.
39 Ibid., sigs. Ccc4^{r}–Hhh3^{v}.
40 Ibid., sigs. Ccc3^{v}, Fff1^{r-v}, Hhh3^{v}.
41 Ibid., sigs. Bb1^{r-v}, Bb2^{v}–3^{r}.
42 Ibid., sigs. Bb4^{r}–Dd2^{r}; Aristotle, *Rhetoric* 2.2.9–26.
43 Vossius, *Commentariorum Rhetoricorum*, sigs. Ss1^{r}–3^{r}.
44 Ibid., sigs. T1^{r}, Vv3^{r}–Xx2^{r}.

ideas.[45] On argument he follows Aristotle and Quintilian; his very brief treatment of the epilogue cites Aristotle and *De inventione.*[46]

Vossius devotes almost three books and more than half his whole work to style. He begins with remarks on the qualities of style which seem to follow Quintilian and *Rhetorica ad Herennium.*[47] Then he turns to sentence construction and rhythmic prose where his main authorities are Hermogenes, Cicero, Scaliger's *Poetics*, Aristotle, and Sturm.[48] He gives a very full account of the four principal tropes, drawing on Quintilian and Aristotle and citing numerous examples from classical poetry and oratory. He claims to follow Scaliger's system of organizing the figures of thought, but his list looks more like an adaptation than a copy.[49] For each figure Vossius gives an explanation, other names it is known by, refers to places where it is discussed, divides, and gives examples. Sometimes he adds suggestions about when a particular figure should be used or avoided.[50] In discussing the kinds of style he first absorbs Pseudo-Demetrius into his account of the grand style, then borrows comments on the Attic and Asiatic styles from Cicero and Quintilian, and finally reports in detail the doctrine of all of Hermogenes's *Ideas of Style.*[51]

Vossius's *Institutiones oratoriae* is immensely long and learned, with an astonishing range of reference to classical authorities, citing and quoting large numbers of instances of each doctrine from Greek and Latin literature. The basis of Vossius's teaching is Aristotle's *Rhetoric*, supplemented by later Greek rhetoricians. When discussing disposition and style he makes important use of the classical Latin tradition, but he largely turns his back on renaissance Latin rhetoric. He makes a few glancing references to Erasmus and Agricola but not in places where their teaching is especially original or influential.[52] Vossius's emphasis on emotion and style prepares for the preoccupations of later seventeenth- and eighteenth-century rhetoric.[53]

CONRAD DIETERICH (1579–1639)

Conrad Dieterich, who was a schoolmaster in Giessen before becoming superintendent and scholarch in Ulm (1614–39), published three works

[45] Ibid., sig. Yy4^{r-v}. [46] Ibid., sigs. Ccc1^{v}–2^{r}.

[47] Ibid. ii, sigs. a1^{r}–c2^{v}. [48] Ibid. ii, sigs. e4^{v}, h2^{r-v}.

[49] Ibid., ii, sig. tt4^{v}. J. C. Scaliger, *Poetices libri septem* (Lyon, 1561; repr. Stuttgart, 1964), 122. Only five sections actually follow: p. 140.

[50] e.g. anaphora, climax: Vossius, *Commentariorum Rhetoricorum*, ii, sigs nn2^{v}, oo3^{v}–pp1^{v}.

[51] Ibid. ii, sigs. hhh4^{r}–lll4^{v}, nnn1^{v}–3^{r}, nnn4^{v}–rrr1^{v}.

[52] Ibid., i, sig. Rr1^{r-v}, ii, sig. e1^{r}.

[53] Conley, *Rhetoric in the European Tradition*, 161–2, 197–8, 209, 213–16, 224.

on rhetoric and dialectic in the early years of the seventeenth century in which he supplemented the Ramist syllabus with materials from Aristotle, Quintilian, and Melanchthon.

His *Institutiones dialecticae* (1609), which was printed seven times before 1620 and twelve times in all, divides dialectic into two parts (invention and judgement) and gives thorough accounts of the topics and the syllogism. Dieterich adds many Aristotelian teachings to his account of the syllogism. The topics are prefaced by short accounts of the Aristotelian predicables and categories, and a full discussion of the fallacies precedes a very brief summary of method.[54] So Dieterich incorporates within a broadly Ramist structure many elements of Aristotelian logic which Ramus had rejected.

His *Institutiones rhetoricae* (1613), which was printed six times up to 1620 and nineteen times in all, is based on Talon's later rhetoric manuals, including Talon's definitions, chief doctrines, and even some of his examples. He adds reports of the views of Quintilian, Aristotle, and Melanchthon and many further examples to each section, especially from scripture. Dieterich includes accounts of several tropes omitted by Talon and adds a section on figures of amplification (organized as in Melanchthon by topics) after Talon's figures of speech and thought.[55] He omits Talon's sections on poetic metre and prose-rhythm. He says nothing about the parts of the oration or emotion.

Dieterich's *Institutiones oratoriae* (1613), which was printed six times before 1620 and seventeen times in all, provided full discussions of several aspects of rhetoric which Talon had excluded, including the parts of the oration, the genres of oratory, and amplification. At the same time it absorbed sixteenth-century innovations, such as the great importance given to demonstrative oratory, the subtypes of deliberative oratory (such as petition and consolation), and amplification. His work assumes a knowledge of the tropes and figures, but otherwise presents most of rhetoric, apart from the emotions, within a new system of organization. He organizes his material in a thoroughly Ramist way, with numbered definitions and axioms setting out his teaching clearly and plainly. He provides many examples to illustrate his rules, writing his own examples of praises of the local prince, the region, the city, and his school.[56] Dieterich's debt to Melanchthon is clear in the didascalic genre, while his division of the deliberative genre into persuasion, dissuasion, exhortation,

[54] C. Dieterich, *Institutiones dialecticae* (Giessen, 1655), 5–37, 332–55.
[55] C. Dieterich, *Institutiones rhetoricae* (Jena, 1630), sigs. B6^{r}–C6^{v}, P1^{v}–Q8^{r}.
[56] C. Dieterich, *Institutiones oratoriae* (Utrecht, 1688), sigs. D3^{v}, E5^{v}, E10^{v}, F5^{r}.

discouragement, requests, prayers, and consolations derives from the letter-writing manuals.

NICOLAS CAUSSIN (1583–1651)

Nicolas Caussin taught rhetoric in the Jesuit colleges at Rouen, at La Flèche, and, from 1619 at the reopened Collège de Clermont, in Paris, where he published his *Eloquentiae sacrae et humanae parallela Libri XVI* (1619). He also wrote *Electorum symbolorum et parabolarum historicarum syntagmata* (1618), combining Egyptian wisdom with Old Testament revelation in the mode of the *prisca theologia* and *La Cour Sainte* (1624), a collection of moral maxims, pious reflections, and historical examples.[57] Caussin became confessor to Louis XIII before being banished in 1637 by Cardinal Richelieu to Brittany, returning to court after Richelieu's death in 1643.

Eloquentiae sacrae et humanae parallela Libri XVI, which runs to 685 folio pages in its elegant first edition (occasionally marred by errors in the numbering of the chapters), was printed sixteen times before 1650 and nineteen times in all in the seventeenth century, mostly in Paris, Cologne, and Lyon. Caussin aims to collect 'the most accurate judgements of illustrious authors concerning the best kind of speaking and the whole method of eloquence with the most famous monuments of Greek and Latin examples'.[58] His address to the reader suggests that he hopes to collect everything that is most valuable in the teaching of rhetoric into one corpus, placing it at the service of sacred eloquence.[59]

The *Parallela* proposes that classical rhetoric finds its most complete realization in Christian eloquence.[60] Caussin argues for the superiority of Christian orators, in particular St Gregory Nazianzenus and St John Chrysostom, in terms proposed by classical rhetoric. Rather than agreeing with St Augustine and Erasmus that Christian oratory will need to be

[57] M. Fumaroli, *L'Age de l'éloquence* (Geneva, 1980), 279–84, 362–71. D. P. Walker, *The Ancient Theology* (London, 1972), 1–21, 63–131.

[58] 'Accurata illustrium authorum de optimo genere dicendi iudicia, totamque eloquentiae rationem clarissimis graecorum, latinorumque exemplorum monumentis.' N. Caussin, *Eloquentiae sacrae et humanae parallela Libri XVI* (Paris, 1619), 1.

[59] 'Quin-imo huius operis instituta est, quicquid in sacra humanaque Eloquentia spectabile, illustri loco ponere, et variorum ingeniorum saeculorumque virtutes in unum veluti perfectionis corpus includere.' Ibid., sig. A4 ^{r}.

[60] Fumaroli, *L'Age de l'éloquence*, 286–98. Conley, *Rhetoric in the European Tradition*, 155–7, 182–3. C. Mouchel, *Cicéron et Sénèque dans la rhétorique de la Renaissance* (Marburg, 1990), 261–70. Conley's outline of the content is based on the 7th edn. (Cologne, 1681).

different in kind from pagan eloquence, Caussin finds that Christian orators are superior because they surpass classical writers in magnificence, in style, and in emotion. There is a little adaptation of classical rhetoric to Christian preoccupations (for example, in including addresses to God within epideictic rhetoric) but more often Caussin endorses the views of the classical authorities. The final three books, devoted to sacred oratory, argue for its importance rather than giving instructions on how to compose sacred oratory. Caussin assumes that the classical four-part oration is the appropriate form for Christian preaching.

Caussin's *Parallela* displays and draws together an immense amount of reading. He is especially keen on Greek authorities. He takes note of sixteenth-century controversies about imitation and discusses the Senecan style. His histories are astonishingly wide-ranging and his chapter on imitation identifies the noteworthy characteristics of a huge range of Greek, Latin, and Christian writers. He includes many illustrative examples from Greek (e.g. Demosthenes, Lysias, Isocrates, Aristides, Synesius) and Christian orators (especially Sts Basil, Gregory Nazianzenus, Chrysostom, and Cyprian) but in spite of this his principal point of reference is always Cicero. Caussin's flourishes of exceptional learning rest on a Ciceronian core.[61] Caussin never cites Agricola, Erasmus, or Melanchthon, but he does occasionally mention Vives.

The *Parallela* includes a wide range of different kinds of material. Alongside chapters outlining rhetorical doctrines, translating passages from Greek authorities, or arguing for a particular perspective we find alphabetical lists, indexes of Cicero's presentations of commonplaces or employment of particular figures, a composed dialogue on the difference between sacred and profane oratory (book 15), collections of examples of different types of oratory, or praises of many different subjects. At times one seems to be reading an anthology rather than a textbook. Even within the more obviously didactic chapters, listing (e.g. of ten sources of invention, six sources for *exordia*, five kinds of love, ten methods of arousing hatred) is one of Caussin's main techniques. Several of the examples he quotes in full are provided with an analysis, listing the main topics which the writer has discussed as a sort of commentary.[62] Caussin is immensely well-read but he always gives the impression of summarizing what he has read and of adapting it into a series of simple rules, which he augments with further observations and numerous examples.

[61] Fumaroli, *L'Age de l'éloquence*, 162–202. Mouchel, *Cicéron et Sénèque*, 271–96.

[62] F. Goyet, 'Les Analyses de discours dans le livre XIII des *Parallela*', in S. Conte (ed.), *Nicolas Caussin: Rhétorique et spiritualité* (Berlin, 2007), 221–68.

Table 9.3 Plan of Caussin, *Eloquentiae sacrae et humanae parallela Libri XVI*

Bk/chs.		Pages
1	ON THE ELOQUENCE OF THE ANCIENTS	1–54
1–8	Importance and usefulness of eloquence	1–8
9–62	Praise of Greek and Roman orators	9–32
63–73	Comparisons	33–54
2	ON THE BEST QUALITIES OF ELOQUENCE	55–102
1–16	Faults of style	55–78
17–27	Orations illustrating, and opinions on, various styles	79–92
28–40	Ideas of style (based on Hermogenes) and decorum	93–102
3	ON SUPPORTS OF ELOQUENCE	103–26
1–6	Different types of natural talent	103–10
7–8	Practice; reasons for decline of eloquence	110–12
9–15	On imitation and authors to imitate	113–21
16	How Cicero imitated Demosthenes	122–26
4	ON INVENTION AND THE TOPICS	127–80
1–12	On invention and ten sources of invention	127–38
13–57	The topics of invention	138–180bis
5	ON AMPLIFICATION	181bis–206
1–11	Methods of amplification	181bis–190
12–30	Examples of amplification from Cicero, Gregory, etc.; diminution; index to commonplaces in Cicero	191–206
6	ON DISPOSITION AND THE PARTS OF AN ORATION	207–42
1–12bis	Preliminaries and *exordium* (with examples)	207–22
13–23	Narration (with examples)	222–32
24–38	Confirmation; argumentation; confutation (examples)	232–41
39–40	Peroration (with examples)	241–2
7	ON STYLE	243–310
1–2	Style and its divisions	243–4
3–15	Composition, periodic style, prose-rhythm	244–56
16–17	On figures and alphabetical list of figures	256–80
18–25	The use of figures in different classes	280–92
	List of figures used by Cicero, with references	293–9
26–7	Figures in Demosthenes and declamations	300–10
8	ON EMOTIONS	311–74
1–13	Emotions in general and how to arouse them	311–28
14–46	Love, fear, hatred, anger, pity	328–74
9	ON DELIVERY	375–88
1–7	General and voice	375–81
8–10	Significances of gesture; gesture in oratory	381–88
10	ON THE EPIDEICITIC ORATION	389–434
1–2	History of epideictic; defence of declamation	389–91
3–25	Precepts for praise of Gods, persons, events, places	391–434

11	ON CHARACTERS OF EPIDEICTIC Ninety-five examples of descriptions	435–506
12	ON CIVIL ELOQUENCE	507–46
1–7	Ideas and topics for deliberative oratory	507–14
8–12	Special types: exhortation, conciliation, consolation	514–19
13–31	Judicial oratory and status-theory	519–39
32–38	Accusation, defence, invective, complaint, etc.	539–46
13	ON CHARACTERS OF CIVIL ELOQUENCE Examples of deliberative and judicial orations	547–92
14	THEORHETOR OR ON THE MAJESTY OF SACRED ELOQUENCE	593–616
1–13	Dignity of sacred oratory and its subjects	593–606
14–19	Location, arguments and style of sacred oratory	606–11
20–5	Examples from Gregory, Basil, Chrysostom	611–16
15	ON THE FORM AND CHARACTER OF SACRED ELOQUENCE: A DIALOGUE	617–40
16	CHRYSOSTOM OR THE IDEA OF SACRED ELOQUENCE	641–71
1–19	Ideas of style in sacred eloquence	641–57
20–35	Chrysostom's fulfilment of these ideas	657–71

The complex structure of the whole work can be understood as falling into four main sections: an introductory section on the history, dignity, and means of learning eloquence (books 1–3), a survey of four of the traditional tasks of the orator: invention, disposition, style, and delivery (books 4–9), the three genres of secular oratory, with examples (books 10–13), and sacred oratory (books 14–16).

Caussin's book relies squarely on the keystones of traditional rhetoric, as interpreted by renaissance writers. Like Agricola and Melanchthon he places the first emphasis on the topics of invention. Like them (and Erasmus) he insists on the role of the topics in amplification and on the importance of commonplaces. Following Aristotle he endorses the traditional contents of the four-part oration (*exordium*, narration, confirmation and confutation, conclusion). He regards style as the essence of rhetoric and focuses above all on the figures of rhetoric, as had *Rhetorica ad Herennium*. To these well-established foundations Caussin adds elements which reflect the preoccupations of sixteenth-century rhetoric, absorbing the lessons of Greek rhetoricians on emotions, ideas of style, and forms of epideictic; taking on board the debate about imitation and the thinking of *De oratore* about the relationship between talent, art, and practice. He has learnt from sixteenth-century scholars much more than his predecessors knew about Greek oratory, and especially the second sophistic.

Caussin's introductory material is original. Unlike textbook authors he does not offer a definition of rhetoric. After asserting that rhetoric is the queen of the other sciences, he identifies three aspects: divine (as exemplified by Christ, Orpheus, Moses, the Prophets, and the Angels), heroic (Sts Basil, Gregory Nazianzenus, Chrysostom, and Cyprian), and human (Cicero and Demosthenes). He compares eloquence to God within the world or to the soul within the body.[63] Among theoreticians of oratory he gives special prominence at the beginning to Greeks, Aristotle, Demetrius, and Longinus.[64] He follows this praise of eloquence with a survey of praises of classical orators, beginning with Pytheus, Homer, Solon, and Themistocles, continuing with Lysias, Isocrates, and Aeschines, before concluding with Caesar, Sallust, and Cicero. The comparisons which follow are all centred on Cicero, primarily comparisons between Demosthenes and Cicero, but also between Cicero and Thucydides, Plato, Lysias, Isocrates, Sallust, and Seneca.

In trying to define the best kind of style Caussin insists on the variety of styles available. The best style is the one which pleases a particular audience most.[65] Longinus is a frequent reference throughout the second book.[66] When Caussin turns to ideas of style he at first follows Hermogenes closely.[67] Gradually he introduces references to other authorities and summarizes Hermogenes's points more selectively, ending with a section on decorum, summarized from Vives's *De ratione dicendi*.[68]

Caussin regards imitation as essential to writing.[69] He offers a complex answer to the much debated question of whether one should imitate one model or many. It may be easier for young pupils to imitate a single author, who should be Cicero, before branching out to other models. There is no reason not to choose as a model the single author who is most appropriate for what you are trying to achieve.[70] In this spirit Caussin offers a survey of the things most worth imitating in Greek, Latin, and Christian authors. He offers a defence of Seneca, though he makes clear his preference for Cicero.[71] The book ends with a collection of parallel passages showing the ways in which Demosthenes and Cicero treated similar subjects and arguing that Cicero imitated Demosthenes.

63 Caussin, *Parallela*, 1–3. 64 Ibid. 1, 2. 65 Ibid. 55.
66 Ibid. 56, 60, 61, 63, 64, 70, 90, 98.
67 Ibid. 93–7. Hermogenes, *On Ideas of Style* 227–69.
68 Caussin, *Parallela*, 102. Vives, *Opera omnia*, 8 vols. (Valencia, 1782–90), ii. 173–86.
69 Caussin, *Parallela*, 112. 70 Ibid. 115. 71 Ibid. 118–19.

Caussin begins his section on invention by stressing the importance of focusing on the question at issue. The writer needs to have a complete and accurate view of the key question and must direct all arguments to winning it. Then Caussin outlines ten sources of invention: history, fables, proverbs, hieroglyphs, emblems, testimony of the ancients, ethical maxims, laws, sacred writings, and, finally, the topics of invention. After listing the topics, which he connects with nine simple questions, he shows with two examples how arguments related to a particular issue can be found using the topics.[72] The questions here have some similarities with Melanchthon's approach and the examples resemble Agricola, but neither is mentioned. Caussin's list of topics resembles Cicero's, with minor omissions and changes in order. For each topic Caussin gives some discussion of the nature of the topic and some examples. The discussion of definition is especially full.[73] He explains the uses of particular topics in argument and in amplification.[74]

Caussin's discussion of amplification is conducted mainly through examples and through summarizing other authorities. After using Longinus to distinguish amplification from the sublime and from the exaggerated, he argues that one must be careful to choose subject-matter that is suited to amplification.[75] Then he summarizes Aphthonius's teaching on the commonplace, setting out ten topics of amplification. After citing Cicero and Longinus, he concludes that amplification requires a proper selection both of topics and of figures of speech.[76] Then he gives examples of amplification from Cicero, the declamations attributed to Quintilian, St Gregory, and Chrysostom. Caussin takes amplification here in the rather narrow sense connected with arousing anger against a criminal. He makes no reference to the broader methods of amplification suggested by Quintilian or to Erasmus's development of the idea of *copia*. Book 5 concludes with an alphabetical index to commonplaces in Cicero's works.

While Caussin relies on traditional teaching on disposition, style, and delivery, he is far more original on emotion. He begins by establishing the importance of the emotions in rhetoric and in the Christian understanding of humanity, considering the views of St Augustine and St Thomas Aquinas. His first positive instruction is pure Cicero: the most important factor in moving other people is the ability to feel emotions oneself and to

[72] Ibid. 137–8. [73] Ibid. 141–8.
[74] Ibid. 150–1, 158, 166–7, 180–1.
[75] Ibid. 185–6.
[76] Ibid. 186–90. Aphthonius's topics as reported by Caussin are: from contraries, exposition, comparison from the lesser, from intention, digression, rejection of mercy, lawful, just, useful, and possible.

project them.[77] The two roots of emotion are pleasure and pain. They are most easily affected by appeals to the senses, and particularly by creating powerful images and lively descriptions of affecting incidents.[78] Certain figures of speech are especially useful in enhancing such effects.[79] Here and at other key points in the chapter Caussin analyses evocations of emotion from literature: Longinus's analysis of Sappho, Euripides, Seneca, Homer, Plutarch's description of Volumnia, and Sophocles's presentation of Orestes.[80] Then he gives eight considerations in moving, among them: the nature of the audience and the time and place of the speech; the need to avoid any suggestion that the desired emotion is uncalled for or is artificially intruded on the subject; the need to avoid argument which is too subtle, since calling on a more intellectual response will diminish the potential for an emotional reaction; the need for forceful expression and plentiful moral *sententiae*; the need for moderation in the way the event is presented so that emotion is built up gradually and to avoid the risk of excess; the understanding that some high points of emotion call for silence rather than words.[81] This is a rather miscellaneous list of topics but it is not obviously dependent on any single authority and it suggests practical reflection on particular examples and situations.

When it comes to individual emotions Caussin is inevitably more reliant on Aristotle, but he concentrates on a smaller group of emotions, beginning with love, joy, and hope, which he discusses mainly on the basis of Plato and Christian authorities.[82] On fear and wrath he makes more use of Aristotle but his ten instructions for arousing of hatred and anger are developments of Aristotle's ideas rather than copies, including: it is easier to move minds to anger which are already wounded with suspicion or moderately moved; people who have already suffered some injury are likely to be aroused to emotion more easily; it helps to compare the innocence of the victim with the dishonesty and savagery of the perpetrator; in bringing a crime before the eyes of the audience one should use high figures of speech such as exclamation, apostrophe, and prosopopeia.[83] Caussin describes pity on the basis of Seneca, St Gregory, and St Bernard, but his notes on the people liable to pity show some overlap with Aristotle.[84]

Caussin significantly adapts the rhetorical tradition to modern opportunities for speaking when he gives epideictic oratory priority over

[77] Ibid. 313. [78] Ibid. 316–18. [79] Ibid. 319.
[80] Ibid. 324–6, 343, 361–2, 369.
[81] Ibid. 326–7. Keckermann's summaries of Agricola might have suggested some of these points.
[82] Ibid. 328–38. [83] Ibid. 346.
[84] Ibid. 364. Aristotle, *Rhetoric* 2.8.

deliberative and judicial. On praises of God he owes most to Christian authors. His instructions for praise of a person begin with the topics of the person in the Roman rhetorical tradition, but he supplements them with examples and other sources.[85] When he turns to speeches for weddings, births, and epithalamia, he closely follows pseudo-Dionysius of Halicarnassus, *On Epideictic Speeches*, adding a list of topics before translating the examples from his source.[86] On funeral oratory, thanks, and salutations, Caussin derives his instructions from study of examples and from letter-writing manuals. Some of his instructions for praises of a city resemble those in Menander Rhetor.[87] He ends with substantial examples from Aristides, adding analysis of the topics employed.[88] Both in epideictic and in civil eloquence, Caussin's category for combining deliberative and judicial rhetoric, much of the weight of Caussin's teaching is carried by the examples. He adds subgenres of deliberative, more suited to seventeenth-century conditions of speaking, which are similar to the subgenres we find in letter-writing manuals. According to Francis Goyet the thirty-eight speeches which Caussin in book 13 chooses from the historians to illustrate civil eloquence are chosen as beautiful examples of the great commonplaces. Caussin's comments neglect structure and focus mainly on emotion and vehemence.[89]

Caussin devotes more attention to showing the superiority of sacred eloquence than to providing specialized instructions for composing it. He argues for its superiority by elaborating on the wonder and majesty of the major subjects for Christian oratory: the incarnation, the nativity, the crucifixion, and resurrection. In describing the forum of sacred oratory he develops a vivid description of Christ's glory at the last judgement, contrasting this with the pettiness of some human occasions for writing.[90] He amplifies the inspired arguments and the exceptional effects of Christian eloquence very impressively.

The dialogue on the form of sacred eloquence in book 15 has three participants: Theophrastus, Logodaedalus, and Neanias. Theophrastus speaks out against the mingling of pagan rhetoric with Christian truth.[91] Logodaedalus opposes this, insisting that the learning of the ancient world

[85] Ibid. 395–400.

[86] Ibid. 406–11. Compare Dionysius, 261–71 (in D. A. Russell and N. G. Wilson, *Menander Rhetor* (Oxford, 1981), 365–71).

[87] Caussin, *Parallela*, 420. Russell and Wilson, p. 33.

[88] Caussin, *Parallela*, 428–34.

[89] Goyet, 'Les Analyses', 223–8, 242–4.

[90] Caussin, *Parallela*, 606. S. Conte, 'La Rhétorique sacrée dans les *Parallela*', in Conte, *Nicolas Caussin*, 282–90.

[91] Caussin, *Parallela*, 618–19.

ought to be used in a Christian way, defending eloquence and arguing that it can help true religion. He points out that the Bible and the Church Fathers employ rhetoric.[92] Although the audience finds this response convincing, Theophrastus reiterates his opposition, declaring that pagan influence is desecrating the Church and pointing out that St Augustine approved only of more restrained forms of oratory. For him the only qualities a preacher really needs are virtue and wisdom. He pours scorn on preachers who refer more to classical literature than to the Bible and the Church Fathers.[93] Neanias responds to Theophrastus by reminding the audience that the mission of the Jesuits was advanced by powerful preaching. He shows that preachers need knowledge of ancient languages and customs in order to interpret the Bible and argues that knowledge of rhetoric enables the word of God to be spread more forcefully, fittingly, and effectively.[94] In book 16 Caussin first outlines the characteristics of Christian high-style oratory and then shows that Chrysostom perfectly exemplifies those characteristics, giving him the place which Hermogenes gave to Demosthenes in his *Ideas of Style*.

The *Parallela* is both a compendium of received rhetorical knowledge and an argument for the importance of sacred oratory. Wide reading, substantial quotation, and textual analysis are essential elements at each stage of the book. For all his knowledge of and respect for previous writers, Caussin also emerges as someone who thinks for himself about the practicalities of writing on the basis of what he has learnt from reading the classical orators, tragedians, poets, and historians. Cicero is his constant point of reference for the first fifteen books, but he also tries hard to persuade us that Chrysostom is an even better model of eloquence for Christians.

These three vast works all put themselves forward as complete courses in rhetoric, collecting the best of the ancient teaching and obviating the need for other textbooks. All insist that style and the emotions are central to rhetoric; all absorb Aristotle's teachings and Greek rhetoric more

[92] Ibid. 619–25.

[93] Ibid. 626–31.

[94] Ibid. 632–40. The exact point at which the third speaker takes over (and even his name) is not absolutely certain. Theophrastus is certainly speaking at the top of p. 631 when he claims to be warning the company about what might happen. The new speaker has certainly taken over by the second column of p. 632 when he contrasts his views with those of Logodaedalus and Theophrastus ('in hac enim parte Logodaedalo . . . ut ait Theophrastus'). The name Neanias is given when he joins the company and questions Theophrastus on p. 630. I presume that a paragraph must have been lost here; later edns. do not supply it. Conte believes that Theophrastus speaks for the whole of this section, 'La Rhétorique sacrée', 286–7.

generally. All emphasize prose-rhythm and the periodic sentence. All three describe the Attic or Senecan style, though all prefer Cicero as a model. All teach genres of expression better suited to seventeenth-century contexts for writing than the classical three genres, basing their teaching on the manuals of letter-writing and preaching, or on Vives. They demonstrate the successful assimilation of a wealth of textual recoveries, Greek rhetoric, and deepened knowledge of the ancient world.

There are also striking differences between the three and it is clear that all three enjoyed localized rather than Europe-wide success. In contrast to Vossius, Keckermann and Caussin place great emphasis on the links between rhetoric and dialectic, on amplification, and on basing their teaching on the analysis of classical literature. They continue to show strong allegiance to aspects of rhetoric promoted by Agricola, Erasmus, and Melanchthon. Caussin and Keckermann engage with the history of rhetoric and logic respectively; both take an interest in the issues concerning talent, teaching, and practice raised by Cicero in *De oratore*; both engage with the Italian debate about imitation and with the criteria for judging literary texts. Vossius and Caussin both use ancient and modern poetics to enrich the teaching of rhetoric.

All three have in different ways absorbed the pedagogic lessons of Soarez and Talon. Keckermann requires that the main principles of each aspect be stated at the beginning of each chapter. Vossius made simplifications and epitomes of his own work for different levels of the Dutch educational system. In spite of its vast length, and enormous variety of exemplification, the main teaching sections of Caussin's *Parallela* are organized as lists of instructions. Caussin discovered that an impressively large book could contain many different kinds of material, which a clerical reader could consult as needed. These works were also the last in a line. The new rhetoric of the seventeenth century would need to respond to the ideas of Descartes and Bacon and would focus mainly on tropes, figures, sentence composition, and different levels of style.[95]

[95] Conley, *Rhetoric in the European Tradition*, 162–87. M. Fumaroli (ed.), *Histoire de la rhétorique dans l'Europe moderne* (Paris, 1999), 539–821.

10

Manuals of Tropes and Figures

Special uses of language which impress and move an audience were considered to be a central part of rhetorical teaching from the Hellenistic period onwards. Brian Vickers has effectively shown how great an impact the tropes and figures had on renaissance writing and on English poetry more generally.[1] When E. H. Gombrich called rhetoric 'perhaps the most careful analysis of an expressive medium ever undertaken',[2] he had in mind primarily the tropes and figures. All the evidence we have suggests that when properly used these forms and strategies are astonishingly effective.[3]

The tropes and figures were very widely available in the renaissance in different ways. Many renaissance grammars, some of which were printed in enormous numbers of editions, included a selection of the figures. The tropes and figures were fully described in two of the most printed classical manuals of rhetoric, *Rhetorica ad Herennium* and Quintilian's *Institutio oratoria*, with a combined total of 278 editions. Almost all the general manuals of rhetoric described in earlier chapters included comprehensive treatments of the tropes and figures. Finally the tropes and figures were described in a group of specialized manuals, with a combined total publication of around 180 editions, which are the subject of this chapter. Together all these works ensured a very wide availability of the tropes and figures, which probably conditioned the way educated people read books and set about constructing sentences of their own. Teachers were instructed to point out the use of tropes and figures when reading classical

[1] B. Vickers, *Classical Rhetoric in English Poetry* (London, 1970); *In Defence of Rhetoric* (Oxford, 1988), 294–339, 491–8.

[2] E. H. Gombrich, *Art and Illusion* (Princeton, 1960), 374–5.

[3] On the figures more generally, see R. Lanham, *A Handlist of Rhetorical Terms* (Berkeley, 1991); H. Lausberg, *Handbuch der literarischen rhetorik*, 3rd edn. (Stuttgart, 1990), 282–455, tr. as *Handbook of Literary Rhetoric* (Leiden, 1998), 248–411; J. Knape, 'Elocutio', in G. Ueding (ed.), *Historisches Wörterbuch der Rhetorik*, ii (Tübingen, 1994), 1022–83; and Gideon Burton's website 'Silva rhetoricae' at http://rhetoric.byu.edu. On the development of the doctrine see G. Calboli, 'From Aristotelian λέξις to elocutio', *Rhetorica,* 16 (1998), 47–80, and 'The Metaphor after Aristotle', in D. C. Mirhady (ed.), *Influences on Peripatetic Rhetoric* (Leiden, 2007), 123–50.

texts with their pupils. Pupils were expected to use particular figures in their school compositions, whether imitated or original.

Manuals of tropes and figures mainly copy from each other, but individual manuals innovate in three main ways. Some manuals aim to be more comprehensive than others, including additional figures, sometimes at the cost of inadvertent repetition. By contrast other manuals aim to simplify the list, so as to make it easier for a pupil to memorize, as a preparation for its practical use in reading and in composition. Many of the manuals respond to the length of the list and the differences in kind between the figures by trying to devise new ways of grouping the figures. The manuals generally name each figure, sometimes giving both Greek and Latin names, then define it, and then give examples from classical literature. Some manuals add subdivisions of particular tropes and figures, and advice on their use.

The verbal patterns and linguistic techniques described through the tropes and figures are much more varied than might at first appear. Figures like anaphora and antistrophe describe patterning of words; homoeoptoton and homoeoteleuton provide for similar case-endings or final sounds in a group of individual words; paronomasia suggests changes in the spelling and sound of a word in order to effect wordplay. Colon, clause, and period analyse the way in which a sentence is built up; asyntedon and polysyntedon discuss the absence or addition of conjunctions within the sentence; hysteron proteron and parenthesis show how normal order within a sentence can effectively be altered. Apostrophe and rhetorical question have clear grammatical markers but describe ways of presenting material to achieve a certain effect. Figures like hypophora (also called subiectio), dubitatio, and permissio suggest attitudes the speaker might take to an audience. Correctio and aposiopesis describe ways of emphasizing something while seeming to retract or to be overcome with emotion. Description, expolitio, character portrayal, and comparison label sections of writing which one might include in a speech. Metaphor and metonymy, while suggesting striking forms of expression, invite questions about the operation of language itself. Renaissance rhetorics set themselves the task of categorizing and ordering these and other figures.[4]

In renaissance schools it seems that the tropes and figures were taught to students after they had learnt the basic Latin grammar and alongside their reading of middle-school texts, such as Cicero's letters, Terence, and Virgil. There is some overlap between grammar and rhetoric textbooks

[4] On the tropes and figures in the renaissance see L. Sonnino, *A Handbook to Sixteenth Century Rhetoric* (London, 1968); S. Adamson *et al.* (eds.), *Renaissance Figures of Speech* (Cambridge, 2007).

here, with some grammars including only figures which describe ways of organizing sentences and others including many figures which rhetoric also discusses.[5] In their reading of classical texts with their classes, teachers were instructed to point out the way in which writers used particular tropes.[6] This assumes that the names and descriptions of a range of figures had already been given to students. Reading texts and their own writing exercises would then have been ways of reinforcing this teaching. Knowing the names of the figures enables students to notice how a particular writer uses a particular technique. The names, which can sometimes seem to us excessively technical, actually make possible observation and the drawing of lessons. Renaissance grammar books often list some figures of speech, as part of the ancillary material, alongside the rules of prosody.[7] Pedagogically, the figures and tropes belong almost as much to the teaching of grammar as to rhetoric.

Our earliest thorough descriptions of the tropes and figures form part of comprehensive Latin rhetorics, *Rhetorica ad Herennium* 4 and Quintilian's *Institutio oratoria* 8 and 9. Book 4 of *Rhetorica ad Herennium* remained the best known classical account of the tropes and figures. It generally provides a Latin name for the figure with description, explanation, and examples, sometimes quite lengthy. Quite a number of the figures are treated at greater length, with subdivisions, instructions for composing, and/or advice on how a particular figure should be used. The work treats sixty-four figures, divided into thirty-five figures of words, ten tropes, and nineteen figures of thought.[8] Quintilian discusses fourteen tropes, some of them at considerable length at 8.6, twenty-nine figures of thought at 9.2.7–71, and fifty-three figures of speech at 9.3.6–87, within a very comprehensive account of style.[9]

We also have short Latin treatises focused entirely on the figures and tropes by Rutilius Lupus (first century AD), Aquila Romanus (third century), and Julius Rufinianus (fourth century). These were rediscovered in the renaissance and first printed in 1519 and 1521.[10] They use Greek

[5] L. Green, 'Grammatica movet', in P. Osterreich and T. Sloane (eds.), *Rhetorica Movet: Studies in Honour of H. F. Plett* (Leiden, 1999), 81–104.

[6] P. Mack, *Elizabethan Rhetoric* (Cambridge, 2002), 14–16, 22–4, 45–6. J. Susenbrotus, *Epitome troporum et schematum* (Zurich, n.d.), sig. A2^{r-v}. Repr. in J. Brennan's dissertation: see n. 12 below.

[7] Green, 'Grammatica movet', 79–83.

[8] On the doctrine of the figures see Cornifici, *Rhetorica ad C. Herennium*, ed. G. Calboli, 2nd edn. (Bologna, 1993), 50–4.

[9] Quintilian, *Institution oratoire*, ed. J. Cousin, v. *Livres VIII et IX* (Paris, 1978), 129–51. On the tropes and figures in classical rhetoric see R. E. Volkmann, *Die Rhetorik der Griechen und Römer* (Leipzig, 1885), 415–505.

[10] C. Halm, *Rhetores Latini Minores* (Leipzig, 1863), pp. v–vii, 1–62.

names for the figures. Rutilius Lupus, who is a source for the others, seems to base his work on the lost first-century BC Greek work of Gorgias.[11] The relatively short lists of Rutilius (forty-one figures, undivided) and Aquila (thirty-eight figures, divided into figures of words and figures of thought) describe some figures not listed in *Rhetorica ad Herennium* and Quintilian. Renaissance rhetoricians also used short treatises on the tropes and figures by the classical Latin grammarians Diomedes and Donatus.[12] They probably also made use of the Venerable Bede's *Liber de schematibus et tropis*, which gives biblical examples for each figure.[13]

Rhetorica ad Herennium 4 remained the most important treatment of the figures and tropes in the middle ages. A highly influential medieval treatise by Marbod of Rennes (*c.*1035–1123) was *De ornamentis verborum*, which paraphrases *Ad Herennium*'s definitions of thirty figures of speech, adding verse illustrations of each figure. This work survives in fifty-one manuscripts and it was printed once (Rennes, 1524).[14] Geoffrey de Vinsauf's *Poetria nova* (*c.*1200), which survives in 204 manuscripts,[15] devotes around a quarter of its 2116 lines to descriptions and (especially) examples of ten tropes, thirty-five figures of speech (examples only), and nineteen figures of thought (as in *Rhetorica ad Herennium*). Later medieval treatments of the figures include those in Eberhard the German's *Laborintus* (after 1213, before 1280), Joannes Balbus of Genoa's *Catholicon* (1280), and the anonymous fourteenth-century *Tria sunt*.[16]

PEROTTI

The earliest renaissance treatment of the tropes and figures and one which was very widely circulated in the late fifteenth century was the relatively brief section *De figuris* in Perotti's *Rudimenta grammatices*, composed in 1468, first printed in 1473, and printed a total of 133 times (115 times

[11] D. A. Russell, *Criticism in Antiquity* (London, 1981), 145–6. G. Kennedy, *The Art of Rhetoric in the Roman World* (Princeton, 1972), 337–8. P. Rutilius Lupus, *Schemata dianoeas et lexeos*, with study by G. Barabino (Genoa, 1967); *De figuris sententiarum et elocutionis*, ed. E. Brooks (Leiden, 1970).

[12] J. Brennan, 'The Epitome Troporum ac Schematum of Joannes Susenbrotus: Text, Translation and Commentary', Ph.D. dissertation, University of Illinois, 1953, pp. iii–vii. H. Keil (ed.), *Grammatici Latini*, i (Leipzig, 1867), iv (Leipzig, 1864).

[13] Halm, *Rhetores Latini Minores*, 606–18. Brennan, 'Epitome', p. xviii.

[14] Marbodo di Rennes, *'De ornamentis verborum'*, ed. R. Leotta (Florence, 1998), pp. xxxiii–xlii, 2–25.

[15] M. C. Woods, *Classroom Commentaries* (Columbus, Ohio, 2010), 289–307.

[16] M. Camargo, 'Latin Composition Textbooks and *Ad Herennium* Glossing: The Missing Link?', in Cox and Ward (eds.), *The Rhetoric of Cicero* (Leiden, 2006), 267–88. I am indebted to Martin Camargo for the information in this paragraph.

before 1500).[17] The division of this section of the work into barbarism, solecism, metaplasm, figures of words, tropes, and figures of construction, suggests that it is based on a Latin grammatical source. Perotti gives Greek names, defines each figure in response to a question, and adds an example of each figure and each subtype.[18]

ANTONIO MANCINELLI (1452–1505)

Some renaissance teachers took the view that their audiences required brief verse texts which could more easily be learned by heart. Antonio Mancinelli was a Latin teacher in Perugia, Rome, and other Italian cities who composed a number of textbooks on grammar and composition. His *Carmen de figuris* (Rome, 1489) was printed forty times up to 1590, latterly together with Mosellanus's *Epitome* which superseded it. Mancinelli's poem of 268 lines describes some ninety-eight figures, divided into faults (twenty-seven), schemes (eighteen), and a rather broad group of tropes (fifty-three). After the three- to four-line segment of the poem devoted to each figure, which generally gives a definition and an example, Mancinelli provides a prose commentary, including definition of the figure, an explanation of how the Greek term denotes the figure, some comments from other authorities (most often Diomedes, Donatus, or Quintilian), and examples of the figure. Mancinelli's main sources are Quintilian, *Rhetorica ad Herennium* (which he refers to as Cicero), and the grammarians Diomedes and Donatus.

> When various words are set out without conjunctions, certainly we achieve dialyton or asyntedon. You may take this example: the thing, the soldier, the people deny that. Dialyton may be called 'set free', for it is derived from the word Dialyo which is 'I untie'. Dialytos means 'dissolved'; Dialysis is 'dissolving'. Dialyton or asyntedon is a phrase without conjunctions. 'Bear arms in haste; hand out weapons; climb up on the walls' (*Aeneid* 9.37). The same in 'I came; I saw; I conquered'... This is also called brachylogia by Diomedes; also in Quintilian book 9 (9.3.50). Asyndetos is called disjoined; Asynthetos uncomposed.[19]

[17] This work is discussed in more detail in the next chapter because of its influential section on letter-writing.

[18] N. Perotti, *Rudimenta grammatices* (Milan, 1480), sigs. I4^v–K1^v.

[19] 'Cum sine iunctura voces variae locitantur / Dialyton certe vel asyndeton efficimus: / Exemplum capies: res miles plebs negat illud. / Dialyton dici potest absolutum: nam descendit a verbo Dialyo quod est dissolvo. Dialytos vero dissolutus. Dialysis dissolutio. Dialyton vel asyntedon est oratio sine coniunctionibus: ut... Ferte citi ferrum; date tela [ascendite muros]... Item in veni vidi vici...Haec etiam Bracchilochia nominatur, ut

Anaphora is called repetitio or relatio . . . Anaphora is, as Diomedes says the placing of the same word or a similar one at the beginning of several verses.[20]

JOHANNES DESPAUTERIUS (JEAN DESPAUTÈRE, *c.*1460–1520)

Johannes Despauterius was a Flemish grammarian who studied and taught at Louvain. His *De figuris* (1512) was printed fourteen times before 1620. Despauterius's work consists of a 100-line poem (heavily dependent on Mancinelli) defining ninety-two figures. He begins by defining a figure as 'a form of speech altered by a certain art', and dividing into metaplasm (the changes which poets make in order to observe the rules of metre), schemes, and tropes.[21] Later he distinguishes between schemes of words and schemes of thought but he only describes the former, perhaps because he regards the latter as part of rhetoric and therefore outside his remit.[22] This may be the reason why frequently used figures like conversio, permissio, dubitatio, correctio, and licentia do not appear in either Mancinelli or Despauterius.

The line of poetry devoted to each figure is followed by a short commentary in which Despauterius defines the figure in prose and adds an example (usually from Virgil). Sometimes he adds a comment on similarities between this figure and others. His list of figures is more thoroughly organized than Mancinelli's, though for the most part he gives the same figures in the same order (with three or four changes of terminology). He begins with fifteen vices of style (subdivided into *barbarum*, *obscurum*, and *inordinatum*, a division Diomedes also made). Then there are fourteen figures of metaplasm, eighteen schemes of words, twenty-seven tropes, and eighteen other figures. Most of his omissions in comparison to Mancinelli are in this last category (which Mancinelli included under tropes). Within the tropes proper Despauterius distinguishes thirteen main types of trope, with the others treated as species of hyperbaton, allegory, and homoeosis.[23]

Diomedes ait; et Fabius libro ix. Asyndetos disiunctus dicitur Asynthetos incompositus.' Sulpitius Verulanus, *Grammatice Quinta recognitio atque additio* (London, 1514), STC 23427a.7, sigs. H2^{v}–3^{r}.

[20] 'Anaphora dicitur repetitio vel relatio . . . Anaphora est, ut Diomedes ait, relatio verbi eiusdem aut similis per principia versuum plurimorum.' Ibid., sig. H3^{v}.

[21] 'Arte novata aliqua dicendi forma figura est.' J. de Spauter, *Artis versificatoriae compendium . . . Item de Figuris liber* (Edinburgh, 1631), sig. C1^{v}.

[22] Despauter, *De Figuris*, sigs. C3^{v}–4^{r}.

[23] Ibid., sigs. C5^{r}, C6$^{r–v}$.

> I call metonymy, I drink Bacchus, Vines crown. Metonymy is a change of names, which occurs when we understand the invention instead of the inventor, the contents instead of the container, the effect instead of the efficient cause, the possessor instead of the thing possessed and vice versa. Metonymy is translated as 'change of name' from meta, that is 'trans' and onoma, that is name.[24]

Despauterius's division of metonymy into these types recalls *Rhetorica ad Herennium* 4.32.43.

PETER SCHADE (1493–1524)

Peter Schade, known as Mosellanus because of his birth in Bruttig on the Mosel, studied with Caesarius and learnt Greek at Cologne (1512–14). He taught Greek in Freiburg and Leipzig where he studied theology and was rector in 1520 and 1523. He was a correspondent and supporter of Erasmus. His *Tabulae de schematibus et tropis* (Frankfurt, 1516) was the most successful of the sixteenth-century handbooks of tropes and figures, with eighty-six printings up to 1590. The main part of the book lists and defines the figures and tropes. In later editions this is supplemented with Georg Major's tabular summary of the whole of rhetoric, based on Melanchthon's *Institutiones rhetoricae*, and his (slightly longer) analysis and summary of Erasmus's *De copia*.[25]

Schade's introduction emphasizes the importance of the figures in capturing the attention of an audience and delighting them. Because there are so many figures and because it is as important to remember them all as it is difficult, Schade thought that it would be useful to collect information about all of them briefly so that students could easily have them all before their eyes. He even suggests that the lists and definitions should be put up on the wall of the school, somewhere where pupils would often see them, in order to refresh their memories. He will start with figures of speech, and then move on to vices and virtues of expression. For each entry he will give the Greek name, a Latin equivalent taken from

[24] 'Dico Metonymiam, Bacchum bibo, Vina coronant. / Metonymia est nominum transmutatio, quoties pro inventore inventum, pro continente contentum, pro efficiente effectum, pro possesso possessorem aut contra capimus. Metonymia transfertur nominis transmutatio, a meta, id est trans, et onoma id est nomen.' Ibid., sig. C5^{v}. Compare: 'Pone tenens lector pro contento: aut vice versa / Nunc pateras libate iovi vel vina coronant / Pone inventorem pro inventis: sive deum quem / Pro re cui praesit: seu pro coitu Venerem dic / Nempe Metonymiam concedimus esse figuram.' Mancinelli, *Carmen de figuris* (as in n. 19 above), H5^{r}.

[25] Mosellanus, *Tabulae de schematibus et tropis* (Antwerp, 1529), sigs. B7^{v}, D7^{r}.

Cicero (by which he means *Rhetorica ad Herennium*), Quintilian, or Diomedes. Then he will give explanations, definitions, and examples. Finally he claims to have included a few figures which others have omitted.[26]

Very clear organization is a strength of Schade's work. Figures are divided into figures of diction, locution, and construction. Schade also recognizes the class of figures of thought, but omits them because they lie outside his present grammatical purpose.[27] He gives fourteen figures of diction, corresponding to Despauterius's category of metaplasm, twenty-four of locution (and three subtypes), most of which are taken from Despauterius's schemes of words,[28] and five types of figures of construction, taken from the grammarians and showing some overlap with the figures of locution. As in Despauterius vices of style are divided into three categories: *obscurum* (eight types), *inordinatum* (six types), *barbarum* (three types). Most of the figures listed are the same as we find in Despauterius and Mancinelli, who took them from Diomedes. Virtues of style are divided into propriety (three qualities) and *ornatus*, whose main element is the tropes. Schade recognizes fourteen main types of trope, with eight subtypes of allegory, five subtypes of hyperbaton, and three subtypes of homoeosis. Like Despauterius he explains why genres like topography and chronography should not be regarded as tropes. In all Schade discusses ninety-three figures, a comparable total to Despauterius and Mancinelli. Like them he includes no figures of thought.

In general Schade's descriptions of figures are very short, offering the Greek name, a transcription into the Roman alphabet (or occasionally a Latin equivalent), a short explanation, and an example. Sometimes he adds a short comment on the use of a topic.

> *Προσωποποιία* Prosopopoeia, a feigning of persons, certainly when speech is given to many things. The poets allowed themselves much in this and the Orators took it over from them, as when Cicero in the speeches against Catilina fits speech to the country.
> *Ἀποσιώπησις* Aposiopesis, which Cicero calls reticence, when because of anger or indignation we stop speaking for part of the speech. 'Which I—but

[26] P. Mosellanus, *Tabulae de schematibus et tropis in rhetorica* (London, 1573), sigs. A1^v–2^r.
[27] Ibid., sig. A2^v.
[28] Eighteen are from Despauterius's figures of words, five are from the miscellaneous figures at the end of Despauterius's work; antimetabole is added from one of the classical lists.

better to still the raging waves.' (*Aeneid* 1. 135). He stops before saying 'will punish'.[29]

There are exceptions to this brevity, notably the discussions of metaphor and synecdoche. Some of the entries show a very clear verbal dependence on Despauterius (and behind him on Mancinelli and Diomedes), though Schade almost always alters the phrasing slightly. In many cases he chooses his own words or relies on a different source. He refers to Erasmus, Diomedes, Cicero, and Quintilian as sources. His uncharacteristically lengthy accounts of metaphor and synecdoche use Quintilian, Erasmus, and *Rhetorica ad Herennium*.[30] But the main features of Schade's account are the clear organization, the short entries for each figure, the reliance on Despauterius's lists, and the absence of figures of thought.

MELANCHTHON

Melanchthon introduced important changes to the presentation of the tropes and figures in his *Institutiones rhetoricae* (1521) and again later in the even more successful *Elementa rhetorices* (1529). As we saw in Chapter 6, these two manuals were published a total of 101 times up to 1610. The 1521 changes appear to have had the greater influence on later manuals of the tropes and figures. In 1521 Melanchthon begins with the tropes, which he has reduced to seven (metaphor, synecdoche, metonymy, antonomasia, onomatopoeia, catachresis, and metalepsis), adding a separate treatment of allegory (with eight subtypes including enigma, irony, sarcasm, proverb, and fable).[31] The figures are divided into grammatical (seven figures) and rhetorical in three orders: figures concerned with individual words (twelve figures: including repetition, polysyntedon, hypallage, and paronomasia), figures of thought (ten figures including question, exclamation, dubitatio, communicatio, prosopopeia, and parrhesia), and figures associated with amplification (thirty-three figures including climax, synonyms, distribution, aitiology, antithesis,

[29] 'Προσωποποιία Prosopopoeia, Personarum fictio, nimirum cum multis sermo tribuitur. In qua quanquam Poëtae multum sibi permittunt, tamen et Oratores usurpant, ut Cicero in Catilinam patriae sermonem accommodat... Ἀποσιώπησις Aposiopesis, quam Cicero reticentiam appellat, cum per iram vel indignationem, orationis partem reticemus. Quos ego, sed motos praestat componere fluctus. Tacet enim, puniam.' Mosellanus, *Tabulae*, sig. A6^{r-v}.

[30] Ibid., sigs. B3^{r}–4^{v}.

[31] Melanchthon, *Institutiones*, C3^{v}–D1^{v}. *Elementa*, 463–6, 472–3. *Elementa* slightly shortens both these lists.

antimetabole, prosopopeia again, and sententia).[32] In 1529 grammatical figures are omitted and figures of amplification are subdivided according to the topics of invention from which they are derived.[33] In comparison with Schade, Melanchthon has considerably reduced the total number of figures (now seventy-nine) at the same time as including the figures of thought, which authors working primarily from the grammatical tradition had omitted. He has also introduced a new and relatively straightforward division of the figures.

> SYNECDOCHE, the use of the part instead of the whole, as when I use the name of 'edge' instead of 'sword', or the name of 'sword' instead of the noun 'war'. The same thing: 'If someone strikes you on the right cheek, you should offer him also the left one'.
> Correctio, in Greek ἐπανόρθωσις, he takes away what he has said replacing it with another more suitable word, as 'Theologian, or rather nitpicker' or 'Cruel man, really not a man at all'. What Rutilius calls μετάνοιαν is obviously correctio.[34]

JOHANNES REUSCH

The Leipzig schoolmaster Johannes Reusch composed a brief *De tropis orationis et dictionis* (1521), which supplements Rufinianus's description of the figures of speech (which Reusch regards as the best explanation of the figures[35]) with an account of the tropes, based on *Rhetorica ad Herennium* and Quintilian. Reusch gives examples from the Bible and Cicero and quotes Erasmus's *De copia* on metaphor. The tropes of diction are metaphor, synecdoche, metonymy, antonomasia, onomatopoeia, catachresis, and metalepsis; the tropes of oration are allegory, irony, and their subtypes, such as enigma. Reusch adds a very brief account of comparisons and examples. The work was printed eleven times, mostly before 1542.[36]

[32] Melanchthon, *Institutiones*, D2r–E3v.

[33] Melanchthon, *Elementa*, 475–92.

[34] 'SYNECDOCHE, partis est pro toto usurpatio, ut cum pro gladii voce, utor mucronis adpellatione, pro belli nomine gladii. Tale est, si quis percusserit te in dextram maxillam tuam, porrige ei et sinistram. Correctio, graece ἐπανόρθωσις, tollit quod dictum est, supponens aliud magis idoneum, ut, Theologus, immo nugator; crudelis homo, immo ne homo quidem. Quam vocat Rutilius μετάνοιαν ea plane est correctio.' Melanchthon, *Institutiones rhetoricae* (Hagenau, 1521), sigs. C3v, E2r. Matthew 5: 39.

[35] J. Rufinianus, *De figuris lexeos,* with Reuschius, *De tropis orationis et dictionis* (Leipzig, 1521), sig. A2r.

[36] Rufinianus, ibid., sigs. B4v–C5v.

SUSENBROTUS (*c.*1485–1543)

Melanchthon's 1521 division of the material and inclusion of the figures of thought was taken up by the Ravensburg schoolmaster Susenbrotus in his *Epitome troporum ac schematum* (Zurich, 1540), which was printed twenty-six times up to 1620. Susenbrotus, however, hugely expanded the number of figures, reinstating many and finding further figures through an exhaustive comparison of sources, to reach a total of 132.[37] He divides the figures into tropes and schemes. Tropes are subdivided into tropes of words (nine kinds: Melanchthon's 1521 list, plus acrylogia and antiphrasis) and tropes of discourse (ten kinds: a slightly expanded list of the species of allegory, plus hyperbole). Schemes can be grammatical, subdivided into orthography (fifteen types), syntactical (thirty-two types, including aposiopesis and figures which involve changes in word-order, such as hysteron proteron and parenthesis; the list also includes some figures which could go in many places[38]) or rhetorical. Among rhetorical schemes, schemes of words include fourteen figures, schemes of thought nineteen figures, and schemes of amplification forty-one figures. A few figures appear in more than one category.[39]

In the address to his students which serves as a preface Susenbrotus insists that teachers need to identify the tropes and figures in texts they are reading just as much as they need to explain unusual words and difficult constructions. Ignorance of the tropes and figures will hinder or even prevent pupils from understanding classical texts. In his own teaching he has always tried to point out the figures both in order to help students interpret the texts correctly and to provide them with materials for their own speaking and writing. Since the students have previously had nothing to help them beyond Mosellanus's *Tabulae* he has now attempted to collect together from ancient and modern authors whatever can help in reading classical literature. In setting out the figures and tropes he has followed the order established by Melanchthon.[40]

Brennan has shown with admirable exactness how Susenbrotus constructed the individual entries through constant references to, and comparisons between: *Rhetorica ad Herennium*, Quintilian, Erasmus's *De copia* (including Weltkirchius's commentary and an epitome) and *Ecclesiastes*, Diomedes, the minor Latin orators Rutilius Lupus, Aquila Romanus, and

[37] Susenbrotus, *Epitome*, repr. in Brennan, 'Epitome', sigs. A2^{v}–3^{v}.
[38] Susenbrotus, *Epitome*, repr. in Brennan, 'Epitome', sig. B5^{v}.
[39] e.g. Susenbrotus, *Epitome*, sigs A7^{v}, B1^{v} (antiphrasis), E2^{v}, F3^{r-v} (prosopopeia).
[40] Ibid., sigs. A2^{r-v}, D1^{r}.

Rufinianus, Mancinelli, Despauterius, Schade, Linacre's *Grammar,* and Melanchthon.[41]

Susenbrotus defines a figure as 'a certain method, by which the direct and simple kind of speaking is altered with a certain strength in the expression'.[42] He explains that figures are supported by the best authorities and are useful in varying our expression and making it more delightful to listeners, in words taken over from Quintilian.[43] His definition of trope ('a variation of a phrase or a word from its proper meaning to a related one for the sake of charm') is close to Quintilian, while the definition of scheme ('a form of speaking and writing altered in some way') is slightly altered from Despauterius.[44] Susenbrotus gives a relatively short account of metaphor, with a definition related to one given by Erasmus, a commendation, various examples, and an explanation that metaphors may be used for necessity (when no appropriate word exists), for emphasis, or for ornament, with examples of each type, taken from Quintilian.[45] In the longer entries on synecdoche and metonymy he follows Schade, who is here drawing on Erasmus.[46]

The general pattern of Susenbrotus's entries on figures of speech is to give a Latin term (often but not always a transliteration of the Greek); the associated Greek term; another Latin equivalent, if appropriate; an explanation; and several examples. Occasionally he adds a division of the figure (with examples of each type); more often he adds at the end a comment on the use of the figure or on alternative names or related figures. He quite often quotes Mancinelli's verse definitions and sometimes invents examples related to religious topics, as Melanchthon had. From time to time he adds a separate note (*Observatiuncula*) on the use of a particular figure or group of figures.

> Subjectio occurs when we reply to our own question. This is effected in three ways. First when we object to ourselves what might be objected by our

[41] Brennan, 'Epitome', pp. xvi–xxii, xxv, 107–41. Occasionally Brennan under-reports the changes Susenbrotus made to his sources. This valuable thesis should be made more widely available.

[42] 'Figura est ratio quaedam, qua de recto ac simplici loquendi genere cum aliquo dicendi virtute deflectitur.' Susenbrotus, *Epitome*, sig. A4^{v}.

[43] Ibid., sig. A4^{v}. Brennan, 'Epitome', 110. Quintilian 9.3.3–4.

[44] 'Tropus est dictionis sive orationis a propria significatione in cognatam ornandi gratia variatio . . . Schema, vel figura proprie, est aliqua novata et scribendi et dicendi forma.' Susenbrotus, *Epitome,* sig. A4^{v}. Brennan, 'Epitome', 110. Quintilian 8.6.1. Despauterius, *De Figuris,* sig. C1^{v}.

[45] Susenbrotus, *Epitome,* sig. A5^{r}. Brennan, 'Epitome', 110. Erasmus, *De copia, Opecoronnia,* i/6, 62–4. Quintilian 8.6.4.

[46] Susenbrotus, *Epitome,* sig. A5^{r}–6^{r}. Brennan, 'Epitome', 110–11. Mosellanus, *Tabulae,* sig. B4$^{r–v}$. Erasmus, *De copia,* 68–72.

> auditors, and we reply just as if the objection had really been made; secondly when we compel our adversaries to respond and we refute them just as though they had responded; third when we propose various replies, as though deliberating, but then confute them one by one. The first method, according to Erasmus is fitting to argument. The second is appropriate for the conclusion and both for the introduction. The third is apt for deliberating. [He gives lengthy examples of each type.] There is another species of subjectio in which we ourselves propose a question and then answer it, and thereby render the hearer attentive. [Another example.] There is yet another form of subjectio by which we concede something as though it were an objection posed by our adversary, and thereupon add a further qualification by which we turn his objection to our own advantage . . . This scheme is somewhat related to *erotemata*, *dialogismus*, *occupatio*, and *dubitatio*. It is not useful for any one occasion in discourse; it makes for perspicuity, for vehemence or gravity, for docility.[47]

While Susenbrotus normally only quotes his examples, sometimes he adds comments on the way a particular author has used a figure or on the interpretation of a particular passage. He gives more advice than other post-classical writers on the uses of particular figures. By allocating a number of figures primarily to amplification and by the way he uses material from *De copia* and the commentary on it by Weltkirchius in describing these figures, Susenbrotus in a way absorbs the teaching of *De copia* into the manual of tropes and figures.[48] The thorough accounts of comparison, types of description, and *sententiae* (also taken from Erasmus) have the effect of incorporating also sections from the *progymnasmata*, so that the book prepares for several different aspects of the grammar-school rhetoric course.[49]

Susenbrotus is very impressive in his scholarship, clarity of expression, and thoughtfulness. The entries are much too long to be learnt by heart

[47] 'Subjectio est cum ipsi nostrae interrogatione respondemus. Id fit tribus modis. Primo cum nobisipsis obiicimus quod ab adversaribus obiici poterat, et quasi obiectum sit respondemus. Secundo, cum adversarios compellamus ut respondeant, et quasi responderint, refellimus. Tertio, cum quasi deliberantes varia proponemus, ac singula confutamus. Primus modus auctore Erasmo convenit argumentatione; Secundus epilogo, uterque convenit introductione. Tertius aptus est ad deliberandum . . . Est praeterea subjectionis species, qua, dum ipsi questionem proponimus ac mox ad eam respondemus, reddimus auditorem attentum ac docilem . . . Est et alia subjectionis forma qua quiddam veluti ab adversario nobis obiectum concedimus, sed subiicimus aliud, quo illius obiectionem ad nos detorquemus . . . Habet autem hoc schema nonnihil affinitatis cum erotemate, dialogismo, occupatione, et cum dubitatione. Nec ad unam orationis commoditatem utilis est. Facit ad perspicuitatem, et ad vehementiam sive gravitatem, et ad docilitatem.' Susenbrotus, *Epitome*, sigs. D6^{r}–7^{r}, tr. Brennan.

[48] e.g. Susenbrotus, *Epitome*, sigs. E3^{r}–4^{r}.

[49] Ibid., sigs. E4^{v}–5^{v}, F3^{r}–4^{v}, F6^{v}–7^{r}.

but the student who read this book frequently and used it as a reference while reading would have access to an immense amount of information about the figures and many examples of each figure.

Lawrence Green has shown that T. W. Baldwin's comments on the ubiquity of Susenbrotus's *Epitome* are overstated in view of the comparatively small number of editions.[50] While we do not know exactly how many editions any of these works went through, it is now safe to assume that there were far fewer editions of any of these handbooks of tropes and figures than there were of standard grammar texts, such as the Lily-Colet grammar in England. Green points out that a few of the figures were taught in the grammar texts, and they may have been supplemented by notes dictated by individual teachers, such as those which survive in Conybeare's *Notebook*.[51]

TALON'S *RHETORICA*

After Susenbrotus, the next major contribution to the study of the tropes and figures was the publication of Omer Talon's *Rhetorica* (Paris, 1548), which went through more than 100 editions before 1620. Since three-quarters of this work (in the later and most printed editions) was given over to the tropes and figures, it must often have been used largely as a guide to them. As we saw in Chapter 7, Talon (and Ramus) reduced the tropes to four (metonymy, irony, metaphor, and synecdoche), treating allegory and hyperbole as types of metaphor.[52] This change proved to be very influential. Later writers who would not contemplate considering themselves as Ramists were nevertheless happy to focus their attention on these four essential tropes (usually in a different order). Equally influential was Talon's decision to place poetic metre and prose-rhythm alongside the tropes at the centre of rhetoric. From now on most handbooks would do the same. This move also helped Talon to reduce the number of figures by including the requirements of rhythm and metre without the need for the numerous figures specified by the grammarians.

More controversial (and less influential on later writers) was Talon's decision to reduce the figures of rhetoric to nineteen. Talon's subdivisions make the whole system much easier to recall, and retain the most frequently used figures. He divides figures of words into those which involve the same sound (seven, including anadiplosis, climax, anaphora, and

[50] Green, 'Grammatica movet', 77, 105–10.
[51] Ibid. 84–104, 110–15. Mack, *Elizabethan Rhetoric*, 45–6.
[52] O. Talon, *Rhetorica* (Cambridge, 1631), sigs. A8^{v}–B1^{r}.

epanados) and those which use similar sounds (two: paronomasia and polyptoton). Figures of thought are divided into monologic (exclamatio, correctio, aposiopesis, apostrophe, and prosopopeia) and dialogic (addubitatio, communicatio, occupatio, permissio, and concessio). Short though the list is, most of the most frequently used and most effective figures are included. Often Talon's accounts of particular figures are preceded by definition and division of the genus to which they belong. Generally he gives a definition followed by several examples, mainly from Cicero, Virgil, and Terence.[53] Because the list is so short Talon can give more examples of each figure and because the system is easier to understand and remember pupils will more quickly move on to the real point of what they are learning, observing how the best classical authors use the tropes and figures in their works. Talon's treatment of the tropes, in particular, is more subdivided and nuanced (and makes more of the logical bases of metonymy and synecdoche) than Susenbrotus or Mosellanus.[54]

> Apostrophe, turning aside, is when the speech is turned to another person than the oration we have undertaken dictates. This figure comes not far short of Exclamatio in its emotional force and is often joined with it. But Apostrophe can be differentiated according to the different condition of the persons. Sometimes the turning is towards a human person. [Examples from Cicero and Virgil.] Sometimes the turning is from men to Gods. [Examples.] In the poets the invocation is a conspicuous example of Apostrophe. [Examples.] At other times the speech is transferred to an inarticulate and inanimate object, as if it were a person. [Examples.] This figure is rare but it is found from time to time, especially in exordia. [Example.][55]

JULIUS CAESAR SCALIGER (1484–1558)

Julius Caesar Scaliger was a Paduan physician, philosopher, grammarian, and naturalist who lived for most of his adult life in Agen in France. His posthumously published *Poetices libri septem* (1561), which was printed ten times up to 1617, contains two treatments of the figures of speech, in books 3 and 4. He defines a figure as 'an acceptable delineation of notions

[53] e.g. ibid., sigs. C4^{r-v}, C7^{r}–8^{r}.

[54] Ibid., sigs. A4^{r}–7^{r}, B1^{r}–3^{r}.

[55] 'Apostrophe, aversio, est quando oratio ad alienam personam convertitur, quam instituta oratio requirit. Figura non multum cedens elationis genere Exclamationi, et persaepe cum ea conjugitur. Sed Apostrophe ex conditione personarum varie distingui potest. Alias enim ad humanam personam sit aversio ... Alias ab hominibus ad deos sit aversio ... In Apostrophe Invocatio insignis est apud poetas ... Alias ad rem mutam et inanimatam, velut ad personam, transfertur oratio ... Haec figura raro quidem, sed tamen aliquando protinus in proemio adhibatur.' Ibid., sigs. C8^{r}–D1^{r}.

which are in the mind, different from ordinary usage' and refuses to distinguish between figures and tropes.[56] Whereas grammar and dialectic have their own kinds of figures (for dialectic Scaliger is thinking of the figures of the syllogism), oratory, history, and poetics share the common figures.[57] Book 3, supposedly concerned with figures of meaning, and using mainly Latin terms, divides ninety-seven figures into five classes. Since figures are a way of representing notions in the mind they must be either equal to (sixty-six figures), greater than (seven), less than (ten), different from (one), or contrary to (thirteen) the idea expressed. Book 4, supposedly devoted to figures of words, and using mainly Greek terms, divides thirty-eight figures into nine classes: from omission (two), from inclusion of the same word (eleven: anaphora, climax, etc.), from inclusion of the meaning (two), from inclusion of similar things (three: allusion, paronomasia, etc.), from different things (nine: pleonasmus, periphrasis, metonymy, etc.), from inclusion of contrary things (six), change of position within the sentence (six: hyperbaton, parenthesis, etc.), from quantity (three: parison, synthesis, tmesis), and from quality (two: homeoptoton and homeoteleuton). This division of the figures is certainly logical and original but not particularly helpful, especially in book 3 where most of the figures lie within the same class. Scaliger's treatment of individual figures is very brief, usually giving only a definition of the figure and an example from Virgil. Rather surprisingly in a work of poetics, metaphor is treated only once and very briefly.[58]

Luc Deitz has shown that in book 3 Scaliger based his account of the figures mainly on Latin sources, especially on Aquila Romanus, Julius Rufinianus, *Ad Herennium*, Quintilian, and George Trapezuntius, while in book 4, as Francis Cairns showed, he worked directly from the Greek *De figuris* by Alexander, son of Numenius, printed in the *Rhetores Graeci* of 1508. Deitz documents the overlaps between the two lists, explaining that Scaliger followed his Greek source very closely, apparently without noticing the repetition, which is explained by a lost common source for Aquila and Alexander.[59]

[56] 'Figura est notionum quae in mente sunt, tolerabilis delineatio, alia ab usu commune.' J. C. Scaliger, *Poetices libri septem* (Lyon, 1561; repr. Stuttgart, 1964), 120. He acknowledges but does not observe the distinction between figures of words and figures of things, p. 121.

[57] Ibid. 121.

[58] Ibid. 127.

[59] J. C. Scaliger, *Poetices libri septem*, ii, ed. L. Deitz (Stuttgart, 1994), 30–59 (esp. pp. 35–6). F. Cairns, 'The Poetices libri septem: An Unexplored Source', *Res Publica Litterarum*, 9 (1986), 49–57.

SIMON VEREPAEUS (*c*.1522–1598)

Simon Verepaeus was a Catholic Dutch grammar-school teacher who wrote textbooks on grammar and letter-writing, and prayers. His *Praeceptiones de figuris seu de tropis et schematibus* (Cologne, 1582), which stretches to 160 octavo pages written in the question-and-answer form of the catechism, was printed six times before 1620, sometimes alongside his *Praeceptiones de verborum et rerum copia*. Verepaeus divides his textbook into faults, tropes, and figures. As in Diomedes, Despauterius, and Schade, the faults are divided into *barbarum*, *obscurum*, and *inordinatum*, though with fewer figures in each class. He discusses eight tropes of words and four of discourse, including seven types of allegory, which is close to Melanchthon (who as a Protestant is not named). He follows Susenbrotus in dividing figures between grammatical and rhetorical. As in Melanchthon and Susenbrotus, the rhetorical figures are divided into figures of words (fifteen figures, including anaphora and its associates), figures of thought (nine), and figures of amplification (thirty), but with some omissions and usually fewer figures assigned to each class. Verepaeus is extremely thorough in his treatment of the tropes, making many subdivisions, particularly in metaphor, metonymy, and synecdoche.[60] He makes considerable use of Schade and Susenbrotus in his treatment of individual figures.

> Gradatio, climax, is what it is called when the sentence rises as if by steps so that the word ending the preceding clause begins the following one.[61]

KECKERMANN, VOSSIUS, CAUSSIN

The large encyclopedic textbooks of rhetoric of the early seventeenth century, which we discussed in the previous chapter, make some use of the specialized textbooks of tropes and figures. Keckermann focuses on Talon's four main tropes (metonymy, synecdoche, metaphor, and irony).[62] He divides figures of thought into six classes according to their uses: explanation, proof, amplification, emotions in general, relation to others (like Talon's category of dialogue), and figures connected with

[60] Verepaeus, *Praeceptiones de figuris seu de tropis et schematibus* (Cologne, 1590), sigs. B8^{v}–C6^{v}.

[61] 'Gradatio, climax, dicitur, cum ita quasi per gradus ascendit oratio, ut dictio finiens clausulam precedentem, inchoat sequentem.' Ibid., sig. h6^{r}.

[62] Keckermann, *Systema Rhetoricae*, M5^{v}–O7^{v}.

specific emotions.[63] Figures of speech are divided into four classes on the basis of form: figures of omission, figures of addition or excess, changes in order, and figures of repetition.[64] Vossius concentrates mainly on four tropes (metaphor, metonymy, synecdoche, and irony), some types of allegory, and three lesser tropes. He tells us that he takes his division of the figures from Scaliger's third book, but it would be better to say that there are some similarities between Vossius's classification and particular sections of Scaliger's two versions of a division. While Vossius's first and second classes resemble the first two groups from Scaliger's fourth book, both in the terms of the description and the content, his third and fourth classes resemble Scaliger's 4.38-41 in description but not in content and his sixth and eleventh groups have some connections with sections 2, 3 and 5 of Scaliger's book 3 division. Caussin's main treatment of the figures combines an inclusive approach with the abandonment of classification, giving brief accounts of 207 figures in alphabetical order, including several repetitions.[65] Later he adds a section on the use of figures, suggesting seven classes for a selection from his longer list: those which express a picture of something in a few words, figures for longer descriptions, repetition, improving the sweetness of the sentence, for weightiness, for argument, and for emotions.[66] He includes tropes and figures of thought but does not separate them from figures of words.

Other new textbooks which were intended for grammar school use were the letter-writing manuals (to be discussed in the next chapter), new versions of the *progymasmata*, particularly from Spanish authors,[67] and adaptations of Erasmus's *De copia*. The latter included Georg Major's summary printed with later editions of Schade's *Tabulae* and Verepaeus's *Praeceptiones de verborum et rerum copia* (Cologne, 1582).[68]

The existence of separate manuals of tropes and figures, of which around 180 editions are known to have been printed between 1489 and 1620, confirms the importance of the tropes and figures within rhetorical education.

[63] Ibid., R2^{r}–V3^{r}.

[64] Ibid., V3^{r}–Y2^{r}.

[65] Caussin, *Parallela*, 256–80.

[66] Ibid. 281–93.

[67] Anon, *Progymnasmata in artem oratoriam* (Paris, 1520), which was printed nine times up to 1620 and see L. López Grigera, *La rétorica en la España del siglo de oro* (Salamanca, 1994), 55, 59, 69–83, 185, mentioning Juan Pérez, *Progymnasmata artis rhetoricae* (Alcala, 1539), Antonio Lulio's *Progymnasmata rhetorica* (Basel, 1548), Lorenzo Palmireno, *Aphthonii progymnasmata* (Valencia, 1553), Juan Mal Lara, *Aphthonii progymnasmata scholia* (Hispali, 1567), Alfonso Torres, *Exercitationes rhetoricae* (Alcala, 1569), and Pedro Juan Nuñez, *Progymnasmata* (Zaragoza, 1596).

[68] Johann Possel, *Calligraphia oratoria linguae Grecae, ad proprietatem, elegantiam et copiam graeci sermonis parandam* (Frankfurt 1585), which went through eight edns., is a Latin–Greek phrasebook organized alphabetically by subject.

These doctrines were also available to readers in *Rhetorica ad Herennium* and Quintilian's *Institutio oratoria*, which together went through more than 280 editions, as well as in all the major renaissance manuals of the whole of rhetoric, totalling more than 550 editions. The large numbers of editions of these manuals confirm the implications of school statutes and instructions for reading, that pupils should be introduced to the figures and tropes once they had passed beyond the elementary stage of Latin reading. Teachers were supposed to point out the ways in which classical authors used the tropes and figures. To do this they needed handbooks of tropes and figures to be studied in advance of the full course in rhetoric. The brevity of the earlier manuals can be explained by the way in which they were to be used. The focus was on learning the names and definitions by heart so that figures could be recognized in reading. Recognizing and naming the figures made it possible to observe the ways in which classical authors used the tools of their trade and made this aspect of their reading available to pupils for imitation in their own writing.

In the course of the sixteenth century textbook writers made various attempts to develop categorizations of the tropes and figures which would help pupils understand and remember them better. None of these attempts was entirely successful, because even those that were followed widely tended to produce some categories (such as Melanchthon's category of figures associated with amplification) which included very numerous and diverse figures. The result was that one of the most important *summae* of rhetoric of the early seventeenth century abandoned classification in favour of a huge and repetitive alphabetical list. Probably the most effective of the new systems of organization was devised by Omer Talon, but at the cost of a radical reduction in the number of figures. His identification of four principal tropes was largely adopted by later writers.

Within the developing tradition of descriptions of the tropes and figures we notice a tension between an expansive impulse, caused by the scholarly desire to incorporate the teaching of a widening range of classical texts, and an impulse to shorten and simplify derived from a pedagogic preference for teaching which can be learnt more quickly and remembered more easily. So while Susenbrotus and Caussin, for example, enlarge the scope of the book, Melanchthon and Talon look for ways to shorten it.

Another characteristic of these manuals is their conservatism. We have seen how Schade copies from Despauterius, who copies Mancinelli, who relies very heavily on the Latin grammarian Diomedes. This tradition also makes a strong impression on all the later writers. One striking effect of this is that the figures of thought only enter the sixteenth-century manuals of tropes and figures at a rather late stage. Thus of the roughly 180 editions of manuals of the tropes and figures, about 140 lack the figures of thought. In later editions of Schade, Major's table of the whole of rhetoric names several figures which Schade's *Tabulae de schematibus* has not described or exemplified.[69]

In contrast we can also see how a little later the manual of tropes and figures begins to incorporate the approach of Erasmus's *De copia*, first in the attachment of Major's summary of *De copia* to later editions of Schade's manual, then in the adoption of the category of figures assisting amplification, and eventually in the reuse of sections from Erasmus in Susenbrotus and Verepaeus.

The overall pattern of publication suggests two conclusions. It very much looks as if independent publication of Mancinelli is superseded by the appearance of Schade's *Tabulae* in 1516. Twenty-four editions of Mancinelli appear before 1518. There are no editions between 1520 and 1540. All the editions after 1540 are part of a collection of texts based on Schade. Considering the group of texts as a whole it seems that there was strong regular production of such manuals between 1500 and 1580, with at least ten editions per decade. There was a peak of around twenty-five editions per decade between 1530 and 1550 and a middle plateau of sixteen editions per decade 1550–1570. Production peaks in the heyday of northern humanism, and tails off at about the same time as Ciceronian rhetoric declines more generally.

[69] Mosellanus, *Tabulae*, sigs. C3^{v}–4^{v}.

11

Letter-Writing Manuals

Latin letter-writing manuals were among the most printed renaissance works on rhetoric with about 900 editions of individual works published between 1460 and 1620. Two manuals in particular, Perotti's *Rudimenta grammatices* (1473), which gave a quarter of its space to letter-writing, and Erasmus's *De conscribendis epistolis* (1521), went through over 100 editions. Several publishers produced omnibus volumes containing manuals by several different authors which were frequently reprinted. Letter-writing was a central feature of grammar-school education, beginning with the imitation of some of Cicero's simpler domestic letters and moving on to several types of letter on subjects related to daily life or to the pupils' reading in classical texts. There were also many letter-writing manuals in the vernacular, some of them quite frequently reprinted, which I shall discuss in Chapter 13 below.

Renaissance letter-writing manuals share many features. They generally define the letter, divide letters into types, provide recipes for and examples of each type, and give advice on formulas of address. There is some conflict in the manuals between those who endorse the medieval pattern of the five-part letter and those who treat the letter as a variant on the form of the oration. While earlier manuals present a variety of fixed elements which the different types of letter should contain, some later ones proclaim that the structure of the letter is free and that writers must devise a form appropriate to their personal relationship to the addressee. Most manuals include some advice on appropriate style or useful formula phrases. While some manuals give simple rules for the construction of different types of letter, others focus more on the relationship between writer and recipient, arguing that this is the foundation for one's whole approach to letter-writing.

Lawrence Green has suggested that letter-writing manuals provided many people with all the rhetoric they needed to know. While I would want to add that schoolboys also learnt rhetoric from their reading of classical authors, from lists of tropes and figures, from their composition exercises, and/or from frequently printed books like Aphthonius's *Progymnasmata* and Erasmus's *De copia*, nevertheless Green identifies an important truth, that for many people the letter-writing manual would be the main or only systematic rhetoric manual which they had read. Some later manuals recognize this probability by expanding the letter-writing manual with further rhetoric teaching (such as the tropes and the figures).

Humanist writers of letter-writing manuals were faced with an acute dilemma in taking up an attitude to their predecessors. Classical manuals said relatively little about the composition of letters, while the medieval *ars dictaminis* had made an extensive and impressive analysis of practical letter-writing.[1] At the same time newly discovered classical collections of letters (by Cicero and Pliny) invited imitation and showed an achievement in letters beyond the utilitarian scope of the medieval manuals. Although they varied in their approach to such 'medieval' features of letter-writing as the five-part structure and the honorific adjectives suitable for different types of addressee, the earliest humanist manuals agreed on the need to teach letter-writing as a part of intermediate grammatical teaching, along with the techniques of artistic Latin prose.

The printed record suggests five main phases of composition of humanist letter-writing manuals. Many compilations and new works were produced in the first thirty years of printing, mainly in Italy, and enjoyed considerable success up to the 1520s. A second group of mainly northern European manuals appeared around 1500. Around 1520 the most successful of all these manuals, Erasmus's *De conscribendis epistolis,* was published alongside Hegendorff's brief *Methodus*. In the 1530s and 1540s new manuals, both Italian and northern, appeared which responded to Erasmus's work and to Melanchthon's reform of rhetoric teaching. The 1570s saw several new works culminating in Lipsius's brief original treatise of 1591. There was no important Ramist contribution to letter-writing.[2]

Although the ancient world produced several important collections of letters, letter-writing played a very minor part in ancient rhetoric textbooks: short sections within Demetrius, *On Style* (first century BC) and Julius Victor's *Ars Rhetorica* (fourth century AD) and two longer late Greek treatises: Pseudo-Demetrius's *Τύποι ἐπιστολικοί* (third to fourth century AD) and Pseudo-Libanius's *'Επιστολιμαῖοι*

[1] G. C. Alessio, 'L'Ars dictaminis nel Quattrocento italiano: Eclissi o persistenza?', *Rhetorica,* 19 (2001), 155–74.

[2] For orientation see M. Fumaroli, 'Genèse de l'épistolographie classique: rhétorique humaniste de la lettre', *Revue d'histoire littéraire de la France,* 78 (1978), 886–905. Luc Vaillancourt, *La Lettre familière au 16e siècle* (Paris, 2003). T. Van Houdt *et al.* (eds.), *Self-Presentation and Social Identification: The Rhetoric and Pragmatics of Letter-Writing in Early Modern Times* (Louvain, 2002). C. Poster and L. Mitchell (eds.), *Letter-Writing Manuals and Instruction from Antiquity to the Present* (Columbia, SC, 2007), esp. pp. 88–177.

χαρακτῆρες (fourth to sixth century AD).[3] Pseudo-Libanius defines the letter as a 'written conversation between two people apart from each other, for a concrete purpose', while Cicero says that 'the property of a letter is that the person addressed should become informed about affairs of which he or she is ignorant' or that 'we should inform people apart from us about things which they should know, either to their or our advantage'.[4] These definitions were widely repeated in renaissance letter-writing manuals. Cicero divided letters into three classes: informative; friendly and jesting; and severe and serious.[5] Julius Victor distinguishes between official and familiar letters.[6] Pseudo-Demetrius and Pseudo-Libanius list twenty-one and forty-one types of letters respectively, including some types which were taken up by renaissance authors: for example, consolatory, admonitory, vituperative, deliberative, petitioning, warning, reconciling.[7] Both give definitions of each type and very brief model letters for each kind. Letters were discussed either within the context of discussing style or alongside discussions of appropriate qualities of style (correctness, clarity, and brevity).[8] Demetrius insisted that the letter should be an expression of the writer's character.[9]

Prompted by the need of kings and popes to express their intentions to distant subjects, the later middle ages developed a new form of epistolary rhetoric based on the principal rhetorical texts available, *Rhetorica ad Herennium* and Cicero's *De inventione*, rather than on classical epistolary theory.[10] From the late eleventh to the late fourteenth century, teachers of letter-writing produced dozens, if not hundreds, of *Artes dictaminis*, some of which dealt with aspects of rhetoric beyond letter-writing strictly considered. By 1135 the essential form of the letter (and the treatise) was established. The letter should be defined (e.g. 'a suitable arrangement

[3] P. Martín Baños, *El arte epistolar en el Renacimiento europeo 1400–1600* (Bilbao, 2005), 27–39. A. Malherbe, *Ancient Epistolary Theorists* (SBL Sources for Biblical Study, 19; Atlanta, Ga., 1988). P.-L. Malosse, *Lettres pour toutes circonstances: Les Traités épistolaires du Pseudo-Libanios et du Pseudo-Démétrios de Phalère* (Paris, 2004).

[4] Baños, *El arte epistolar*, 43, 46, 59; Malherbe, *Ancient Epistolary Theorists*, 20, 66; Cicero, *Ad Quintum fratrem* 1.1.37, *Ad familiares* 2.4.1 (to Curio).

[5] Cicero, *Ad familiares* 2.4.1.

[6] Halm (ed.), *Rhetores latini minores* (Leipzig, 1863; repr. Frankfurt, 1964), 447.

[7] Malherbe, *Ancient Epistolary Theorists*, 30, 66. Baños, *El arte epistolar*, 51–4.

[8] Baños, *El arte epistolar*, 64–74. Demetrius, *On Style* 223–9.

[9] Demetrius, *On Style* 227.

[10] M. Richardson, 'The *Ars dictaminis*, the Formulary and Medieval Epistolary Practice', in Poster and Mitchell, *Letter-Writing Manuals*, 52–66. J. J. Murphy, *Rhetoric in the Middle Ages* (Berkeley, Calif., 1974), 194–268. M. Camargo, *Ars Dictaminis, Ars Dictandi* (Turnhout, 1991). For edns see Camargo, *Ars Dictaminis*, 51–5, and L. Rockinger, *Briefsteller und Formelbücher*, 2 vols. (Munich, 1863).

of words set forth to express the intended meaning of the sender').[11] Each of its five parts (*salutatio*, *exordium* or *captatio benevolentiae*, *narratio*, *petitio*, *conclusio*) should be described, giving special attention to the forms of salutation appropriate to different levels of noble and ecclesiastical addressee. Then there should be some discussion of style, for example, of methods of amplifying or shortening the text or a description of the Latin *cursus* in place of the classical theory of sentence composition.[12] From the second half of the twelfth century, letter-writing manuals always include a treatment of prose-rhythm, something which is not usually found in the humanist manuals. Alongside the *Artes dictaminis* proper we also find a number of formulary manuals, which provide model letters for a range of possible situations. In some collections the model letters are organized by subject-matter or function; in others they are grouped according to the status of sender and recipient.[13] These model letters were sometimes added to a treatise on letter-writing to form a *Summa dictandi*.[14]

Paul Kristeller saw the earliest humanists as the direct professional heirs of the medieval teachers of letter-writing.[15] Ronald Witt has argued that humanism originated in Lovato dei Lovati's poetic experiments in mid-thirteenth-century Padua. According to Witt the earlier humanists, up to the late fourteenth century, continued to follow the medieval *ars dictaminis* in their teaching and practice of letter-writing. He sees Salutati's experience as split between a private interest in Cicero and classical standards of Latin prose and a public adherence to medieval forms.[16] The recovery of Cicero's letters by Petrarch and Salutati in the fourteenth century prompted imitation of classical forms of letter.[17] The earliest humanist manuals on letter-writing were overwhelmingly composed in Italy, though the earliest of all, the writings of Barzizza (see Chapter 3 above), Fliscus, and work attributed to Aeneas Sylvius Piccolomini were first transmitted in print in the collection *Margarita poetica* (1472)

[11] Murphy, *Rhetoric in the Middle Ages*, 222.

[12] Camargo, *Ars Dictaminis*, 23–6. Murphy, *Rhetoric in the Middle Ages*, 248–53.

[13] I owe these last three sentences to comments by Martin Camargo who kindly looked over this chapter.

[14] Camargo, *Ars Dictaminis*, 27–8. Murphy, *Rhetoric in the Middle Ages*, 199–202.

[15] P. O. Kristeller, *Renaissance Thought and its Sources* (New York, 1979), 93–4.

[16] R. Witt, 'Medieval "Ars Dictaminis" and the Beginnings of Humanism: A New Construction of the Problem', *Renaissance Quarterly*, 35 (1982), 1–35; *In the Footsteps of the Ancients* (Leiden, 2000), 96–105, 295–323, 443–5.

[17] J. Rice Henderson, 'Erasmus on the Art of Letter-Writing', in J. J. Murphy (ed.), *Renaissance Eloquence* (Berkeley, Calif., 1983), 332–6); R. G. Witt, *Coluccio Salutati and his Public Letters* (Geneva, 1976).

compiled by the German humanist Albrecht von Eyb (1420–75), which was printed twenty-two times up to 1503.

Margarita poetica is better considered as a resource for letter-writers than as a letter-writing manual. The book is in five sections. The first tractate (attributed in some editions to Barzizza and Fliscus) discusses sentence composition and rhythmic prose, ending with a poem describing twenty-five figures of speech. The second (also said to be Barzizza's) collects phrases (for example, expressing friendship or thanks, or saying how much pleasure letters received gave) likely to be useful to someone composing a letter. These phrases are grouped according to the six parts of an oration. The third section collects elegant phrases from the letters of Cicero (ordered by the book of letters from which they are taken) and recent writers such as Barzizza, Bruni, and Poggio organized according to topics relevant to letters (such as love, goodwill, inviting someone to dinner, praising the liberal arts), and closing with a long sequence of extracts from poetry. The fourth section lists impressive phrases, proverbs, moral narratives, and similes taken from works by Cicero (starting with *De officiis*), Lactantius, Macrobius, Terence, Seneca's tragedies, and Petrarch. The final section consists of orations including praises of the Eucharist and of St Jerome, a lament for the death of Lorenzo de' Medici, and an argument that someone should be willing to serve as rector. Prefaces to the different sections indicate that the aim of the work is to collect materials which would be useful for letter-writing.[18] Some other early manuals, such as the very successful *Elegantiarum viginti praecepta* (1477; forty-three editions) present themselves as directed to letter-writing while providing fairly standard grammatical advice on varying sentence order, while others, such as Maneken's *Formulae epistolarum* (1476; forty-three editions) or the anonymous *Formularium instrumentorum* (1474; thirty-one editions), consist of models for letters or ecclesiastical and legal documents.

In some of its early editions the *Elegantiolae*,[19] or rules for composition of elegant Latin sentences, of Agostino Dati (1420–78) are accompanied by two letter-writing manuals, one which forms part of pseudo-Dati's *De variis loquendi figuris* (1472), the other is by Antonius Haneron (*c.*1400–90): *De epistolis brevibus edendis* (1477).[20] Pseudo-Dati begins with salutations to persons of different ranks, before describing the four parts of the letter (*exordium*, *narratio*, *petitio,* and *conclusio*) and six types

[18] Albertus de Eyb, *Margarita poetica* (Strasbourg, 1503), sigs. c6^{v}, f6^{v}–7^{r}, v4^{r-v}.

[19] Ann Moss, *Renaissance Truth and the Latin Language Turn* (Oxford, 2003), 52–4.

[20] A. Dati, *Elegantiolae* (Antwerp, 1487–90), RRSTC 1302, sigs. e3^{v}–h2^{r}. R. Black, *Humanism and Education in Medieval and Renaissance Italy* (Cambridge, 2001), 359–64.

of letter. Haneron distinguishes three internal elements of the letter (cause, intention, and effect) from external factors like superscription and salutation, which he deals with last. He discusses four types of letter (request, thanks, information, and mixed) and replies to each of his three principal types. There appears to be some connection between his approach and that of Traversagni (see below). These manuals confirm the strength of the link between letter-writing and early teaching of Latin composition. Green and Murphy list thirty-nine editions of Pseudo-Dati and six editions of Haneron.

NICCOLÒ PEROTTI (1430–1480)

The *Rudimenta grammatices* of Niccolò Perotti, composed in 1468 and first printed in 1473, was the first comprehensive Latin grammar produced by a renaissance humanist.[21] Because this work included an accidence, a syntax, a treatise on letter-writing, and a section on metre, it in effect constituted, as Percival observes, a complete elementary course in Latin. Its 133 editions up to 1535 (the great majority of them prior to 1501) make it the most printed of all renaissance letter-writing manuals, and it is with this aspect of the work, amounting to about one-quarter of the whole, that we are concerned in this chapter. Perotti begins by briefly setting out the aim of letters, giving an etymology and identifying ten types of letter. Then he devotes a long section to epistolary style, first explaining that letters are generally written in the low style, though style will vary with subject-matter, and that they should be brief but not too brief and giving further general advice. Most of the discussion of style (almost thirty folio pages) is devoted to elegant expression culminating in a model letter which includes many of his suggestions. In a section which must have influenced Erasmus's *De copia*, Perotti discusses different ways of saying 'I received your letters' and 'they gave me great pleasure'.[22] Like Valla, Perotti weighs up the implications of using different expressions in considerable detail (e.g. What is the difference between *deligere* and *amare*?

[21] Perotti, *Grammatica* (London, 1512). W. K. Percival, 'The Place of the *Rudimenta Grammatices* in the History of Latin Grammar', *Res publica litterarum*, 4 (1981), 233–64; 'Early Editions of Niccolò Perotti's *Rudimenta Grammatices*', *Res publica litterarum*, 9 (1986), 219–29. Both articles are now collected in Percival's *Studies in Renaissance Grammar* (Aldershot, 2004). His 2003 paper on the epistolary part of the manual is available at http://people.ku.edu/~percival/Sassoferratoscript2003. G. C. Alessio, 'Il *De componendis epistolis* di Niccolò Perotti e l'epistolografia umanistica', *Res publica litterarum*, 11 (1988), 9–18.

[22] Perotti, *Grammatica*, sigs. M1^{r}–2^{r}.

How does *ludere* differ from *iocari*, or *gaudere* from *gratulari*?).[23] In these sections Perotti cites examples of usage from classical Latin literature to explore the effects of particular words.

After his example of an elegant letter, Perotti gives a definition of the letter, a discussion of each of the four parts (*salutatio*, which seems to include *exordium*; *narratio*; *petitio*; and *conclusio*) which follows the medieval scheme of the letter. Then he provides eight tables of the words one might use in saluting eight classes of recipient (organized hierarchically from the pope, to cardinals and kings, down to inferiors (table 7) and Saracens, Jews, apostates, and heretics (table 8)) at the four different stages of the letter. Each table is followed by examples of introductions and conclusions to letters. The ninth table suggests some phrases for replying to letters and gives some examples. So one could suggest that the work falls into four sections: introduction (one page), style, culminating in an example (thirty-three pages), definition and four-part structure (two pages), and tables of salutations with examples (nine pages). Whereas Perotti's surveys of classical Latin usage align him strongly with humanist grammarians, his analysis of the structure of the letter and his extensive treatment of forms of salutation depend on the heritage of the *ars dictaminis*.

Neither of Perotti's two definitions of letter has a particularly classical flavour: 'the letter is a full litteral instruction (*legatio*) conveying the intention of the instructor' and 'the letter is a fruitful indirect declaration in human language of the will of absent persons'.[24] The purpose for the letter, stated at the outset, is slightly more reminiscent of Cicero: 'that we should be able to inform those with whom, either for reasons of absence or embarrassment, it was not appropriate for us to speak, if there was something which we ought to write to them either for our sake or theirs or someone else's'.[25] His division into ten classes, while thoroughly sensible and reflecting classical practice, does not correspond exactly to any other manual that I know: divine matters, moral issues, daily events, informing absent people of news, consolation, recommendation to friends of someone they don't know, exhortation, love, friendly and domestic affairs, and amusement (*iocose*). For several of these classes Perotti cites

[23] Ibid., sigs. M4^{v}, M8^{v}, N3^{r}.

[24] 'Epistola est litteralis legatio plenum legantis affectum insinuans ... epistola est humanae linguae fecunda vicaria voluntatis absentium declarativa.' Ibid. sig. O4^{v}. Possibly the latter, with its emphasis on communication with someone absent, has a slight connection with pseudo-Libanius.

[25] 'Ut eos cum quibus sive propter absentiam sive propter ruborem ... loqui non licet, certiores facere possumus si quid sit quos eos scribere oporteat sive nostra sive illorum sive aliorum causa.' Ibid. sig. L4^{r}.

examples from classical epistolography.[26] In contrast to later writers he gives no suggestions for composing letters in any of these genres.

The Viennese grammar-school teacher Bernhard Perger (d. *c.*1502) produced an abridged and simplified version of Perotti, the *Grammatica nova* (1481), which was printed thirty times, mostly in Germany. His definition ('The letter is a faithful messenger'), etymology, and division into types look like careful abbreviations and adaptations of Perotti.[27] Unlike Perotti he moves from a short comment on the appropriateness of low style to letters to an exposition of the traditional five-part letter, which explains that not all these parts are needed, especially in familiar letters. He gives a short account of salutations for different classes of recipients and of the use of the *exordium*, before summarizing the plan of the letter.

> Therefore you will order your letter in this way. First you will take your beginning from a salutation or commendation. Then if the material requires it you will add an exordium. In the third place you will relate what needs to be narrated. You will position fourth the request if you have one, expressed with a certain modesty and in words suited to it. Lastly in concluding the letter you will explain briefly your intention on the basis of what you have already said.[28]

He then imitates Perotti by giving different Latin ways of expressing a series of German phrases (*Ich hab empfangen dyne brieffe* . . . *Dyne brieff haben mich fast erfreut*),[29] abbreviating Perotti's comments on the different uses of particular Latin words and culminating in the same Latin letter which Perotti had included.[30] Perger's short account preserves some of the humanist stylistic concerns of Perotti while setting out for German pupils the basic principles of writing a five-part dictaminal letter in a simple, orderly, and traditional way.

[26] Ibid.

[27] B. Perger, *Grammatica nova* (Memmingen, 1485), sig. e5^{r}.

[28] 'Ordinabis igitur epistolam tuam hoc modo. Primum a salutatione aut commendatione epistolae tuae initium dabis. Deinde si materia exposcit exordium subiicies. Tertio loco quae narranda sunt narrabis. Quarto petitionem si quam habes cum quadam modestia et verbis ad eam rem congruis ordinabis. Tandem concludendo epistolam breviter intentionem tuam ex dictis prioribus explanabis.' Ibid., sig. e6^{v}.

[29] Ibid., sigs. e6^{v}–7^{r}.

[30] Ibid., sig. f4^{v}–g1^{r}; Perotti, *Grammatica*, O4$^{r–v}$. I presume that Perotti composed this letter and Perger copied it.

PUBLICIUS AND FILELFO

The Florentine Jacobus Publicius's *Epistolarum institutiones* (1475; fifteen editions prior to 1510, mostly northern) adapts Cicero's approach to the definition of the letter and the division into types.

> It seemed evident to our predecessors that the duty of the epistle was to inform absent people in writing about either external affairs or attitudes of mind. There are three kinds: the first of teaching, the second of enjoyment and the third of seriousness.[31]

Subjects of serious letters include religion and affairs of state. Publicius discusses topics which provide material for each of these types. He describes the letter as constructed in four sections (beginning, proposition, proof, close) which seem to be adapted from the four-part oration. He discusses two kinds of letter in more detail, explaining the reasons for writing thank-you letters and the types of argument which need to be made in a letter of recommendation. He allows that sometimes letters will need to be quite long, especially if they are on a religious or serious topic.[32] The book concludes with a thorough discussion of sentence composition and rhythmic prose, and accounts of the epithets suited to different kinds of addressee.

Giovanni Mario Filelfo (1426–80), son of the famous humanist Francesco Filelfo, composed his *Novum epistolarium* in 1477. It was first printed in 1481 and appeared twelve times up to 1511. He assumes that letters should follow the form of the six-part oration, allowing that the *exordium* can begin with a title (equivalent to the superscription) and that a valediction should end the conclusion. He adds examples of each section, giving most space to the *exordium*.[33] After discussing the parts of the letter he says a little about figures of speech and delivery. He finds that there are eighty different types of letter and a threefold method: familiar (corresponding to the moderate style), most familiar (low style), and serious (high style).[34] He closes the introductory section with lists of complimentary epithets for different classes of people, starting with the pope, church dignitaries, and princes.

31 'Epistolarum officium preclare maioribus nostris visum est absentes litteris de rebus quae extrinsecus animove geruntur certiores facere. Earum genera tria sunt quorum doctrinae unum, alterum iocunditatis tertium severitatis.' J. Publicius, *Epistolarum institutiones* (Toulouse, 1475), sig. a2^{r}.

32 Ibid., sigs. b6^{r}–7^{v}.

33 G. M. Filelfo, *Novum epistolarium* (Milan, 1484), sigs. a1^{v}–b4^{r}.

34 Ibid., sig. b7$^{r–v}$.

The bulk of the long manual is taken up with his eighty types. For each he gives three exemplary letters (one for each of his three approaches), followed by a set of useful phrases adapted to the subject-matter of each type. The eighty types include familiar kinds like commendation, consolation, persuasion, dissuasion, joking, lamenting, but also useful types not included in other manuals, such as son to mother, client to patron, making peace, argumentative, on the birth of a prince's daughter, medical, making yourself known to strangers, and merchanting.[35]

TRAVERSAGNI AND BRANDOLINI

Lorenzo Traversagni of Savona (1425–1503), a Franciscan friar with humanist interests who taught in Vienna and Cambridge, first published his *Modus conficiendi epistolas* around 1480. There were thirteen editions up to 1499, some of them undated. Traversagni insists on the usefulness of letter-writing, both in practical life and for teaching Latin.[36] He follows Perotti in defining the letter as 'a fruitful indirect declaration in human language of the will of absent persons'.[37] Unusually, but logically, he divides letters into those sent (*missiva*) initially and replies, suggesting that other divisions (for example, into narrative, congratulatory, condoling, and threatening) are always incomplete.[38] He asserts that all letters have three parts (cause, intention, and consequence), perhaps relying on Haneron, and provides examples of letters in which he marks these three logically connected sections,[39] but he also recognizes the division into six sections based on the classical oration.[40] He reports suggestions on how one should go about making requests, but insists that not all letters contain petitions.[41] He urges writers to think carefully about the person they are addressing and emphasizes the need to write differently to different types of people. About a quarter of the manual is given over to listing forms of address for civil and religious dignitaries,[42] and the work closes with a discussion of brevity. Traversagni presents some original views on the staples of the letter-writing manual but the innovatory

[35] Ibid., sigs. c4^{r}–t4^{v}.
[36] Guglielmus Saphonensis, *Modus conficiendi epistolas* (Leipzig, 1499), sig. a2^{r}.
[37] 'Epistola . . . est humanae linguae fecunda vicaria voluntatis absentium declarativa.' Ibid., sig. a2^{v}.
[38] Ibid., sig. a3$^{r–v}$.
[39] Ibid., sigs. a4^{r}–5^{r}, B2^{r}–3^{v}.
[40] Ibid., sigs. a5^{v}–6^{r}, D3^{r}–4^{r}.
[41] Ibid., sig a6$^{r–v}$.
[42] Ibid., sigs. C1^{v}–D2^{v}.

elements were only partly taken up, much later, in the vernacular manuals by Fabri, Durand, and Fulwood.

De ratione scribendi libri tres by Aurelio Lippo Brandolini (1454–97) was probably written around 1485.[43] It was first printed in Basel in 1549 as part of an anthology of letter-writing manuals and in that form was printed six times. The first book defines the letter ('conversation directed to absent people'[44]) and outlines a five-part structure based on the classical oration (with a salutation, considered in the simple classical form). The second describes the three kinds of oratory, giving most emphasis to demonstrative, and twenty-five types of letter. The third is concerned with emotion, disposition, and style. The original feature here is the account of several emotions: love, desire, contempt of worldly success, hope, despair, wrath, and others. This section is probably based on St Thomas Aquinas.

FRANCESCO NEGRO (b. 1452)

Francesco Negro's *Modus Epistolandi* (1487) was one of the most successful letter-writing textbooks of the renaissance, appearing in sixty-two editions up to 1588, in northern Europe as well as Italy. Most of the independent editions of Negro's work, which was also published in collections of letter-writing manuals, appeared before 1520. It was an immediate bestseller, with forty-three editions between 1487 and 1501. The work is divided into three short books (*libelli*), the first describing twenty types of letter, the second giving thirty rules for writing elegant Latin, and the third providing forms of address for eighteen classes of recipient, beginning with the pope and ending with women.

For Negro the purpose of letters is 'to make ourselves present to absent friends using this remedy'. The letter is defined as 'prose discourse which makes absent friends present as much for pleasure as usefulness both public and private'.[45] The first book is divided into twenty chapters corresponding to the twenty types of letter. Within each chapter the main type is subdivided; each subtype is defined, provided with rules (usually four), indicating the main points to be made, and an example of a model letter, preceded by a proposition stating its purpose. Marginal notes

[43] J. W. O'Malley, *Praise and Blame in Renaissance Rome* (Durham, NC, 1979), 44–50.

[44] 'Est igitur epistola sermo ad absentes, de re ad eorum alterum pertinente conscriptus.' Brandolini, *De ratione scribendi* (Basel, 1549), sig. A5^{r}.

[45] 'Ut absentes amicos hoc tantum remedio praesentes redderemus . . . Epistola est oratio pedestris, quae absentes amicos praesentes facit tam ad voluptatem quam ad utilitatem tum publicam tum privatam.' F. Negro, *De modo epistolandi* (Venice, 1492), sigs. A2^{v}–3^{r}.

to the model letter show how it follows the rules. Negro's twenty types of letter are: commendation, request, giving (*munificum*), praise and blame, giving thanks, love letters, lamentation, consolation, exposition, rejoicing, exhortations, dissuasions, invectives, justification, domestic, ordinary (informing a friend), humorous, entrusting business (*commissiva*), royal, and mixed.[46]

Since Negro's instructions are an important source for later writers it will be worthwhile to give two examples of his instructions; the overlap between the two is also typical of Negro's manner of proceeding.

> (Letter of Recommendation for a position) if we want to write a letter which is called *epentica*, we shall divide this into four parts. In the first we shall obtain goodwill from the person we address, praising them for their liberality or magnificence, which is customary in all cases in which we have great confidence in coming to someone with the hope of easily obtaining what we want, or even for another virtue, and especially for one which the person we wish to commend particularly possesses, saying that that person we are approaching has always been accustomed to favour people with this virtue because he is one of them. In the second place we obtain goodwill from the person we intend to recommend, praising him greatly and saying also that he pleases everyone on account of his virtues and especially we ourselves who have known him for such a long time. In the third place we shall explain the thing which we want to obtain, arguing that it is just, honourable, and easy and that it will bring great honour to the person we are writing to if he should wish to favour that friend of ours whom we recommend. In the final part we shall either promise some reward or more likely offer our continuing service, if we obtain what we want, saying that we shall regard whatever he has done for our friend as if he had done it for ourselves.[47]

[46] 'Commendatitia, petitoria, munifica, demonstrativa, eucharistica sive regratiatoria, amatoria, lamentatoria, consolatoria, expositiva, gratulatoria, exhortatoria, dissuasoria, invectiva, expurgativa, domestica, communis, iocosa, commissiva, regia, mixta.' Ibid., sig. A3r.

[47] 'Si commendatitiam epistolam quae epentica dicitur scribere voluerimus, illam in partes quatuor dividemus. In quorum prima ab ea persona benivolentiam captabimus ad quam scribimus, laudantes illam vel a liberalitate sive magnificentia, qua in omnes utitur unde nobis maxima exoriatur fiducia ad ipsam veniendi cum spe id facile obtiniendi quod cupimus, vel etiam ab alia virtute, et maxime ab illa cuius est is plenus, quem commendare volumus, dicentes eam personam semper fuisse assuetam talibus viris favere, cum ipsa ex eorum numero sit. In secunda vero benivolentiam captabimus ab eius persona quam commendare intendimus, ipsam maxime laudantes, dicentes quoque ipsam propter virtutes suas omnibus esse gratissimam, et nobis praecipue qui eius consuetudine diutius usi fuerimus. In tertia autem rem ipsam exponemus quam impetrare cupimus, illam esse iustam, honestam et facilem arguentes, et ex quo maximum sit honorem consecuturus ille ad quem scribimus, si voluerit illi amico nostro favere quem commendamus. In ultima parte vel aliquod praemium pollicebimur, vel potius perpetuam servitutem nostram offeremus, si quod petimus consequi poterimus, dicentes quod quicquid in ipsum amicum factum fuerit tanquam in nos ipsos factum existimabimus.' Ibid.

(Request for a thing) We shall divide this letter into five parts. In the first we shall obtain goodwill from the person to whom we write, praising him first for his liberality and then from his authority to grant the thing which we request. In the second place we shall show that our request is honourable, together with its great necessity to the point where we will scarcely be able to do anything without it. In the third place we will show that it will be easy for a person like this to give us what we want. And in this place we will show his power not just in this matter but in granting greater things. In the fourth place we shall promise some reward either of a material kind or better in some sort of service which will show our goodwill. We shall place the final part, that is the request itself, wherever among these parts it seems best to us, as in the previous genre of letters.[48]

For Negro the structure of the letter will vary according to the different types and the different arguments to be made. In the last example he leaves the precise positioning of the request itself up to the judgement of the writer.

Between them these early manuals announce what will become an almost century-long consensus about the required contents of a letter-writing manual: a definition of the letter, a division into types of letters (for which models, topics, or suggested contents may be provided), a statement of the structure of the letter (either based on the classical oration or the five-part structure of the *ars dictaminis* or sometimes a compromise between the two) with a discussion of the contents of each part; some discussion of salutation, valediction and titles; some account of prose style; and some provision of model phrases.

Two different aspects of this consensus are represented by two manuals often printed together. Giovanni Sulpizio's *De componendis epistolis* (1489) adapts a summary of most of classical rhetoric (including five tasks of the orator, six parts of the oration, prose rhythm, figures of speech, and status-theory) to letter-writing by adding sections on superscription and valediction, following Cicero on the three types of letter and commenting on the style appropriate to letters.[49] Josse Badius (1461–1535) in

[48] 'Istam epistolam in partes quinque dividemus. In quarum prima benivolentiam captabimus ab ea persona ad quam scribimus, laudantes ipsam prius a liberalitate, deinde potissimum ab auctoritate illius rei concedendae quam petimus. In secunda vero demonstrabimus petitionis nostrae honestatem una cum summa ipsius rei petitae necessitate sine qua vix facere possimus. In tertia autem ostendemus tali viro facile esse nobis illud tribuere quod petimus. Et in hoc loco aperiemus ipsius viri facultatem, non solum in tali sed etiam in maiore multo eroganda. In quarta praeterea praemium aliquod pollicebimur, vel in praecio constitutum, vel potius in aliqua servitute, quae animum nostrum ostendat. Ipsam demum propositionem inter partes istas prout nobis melius videbitur interponemus sicut in superiore praeceptum est.' Ibid., A4^{v}–5^{r}.

[49] Badius, *In hoc codice contenta* (Nuremberg, 1504), sigs. a8^{r}–b1^{r}.

his *De epistolis componendis compendium* (1501) copies Cicero's threefold division (information, serious matters, or friendship) in his definition of the letter.[50] He describes the five medieval parts of the letter (salutation, *exordium*, narration, petition, and conclusion) in order, with examples, describing the topics of praise as part of the *exordium*, and ending with comments on style and vocabulary. Badius printed these two letter-writing treatises together with grammatical works by Dati and Negro, giving rules for elegant Latin expression and Giorgio Valla's work on orthography, to make an intermediate level compendium of grammar, which was printed twenty times between 1501 and 1540, in addition to about eleven separate printings of Badius's work.[51] The popularity of such compilations of letter-writing manuals suggests that in practice the structures based on the classical oration and on the five-part dictaminal letter frequently coexisted. Pupils may have constructed compromises between them, just as authors of letter-writing manuals did.

Methodus conficiendarum epistolarum (1492) by Konrad Celtis (1459–1508) was originally published as an appendix to his epitome of *Rhetorica ad Herennium* and Cicero's *De inventione*. Later it was reprinted fifty-five times, usually as part of an anthology of letter-writing texts (for example, alongside Vives, Erasmus, and Hegendorff).[52] His definition emphasizes the letter's role in conveying our intentions, desires, and state of mind to absent friends or transmitting information.[53] He gives most attention to five types of letter: serious, consolatory, commendatory, amatory, and exhortative or instructive, giving examples of each type.[54] He suggests a rather unusual four-part structure: beginning (preparing the recipient), cause (explaining why we are writing), narration (explaining what we want to say), and *enumeratio* (which explains who is writing, when, and from where).[55]

ERASMUS

Erasmus's *Conficiendarum epistolarum formula* was probably written before 1498 as an aid to the private teaching which Erasmus undertook

50 Ibid., sig. a2^{r}.

51 Green and Murphy, *Renaissance Rhetoric Short-Title Catalogue* (Aldershot, 2006), 56–7, 421.

52 Ibid. 80, 86, 103, 183, 184, 271, 448.

53 Vives, *De conscribendis epistolis*, with Celtis and others (Cologne, 1537), sig. G4^{v}.

54 Ibid., sigs. G4^{v}–5^{r}, G7^{r}–H1^{v}.

55 Ibid., sigs. G5^{r}, H1^{v}.

in Paris in the 1490s.[56] This short work was first printed in 1520, achieving nineteen independent editions up to 1573 (though it is the type of short schoolbook of which many editions could have disappeared altogether), mostly in the 1520s. It was reprinted forty times as part of different collections of letter-writing manuals, giving a total of fifty-nine sixteenth-century editions. The work is divided into three sections: introduction, including a definition of the letter and observations on style; training, imitation, and practice; and types of letter, based on the three genres of classical oratory.

Erasmus deliberately follows Libanius in defining the letter as 'a conversation between absent persons'.[57] He refers to Libanius's opinion that letters should be written in a simple conversational style, though his own preference is for a correct, clear, ornate Latin which gives the impression of simplicity, like the style of the younger Pliny's letters.[58] Good writing requires training, imitation, practice, and the exercise of judgement. Pupils should choose Cicero, Pliny, and Poliziano as models of good epistolary style for imitation. Seneca may have a bad effect on the style of young people but should be read by adults.[59] Good writing requires literary art and deliberate variation. Erasmus rejects the five-part structure of the letter (*salutatio*, *exordium*, *narratio*, *petitio*, *conclusio*) suggested by the tradition of the *ars dictaminis*.[60]

In this work Erasmus insists that all types of letters can be considered as falling within the three classical genres.[61] Under demonstrative he gives advice on topics for letters of praise of persons and descriptions of places. Under deliberative he mentions letters of persuasion and dissuasion, encouragement and discouragement, petition, advice, and love letters. He discusses the topics of deliberation (the honourable, the useful, and the possible) and suggests several arguments for letters of recommendation:

> In praising the one whom we recommend we show that our recommendation is honourable. In this class we begin with an introduction, winning goodwill through our modesty . . . then by describing the character and pursuits [of the person recommended] we shall show that they are worthy of either the friendship and intimacy or the kindness and assistance of the person to whom we are writing. We shall sometimes praise them for their distinction of lineage and native origin, or, what is much more effective, for

[56] Baños, *El arte epistolar*, 330–1.

[57] 'Epistola est absentis ad absentem colloquium.' Vives, *De conscribendis epistolis*, with Erasmus, Celtis, Hegendorff (Cologne, 1537), sig. f3^{r}. Tr. Fantazzi, as in note 62, 258.

[58] Ibid., sig. f3^{r-v}. Tr. Fantazzi, 258.

[59] Ibid., sig. f5^{r}. Tr. Fantazzi, 257–60.

[60] Ibid., sig. f6^{v}. Tr. Fantazzi, 261–2.

[61] Ibid., sig. f7^{v}. Tr. Fantazzi, 262.

> their gifts of intellect and learning, such as modesty, reliability, industry, speaking ability, or some other intellectual capacity. A very effective manner of recommendation is to mention that the candidate is a grateful person and one mindful of benefits received.... Concerning the possibility of granting favour we must show that the candidate can be helped or his career advanced by the person to whom we are writing, or by others, namely the friends of the person addressed.[62]

Erasmus shows how the general topics of deliberation are linked to the specific arguments useful in letters of recommendation, before referring to examples of this type by Pliny and Horace. He explains that letters of encouragement and advice can be created in a similar way, insisting that the writer's judgement is the most important factor and that the rules of art seem to take their origin from this practical judgement. Under the judicial genre, Erasmus includes letters of accusation, rebuke, vituperation, and justification (*deprecatoria*). He emphasizes the importance of the emotions in letters of this type and provides some model phrases for *exordia* intended to win favour.[63] In this work Erasmus takes a rather relaxed view of letter-writing, suggesting that the art consists mainly in applying the general rules of rhetoric to particular letter-writing assignments. He rejects the special rules for letters formulated in the *ars dictaminis*.

The Tübingen rhetoric teacher Heinrich Bebel (1472–1518) took an equally hostile attitude to *ars dictaminis* in his *Commentaria epistolarum conficiendarum* (1503), printed ten times up to 1516 and abbreviated, together with pseudo-Dati, Sulpitius, Negro, and Badius in Despauterius's *Ars epistolica* (1519), printed twelve times up to 1550. After a general attack on earlier letter-writing manuals he rejects the five-part plan, preferring to cite comments by Cicero and St Ambrose on the letter as a way of giving information and on the prevalence of the low style. The way to learn to write letters is to read classical letters and to concentrate on

[62] 'Nam laudantes eum quem commendamus, honestam commendationem nostram ostendimus. Ac primum quidem in hoc genere utimur principio aliquo, velut captantes benivolentiam a modestia nostra... Deinde describendo eorum studia et mores, dignos monstrantes vel amicitia et familiaritate, vel beneficio aliquo ac munere eius ad quem scribimus, laudamusque interdum eos a generis claritate aut a patria, sed multo efficacius ab ingenii doctrinaeque dotibus, ut a modestia, fide, diligentia, dicendi facultate, aut alia quaquam insigni eruditione. Efficacissima tamen illa ratio est commendandi, cum gratos illos, et memores beneficiorum esse dicimus... De facultate autem necesse est ostendere, posse ab illo ad quem scribimus, hunc nostrum iuvari aut ornari, quod etiam interdum per alios fieri potest, nempe amicos eius ad quem scribimus.' Ibid., sig. g1^{v}. Tr. C. Fantazzi from *Collected Works of Erasmus*, xxv (Toronto, 1985), 265.

[63] Vives, *De conscribendis epistolis*, sig. g2^{r}–3^{v}. Trans Fantazzi, 265–7.

expressing your message clearly.[64] Nevertheless he adds sections on the periodic prose style and on epithets suitable for different classes of addressee.[65]

Margarita philosophica (1503), the encyclopedia composed by the Freiburg Carthusian Gregor Reisch (*c.*1467–1525), printed twelve times up to 1583, includes a wide-ranging summary of rhetoric (covering the three genres, the four parts of the oration, and the orator's five tasks) and appends a short treatise on letter-writing. Reisch divides letters into divine and human, subdivided into serious, consolatory, amatory, recommending, and encouraging. He refers to Filelfo's eighty types of letter for further reading.[66] He produces a new composite version of the five-part letter (salutation, *exordium*, *narratio*, conclusion, superscription), giving examples of each, but treats the conclusion mainly as the occasion for giving the date and place of writing. For the superscription he lists epithets suitable to the status of the recipient.[67]

CRISTOPH HEGENDORFF (1500–1540)

The Leipzig humanist Cristoph Hegendorff composed a brief *Methodus conscribendi epistolas* (1520) which went through fifteen independent edtions up to 1558, but was printed a further fifty-six times as part of compilation volumes of letter-writing manuals.[68] Hegendorff takes his opening from pseudo-Libanius and Cicero.

> A letter is a conversation from one absent person to another. Why was it invented? So that we could inform absent people if there was something which they should know either for our or their benefit, as Cicero says in the second book of letters.[69]

Hegendorff organizes the treatise according to the types of letter, which he derives from the three genres of rhetoric: demonstrative, deliberative, and judicial. He treats three types of demonstrative letter, of person, of action, and of thing. For demonstrative of person he begins by listing topics of

[64] H. Bebel, *Commentaria epistolarum conficiendarum* (Strasbourg, 1516), sigs. a1^{r}–2^{r}.
[65] Ibid., sigs. a4^{r}–b2^{r}.
[66] Reisch, *Margarita philosophica* (Strasbourg, 1504), sig. l8^{v}.
[67] Ibid., sigs. m1^{v}–2^{r}.
[68] Green, *Renaissance Rhetoric STC*, 80, 184, 271, 284–5, 448. J. R. Henderson, 'Humanism and the Humanities', in Poster and Mitchell, *Letter-Writing Manuals*, 152–6.
[69] 'Epistola est sermo absentis ad absentem. *Cur inventa?* Ut faceremus certiores absentes, si quid esset quod eos scire, aut nostra, aut ipsorum interesset: author Cicero libro epistolarum secundo [*Ad Familiares* 2.4].' Macropedius, *De conscribendis epistolis*, with Hegendorff's *Methodus* (London, 1609), sig. O6^{r}.

praise (such as birth, childhood, old age, death, body, health, honours, and riches), then writes a praise of Hannibal based on those topics, before printing examples from Cicero and the younger Pliny.[70] Constructed and classical examples are provided throughout the work, though sometimes he refers to places where examples may be found rather than printing the text in full. In all Hegendorff discusses thirteen types of letter: demonstrative of person, action, and thing, persuasive, dissuasive, conciliatory, exhortatory, dehortatory, petitioning, recommending, consolatory, accusatory and defensive. In addition he lists five further types of judicial letter which can be dealt with in the same way: complaint, expostulation, expurgation, exprobration, and invective.[71] For some of these types Hegendorff offers several arguments; for others only very brief suggested contents.

> A letter is conciliatory, by which we reconcile either ourselves with others or other people with third parties. The topics are the same as for letters of persuasion. We shall say that it is honourable to set aside anger, hatred and feuds, that becomes brave men to overcome their own feelings. We shall say that it is irreligious for Christians to fight each other when Christ brought them both together with his blood: for he is our peace. We shall show the disadvantages which grow from mutual hatreds and feuds . . . and how easy it is to be reconciled.[72]
> *Requesting.* We request things which are honourable useful and easy to be done and possible and necessary to be provided.[73]

Hegendorff ends the treatise by giving examples of, and topics for, *exordia* and by listing some epithets suitable for superscriptions to different classes of addressee.[74] Both Hegendorff's list of letters and a couple of direct references made under exhortation suggest that Hegendorff may have had access to a copy of Erasmus's *De conscribendis epistolis*, either in advance of publication or during revision.[75]

Seeing Erasmus's *De conscribendis epistolis* (1521), the second most printed renaissance letter-writing manual with ninety-two editions, in the light of earlier renaissance treatises on letter-writing prompts some

[70] Macropedius, *De conscribendis epistolis*, sigs 06^r–7^v.
[71] Ibid., sigs. 06^r–Q2^r.
[72] 'Conciliatrix epistola est, qua conciliamus vel nosmetipsos aliis, vel alios aliis. Loci sunt iidem qui suasoriae epistolae: dicimus honestum esse, ut iram, simultatem, odium deponat: siquidem fortium virorum esse, seipsos vincere. Dicimus impium esse, Christianum cum Christiano dissidere, cum utrumque Christus suo sanguine coniunxerit: ipse enim est pax nostra. Ostendimus multa incommoda, quae ex illis odiis mutuis et simultatibus gliscant; facile vero eos posse reconciliari docemus.' Ibid., sig. P4^v.
[73] '*Petitoria.* Petimus honesta, utilia, facilia et factu, et praestitu possibilia, necessaria.' Ibid., sig. P6^r.
[74] Ibid., sigs. Q2^r–5^r.
[75] Ibid., sig. P5^r.

additions to the account given in Chapter 5 above. The introductory sections of the manual promote a less dogmatic view of letter-writing than earlier manuals. Letters should usually be short, although they cannot always be. There will be occasions when the subject and addressee of a letter demand length or when they require a style which is higher than the low style normally favoured in familiar letters. Erasmus has also relaxed some of his own earlier positions, now accepting that complimentary epithets may form part of the salutation of a letter, while giving less direction on this than some of his predecessors. *De conscribendis epistolis* is longer than most (but by no means all) other manuals; Erasmus discusses more types of letter than most renaissance writers and some of the examples he gives are very long. Erasmus's types of letter seem to be based on the classical manuals (he summarizes the list from pseudo-Libanius[76]) and on Negro. In some cases (such as *petitio*) the suggestions for the content of the letter are close to Negro, but Erasmus also treats some of Negro's types in different ways, and includes types of letter not discussed by Negro.

Erasmus is one of the earliest writers (if not the earliest) to emphasize thinking about the addressee, and the writer's relationship to the addressee, as (together with the nature of the letter's subject) the chief factors in determining the approach and style to be adopted in a letter. He adds to the normal repertory of the letter-writing manual comments on using examples and on amplification, which are characteristic of his other works. He is unusual but not unique in addressing part of his manual to teachers of letter-writing (rather than students) and in the attention he gives to argumentation, in a section he seems to have borrowed from George Trapezuntius.

Together with Bebel, Erasmus inaugurates a counter-movement in renaissance letter-writing which Vives and Lipsius will take further. Where writers preoccupied with the role of letter-writing in grammar-school education had wanted to give simple rules for pupils to use in constructing different types of letter, the new emphasis is on reading classical letters and focusing on the relationship between writer and addressee. The writer's judgment and thinking about the addressee will determine the content of the letter. All the existing rules about content, brevity, or low style can be adapted or even ignored if they conflict with what seems appropriate to the situation. These new ideas are truer to the practical situation of writing letters but they may be less helpful in elementary training.

[76] *Opera omnia*, i/2. 312–13.

JUAN LUIS VIVES (1492–1540)

Juan Luis Vives probably had Erasmus's work before him when he wrote his own *De conscribendis epistolis* (1534) which was printed seventy times up to 1620, in northern Europe usually with a collection of other letter-writing manuals (such as Celtis, Hegendorff, Erasmus's *Formula,* and pseudo-Libanius), and in Italy very often with Vives's own dialogues for learning spoken Latin, the *Colloquia.*[77] This Italian version was especially successful after 1580 (twenty-seven editions 1580–1620) when other humanist rhetorics were in decline. Vives's manual is thorough, thoughtful, and practical but not all that well organized as a first teaching book. Probably Vives assumed that his book would be used in conjunction with a simpler more dogmatic work, to which he was adding (in the manner of *De oratore* perhaps) finer shading and reflections on the basis of experience, which would be helpful once the basic material had been mastered.[78] Vives's work falls into six main parts: introduction and definition (1–4); invention and *exordia* (5–12); subject-matter and types of letter (13–44); disposition, conclusions, and superscriptions (45–70); style with useful phrases and formulae, and the issue of brevity (71–105); and comments on classical and modern writers of letters (106–12).[79]

Vives amplifies pseudo-Libanius's definition of the letter, before quoting St Ambrose's words at more length.

> A letter is a conversation through the written word between persons separated from each other. It was devised so that a faithful and informative interpreter of instructions should deliver the thoughts and mental concepts of one person to another. 'The usefulness of the letter', said St Ambrose to Sabinus, 'is that though separated in location we may be united in our emotions. In a letter the image of presence shines among people who are

[77] Green and Murphy list a total of forty-three edns (pp. 80, 184, 270–1, 448). Enrique González González and Víctor Gutiérrez Rodríguez, *Los diálogos de Vives y la imprenta* (Valencia, 1999), 233–64, list a further twenty-seven Italian (mainly Venetian) edns (with the *Colloquia*) before 1620. Most of these edns are found only in Italian libraries and are not recorded in union catalogues or databases. I am grateful to Charles Fantazzi for this reference.

[78] J. R. Henderson, 'Defining the Genre of the Letter: Juan Luis Vives' *De conscribendis epistolis*', *Renaissance and Reformation,* 19 (1983), 89–105. C. Fantazzi, 'Vives versus Erasmus on the Art of Letter-Writing', in Van Houdt *et al.*, *Self-Presentation*, 39–56. P. Mack, 'Vives's Contribution to Rhetoric and Dialectic', in C. Fantazzi (ed.), *A Companion to Juan Luis Vives* (Leiden, 2008), 227–76.

[79] Paragraph numbers based on Vives, *De conscribendis epistolis*, ed. C. Fantazzi (Leiden, 1989), with useful introduction.

> apart and the written conversation unites those who are separated. In it we share our thoughts with a friend and infuse him with our mind.'[80]

Vives adds to this by discussing the etymology of *epistola*, the ancients' use of writing tablets, and by quoting more fully than other writers Cicero's comments to Curio about the types of letter he particularly enjoys. Throughout the work Vives keeps the emphasis on the relationship between sender and addressee.

> One who is about to write a letter must consider who he (the writer) is, to whom he writes, and the subject; who we are to the addressee and who he is in his own right. For we may be strangers or acquaintances, friends or enemies, casual or doubtful friends, or open and close, equals or unequals (which may be in different ways: in family, fortune, education, or age). Then, concerning the addressee, we must consider family background . . . personal resources: opulent, conspicuous, moderate humble, non-existent . . . We must determine whether he is outspoken or secretive, of good or bad reputation, leisurely or occupied. . . . All these things may easily be surveyed in a single mental reflection and a moment of time.[81]
>
> To a prosperous, haughty person the letter must be more respectful but without flattery; to one who is stern and disagreeable, it should be lighter and more reserved; to an unlearned or dull person the letter should be simpler and clearer, to a clever person more studied and ornate if that would please him and make him feel respected; to a learned man the letter should be suited to the manner of the classics, briefer to a busy man, more expansive to a man of leisure, if you are dealing with something he will like.[82]

[80] 'Epistola est sermo absentium per litteras. In hoc enim ea est reperta ut conceptus animi et cogitata aliorum ad alios fida mandati interpres et nuntia perferat. "Epistolarum usus est", inquit D. Ambrosius ad Sabinum, "ut disiuncti locorum intervallis affectu adhaeremus, in quibus inter absentes imago refulget praesentiae et collocutio scripta separatos copulat, in quibus etiam cum amico miscemus animum et mentem ei nostram infundemus."' Vives, *De conscribendis epistolis* 2, p. 22, tr. Fantazzi (adapted).

[81] 'Scripturus epistolam consideret quis et cui scribat et quibus de rebus, qui sumus nos ad illum, qui ille in se. Aut enim ignoti sumus aut noti, amici aut inimici, leviter seu dubie amici, aut aperte et arcte, pares aut impares, et hoc variis in rebus: genere, fortunis, eruditione, aetate. Tum ille quo genere . . . qua fortuna: summa, magna, mediocri, infima, nulla . . . opiniosus an obscurus, bonae an malae famae, otiosus an occupatus . . . Haec enim uno mentis intuitu facile percurremus omnia et momento temporis.' Ibid. 6, p. 28, tr. Fantazzi.

[82] 'Ad fortunatum et superciliosum reverentius, modo absit assentatio; ad morosum et asperum parcius et levius, ad rudem aut hebetum apertius, ad ingeniosum accuratius et maiore apparatu, si eo delectatur et sic se venerari arguit; docto ad antiquitatem accommodatius, ad occupatum breviter, ad otiosum fusius, si rem non ingratam facturus es.' Ibid. 11, p. 34, tr. Fantazzi (adapted).

Vives's general principle is that finding material for a letter depends on practical wisdom, that is, on intellect, memory, judgement, and experience. The principles of rhetoric can assist but not replace these natural and learnt qualities.[83] He derives the common types of letter from thinking of things we need to convey about ourselves or about other people. Thus letters of advice may have to do with strengthening someone materially or morally, while letters of conciliation are concerned with the emotions and the winning of goodwill. We may write for the addressee's advantage in letters of instruction, advice, and exhortation.[84] After this deliberately general approach to the types which dominated so many letter-writing manuals, Vives gives more detailed advice about three of the most common types of letter: petition, recommendation, and consolation. Here too, however, Vives's approach is general and wide-ranging, as if he wishes to remind the reader/writer of things to think about, rather than to lay down topics to be included in each of these types of letter.[85] In this third section of the book, Vives also gives advice about letters of praise and criticism, palliative letters, jesting letters, and replies.

When he turns to disposition, Vives insists that, once the introduction is finished, there are no rules for ordering the main body of a letter; one must adapt to the circumstances and begin wherever it seems best.[86] He makes some suggestions for transitions in this fourth section, but gives most attention to greetings and dating at the conclusion of the letter, and to superscription, which should be without complimentary epithets. The style of the letter should be conversational, correct but not ornamented. Vives observes that Cicero and other classical writers would write in a simpler style in letters about the same subjects which would be decorated with stylistic ornaments in orations or philosophical works.[87] In writing to learned men of leisure you may use more proverbs, quotations, and historical allusions.[88] Much of this section is devoted to examples of useful phrases. Letters are usually brief but they may be longer where it suits the subject-matter or our relationship to the addressee.[89] Vives's review of ancient and modern letter-writing demonstrates the breadth of reading and the acuteness of judgement, which characterize this work, whose simple, well-thought-out and practical advice is always stimulating.

[83] Ibid. 5, p. 26.
[84] Ibid. 13–16, pp. 36–8.
[85] Ibid. 19–28, 36–7, pp. 40–50, 58–60.
[86] Ibid., 58, p. 82.
[87] Ibid. 71–2, pp. 96–8.
[88] Ibid. 78, p. 104.
[89] Ibid. 101–3, pp. 124–6.

GEORGIUS MACROPEDIUS (1487–1558)

Georgius Macropedius was a Dutch humanist schoolmaster (headmaster of St Jerome's school Utrecht, 1530–57) and Latin playwright.[90] His *Methodus de conscribendis epistolis* (1543) was printed thirty-two times up to 1649, in Antwerp, Cologne, Dillingen, and latterly in London. The book combines a treatise on letter-writing with many of the elements of a full course in rhetoric, including, for example, a full treatment of status-theory and a lengthy description of the tropes and figures. The work is divided into six main sections: an introduction on the nature and style of letter-writing; a description of the *partes generales*, which appear in all letters, the salutation, valediction, and superscription (generally treated in the plain classical way but including a section on epithets suitable for different classes of addressee);[91] a thorough treatment of invention; a brief section on disposition; a description of twenty-three tropes (in two classes) and seventy-seven figures (in three groups),[92] which looks like an expanded version of the list found in Melanchthon's *Institutiones rhetoricae* (1521); and a short collection of ancillary treatises: rules for elegant sentence construction, questions on generating *copia* of both kinds, and nine forms of rhetorical argumentation.

At the outset Macropedius defines the letter in a way which reflects both a reading of classical sources and his practical understanding of writing letters.

> Since a letter is mainly familiar, a sort of reciprocal conversation (*sermo*) between absent friends, ἀπὸ τοῦ ἐπιστέλλω, which is 'I send', or I signify something to an absent person by letters, it ought to be like reciprocal conversations (*confabulationes*) between friends. Therefore it loves the humble style, the one which comes closest in phrasing to comedy, and (to put it more plainly) simple, joyful, clear, as little as possible of the artful method of writing, which yet does not disregard its own kind of elegance.[93]

[90] Henk Giebels and Frans Slits, *Georgius Macropedius 1487–1558: Leven en Werken van een Brabantse humanist* (Tilburg, 2005). Thomas W. Best, *Macropedius* (New York, 1972). Henderson, 'Humanism and the Humanities', 157–60.

[91] Macropedius, *De conscribendis epistolis,* sigs. A3^{v}–6^{r}.

[92] Ibid., sigs. H6^{v}–L2^{r}.

[93] 'Cum sit epistola praecipue familiaris, absentium amicorum quasi mutuus sermo, ἀπὸ τοῦ ἐπιστέλλω, quod est mitto, aut per litteras absenti aliquid significo, talem eam esse oportet, quales sunt amicorum mutuae confabulationes. Amat igitur characterem humilem, proximeque ad comicam phrasin accedentem, et (ut planius dicam), simplicem, festivam, dilucidam, minimeque fucatam scribendi rationem, quae suam tamen elegantiam non negligat.' Macropedius, *De conscribendis epistolis* (London, 1609), sig. A3^{r}.

He rapidly adds that the method of inventing, disposing, and embellishing letters is not really different from the approach required in composing an oration. After claiming (like the earlier Erasmus) that all the types of letter can be included in the three genres of rhetoric, to which (like Melanchthon) he adds a fourth dialectic or didascalic genre, he gives a general account of the topics of demonstrative and deliberative rhetoric and of the theory of status from judicial rhetoric. Within this structure he identifies twenty types of letter, some familiar from earlier manuals, some owed to his incorporation of status-theory: demonstrative of person, action, and thing, recommendation, persuasion, dissuasion, exhortation, petition, consolation, reconciliation, accusatory in the conjectural status, defensive in the conjectural status, expostulating, apologetic (*purgatoria*), accusatory in the juridical status, defensive in the juridical assumptive status, defensive in the absolute status, didactic, and familiar, subdivided into mixed and simple.[94] For each type Macropedius gives rules and an example letter, with the topics marked in the margin to show how the rules are carried out in the example. The rules seem to owe a little to the topics set out in Negro's and Erasmus's manuals. For example:

> (Letter of recommendation in four or five parts) In the first we obtain goodwill (if it seems necessary) from the humanity, kindness, and generosity of the person to whom we are writing, but this part can be left out in the case of close friends. In the second we write the reasons which move us to commend this person, such as the friendly custom of recommending, a benefit received, pity, or something else of the kind. In the third we praise the person being recommended as far as the length of a letter will allow using the instructions in the genus demonstrative of persons, from birth, from nature, etc. In the fourth we set out the thing itself which we are asking on behalf of our friend, showing by various arguments that it is honourable, just, pious, or compatible with virtue, also useful or necessary, above all not only possible but easy for the person to whom we write, according to the topics of confirmation of the deliberative genre. We shall also promise in the fifth place that both we and our friend whom we are commending will be grateful and that we will also both offer our hard work and devotion.[95]

[94] Ibid., sigs. A8^{v}–H3^{r}.

[95] 'In prima captamus benevolentiam (si necessarium videatur) ab humanitate, benignitate, vel liberalitate eius ad quem scribimus, licet inter familiares amicos haec pars plerunque negligatur. In secunda causas scribimus, quae nos movent ad aliquem commendandum, ut est amica commendandi consuetudo, beneficium acceptum, commiseratio, vel id genus alia. In tertia commendandum laudabimus pro quantitate Epistolae, eo quo praescriptum est modo in genere demonstrativo personarum, a natalibus, ab indole etc. In Quarta rem ipsam exponemus, quam in commendatione pro amico postulamus, ostendentes eam variis argumentis honestam, iustam, piam, aut virtuti cognatam, item utilem aut necessariam, praeterea non modo possibilem, sed etiam facilem ei, ad quem scribimus, secundum locos

For the letter of consolation ('by which we console a sad friend in difficult circumstances'), Macropedius proposes a five-part structure based on the oration, whose last two sections are confutation and conclusion. Here are the first three parts.

> In the first we obtain goodwill either indirectly from the wisdom of being consoled or from our duty etc. In the second we briefly narrate his misfortune and propose that either it should not be lamented at all or not so much. In the third place, depending on different conditions of the sorrow or the sorrower, either we proceed using the topics of deliberative oratory to show that sorrow is neither sufficiently honourable, nor sufficiently pious, not sufficiently just, not useful etc., or according to the topics of exhortation we attempt to arouse emotions either by pleasing or by rebuking, or we use other arguments taken from philosophy or holy scripture, etc.[96]

Macropedius provides a grammar-school-level compendium of rhetoric, focusing on letter-writing but providing much material which will aid pupils' later studies. He draws on the structural formulae devised by Negro, and to some extent endorsed by Erasmus, but his recipes also reflect the structure of the classical oration and the freer approach advocated by Erasmus and Vives. It seems like a typically Melanchthonian compromise between different approaches, reflecting the fact that the popular collections of several manuals ensured the continuing availability of different approaches to teaching letter-writing.

Two manuals illustrate Italian approaches to letter-writing in the 1540s. *Grammatice, de epistolis componendis* (1539), by Lucio Scoppa (d. 1543), printed thirteen times up to 1598, always in Venice, incorporates a very short discussion of letters within the small part of his grammar devoted to rhetoric. His definition of letter seems to be based on Vives and he uses the same quotations from Augustine and Cicero directly after it.[97] He gives most attention to beginning the letter (perhaps as the part which differs most from the oration) and to appropriate style. Girolamo Cafaro's

confirmationis generis deliberativi. Pollicebimur quoque in quinto loco et nos et commendatum amicum nostrum gratos futuros mutuam quoque nostram operam et studium deferemus.' Ibid., sig. C4^{r-v}.

[96] 'Consolatoria epistola est, qua amicum in rebus adversis contristatum consolamur . . . In prima benevolentiam captamus aut per insinuationem a prudentia consolandi, aut ab officio nostro etc. In secunda, narramus breviter infortunium eius, et proponimus non dolendum, aut non usque adeo dolendum, etc. In tertia pro diversa desolati aut doloris conditione, aut procedimus secundum locos deliberativos, probantes neque satis honestum, neque satis pium, neque satis iustum, neque utilem esse dolorem etc., aut secundum locos praescriptos in exhortationibus, studemus vel blandiendo vel increpando movendis affectibus, aut aliis argumentis ex philosophia seu Scriptura sacra depromptis utimur etc.' Ibid., sig. D4^{v}.

[97] L. J. Scoppa, *Grammatice, de epistolis componendis* (Venice, 1540), sig. EE5^{r-v}.

De conscribendis epistolis (1546), which was printed twenty-five times, mostly as part of his *Grammatice* (1555), defines the letter as 'an interpreter of our mind and our affairs' and divides letters into thirteen types (divine, serious, persuading, dissuading, warning, consoling, exhorting, dehorting, love, mixed, announcing news, lamenting, joking). He outlines a six-part letter based on the classical oration.[98] Most space is devoted to rhythmic prose, instructions for elegant Latin, and collections of useful Latin phrases (derived from Fliscus) for ideas first expressed in Italian, for each section of the letter. Both manuals regard letter-writing as a part of elegant Latin composition, on the border as it were between intermediate grammar and elementary rhetoric. Scoppa is more alert to recent developments than Cafaro.

De epistolis Latine conscribendis libri V (1571) by the Dutch grammarian Simon Verepaeus (1522–98) was printed twenty-nine times before 1620, mainly before 1600 and mainly from Antwerp, Cologne, and Wittenberg. Verepaeus uses a traditional definition, putting his emphasis on conversational style, studying examples of the best letter-writers, and crafting material and order by thinking about the writer, the addressee, and their relationship.[99] In his six-part analysis of the letter, he distinguishes, like Macropedius, between parts which are specific to the letter, for which he provides model phrases from Cicero and others: salutation, valediction, and inscription; and parts which are shared with rhetoric generally: *exordium*, narration, and conclusion.[100] The second book is devoted to style, vocabulary, and the question of why Cicero is the best model. The third book outlines eighteen types of letter, with reference to examples by Cicero, advice, and suggested contents for each type. The types seem to be adapted from Erasmus's list: announcing or narrating, recommending, requesting, exhorting, praising, accusing, reproaching, invective, excusing, asking forgiveness (*deprecatoria*), joking, lamenting, consoling, dutiful, congratulation, thanking, ordering, and dedicating.[101] The fourth and fifth books are given over to model phrases and formulae useful for the *exordium* (4) and the other parts of the letter (5).

The French Jesuit rhetoric professor Jean Voëllus (1541–1610) composed his *De ratione conscribendi epistolas* (1578) as a clear, brief guide for Jesuit schools.[102] It was printed eleven times up to 1614. After quoting

98 'nostrae mentis interpres et quasi rerum nostrarum sive alienorum certa nuncia.' G. Cafaro, *De conscribendis epistolis* (Cortona, 1546), sigs. A4^r–5^r.

99 Verepaeus, *De epistolis latine conscribendis libri V* (London, 1592), sigs. A5^v–8^v.

100 Ibid., sig. B1^r.

101 Ibid., sig. E3^v.

102 J. Lipsius and J. Voellus, *De ratione conscribendi epistolis* (Brescia, 1601), sig. C1^r. C. Mouchel, *Cicéron et Sénèque dans la rhétorique de la Renaissance* (Marburg, 1990), 192–7.

Libanius's and Cicero's definitions of the letter, Voëllus gives instructions for writing fourteen types of letter, referring to examples of each type in classical literature.[103] He envisages a five-part letter (salutation, *exordium*, narration, confirmation, valediction) but explains that the most important guide to what to include is to think about what is appropriate to author, recipient, and subject.[104] He includes a short section on the qualities of style appropriate to the letter, and an exhortation to pupils to study Cicero's letters and practice by writing letters of their own.

JUSTUS LIPSIUS (1547–1606)

The last successful letter-writing manual of the sixteenth-century, Lipsius's *Epistolica Institutio* (1591), which was published independently nineteen times before 1620, as well as in various editions of his complete works and other collections, was also one of the best. It is methodically organized into two main parts: chapters 1–6 on the nature of letters, their different types, and their content; chapters 7–14 on style and imitation; followed by a Greek text of the section on letters from Demetrius, *On Style*, with parallel Latin translation.

After discussing the etymology of *epistola*, various synonyms, and the physical form of early letters (drawing on his immense knowledge of classical literature), Lipsius defines the letter as 'writing announcing one's mind to people who are absent or almost absent'.[105] He justifies each phrase of this, pointing out that a letter can convey emotion or fact, citing definitions by St Ambrose, Cicero, and Turpilius, and showing that Augustus, Tiberius, and Seneca wrote letters to people in the same building as them. The subject-matter of the letter is partly invariant (as in Macropedius): the salutation (which should give name of sender and recipient, without any complimentary adjectives, in the classical fashion), valediction (presented as a four-part formula), and superscription.[106] The variable material is dictated by the occasion and reason for writing the letter, but it can be regarded as falling into three types: serious, learned (subdivided into philological, philosophical, and theological), and familiar, which concerns the daily life of our selves, family, and friends. Public serious letters involve narratives, disputations, deliberations on the state of

[103] J. Voellus, *De ratione conscribendi epistolis*, sigs. C1^{v}–3^{r}, E1^{v}.
[104] Ibid., sig. E5$^{r–v}$.
[105] 'Scriptum animi nuntium ad absentes, aut quasi absentes.' Lipsius, *Opera omnia* (Wesel, 1675; repr. Hildesheim, 2003), ii/2. 1068.
[106] Ibid. 1069–72.

affairs, on war and peace, and similar topics. Private serious letters are concerned with consolations, warnings, requests, reproaches, excuses, persuasions, praises, and whatever else we want to take up a position on. There is not much to say about invention, since we would not trouble to write a letter if we did not have something in mind which we wanted to say.[107] There may be some need for amplification in learned or serious letters but in familiar letters one should just say whatever one wants to say. The best order for a letter is whatever one chooses, as in a conversation. Even in replying it is better not to answer point by point but to focus on what one wants to say. In serious letters there may be more need of order, but there the precepts of rhetoric will be the best guide.

Lipsius describes five qualities of epistolary style. Brevity is essential, but the letter must be long enough to make its meaning clear. Learned and serious letters may need to be longer. Clarity depends on using appropriate and familiar words and positioning them correctly. Simplicity is a matter of straightforward and honest exposition of one's thought and of using a language which may be heightened but should never be pompous, ostentatious, or overdressed. Cicero is the model to imitate here. Charm (*venustas*) depends on good judgement and the use of proverbs, *sententiae*, and jokes. *Decentia* requires thought and language which is appropriate to the people involved and the subject. Words should be good Latin used in the customary way; phrases should have elegance and brightness.[108]

Lipsius identifies three aspects of imitation: reading, selection, and practice. Boys should read Cicero; young men should expand their reading to a range of other writers; adults should read all types of books, most of all Sallust, Seneca, and Tacitus, but they too should continually read Cicero. Under selection, Lipsius suggests that people should copy materials they wish to imitate into three notebooks. The first is a formulary in which one should collect on the one hand formulae which organize a text, such as narrations, divisions, and transitions, on the other hand materials for particular epistolary purposes, such as asking, thanking, offering, praising. For this book one should especially read Cicero, the younger Pliny and Poliziano. The second book is for ornaments: similes, allegories, images, descriptions, sharp phrases, *sententiae*. These should be taken from the historians, Seneca, Plutarch, Cicero, Quintilian, and Pliny. The final book is for diction: striking or brilliant phrases or words which are unusual, new, or used in new senses. But the most important part of imitation is writing.

[107] 'Nam ad Inventionem uberibus praeceptis quid opus? Cum semper ea prompta; nec ad Epistolam scribendam veniatur nisi argumento concepto, et mente (ut ita dicam) tumente.' Ibid. 1073.

[108] Ibid. 1074–8.

Schoolboys should borrow words and phrases from their reading and should imitate the style of Cicero. Young men should avoid stealing too much and should be more choosy about whom and when to imitate. Adults should aim at imitation of spirit rather than surface features.[109]

Lipsius has thought hard about the nature of the letter and about what can be achieved in a short manual. Consequently he has understood that it may be better to make use of wider principles taught elsewhere in the rhetoric syllabus rather than try to teach everything again here. He is refreshingly practical about invention and disposition. His five categories for epistolary style are striking and well thought out. He adds the best short account of stylistic imitation in existence to fill out his requirements for clarity and simplicity and his advocacy of charm and appropriateness. Lipsius's well-known preference for Seneca and Tacitus does not exclude repeated expression of his admiration for Cicero. His final assertion of imitation of the spirit rather than the exact vocabulary is close to Erasmus's view in the *Ciceronianus*.

Sixteenth-century letter-writing manuals mostly resemble each other more than they follow the principles of different authors of manuals of the whole of rhetoric, or different schools. Generally they define the letter, divide it into types, some of which may be discussed in detail, provide examples, analyse the structure of the letter, and give some comments or instruction on prose style. Some manuals incorporate their teaching of letter-writing within a wider ranging picture of rhetoric, treating letter-writing as a way of introducing some of the issues which will dominate the full course. The format for these basic instructive manuals is fixed by the 1530s in manuals which are reprinted, often in collections of letter-writing texts, for the rest of the century. These manuals were probably used mainly in grammar schools.

Alongside this pedagogical approach which gave simple rules for the construction of different kinds of letter, we also find a more pragmatic approach which insists that letters are extremely varied and that content, order, and style depend more on what the writer wants to convey to the addressee and on the perceived relationship between them than on any rules of genre. Some of these manuals, such as Vives and Erasmus's *De conscribendis epistolis* (which has elements of both types) were reprinted so often that they must have been used in schools. Towards the end of the sixteenth century mainstream rhetoric textbooks began to absorb from letter-writing manuals the idea of different types of deliberative and demonstrative oratory, better adapted to contemporary concerns.

[109] Ibid. 1078–83.

12

Preaching Manuals and Legal Dialectics

Preaching is the most Christian form of public speaking, the occasion on which Christians have most opportunity to make use of rhetoric, but most need to justify employing classical culture. Preaching also requires an adaptation of classical rhetoric, with special attention to interpreting scripture, to the life and self-presentation of the preacher, and to different emotions from those required in the courtroom. The medieval tradition of preaching, accompanied by a rich corpus of *artes praedicandi*, was challenged first by humanists, who wanted to make more use of classical forms and teaching, and later by Protestants, who emphasized understanding scripture and teaching a congregation, and Counter-Reformation Catholics, who demanded a fervent advocacy of basic doctrine and moral instruction.

Renaissance preaching manuals tended to agree on the usefulness of rhetorical principles in exegesis and on the need to show that scripture and the church fathers employed rhetoric. There was more variety of opinion about how much classical principles should inform the structure and content of the sermon and about identifying the different types of sermon. In contrast to the classical consensus on the six- (or effectively very similar four-) part structure of the oration, renaissance preaching manuals propose many different plans for sermons, which reflect different ways of mediating between the teachings of classical rhetoric and the requirements of different types of sermon. Preachers would normally have studied classical rhetoric at school and university. It is possible that preaching manuals were used in seminaries or in the theology faculty, but they may have been intended for private study by practitioners. There were far fewer editions of preaching manuals than letter-writing manuals, partly because the intended readership was smaller and more advanced.

About 150 editions of preaching manuals were produced between 1477 and 1620; the most successful were Melanchthon's *De officiis concionatoris* (after 1529) with fifteen editions and Francisco de Borja's *Ratio concionandi*, written in the 1550s but first printed in 1579, with nineteen.[1] Two Catholic works which provide resources for the preacher, based on the Gospel texts for each Sunday and major feast, were frequently printed: Thomas Stapleton's *Promptuarium Catholicum* (1547) with fifteen editions and Tomás de Trujillo's vast *Thesaurus concionatorum* (1570), with fifteen editions, mostly in southern Europe, up to 1596. Twelve editions of Stapleton, including three from Venice, were printed after 1594, so Stapleton may have replaced Trujillo. The most influential preaching manuals are usually said to be Erasmus's *Ecclesiastes* (1535) and Luis de Granada's *Ecclesiasticae rhetoricae libri VI* (1576), both with ten editions. Perhaps because the majority of sermons were preached in the vernacular, there were also seven preaching manuals composed in vernacular languages, which I will discuss in the next chapter, and several translations of works originally written in Latin. There were very few rhetoric and dialectic manuals dedicated to legal practice and only a handful of editions of each. I will discuss them at the end of the chapter.

The manuscript and printing record suggests four main phases in the circulation of preaching manuals in the renaissance. In the fourteenth and fifteenth centuries medieval manuals and preaching aids continued to be copied widely and some new ones were composed. Humanist manuals began to appear in the early days of printing, including works by Traversagni (1478), Reuchlin (1504), and Erasmus (1535). Closely related to these were a group of Protestant preaching manuals by Dietrich (after 1529), Melanchthon (after 1529, and 1540), Bullinger (1532), Hemmingsen (1552), and Hyperius (1553). Far more numerous were the Counter-Reformation manuals, several by Spanish and Italian authors, notably Francisco de Borja (1550s), Lorenzo de Villavicencio (1564), Agostino Valier (1574), Luis de Granada (1576), Diego Valadés (1579), and St Carlo Borromeo (1581). In some cases these manuals must have been studied towards the end of a lengthy programme of education including a good deal of rhetoric, like that outlined in the Jesuit *Ratio Studiorum*; in others the preaching manual may have been intended to remedy the omissions of previous clerical education. By the end of the century there was considerable overlap between the preaching manuals strictly defined and the treatments of rhetoric more generally by Keckermann, Vossius, and Caussin, described in Chapter 9 above.

The earliest examples of Christian preaching are found in the Gospel accounts of Christ's ministry and in St Paul's letters. The form of preaching depicted there shows some connections to exposition of scripture in

[1] Johannes Melber's *Vocabularius praedicantium* (1477), listed with twenty-two editions in Green and Murphy, *Renaissance Rhetoric Short-Title Catalogue* (Aldershot, 2006), is a Latin–German dictionary, with no special adaptation to preaching.

the Jewish tradition.[2] Hellenistic discussion of epideictic rhetoric, for example by Menander Rhetor and Dionysius of Halicarnassus, included sections on praise of the gods.[3] But the only substantial work on Christian preaching from the ancient world was St Augustine's *De doctrina Christiana* (most of first three books written about 396; completion and fourth book, 427). This book was well-known in the middle ages and the renaissance. It was printed nineteen times independently between 1466 and 1620, and a further thirty-seven times in editions of St Augustine's collected works. These figures are rather small for a classical rhetoric but quite large for a preaching manual.

The first three books show how ancient grammatical and rhetorical teaching is helpful in analysing scripture; the fourth is concerned with preaching to others. Augustine assumes that the technical teaching of rhetoric is available to his readers through classical rhetorical texts. He makes four main points. First, he emphasizes that in order to serve Christ and their fellow Christians better preachers need eloquence combined with wisdom; that is, they need rhetoric. He supports this point by showing that scripture uses techniques of style depicted in rhetoric.[4] Secondly, Christian rhetoric must focus on clarity. The preacher, like the orator, should aim to teach, move, and delight, but teaching is the most important and delight should not be over-emphasized.[5] Thirdly, Augustine describes the three classical levels of style, showing that the Christian orator can achieve persuasion and eloquence in all three styles and arguing for variation of style within a single sermon, while insisting that the grand style will be important for its effect on the emotions of the congregation.[6] Finally he stresses the persuasive effect of Christian ethos, meaning that preachers need to demonstrate Christian virtues in their lives, and that they need to seek God's help in order to preach effectively.[7] His work has nothing to say about the structure of the sermon and nothing about amplification or techniques for elevating style.

St Gregory's *Cura pastoralis* (591) places most emphasis on the need for the preacher to lead an exemplary life and to adapt his preaching to different audiences. The section of Rabanus Maurus's *De institutione clericorum* (819) devoted to preaching combines passages from Augustine and Gregory.[8] Murphy argues that by 1220 a new rhetoric of preaching

[2] J. J. Murphy, *Rhetoric in the Middle Ages* (Berkeley, Calif., 1974), 269–85.
[3] D. A. Russell and N. G. Wilson, *Menander Rhetor* (Oxford, 1981), 6–29, 62–5, 363.
[4] Augustine, *De doctrina Christiana* 4.3–21.
[5] Ibid. 4.24–30.
[6] Ibid. 4.34–58.
[7] Ibid. 4.32, 59–63.
[8] Murphy, *Rhetoric in the Middle Ages*, 292–7, 300.

became prominent, spreading throughout Europe and inspiring over 200 preaching manuals produced between 1200 and 1503.[9]

This new approach centred on the 'thematic sermon', which generally had four main parts: an introduction (consisting of a prayer and an introduction to the theme); a reading of the text from scripture, called the theme; a logical division of the theme into parts and subparts, each of which would be explained, using a variety of arguments and parallels from scripture, and amplified; and a conclusion. Sermon manuals of this period typically give advice on each of these sections, on the choice of themes, on the types of argument to be employed, and on techniques of amplification. Preachers' aids might give in addition: collections of exempla; concordances and lists to aid in the finding of parallel passages from scripture useful for proving or amplifying a theme; and collections of sermons and sermon outlines.[10] A really extensive medieval preaching manual, like Robert of Basevorn's *Forma praedicandi* (1322) adds: definitions of preaching and advice on the preacher's character and on preparing to preach; models of preaching from Christ, the Apostles and the church fathers; advice on winning over the audience, developing a theme (using authorities and arguments) and dividing the theme; digression; style; delivery; humour and allusion.[11] While thirteenth- and fourteenth-century manuals continued to be copied, the fifteenth century also produced some new manuals of this type, culminating in *Manuale curatorum praedicandi praebens modum* (Basel, 1503), by Johannes Ulrich Surgant (d. 1503), printed nine times up to 1520.[12] According to Wenzel, old-style homilies continued to be preached alongside these newer thematic sermons, from the thirteenth to the fifteenth century.[13]

Margarita eloquentiae castigatae (London, 1478) by the Franciscan humanist Lorenzo Traversagni of Savona (1425–1503) was the first humanist preaching manual and the first rhetoric manual to be printed in England, where Traversagni taught (mainly at Cambridge) between 1476 and 1487. It was printed twice in full and once in epitome. Since all three editions were English, the work, which also survives in a Vatican manuscript, may not have circulated much in continental Europe.

[9] Ibid. 300. S. Wenzel, 'The Arts of Preaching', in A. Minnis and I. Johnson (eds.), *The Cambridge History of Literary Criticism*, ii. *The Middle Ages* (Cambridge, 2005), 87.

[10] Murphy, *Rhetoric in the Middle Ages*, 315–43. See also Marianne Briscoe, *Artes praedicandi* (Turnhout, 1992), 11–76.

[11] Murphy, *Rhetoric in the Middle Ages*, 344–55; T. Charland, *Artes praedicandi* (Paris, 1936), 233–323; see also J. J. Murphy (ed.), *Three Medieval Rhetorical Arts* (Berkeley, Calif., 1971), 114–215.

[12] Briscoe, *Artes praedicandi*, 45–53.

[13] Wenzel, 'Arts of Preaching', 88.

The *Margarita* is largely a digest of the teaching of *Rhetorica ad Herennium* with examples from the Bible and church history and with a little adaptation to modern speaking practices. In the middle of the work Traversagni discusses arguments suitable for three different occasions for oratory: speaking before princes (for example, as an ambassador); speaking to the learned; and addressing a popular audience.[14] But rather than crafting a rhetoric for these situations, Traversagni tends to repeat classical teaching. His first book is devoted to invention, following the same order as *Rhetorica ad Herennium*, the second to deliberative and demonstrative oratory (where he takes over a great deal of material from *De inventione*), and the third to style. Here he first copies the entire list of figures from *Rhetorica ad Herennium* and then adds the whole of Bede's discussion of the tropes from *De schematibus et tropis*, apparently without noticing that the same tropes are described, using their Greek rather than their Latin names.[15] Traversagni omits judicial oratory and the associated theory of status. While much of the book concentrates on classical demonstrative oratory, in line with O'Malley's presentation of Roman rhetoric in the later fifteenth century, Traversagni also recognizes the division of the biblical text typical of thematic preaching.[16]

Liber congestorum de arte praedicandi (1504) by the famous Hebrew scholar Johann Reuchlin (1455–1522), printed four times, concentrates on invention, memory, and delivery, giving a mainly classical account of the six-part oration (*exordium*, reading, division, confirmation, confutation, conclusion),[17] the three types of rhetoric, and the topics of invention. He divides sermons into three types: moral, civil, and theological; and asserts that sermons have three aims: equity, usefulness, and honour. Preachers must take care to conceal art. They must adapt what they intend to say to the audience and their views and to the time and place of the sermon. The preacher must speak suitably for persuasion, and with a certain dignity.[18] As well as making the audience attentive and well-disposed, the *exordium* should set out the general subject (*thesis* or *thema*) of the sermon and include a prayer for divine assistance.[19]

[14] L. G. Traversagni, *Margarita eloquentiae castigatae* (St Albans, 1480), sigs. g2^{r}–3^{v}, edn. by G. Farris (Savona, 1978). G. Farris, *Umanesimo e religione in L. G. Traversagni* (Milan, 1972). L. D. Green, 'Classical and Medieval Rhetorical Traditions in Traversagni's *Margarita eloquentiae*', *Quarterly Journal of Speech*, 72 (1986), 185–96.

[15] Traversagni, *Margarita*, sigs. q7^{v}–t7^{r}; the section taken from Bede starts at s8^{v}.

[16] Ibid., sigs. d8^{r}–e1^{v}. J. W. O'Malley, *Praise and Blame in Renaissance Rome* (Durham, NC, 1979), 48.

[17] Reuchlin *et al.*, *De arte concionandi formulae* (London, 1570), sig. A3^{v}.

[18] Ibid., sigs. A3^{r}–4^{r}.

[19] Ibid., sig. A4$^{r–v}$.

Later renaissance preaching manuals illustrate the same basic dependence on classical rhetoric, but they find more, different, and more consistent ways to adapt it. Several of them recognize that their proposal for a more classical form of preaching is opposed to the tradition of the thematic sermon, though some soften this by recognizing different types of preaching. Most of them add sections on the grandeur of preaching, the purity of life required of the preacher, and religious preparations for preaching, such as prayer and meditation. Indeed, a few successful manuals focus almost entirely on this aspect. Since preaching always involves commentary on and interpretation of the Bible, many preaching manuals follow St Augustine in giving advice on ways to read and understand scripture. In general they take a classical rhetorical approach to invention (and the use of the topics) but they often give extra importance to emotion (following St Augustine) and amplification (following Erasmus). They copy the classical teaching on tropes and figures, while showing that the Bible and the church fathers made use of these same techniques. Delivery is treated more prominently than in many renaissance rhetoric treatises.

PROTESTANT PREACHING MANUALS

Ratio brevis et docta piaque sacrarum tractandarum concionum (after 1529) by Luther's friend and amanuensis Viet Dietrich (1506–49), printed five times, was heavily influenced by Melanchthon, whose short *De officiis concionatoris* was usually printed with it. Dietrich insists that rhetoric and dialectic have to be studied together. He proposes a classically based eight-part outline for the sermon (*exordium*, narration, proposition, argument, confirmation, ornament, amplifications, epilogue).[20] Like Melanchthon he divides themes into simple and complex. Simple themes should be investigated using a short list of topics (definition, causes, parts, duty). He illustrates this approach with an example of a sermon on faith, marking the different sections in the margin.[21] He praises the organization of Luther's sermons and his example of a complex sermon treats the theme 'saved by faith alone, without works', using testimonia, examples, and contraries.[22] He ends with a discussion of another kind of complex theme, the deliberative sermon, which depends on the topics of the honourable and the useful, writing an example of St Paul giving advice to Timothy.[23]

[20] Ibid., sigs. C4^{r}–6^{r}. In this edn. Dietrich's work is misattributed to Melanchthon.
[21] Ibid., C7^{r}–E1^{v}.
[22] Ibid., E2^{r}–F2^{r}.
[23] Ibid., F5^{v}–G5^{v}.

The Swiss reformer Heinrich Bullinger (1504–75) in his *De prophetae officio* (1532), printed twice, assumes that readers will already have studied rhetoric and dialectic. The role of the preacher is to interpret scripture, to reprove errors and crimes, to fight for piety and truth, and to inculcate justice, faith, and mutual love in his hearers.[24] Bullinger describes the interpretation of scripture, the construction of sermons on simple themes (such as grace, faith, Christ, justice), and preaching against errors (including arguments against the Mass drawn from the Bible and St Paul). He cites St Augustine on interpreting the Bible and Cicero's *De oratore* on the importance of devoting all one's efforts to the main point at issue, the *status quaestionis*.[25] Just as charity is the greatest help in interpreting scripture so purity of life and integrity are of most assistance to the preacher in persuading his congregation.[26] The work ends with an oration praising Zwingli as an example of the ideal preacher.[27] Bullinger's work relies on classical rhetoric but does not attempt to go over the same ground, focusing on the specific task of the preacher.

Erasmus's *Ecclesiastes* (1535), printed ten times up to 1554, is analysed in Chapter 5 above. Erasmus places great emphasis on the person and moral obligations of the preacher in book 1. Books 2 and 3 present a classical rhetoric adapted to preaching, focusing on the classical six-part oration. Erasmus gives special attention to amplification, emotion, the use of the figures and tropes in interpreting scripture, and decorum. Book 4, which is unfinished, collects materials which are likely to be helpful in composing sermons on different subjects, such as the nature of God, the Son, the Holy Spirit, angels, concord, and discord.

Philipp Melanchthon (1497–1560) never completed a comprehensive account of preaching, but two short manuals of homiletics were published over his name. *De modo et arte concionandi* (1540) first appeared with his commentary on Timothy and was printed four times in Strasbourg and Wittenberg. This work recognizes three types of preaching: methodical teaching, interpretation of scripture, and exhortation to good works, patience, obedience, chastity, and almsgiving. Methodical teaching must follow the rules of dialectic.[28] Four rules are offered for the interpretation of scripture.[29] Melanchthon urges preachers to make connections between

[24] H. Bullinger, *De prophetae officio* (Zurich, 1532), sigs. B5^{r}, A3^{v}, D5^{r-v}. F. Busser, *Heinrich Bullinger (1504–1575): Leben, Werk und Wirkung*, 2 vols. (Zurich, 2004–5).

[25] Bullinger, *De prophetae officio*, sigs. A4^{r}, A8^{r}, A4^{v}.

[26] Ibid., sigs. B1^{v}, D6^{r}.

[27] Ibid., sigs. D8^{r}–E5^{r}.

[28] *Philipp Melanchthons Schriften zur praktischen Theologie*, ed. D. Drews and F. Cohrs, ii. *Homiletische Schriften* (Leipzig, 1929; repr. Frankfurt, 1963), 33–5, 51.

[29] Ibid. 35, 46, 48.

Bible texts and theological commonplaces, giving several examples. All these types of preaching will need to make an emotional appeal to the audience.[30]

His very brief *De officiis concionatoris* first appeared after 1529 together with Dietrich's *Ratio brevis*. In total it was printed fifteen times, always with other works.[31] This work defines the main aim of preaching as 'teaching the force and nature of religion', with 'exhorting to faith and good behaviour' as a subsidiary aim.[32] This leads Melanchthon to recognize three genres of preaching: didactic, epitretic (teaching you what to believe), and paraenetic (concerned with behaviour).[33] The didactic genus is subdivided into interpretation and method.[34] Melanchthon gives instructions for interpretation based on a rejection of the fourfold interpretation of scripture and very brief advice on method.[35]

The Danish Lutheran theologian Niels Hemmingsen (1513–1600) acknowledged his debts to Melanchthon's logic and rhetoric in his *Ecclesiasten* (1552), printed seven times, mainly in Wittenberg and Leipzig, up to 1578, and translated into English.[36] His treatise is organized into three main sections: advice on the interpretation of the Bible, going through each section of the structure of the sermon, and discussing the different types of sermon. He divides the sermon into four sections: the *exordium*, in which after a prayer and the reading of the Bible text, the preacher briefly outlines what he will say; the treatise (subdivided into division and exposition), which will vary according to the type of sermon; the digression, which applies the teaching of the sermon to the audience; and the conclusion.[37] Hemmingsen divides sermons into teaching and exhortation. Teaching can focus on persons, things, or propositions; exhortation involves persuading, rebuking, or consoling.[38] Sermons involving teaching of simple elements will use topics related to Melanchthon's invention of simple themes: definition, division, causes, effects, use and abuse, and contraries. Hemmingsen explains the topic of definition by constructing definitions of marriage and the gospel.[39] In using Bible texts preachers will

[30] Ibid. 37–45, 51.

[31] Green and Murphy, *Renaissance Rhetoric STC*, 147, 167, 296, 375.

[32] 'Praecipuum est docere quae sit vis et natura religionis. Alterum est hortari tum ad fidem, tum ad bonos mores.' *Melanchthons Homiletische Schriften*, ed. Drews and Cohrs, 5.

[33] Ibid. 5–6.

[34] Ibid. 7.

[35] Ibid. 10–14.

[36] This work originally formed the second book of Hemmingsen's *De methodis*.

[37] N. Hemmingsen, *De methodis* (Leipzig, 1578), available electronically from the Bayerische Staats Bibliothek, sigs. K7^{r}–8^{r}.

[38] Ibid., sig. K8^{r}.

[39] Ibid., sigs. L1^{r}, L5^{r}–7^{r}.

want to locate the general teaching which Hemmingsen associates with Melanchthon's *Loci communes*, and will then amplify it using techniques of *copia*.[40] Hemmingsen gives a worked example of a persuasive sermon and careful advice on the method of consolation and the texts to be employed.[41] He assumes that his readers will make use of their training in rhetoric and dialectic to develop what he has to say about the sermon.[42] This may explain the absence of any comment on amplification or style.

De formandis concionibus sacris (1553) by the Marburg schoolteacher Andreas Gerardus Hyperius (1511–64) was printed seven times up to 1581 and translated into English and French.[43] His first, relatively short book announces the types of sermons and describes the contents of each section of the sermon. The second book, which offers many examples, discusses the technique for handling scripture, theological commonplaces, and material to use in the different kinds of sermon. Hyperius finds the three genres of rhetoric inappropriate to preaching, arguing on the basis of 2 Timothy 3: 16 that there are five types of sermon: doctrinal, confuting (of false doctrines), institution (teaching holiness and good behaviour), correcting (of corrupt behaviour), and consolation.[44] Every sermon must have a theme (here used in the sense of principal subject or *status causae*), either one word, or a proposition, which will be derived from the passage of scripture read at the outset. Hyperius envisages the sermon as having seven sections, adapted from the classical oration: reading of scripture, invocation, *exordium*, proposition, confirmation, confutation, and conclusion.[45]

Like Augustine and Erasmus, Hyperius explains the importance and the difficulty of the preacher's task. The preacher will need a training in rhetoric and will need to be well-versed in the Bible and the church fathers, especially Chrysostom and Augustine.[46] Hyperius gives particular attention to amplification and the commonplaces used to arouse different types of emotion.[47] Within his treatment of the doctrinal sermon he sets out twenty-eight topics of invention (taken from Agricola) and

40 Ibid., sigs. M5^{r}–N4^{r}.
41 Ibid., sigs. O2^{v}–4^{v}, O5^{r}–8^{v}.
42 Ibid., sig. K7^{r}.
43 The English tr. is somewhat elaborated from the Latin text.
44 Hyperius, *De formandis concionibus sacris* (Marburg, 1553), accessed via Bayerische Staats Bibliothek, sigs. B4^{v}–5^{r}, K4^{v}–6^{r}. See J. Lares, *Milton and the Preaching Arts* (Pittsburgh, 2001), 56–77; O. Millet, 'La Réforme protestante et la rhétorique (circa 1520–1550)', in M. Fumaroli (ed.), *Histoire de la rhétorique dans l'Europe moderne* (Paris, 1999), 302–9.
45 Hyperius, *De formandis concionibus sacris*, sig. C7^{r}.
46 Ibid., sigs. A3^{v}, A5^{v}–B1^{r}, B5^{r}–6^{r}.
47 Ibid., sigs. G8^{r}–K4^{r}.

twenty-two theological topics.[48] Then he gives eight rules to be observed in writing sermons of this type, including: the preacher must concentrate on questions which develop piety in his audience; his reasoning should not be too convoluted; he should illustrate his points with comparisons and allegories. Finally he cites examples of various subtypes of doctrinal sermon.[49] Hyperius also gives examples of doctrinal sermons based on simple and compound subjects. Preachers should especially strive for the benefit of their listeners, comeliness of gesture, and the promotion of concord.[50]

According to Hieronymus Weller (1499–1572) in *De modo et ratione concionandi* (1558), which was printed four times up to 1565, in Wittenberg and Nuremberg, the preacher should be diligent, humble, should avoid paradoxical subjects and starting quarrels, and should not speak for too long.[51] There are three kinds of sermon: teaching, reproving, and exegetic; and the preacher has four main duties: to teach, to argue, to console, and to exhort.[52] The sermon has six parts: *exordium* (or invocation of God's name), reading of the scripture text which will be explained, proposition of the theme, confirmation, confutation, peroration.[53] Weller examines four methods of confirmation (definition, division, argumentation, and citation of authorities) and six forms of amplification (movement from hypothesis to thesis, digression, allegory, similitudes, *sententiae* and *prosopopeia*), providing some striking examples of each type.[54] For all their differences, Hyperius and Weller are clearly working out of similar Lutheran traditions of preaching (and Melanchthonian traditions of rhetoric), with Hyperius focusing more on scriptural exegesis, Weller more on literary amplification.

COUNTER-REFORMATION MANUALS

Even before the first meetings of the Council of Trent (1545–63), Catholic thinkers believed that the rapid advance of Protestant ideas in the 1520s and 1530s could be explained by the rhetorical force with which Protestants had promulgated their new doctrines and their criticisms of the church, and by corresponding weaknesses in Catholic preaching.

48 Ibid., sigs. K6ʳ–L3ᵛ.
49 Ibid., sigs. L3ʳ–7ʳ.
50 Ibid., sigs. Q8ʳ–R7ʳ.
51 H. Weller, *De modo et ratione concionandi* (Nuremberg, 1565), sigs. b2ᵛ–4ᵛ.
52 Ibid., sigs. b7ʳ, b8ᵛ.
53 Ibid., sig. c1ᵛ.
54 Ibid., sigs. c5ʳ, e2ᵛ, f6ᵛ–i1ᵛ.

Regional councils and individual bishops took up the challenge of improving the quality of clergy and preaching.[55] In the 1550s the third General of the Jesuits, Francisco de Borja (1510–72), composed a *De ratione concionandi* (1579) printed fifteen times before 1620 and translated into Spanish, which concentrates on the preacher's experience of preaching. The preacher should be fearful before God but have faith. He should read widely in the Bible, following the interpretations of the church fathers.[56] The sermon should be well-organized, including commonplaces, metaphors, passages from scripture, examples, and narratives, but there should be no more than three or four sections and it should not be too long.[57] Before preaching the priest should seek God's help; afterwards he should meditate on his shortcomings.[58] In reprimanding others the preacher should act as if reprimanding himself. He should correct in a fraternal way, showing pity for sinners rather than indignation. He should avoid difficult theological issues but should speak up strongly for Catholic doctrine.[59] Borja's emphasis on the preacher's preparation for an almost theatrical delivery of his sermon is widely taken up in Tridentine preaching manuals.

De formandis sacris concionibus (1564) by the Augustinian friar and adviser to Philip II of Spain, Lorenzo de Villavicencio (*c.*1518-1583), was printed five or six times in the sixteenth century, mostly in Antwerp and Cologne. Villavicencio demonstrates the importance of preaching from scripture and from the church fathers. The preacher must show charity, plainness of speech, and probity of life. He must have a vocation, must call on the help of the Holy Spirit, and must be willing to confront Protestant heretics and point out the errors of the Jews.[60] The sermon should have seven parts, adding a reading and a prayer to the structure of the classical oration: reading of holy scripture, invocation, *exordium*, proposition or division, confirmation, refutation, and conclusion. He gives examples to show that Christian preachers wrote *exordia*.[61]

Following the same interpretation of 2 Timothy 3: 16–17 as Hyperius, Villavicencio declares that there are five types of sermon, corresponding to

[55] F. McGinness, *Right Thinking and Sacred Oratory in Counter-Reformation Rome* (Princeton, 1995), 33–7.

[56] F. Panigarola and F. Borgia, *Rhetoricae ecclesiasticae . . . libri tres* (Cologne, 1612), sigs. f11^{v}–G4^{r}.

[57] Ibid., sigs. G7^{v}–9^{r}, H3^{v}.

[58] Ibid., sigs. H2^{r-v}, H8^{v}–10^{v}.

[59] Ibid., sigs. H4^{r}–6^{v}. McGinness, *Right Thinking*, 38–9.

[60] L. a Villavicentio, *De formandis sacris concionibus seu de interpretatione scripturarum populari*, in G. Aromatari ed., *Degli autori del ben parlare*, 5 parts (1633), ultima parte, sigs. g1^{r}–i4^{v}.

[61] Ibid., sigs. l3^{r}–5^{v}.

five kinds of status of religious speech: doctrine, reproof of error, correction of sinful behaviour, instruction in religion, morality, and good works, and consolation. Later he adds a mixed type.[62] He gives instructions on developing commonplaces, on amplification, and on the arousing of Christian emotions, such as joy, hope, fear, and grief. In Aristotelian fashion he lists topics for arousing these emotions.[63] The simple doctrinal sermon should be developed according to six topics (definition, parts, cause, effects or duties, similars, and contraries) which resemble Melanchthon's didascalic genre of rhetoric. The complex doctrinal sermon will need to employ topical invention. The list of topics, which is not developed at length, owes something to Agricola.[64]

Throughout Villavicencio emphasizes the need to keep things simple for the sake of the people, to restrict the number of proofs offered, and to adapt what one says to time and place and to what will be useful to, and suitable for, the audience.[65] The final section of the work is a defence of the fourfold interpretation of scripture and a discussion of the use of theology in preaching.[66] Although Villavicencio is famous for urging Philip II to attack Protestantism in the Netherlands, his preaching manual shows some influence from Melanchthon and Hyperius.

The bishop of Verona Agostino Valier (1530–1606) in his *De rhetorica ecclesiastica* (1574), printed ten times up to 1585, defined ecclesiastical rhetoric as

> the art or faculty of discovering, ordering and expressing in words the things which are required for saving souls. The tasks of the ecclesiastical orator are to open the secret truth of God to the people, to teach pious and virtuous living, to destroy most disgraceful errors, pestilential superstitions and wicked customs, and to call men to the pious, true and divine wisdom of the Christian religion and to feed the souls of his audience with knowledge of the truth, which is the sweetest food of all.[67]

The crucial point is to speak in a way that suits the audience. In the schools one can speak briefly and perceptively about difficult issues, but to

[62] Ibid., sig. l7^{v}, n6^{r-v}, p8^{r}.
[63] Ibid., sigs. m3^{v}–n4^{v}.
[64] Ibid., sigs. n6^{v}–8^{r}.
[65] Ibid., sigs. l2^{v}–3^{r}, l7^{v}–8^{v}, p8^{r}.
[66] Ibid., sigs. q4^{r}–r6^{r}.
[67] 'Quae est ars sive facultas inveniendi, disponendi et eloquendi ea, quae ad salutem animarum pertinent. Oratoris enim ecclesiastici officium est veritatem arcanum dei aperire populo, docere pie et innocenter vivere, errores turpissimos, pestiferos superstitiones, pravas consuetudines tollere, ad piam, veram, divinamque sapientiam, christianam religionem homines compellere, cognitione veritatis, qua nullus est suavior cibus, auditorum animos nutrire.' A. Valerius, *Libri tres de rhetorica ecclesiastica* (Paris, 1575), sig. a2^{r-v}.

a popular audience one should be copious and clear, and should concentrate on subjects which help in the saving of souls.[68] Book 1 is devoted to invention, book 2 to emotion, and book 3 to style. Although Valier upholds the three classical genres of rhetoric, in practice he concentrates on deliberative (which he divides into five types: what should be believed, what hoped, what feared, what avoided, and what done) and demonstrative oratory. His account of invention focuses on the topics of invention and on finding support in scriptural and patristic authorities.[69]

The arousal of emotion is of central importance to the Christian orator because, as Augustine observes, it obtains victory and teaches the audience what they ought to do.[70] Valier gives four general rules for eliciting an emotion in others: that you should feel the emotion yourself, that you should read what scripture and the prophets say on your subject, that you should paint scenes of human calamity before the eyes of the audience, and that you should pray for the help of the Holy Spirit.[71] The sacred orator must strive above all to encourage the love of God, since this is the source of all good emotions.[72] Suggestions are provided for arousing specific emotions and for achieving an emotional effect on different types of audience. Examples, enthymemes, and proverbs may be particularly helpful. All the resources of style may be employed to promote the glory of God and the saving of souls.[73] Valier shows that scripture and the fathers used the whole range of tropes and figures. An understanding of them may also be helpful to the preacher in interpreting scripture.

LUIS DE GRANADA (1504–1588)

Luis de Granada, provincial of the Portuguese Dominicans and confessor to the queen, published his *Ecclesiasticae rhetoricae sive De ratione concionandi libri sex* in Lisbon in 1576. It was printed ten times up to 1611, and translated into French. In his preface Luis declares that the most important aspects of rhetoric are invention, style, and delivery. Existing rhetorics teach the whole art in a way that is suited to civil oratory. His manual, which is aimed not at schoolboys but at adult preachers, will adapt the precepts to preaching and present examples from scripture and the church fathers. Divinely inspired language is even more impressive

68 Ibid., sig. a3^{v}.
69 Ibid., sigs. c6^{r}–e4^{r}.
70 Ibid., sig. e5^{r}.
71 Ibid., sigs. e5^{v}–6^{r}.
72 Ibid., sig. e7^{r}.
73 Ibid., sig. k4^{r}.

Table 12.1. Plan of Luis de Granada, *Ecclesiasticae rhetoricae... libri six*

Bk	Contents	Pages
I	Christian rhetoric and the importance of emotion	1 (A1^{r})
II	Defining rhetoric; invention; topics; argument; emotion	33 (C1^{r})
III	Techniques for amplification; how to arouse emotion	94 (F7^{v})
IV	Disposition: six parts of the sermon; five types of sermon	150(K3^{v})
V	Style: tropes and figures	189(M7^{r})
VI	Techniques and practice in delivery; advice to the preacher	294(T3^{v})–362(Z5^{v})

than secular oratory.[74] The structure of Luis's work combines justification of Christian rhetoric (based on St Augustine), practical reflections on preaching (like those in Borja), and summaries of the whole syllabus of Ciceronian rhetoric.

According to Luis, the most important element in preaching is that the preacher should display charity and the ardent love of divine glory. As well as showing integrity of life and purity of intention, the preacher needs enthusiasm and hard work in order to succeed.[75] Like Valier, Luis quotes St Augustine on the three aims of the orator (to teach, to please, and to move) and the importance of emotion for achieving victory. Luis cites Agricola on the connections between rhetoric and dialectic and on the topics of invention.[76] His discussion of the forms of argumentation draws in figures of speech like *subjectio*, which he treats as a more elegant way of presenting arguments by enumeration.[77] In this section he also emphasizes *accommodatio*, the process of drawing from a generally established moral truth, instruction about specific virtuous or vicious actions, explaining this type of teaching with examples and comments.[78] Advice on the use of *sententiae* and narratives also forms part of his treatment of invention.

Luis treats amplification as one of the major aspects of rhetoric, embracing both the use of the topics of invention and Quintilian's instructions for amplification. Towards the end of the work he comments on the

[74] Luis de Granada, *Ecclesiasticae rhetoricae sive De ratione concionandi libri sex* (Lisbon, 1576), sigs ¶6^{v}–7^{v}. M. Fumaroli, *L'Age de l'éloquence* (Geneva, 1980), 144–8. C. Mouchel, *Cicéron et Sénèque dans la rhétorique de la Renaissance* (Marburg, 1990), 111–22. McGinness, *Right Thinking*, 50, 54–5, 58–61. M. López Nuñez, *Fray Luis de Granada y la rétorica* (Almería, 2000).

[75] Luis de Granada, *Ecclesiasticae rhetoricae*, sigs. B4^{r}–8^{r}.

[76] Ibid., sigs. C2^{r}, C2^{v}, C6$^{r–v}$.

[77] Ibid., sig. D8$^{r–v}$.

[78] Ibid., sig. E5^{v}–8^{r}.

importance of *copia* for the preacher.[79] Vivid description and personification have particularly strong effects on an audience and Luis gives detailed instructions and several examples from Christian orators. For his theoretical treatment of emotion Luis quotes Quintilian and refers to Aristotle. He shows that the Christian orator will use several emotions beyond those employed in secular oratory, including love of God, hatred of sin, hope of divine compassion, fear of retribution, spiritual joy, admiration of God, contempt of the world. In discussing these emotions he refers mainly to other Christian writers. As an example of what could be done he gives a series of arguments which should help arouse love of God.[80] The section concludes with detailed discussion and exemplification of particular figures (such as *exclamatio*, *apostrophe*, *interrogatio,* and *admiratio*) suited to arousing emotions. Perhaps Luis is more effective in asserting the importance of emotional manipulation than in providing a thoroughly Christianized account of the subject.

Luis promotes a thoroughly classical structure for the sermon, in six parts: *exordium*, narration, proposition (with division), confirmation, confutation, and conclusion.[81] Luis established five types of sermon: persuasive, demonstrative, narrating the gospel, mixed, and didascalic.[82] The structure of the third type will be simpler, consisting mainly of a reading of the text, a brief exposition of it, and an explanation, in which the teaching of the text will be related to the needs of the audience, under three or four headings. Alternatively a sermon of this kind may begin with a moral *sententia* or a commonplace.[83] In the manner of Melanchthon the didascalic sermon will treat a single subject (such as grace), looking into what it is, what qualities and emotions it has, what causes, what effects, and what parts.[84]

Luis provides a lengthy and thorough treatment of the tropes and figures, dividing the figures into six classes (figures of speech involving repetition, similarity, contrariety, and the remainder; figures of thought connected to teaching or to greater vehemence), quoting classical definitions and providing numerous classical and Christian examples. The final book begins with a thorough treatment of delivery, including many Christian examples to assist in practising delivery.[85] It concludes with

[79] Ibid., sigs. C4^{r}, F7^{v}–G6^{v}, Y4^{r}–5^{v}.
[80] Ibid., sigs. I4^{v}–7^{r}.
[81] Ibid., sig. K4^{r}.
[82] Ibid., sigs. L3^{r}–M6^{v}.
[83] Ibid., sigs. M1^{v}–4^{r}.
[84] Ibid., sigs. M5^{v}–6^{v}.
[85] Ibid., sigs. T3^{v}–X7^{r}.

Table 12.2. Plan of Valadés, *Rhetorica Christiana*

Bk	Contents	Pages
I	Rhetoric, Christian rhetoric, reading, preaching	1
II	Divisions of rhetoric, religious truth, five tasks, memory	48
III	How to read and interpret the Bible, delivery, emotion	125
IV	Three types of speech, Indian customs	163
V	Six parts of the oration, emotion and two model orations	228
VI	Style, figures and tropes, status-theory, topics of invention	249–378

discussions of the preacher's life, virtues, reading, practice, and preparation for preaching.

Diego Valadés was born in Mexico to an Indian mother in 1533, and was a Franciscan missionary in New Spain for about twenty years. He wrote and published his *Rhetorica Christiana* (1579, printed four times up to 1587) in Italy, where he was procurator-general of the Franciscans, a role which would have involved preaching in Latin before the pope. He died in Italy, probably in 1582.[86] Many of the examples and illustrations in his book refer to indigenous customs and to the conversion of Amerindians to Christianity. His six books combine coverage of the essential topics of classical rhetoric, advice to the preacher, principles of biblical interpretation, and examples which describe Amerindian customs.

All the main elements of a course in classical rhetoric are included, though the placing of some of them (e.g. delivery, emotion, status-theory, topics) is unusual. Valadés repeats the classical doctrine on the three types of case (placing his descriptions of Indian customs within demonstrative oratory) and the parts of the sermon (*exordium*, narration, digression, partition, confirmation and confutation, conclusion). His first treatment of emotion cites Quintilian and owes something to Luis de Granada's account of the emotions which the Christian orator needs to arouse, while the second refers to Aristotle's *Rhetoric*.[87] He writes a short speech for a father urging his son to marry and a longer reply from the son, extolling the benefits of celibacy.[88] He briefly defines the major figures and tropes, showing, with examples, that scripture and the fathers made use of them.

[86] D. P. Abbott, *Rhetoric in the New World* (Columbia, SC, 1996), 41–59. E. J. Palomera, *Fray Diego Valadés OFM* (Mexico City, 1962). C. Finzi and A. Morganti (eds.), *Un francescano tra gli Indios* (Rimini, 1995). See the collection *Acerca de Fray Diego Valadés y su Retórica cristiana* (Mexico City, 1996).

[87] D. Valadés, *Rhetorica Christiana* (Perugia, 1579), sigs. X2^{r-v}, HH1^{v}–2^{v}. There is a facsimile edn. with notes by E. J. Palomera (Mexico City, 1989).

[88] Ibid., sigs. HH2^{v}–II2^{v}.

St Carlo Borromeo (1538–84) in *Pastorum concionatorumque instructiones* (1581), printed eleven times before 1620, describes the preacher's training and preparation without summarizing rhetorical teaching more generally. The preacher must act virtuously and have a good theological education. Greek and Hebrew will be helpful in interpreting the Bible, as will knowledge of everyday life and agriculture in suggesting metaphors.[89] Borromeo emphasizes the importance and difficulty of preaching, the need for the preacher to carry out his bishop's instructions, and the importance of emotion in preaching. This is more likely to be achieved where the preacher writes his own sermon and prays for divine assistance as he mounts the stage.[90] Preaching should concentrate on moral teaching and on upholding the truths of the Catholic Church, avoiding difficult and contentious doctrines. The style and delivery should be restrained and moderate.[91] Borromeo evidently envisages a less elaborate, less emotional form of preaching than Luis de Granada.

PERKINS AND KECKERMANN

The *Prophetica* (1592) by the moderate Cambridge Puritan William Perkins (1558–1602) was printed five times in Latin, once in English, and twice in Dutch prior to 1620. His treatise is organized through definition and division, like a Ramist manual. He supports or illustrates each doctrine with a mass of quotation from scripture. *Prophetica* is the holy teaching of correctly practising prophecy. Prophecy is either preaching the word or prayer.[92] Preaching the word is 'prophecy in Christ's name and on his behalf which brings men to a state of grace and keeps them there'.[93] Since preaching depends on understanding the word of God, Perkins describes the different kinds of material found in the Bible and explains methods of interpreting each of them. Understanding the grammar, rhetoric, and logic of the text is fundamental.[94] The first section of Perkins's book offers a thorough and carefully exemplified discussion of Protestant principles of biblical interpretation.

[89] C. Borromeo, *Pastorum concionatorumque instructiones* (Cologne, 1587), sigs. E3^{v}, 5^{v}, 6^{v}. McGinness, *Right Thinking*, 43–4.

[90] Borromeo, *Pastorum concionatorumque instructiones*, sigs. E8^{v}–F2^{v}, F6^{v}–7^{v}, I3^{r}.

[91] Ibid., sigs. g5^{v}–H2^{v}, I1^{v}, I6^{v}–7v.

[92] W. Perkins, *Prophetica* (Cambridge, 1592), sig. A1^{r-v}.

[93] 'Praedicatio verbi est Prophetia Christi nomine et vice habita, qua vocantur homines ad statum gratiae et in eodem conservatur.' Ibid., sig. A2^{v}.

[94] Ibid., sigs. B1^{r-v}, C8^{v}–D3^{v}.

Preaching depends on resolution and application. Resolution finds the teaching in the text either by noting the words of the text or by discovering their implication through nine topics, which seem to be taken from Ramus: causes, effects, subjects, adjuncts, disagreements (including contraries), comparisons, etymology, division, and definition.[95] Application has seven modes, depending on the approach to be taken to seven types of audience (e.g. resisting non-believers, ignorant but willing to listen, believers, lapsed, mixed). On the basis of 2 Timothy 3, application is divided into two main kinds (intellectual and practical) and four subtypes: instruction as to belief, correction of theological error, moral education (including consolation and exhortation), and admonition.[96] Perkins includes no chapter on disposition (though he implies that in a sermon analysis of the Bible text precedes the section in which it is applied) or style, but he includes memory and delivery, under which he urges that one invoke the Holy Spirit and avoid human art. The preacher should use plain and clear language; his life should exhibit grace and holiness.[97] With its rich quotation of scripture and its logical approach to the subject, *Prophetica* collects familiar materials in a new way. It serves more as a methodical survey than a training in preaching.

While early seventeenth-century Catholic writers tended to unite the *summa* of rhetoric and the preaching manual in one text of sacred rhetoric, the Protestant Bartholomaeus Keckermann (1571–1609) continued to publish a separate preaching manual to be studied after his comprehensive textbooks on rhetoric and dialectic. Keckermann's *Rhetoricae ecclesiasticae sive artis formandi et habendi conciones sacras, libri duo* (1600) was printed six times up to 1616, mainly in Hanau. Keckermann builds a careful account of the writing of evangelical sermons around a simple Ramistic structure (two books: figures in the first, delivery in the second), adding accounts of invention, emotional manipulation, and advice on practical application of the rules. He divides sermons into free (mainly given by Catholics) and textual. Textual sermons comprise (after a reading of the Bible text) an introduction, an explication of the text, amplification and application of the text, and a conclusion.[98] Thinking about the Bible text will involve considering the commonplaces to which it can be applied and the emotions which the preacher must evoke. The Christian orator must know how to evoke emotions like shame, penitence, hatred of sin, love of

95 Ibid., sigs. E1^{v}–2^{r}.
96 Ibid., sigs. E6^{v}–F6^{r}.
97 Ibid., sigs. G1^{v}–3^{v}.
98 B. Keckermann, *Rhetoricae ecclesiasticae . . . libri duo* (Hanau, 1606), sigs. B8^{v}–C1^{v}, G5^{r}–6^{v}.

God, one's neighbours and virtue, fear of God, consolation, happiness, patience, and hope. In his advice on arousing emotions, Keckermann refers to Aristotle, Agricola, and Calvin.[99] Keckermann provides rules for dividing and interpreting scripture, guides to amplification (using the topics), and advice on ways to apply the teaching of a scripture text to the needs of a particular audience.[100] Aids to the practice of preaching include wide reading in scripture and good commentaries (especially by the fathers, the doctors, Calvin and Luther), imitation (on the model of St Augustine's *De doctrina christiana* 4), and practice on simple examples with the help of a friend.[101] Keckermann concentrates on the sermon on a scriptural text, leaving the classical oration to his rhetoric textbook. He adds a Protestant version of the Counter-Reformation manuals (like Borja and Borromeo) which focus on the preacher's experience.

CARLO REGGIO (1540–1612)

The *Orator Christianus* (1612) by the Jesuit professor of rhetoric at Rome, Carlo Reggio, was printed three times before 1620. This very long book is organized into three main sections: the preacher (books 1–4); the sermon (5–8); practical wisdom and labour of the preacher (9–10).

Reggio absorbs the lessons of Borja and Borromeo. The essential part of preaching is the gift of the Holy Spirit but the Christian orator can prepare himself for this gift both by the morality of his life and by studying languages and theology.[102] Reggio puts great emphasis on hearing good preachers, thinking about the occasion and audience of one's preaching, on imitation (for which the principal model should be St Paul, followed by Chrysostom, St Gregory, and St Bernard) and on practising, with the aid of an adviser.[103]

Reggio proposes an original classification of sermons. There are three main types, related to three kinds of audience: the purgative sermon which aims to convert non-believers; the illuminative sermon, which leads believers towards Christ and Christian behaviour; and the unitive sermon, which helps the virtuous towards greater perfection by discussing theological or mystical issues. These three types, which mark out a progression of religious improvement in the audience, are then mapped on to ten more

[99] Ibid., sigs. C6^{r}–D8^{r}.
[100] Ibid., sigs. E1^{r}–G2^{v}.
[101] Ibid., sigs. I6^{r}–K4^{v}.
[102] C. Regius, *Orator Christianus* (Mainz, 1613), sigs. b1^{r}–2^{r}, B4^{r}, N4^{r}, O1^{v}. Fumaroli, *L'Age de l'éloquence*, 186–90.
[103] Regius, *Orator Christianus*, sigs. O4^{v}–P1^{v}, P4^{r}–Q3^{r}.

Table 12.3 Plan of Reggio, *Orator Christianus*

Bk	Title and contents	Page
I	The duty of the Christian orator: dignity, difficulty, vocation	1
II	The virtues of the Christian orator: love of God, faith, zeal	48
III	Knowledge required and exercises: theology, imitation	86
IV	Justification of Christian eloquence, types of sermon	126
V	Topical invention of material and arguments, types of sermon	171
VI	Topics from Christ and Christianity, argumentation, amplification, similitudes	211
VII	On arousing emotions: Aristotle, then Christian emotions	285
VIII	Disposition, style, memory, and delivery	332
IX	Practical advice for the preacher, on preparation, audiences, types of sermon	380
X	Labours of the preacher: alms collecting, encouraging spiritual life of parishioners, preparing sermons	465
	Synopsis of training of the preacher	522
	List of things which need to be corrected in a preacher	529–36

familiar types of sermon. The sermon of exhortation belongs to all three classes; refutations of error and reprehensions of bad behaviour belong to the purgative kind; dogmatic, moral, advisory, consolatory, and laudatory sermons belong to the illuminative kind, and descriptions and praise of heavenly things form the unitive genre.[104] The sermon should generally be modelled on the classical six-part oration but other types of sermon, for example, the didascalic and the evangelical, may be organized in different ways. Disposition ultimately depends on the judgement of the preacher and must make his teaching as clear as possible to the audience.[105]

Reggio's book absorbs the major teachings of classical rhetoric within the framework of a sermon manual but often in such a summary form that an earlier study of, for example, the topics of invention and the tropes and figures seems to be assumed. In these areas Reggio's main addition to short definitions is the Christian examples which show that these techniques are useful for the preacher. Like St Augustine, whose *De doctrina Christiana* he frequently cites, Reggio recognizes the importance of emotion to the preacher, offering an account which first summarizes Aristotle's account from *Rhetoric* 2 and then adds discussions of Christian emotions such as love of God, love of one's neighbour, sins, hope, fear, and desperation.[106] Like earlier renaissance rhetoricians Reggio gives special attention to

[104] Ibid., sigs. V4^{v}–X2^{v}.
[105] Ibid., sigs. Tt2^{v}, Vv2^{r}–Xx4^{r}.
[106] Ibid., sigs. Oo1^{v}–Rr4^{r}.

amplification, descriptions, and similitudes.[107] Not long afterwards Reggio's successor Caussin would adapt Luis's combination of Cicero and Augustine into a full-blown *summa* of rhetoric in which preaching is presented as the highest contemporary expression of the classical tradition of rhetoric.

The preaching manual is an obvious area of overlap and conflict between classical and Christian rhetoric. For the most part humanists agree to incorporate the main tenets of classical rhetoric into preaching manuals with some additions and changes. Usually they add sections (sometimes very extensive) on biblical interpretation and the importance of preaching. Most theorists propose a version of the four- (or six-)part classical oration which has been adapted for preaching by the inclusion of additional sections. Some identify different types of sermon which may employ structures which differ more from the classical oration. Most recognize that the preacher's purity of life will contribute to his ability to persuade his audience. Some manuals emphasize the priest's preparation for and experience of preaching, which leads them to give more attention to delivery than is usual in renaissance rhetoric manuals.

Where earlier humanists and Protestants tend to favour a restrained style in preaching, some Counter-Reformation manuals prefer the magnificence of the Christian grand style. Preaching manuals often put more emphasis on emotional persuasion than other rhetoric manuals, perhaps because the preacher is envisaged as inspiring devotion to God in ordinary people, where other renaissance orators mostly address the élite. They often emphasize different emotions from those discussed in the rhetorical tradition, since their most important task is to inflame the love of God in their audience. This adaptation was generally based on ideas about emotion discussed by St Augustine, St Thomas Aquinas, or Calvin. Some manuals draw on humanist ideas about amplification and *copia*. Most preaching manuals assume that pastors will already have learnt classical rhetoric at school or university, but in their different ways both Melanchthon and Caussin wrote manuals of the whole of rhetoric which could be read (in the former case) or were intended (in the latter) as preparations for Christian preaching. So preaching had some effect on mainstream manuals of rhetoric, but most churches were committed to the idea that preaching was a specialized task for an ordained priest rather than an oration in which any educated Christian might express their faith. Even more than in other aspects of rhetoric, the choice of manual to print or teach depended on the confessional allegiance of writer and teacher.

[107] Ibid., sigs. Kk3^{v}, Mm3^{v}, Nn1^{r}–2^{v}, Zz3^{v}–Aaa2^{r}.

Because they were aimed at people with a higher level of education preaching manuals were produced in much smaller numbers than letter-writing manuals or textbooks of general rhetoric.

LEGAL DIALECTIC

While there is a long history of connections between classical rhetoric and the practice of law, the production of manuals of legal dialectic is a sixteenth-century phenomenon, linked to humanist reforms of education and jurisprudence.[108] Judicial oratory was one of the three genres of rhetoric. Much of the theory of status expounded in *De inventione* and *Rhetorica ad Herennium* depended on Roman legal practice, as did much of ancient declamation. Cicero's *Topica* was a dialectic manual which took all its examples from law cases, real or imagined. Everyone who studied civil law had first received some sort of training in logic and rhetoric. Medieval Italian jurists like Dino da Mugello and Baldo degli Ubaldi had given some theoretical consideration to the logical forms used in law.[109] Legal dialectic, which was a product of humanism, took two typical forms: the manual on how to argue in legal practice, subdivided into those which focused on the topics, and those which covered the whole of dialectic; and textbooks reorganizing the law on the basis of dialectical principles. None of these books went through many editions, perhaps because of the relatively small target audience.

Legalis dialectica (1507) by Pietro Andrea Gammaro (1480–1528) was printed six times up to 1545. It is framed as a dialogue, one of whose participants, Ferabric, may represent an English logic professor. Socinius, the main speaker, explains that dialectic, and especially topical invention, is a great help in constructing arguments and brings embellishment and *copia* to the law.[110] Book 1 defines argument, case, and question, briefly outlines the four main types of argumentation, and sets out the internal topics. Book 2 is devoted to intermediate and external topics and hypothetical syllogism. Book 3 is concerned with predicables, categories, and sophisms. The focus is firmly on the topics, treated with reference to

[108] V. Piano Mortari, 'Dialettica e giurisprudenza', *Annali di storia del diritto,* 1 (1957), 293–401. H. J. Berman, *Law and Revolution*, ii (Cambridge, Mass., 2006), 87–94, 110–26.

[109] Piano Mortari, 'Dialettica e giurisprudenza', p. 295.

[110] P. Gammaro, *Dialectica legalis*, with C. Cantiuncula, *Topica legalia* (Basel, 1545) sig. o6^{v}.

Boethius, Cicero, Aristotle, and many legal authorities. The topic of similars is used to set out a range of types of legal argument.[111]

Nicolaas Everaerts (1462–1532) was a law teacher, Habsburg councillor and correspondent of Erasmus. His *Topicorum seu locorum legalium centuria* (1516), which was printed at least five times in the sixteenth century, lists 100 legal topics, combining logical arguments based on Cicero's *Topica*, such as from etymology, from effects, and from contraries, with more strictly legal forms of argument, such as from the conjunction of two laws, from the ambassador to the commission, and from contract to intentions. Under each heading Everaerts collects references to statutes and cases, which are separately indexed at the start of the volume.

Another correspondent of Erasmus, the Basel professor of law Claude Cantiuncula (*c.*1490–1549) establishes a distinctively humanist approach in his *Topica* (1520), printed at least three times.[112] For him the topics offer a helpful way of collecting the numerous available opinions and commentaries in a way which will contribute to the advocate's aim. Knowledge of the topics assists in speaking gracefully and forcefully, in explaining difficult points of legal theory and cases, and in understanding the best authors.[113] He reprints the whole first chapter of Agricola's *De inventione dialectica* under the title 'Concerning the origin and usefulness of the topics' and makes frequent reference to Agricola's views on individual topics.[114] He cites classical rhetorical manuals and literary texts, legal authorities and humanists, including Melanchthon's recently published rhetoric. Cantiuncula's list of topics represents a compromise between Cicero and Agricola, with the addition of thirty-seven topics covering juridical arguments.[115]

The Leipzig humanist Christoph Hegendorff (1500–40) in *Dialecticae legalis libri quinque* (1531), printed twelve times, which refers to Cantiuncula's *Topica*, aims to give lawyers a full account of dialectic and show how it can be useful to them.[116] Book 1 covers the divisions of dialectic, the difference between dialectic and rhetoric, the predicables and the categories; book 2 the subject-matter of Aristotle's *De interpretatione*; book 3 the forms of argumentation (mainly a full treatment of the syllogism, but also induction, example, sorites, and dilemma); book 4

111 Gammaro, *Dialectica legalis*, sigs. s3^{r}–5^{r}.
112 Basel 1520, Venice 1534, Basel 1545.
113 C. Cantiuncula, *Topica* (Basel, 1520), sigs. A2^{v}–3^{r}. G. Kisch, *Claudius Cantiuncula: Ein Basler Jurist und Humanist* (Basel, 1970).
114 Cantiuncula, *Topica*, sigs. A4^{r-v}, B1^{r}, C1^{r}, C5^{v}–6^{r}, D1^{r}, E1^{v}, F2^{v}, G5^{v}.
115 Ibid., sigs. B2^{v}–3^{r}, B4^{v}, B6^{v}, C1^{r}–2^{v}.
116 C. Hegendorff, *Dialecticae legalis libri quinque* (Lyon, 1534), sig. A3^{r-v}.

the topics; and book 5 the sophisms. The topics and definitions are taken mainly from Cicero and Boethius, but the treatment of invention on a simple theme resembles Melanchthon and the additional legal topics under similarities resemble Gammaro and Everaerts.[117] The work presents the whole syllabus of Aristotelian dialectic (in the manner of Melanchthon's middle period dialectics) with legal examples.

Johann Apel (1486–1536) in *Methodica dialectices ratio ad iurisprudentiam adcomodata* (1535) includes a letter of encouragement from Cantiuncula. His book is organized in seven sections which reflect Melanchthon's topics for discussing simple themes (definition, division, cause, duty (or effect), similars (literally neighbours, *adfines*), contraries, and circumstances).[118] Under definition, his largest section, Apel includes the predicables, the categories, and Melanchthon's five types of definition, as well as definitions of many legal concepts with references to legal authorities.[119] Many legal issues are considered within division, causes, and effects. Obligations are altered by circumstances.[120] The legal historian H. Berman regards Apel's book, for which Green and Murphy list only one edition, as an attempt to organize and systematize the entire body of the law on a new basis, which encouraged similar work by Lagus and Vigelius.[121]

Joannes a Reberteria (fl. 1575–90) wrote his *Topicωn* [sic] *iuris libri quatuor* (1575), which was printed four times up to 1590, first in Paris and later in Wittenberg, to introduce order into the labyrinth of the civil law.[122] For the first two books he follows the outline of Cicero's *Topica*, though in each chapter the Ciceronian material rapidly gives way to listing and classifying legal authorities. The topic of authority, which he subdivides according to different types of legal authority, takes up most of the second book. The third and fourth books are devoted to presumptions, privileges, instruments, and other legal categories. The dialectical content of this work is rather slight. Reberteria uses the framework of the topics to attempt a new classification of the sources of legal arguments. There are a few references to literary and humanistic texts, including Horace, Agricola, and Valla.[123]

[117] Ibid., sigs. F6^{r-v}, G5^{r}–H2^{r}.

[118] J. Apel, *Methodica dialectices ratio ad iurisprudentiam adcomodata* (Nuremberg, 1535), sigs. A1^{v}, 3^{v}.

[119] Ibid., sigs. B2^{r}–H4^{r}.

[120] Ibid., sigs. L2^{r}–N2^{r}, O2^{v}.

[121] Berman, *Law and Revolution,* ii. 110–26.

[122] Reberteria, *Topicωn iuris libri quatuor* (Paris, 1580), sig. a1^{r-v}.

[123] e.g. Reberteria, *Topicωn iuris libri quatuor,* sigs. a4^{v}, a5^{r}, a5^{v}.

The Ramist Thomas Freigius (1543–83) produced both a dialectically organized tabulation of the whole subject of law, *Partitiones iuris utriusque* (Basel, 1571) and a Ramist logic manual with legal examples, *De logica iureconsultorum libri duo* (Basel, 1582), which was printed three times. This work ends with logical analyses of some sections from the *Digest* and some cases which illustrate legal dialectic in practice.[124]

Humanist legal educators expect that their pupils will have studied classical rhetoric. They recognize the overlap between rhetorical and legal studies in the field of invention, especially in status-theory and in Cicero's *Topica*. Some try to organize the teaching of legal argument along the lines set out in the topics, while others aim to incorporate arguments derived from later legal thinking alongside topics and status-theory. Overall this does not seem to have been a very influential part of legal training, with a total of only about forty editions recorded by Green and Murphy.

124 J. T. Freigius, *De logica iureconsultorum libri duo* (Basel, 1582), sigs. k7^r–m7^r.

13

Vernacular Rhetorics

In the renaissance large numbers of rhetoric manuals in vernacular languages were written and circulated in print. Green and Murphy record a combined total of 436 editions of 100 vernacular rhetorics between 1472 and 1620. In addition there were forty-five editions of seventeen vernacular translations of classical rhetoric texts. The vast majority of these translations were into Italian (thirty-nine editions). The most frequently translated works were: *Rhetorica ad Herennium* (nine editions), Aristotle's *Rhetoric* (eight editions), and Quintilian (seven editions). The absorption of classical culture into writing in the European vernacular languages was one of the most significant and enduring changes brought about in the renaissance. Most sixteenth- and seventeenth-century readers and writers learnt rhetoric through their Latin-based educational system, applying its lessons to their own writing and speech-making which largely and increasingly was conducted in the vernacular languages. Moreover, speakers of vernacular languages regarded the existence of rhetoric in that language as a sign of its maturity, less important than possessing a vernacular literature but thought of as a contribution to producing that literature. Vernacular rhetorics could also be promoted for political reasons. For the most part vernacular rhetoric textbooks were entirely based on classical or renaissance Latin works. In general, vernacular manuals of rhetoric played no part in formal education, since grammar-school and university education was exclusively aimed at literary competence in Latin. Few of the vernacular manuals were printed more than a handful of times and those few were generally letter-writing manuals.

In this chapter I shall try to give a sense both of national characteristics and of pan-European trends, and to comment on, or at least mention, the most important texts. I shall begin by surveying the production of rhetoric manuals in the major European languages; then I shall illustrate the dependence of vernacular rhetoric texts on Latin sources, using French examples. Later I shall consider letter-writing manuals, preaching manuals, style manuals, and textbooks of the whole of rhetoric. I shall also notice vernacular contributions to the debate about imitation and Ciceronianism, and two discussions of rhetoric by renaissance philosophers. Comments on rhetoric also play a significant part in renaissance manuals of courtly behaviour, education, and conversation.

THE PRODUCTION OF RHETORIC TEXTS IN VERNACULAR LANGUAGES

Italy produced thirty rhetorical texts printed in 129 editions before 1620, starting in 1472 with *Fiore di retorica* by Guidotto da Bologna (fl. *c.*1266), based on *Rhetorica ad Herennium*. The most successful of these works were the letter-writing manual *Formulario* by Landino (forty-nine editions from 1485 to 1567; some of them attributed to Miniatore) and Sperone Speroni's *Dialogo della rhetorica*, one of his *I dialogi* (1542) with eleven editions.[1]

Germany published 164 editions of twenty titles between 1476 and 1620. The great majority of these (125 editions of eleven titles) were in the German-language speciality of notarial formularies and letter-books, among them *Formulare und tutsch rhetorica* (1476) by Heinrich Gessler (d. 1518), which had twenty-three editions and Ludwig Fruck's *Rhetoric und teutsch formular* (1530) with thirty-two editions. The remaining nine German titles, whose total output of thirty-nine editions is more similar to trends in other vernacular languages, included thirteen editions of two letter-writing manuals and eleven editions of the preaching manual *Postilla* (1567) by Simon Pauli (1534–91).[2]

There were sixteen titles in French, with a total of fifty-five editions, beginning with *L'art et science de rhétorique pour faire rigmes et ballades* (1493), by Jean Molinet (1435–1507), which was printed seven times. The most printed works were *Le grant et vray art de pleine rhetorique* by Pierre Fabri (fl. 1483–1515), with ten editions (1521–44), *Lettres missives et familières* by Estienne Du Tronchet (?1510–?1585), with ten editions (1567–1608), and *De l'eloquence francaise* by Guillaume Du Vair (1556–1621), which was printed five times on its own (1590–1610), and a further thirteen times in Du Vair's *Oeuvres* (1610–20).

Among the countries which developed their printing industry later, ten editions of seven titles appeared in Spanish, including three editions of *Aviso de curas...para todos los religiosos y predicadores* (1530) by Diaz de

[1] G. Tagliente, *Lo presente libro insegna la vera arte de lo excellente scrivere* (1524), listed with 12 edns. by Green and Murphy, *Renaissance Rhetoric Short Title Catalogue* (Aldershot, 2006), is a handwriting manual.

[2] I regret that I only came across J. Knape, *Poetik und Rhetorik in Deutschland 1300–1700* (Wiesbaden, 2006) too late to use it.

Luco (d. 1556), two editions of Jerónimo Paulo de Manzanares's *Estilo y formulario de cartes familiares* (1600), and one each of *Rhetorica en lengua castellana* (1540) by Miguel de Salinas (d. 1577), Espinosa de Sanctayana's *Arte de retorica* (1578), Juan de Guzmán's *Primera parte de la rétorica* (1589), Bartolomé Jiménez Patón's *Eloquencia española in arte* (1604), and Francisco Terrones's *Arte e instrucción . . . que ha de tener el predicador evangélico* (1617).[3]

There were seventy-two editions of twenty-two titles in English between 1550 and 1620, including seven editions of the dialectic *Rule of Reason* (1551) by Thomas Wilson (1525–81), eight of his *Art of Rhetoric* (1553), nine of William Fulwood's letter collection *Enemie of Idlenesse* (1568), and six of Angel Day's letter-writing manual *The English secretorie* (1586).[4] Three rhetorics in Dutch are recorded with four editions in total: M. de Castelein's *De const van rhetoriken* (1555, 1616),[5] Loys Van der Gruythuyse's *Rhetorijcke ende gehebeden bouck* (sixteenth century), and Willem Teellinck's *De maniere om predekatien te stellen* (1620). Judah Messer Leon's Hebrew *Nofet Tsufim* (1474), which is based on *Rhetorica ad Herennium*,[6] and Henry Perry's Welsh *Egluryn phraethineb* ('elucidator of rhetoric') (1595), were printed once each.

THE DEPENDENCE OF VERNACULAR RHETORICS ON THE LATIN TRADITION

Impressive though these lists of titles and editions are, the vernacular rhetorics are generally either dependent adaptations of Latin works or of slight value for the teaching of rhetoric,[7] with the notable exceptions of Bartolomeo Cavalcanti's *La retorica* (1558), ten editions, Daniele Barbaro's *Dialogo della eloquenza* (1557), one edition, both discussed in Chapter 8 above, and Francesco Panigarola's *Modo di comporre una predica*

[3] All the above figures are extracted from Green and Murphy, *Renaissance Rhetoric STC*. Because of the bibliographical resources available to them in compiling this invaluable work, it is quite likely that there were more titles and edns of Italian- and Spanish-language rhetorics than they record. A. Martí, *La preceptiva retórica española en el Siglo de Oro* (Madrid, 1972), 89–95, 205–19, 263–70. J. Rico Verdú, *Le retórica española de los siglos XVI y XVII* (Madrid, 1973), 113–17, 120–3, 137–40, 147–52, 195–200.

[4] W. S. Howell, *Logic and Rhetoric in England 1500–1700* (Princeton, 1956). P. Mack, *Elizabethan Rhetoric* (Cambridge, 2002), 76–102.

[5] Dirk Coigneau, '*De const van Rhetoriken*', in J. Koopmans (ed.), *Rhetoric-Rhétoriqueurs-Rederijkers* (Amsterdam, 1995), 123–40.

[6] Judah Messer Leon, *The Book of the Honeycomb's Flow*, tr. Isaac Rabinowitz (Ithaca, NY, 1983), pp. lvi–lvii.

[7] Mack, *Elizabethan Rhetoric*, 76–80.

(1584), six editions, discussed in the section on vernacular preaching manuals below. For example, as Alex Gordon observes, Pierre de Courcelles's *Premier livre de la rhétorique* (1557) gives a very straightforward account of the content of the six parts of the oration, adding to the classical examples some modern ones from the works of Marot, Des Masures, and Ronsard.[8] The anonymous manuscript *Rhétorique françoise*, dedicated to Henri III, repeats Ramist teaching on invention and style, adding examples from Garnier's tragedies.[9] Du Vair's *De l'éloquence françoise* (1590) criticizes the orators of his time and offers reasons for the weakness of French oratory, while the *Avant-discours de Rhetorique* by Cardinal Du Perron (1556–1618), first published in a now lost edition of 1579, is more a preface than a textbook, arguing for the usefulness and difficulty of rhetoric and for the orator's need of a wide education, and defending the art against those who believe that natural talent is enough.[10] Robert Sealy and Claude La Charité argue that the manuscript *Rhétorique françoise*, Du Perron's *Avant-discours,* and Amyot's *Projet de l'éloquence royale* (first printed in 1805), were read together at a meeting of the Academie du Palais in 1576 and formed part of Henri III's plan for acquiring skill in speaking and improving the rhetorical attainments of his courtiers.[11] Amyot's *Projet* based its general material on Plutarch and its teaching on Quintilian.[12]

Jean Molinet (1435–1507) belonged to the group of French poets known as the *Grands Rhétoriqueurs*. His *L'art et science de rhétorique pour faire rigmes et ballades* (1493), which was printed seven times, belonged to the French tradition of *seconde rhétorique*, manuals setting out the rules for different verse forms.[13] Pierre Fabri's *Le grant et vray art de pleine rhétorique* (1521), printed seven times, combines a general rhetoric, based loosely on the precepts of *Rhetorica ad Herennium*, and a letter-writing manual with (in the second book) a *seconde rhétorique*, which sets out rules for poetic compositions, and a short list of faults of

[8] Alex Gordon, *Ronsard et la rhétorique* (Geneva, 1970), 15–16.

[9] G. Camus (ed.), *Precetti di retorica scritti per Enrico III* (Modena, 1887), cited in Gordon, *Ronsard et la rhétorique*, 17. C. La Charité, 'Les Trois Institutions oratoires de Henri III', *Renaissance et réforme*, 31/4 (2008), 43–66.

[10] G. Du Vair, *De l'éloquence françoise*, ed. R. Radouant (Paris, 1908). Du Perron, *Les Oeuvres diverses* (Paris, 1633; repr. Geneva, 1969), 759–70. Gordon, *Ronsard et la rhétorique*, 18.

[11] R. J. Sealy, *The Palace Academy of Henri III* (Geneva, 1981), 153–66. La Charité, 'Les Trois Institutions', 43–4.

[12] F. Amyot, *Projet de l'éloquence royale*, ed. P.-J. Salazar (Paris, 1992). La Charité, 'Les Trois Institutions', 48–52.

[13] F. Rigolot, '1493. The Rhétoriqueurs', in D. Hollier and H. Bloch (eds.), *A New History of French Literature* (Cambridge, Mass., 1994), 127–33. F. Cornilliat, *Or ne mens: Couleurs de l'éloge et du blâme chez les 'Grands Rhétoriqueurs'* (Paris, 1994).

expression and barbarisms. According to Dirk Coigneau, Fabri borrowed his treatise on poetic forms partly from Molinet but even more from *L'instructif de la seconde rhétorique* attributed to Regnaud Le Queux.[14]

Fabri defines rhetoric as 'the political science concerned with deliberately speaking and writing well according to the teaching of the art to persuade or dissuade in its subject-matter and to organize it into parts and to apply good words to each part, to keep them in the memory and to deliver them well'.[15] After describing the five skills of the orator he discusses in detail the contents of the five parts of the oration, adding some sections suited to each of the three genres (for example, on the *exordium* of the judicial genre). Although Fabri here summarizes a good deal of familiar classical material there are also many unfamiliar elements, such as lists of three kinds of narration and nine ways to make the narrative more believable.[16] The second major section of the first book is given over to a reasonably full but slightly disorganized account of the figures of thought and diction.[17]

The last third of the first book is a complete treatise on letter-writing. Fabri begins by explaining that there are three types of person one can write to: superiors, equals, and inferiors.[18] He defines the letter as 'speaking to absent persons as if they were present and declaring one's will to them'.[19] He fills out this definition with a list of nine main kinds of letter: theological, important matters of war and peace, news, consolation, recommendation, advice, love, domestic familiarity, happiness. Following Haneron or Traversagni he declares that there are three parts to all letters (cause, intention, and consequence).[20] All letters must contain salutations, superscriptions, and subscriptions.[21] The greater part of the section consists of instructions for particular types of letter (e.g. letters of recommendation, request for a favour, reply to a request, letter of thanks), followed by an example of each type, divided up to show that the letter follows the rules he has set out. Some of these letters are specially constructed; others

[14] Coigneau, '*De Const van Rhetoriken*', 131–2.

[15] Pierre Fabri, *Cy ensuit le grant et vray art de pleine rhétorique* (Rouen, 1521; repr. Geneva, 1972), sig. A4^{r}: 'Rethorique donc est science politique qui est appenseement bien dire et parler selon enseignement de lart pour suader ou dissuader en sa matiere, et a disposer par parties, et chascune aorner par beaux termes, et la retenir par ordre en memore et bien la pronuncer.'

[16] Ibid., sigs. D6^{r}–8^{r}.

[17] Ibid., sigs. K2^{r}–M3^{v}.

[18] Ibid., sig. M4^{r}.

[19] Ibid., sig. N1^{r}: 'Toute epistre ou lettre missive nest austre chose que aux absens parler, comme presens et parler a eulx et leur desclarer la volunte.'

[20] Ibid., sigs. N1^{r}–2^{v}.

[21] Ibid., sig. N4^{r-v}. He has much less to say on salutations than most authors of letter-writing manuals.

purport to be letters from Cicero, popes, or kings. This section of Fabri's work closely resembles the letter-writing manuals of Durand and Fulwood described below. Fabri may be their source or he may be summarizing an earlier treatise to which Durand and Fulwood also had access. In any event Fabri provides the francophone public with a complete course in classical rhetoric, letter-writing, and poetry in order to enrich the language and encourage the flowering of literature in French.[22]

VERNACULAR LETTER-WRITING MANUALS

Letter-writing manuals were the most popular genre of vernacular rhetoric, with 115 editions of thirteen titles between 1485 and 1620, or if the German formularies are added, as they probably should be, 240 editions of twenty-four titles (1476–1620), amounting to more than half the total production of rhetoric manuals in the vernacular, far higher than the proportion among Latin rhetorics, though smaller in absolute numbers. On average there were around ten editions of each vernacular letter-writing title, whereas other vernacular titles achieved on average only 2.6 editions. There was clearly a considerable demand for instruction in and models of letter-writing in the mother tongue. This demand probably came mainly from those who did not know Latin, but even those who did may have found vernacular manuals (whose teaching generally depended on Latin originals) useful for the examples. Some of the successful vernacular letter-writing manuals consisted almost entirely of examples. By 1620 letter-writing manuals were available in English, French, German, Italian, and Spanish, a handful of them in large numbers of editions. Although all these manuals were ultimately dependent on the Latin tradition outlined in Chapter 11, some of them copied directly from previous vernacular works in other languages.

Formulario di epistole vulgare missive e responsive (1485) by Cristoforo Landino (1424–1504) contains no discussion of the theory or rules of letter-writing. Instead it offers model paragraphs with headings like '*Exordium* and handsome apology when one has been negligent in writing to a good friend', and '*Exordium* and apology to a great master to whom one has not previously written, seeking to win goodwill'.[23] Some of the model

[22] Ibid., sig. A3^{r-v}.

[23] 'Exordio et excusatione optima et bella quando si fusse stato hegligente a scrivere a uno amico suo maggiore... Exordio et excusatione a un gran maestro che mai piu non sigli havesse scripto captando benivolentia.' C. Landino, *Formulario di epistole vulgare missive e responsive* (Florence, 1497–1500), sigs. a1^{v}, a2^{r}.

paragraphs reply to previous ones; some are intended for short orations, as in 'Visitation made to some grand ambassadors by a delegate in the name of a worthy man' and 'Short oration one might give when sent to Bologna by the Pope as legate or governor'.[24] Occasionally notes indicate that a particular paragraph could be adapted for a different occasion or from a letter to an oration.[25] Landino treats letters and short orations as closely related. Some of the examples cover recognized letter types, such as letters of recommendation, petition, and thanks, using similar arguments to those set out in letter-writing manuals.[26] A few of the paragraphs are said to be arguments.[27] Landino's model paragraphs show some similarities with Barzizza's examples of *exordia*, but there are no parallels of detail to indicate dependence.[28] Landino's work ends with a list of model superscriptions to people of different ranks, in both Latin and Italian,[29] like those found in some letter-writing manuals.

P. Durand's *Le stile et maniere de composer, dicter et escrire toute sorte d'epistres* (1553) was printed three times in the sixteenth century. The work begins by setting out a number of preliminary divisions, before giving examples of about 100 letters written for different purposes. Letters may be written to persons greater, to equals, and to inferiors. Appropriate superscriptions must be provided in each case. Following Traversagni (or perhaps Haneron), Durand suggests that each letter must contain a cause, an intention, and a consequence. He shows that the order of these three sections may be varied. In every letter you should show that what you are asking is, just, possible and will be recompensed. Adapting the teaching of *Rhetorica ad Herennium*, he says that conclusions may be made by amplification, the arousing of pity, or the summary of points made. The length, content, and style of the letter will depend on the competence of the writer and the relationship between writer and recipient.[30] Both in these preliminary instructions and in the first forty-five letters Durand's treatise follows the letter-writing section of Pierre Fabri's *Le grant et vray art* (discussed above) very closely. However Durand gives the model letters

[24] 'Visitatione facta per seconda persona a qualche magnifici ambasciadori in nome di uno huomo degnissimo . . . Risposta facta per gli decti ambasciadori alla decta visitatione . . . Essendo mandato per lo beatissime Padre uno legato o governatore a Bologna siglidiva questo orationcella.' Ibid., sigs. a4^{r-v}, a5^{r}–6^{r}, b6^{v}.

[25] Ibid., e.g. sigs. a4^{r}, a5^{r}.

[26] Ibid., sigs. a8^{r}–b1^{r}, c1^{r}–2^{v}, c4^{v}–7^{r}.

[27] Ibid., sig. b2^{r-v}.

[28] G. Barzizza, *Exempla exordiorum* (Padua, 1483). Mercer, *The Teaching of Barzizza* (London, 1979), 98.

[29] Landino, *Formulario*, sigs. f3^{r}–6^{v}.

[30] P. Durand, *Le stile et maniere de composer, dicter et escrire toute sorte d'epistres* (Paris, 1553), sigs. A3^{r}–B1^{v}.

without the preceding instructions for each type of letter which Fabri had written. Later Durand adds many letters from Italian humanists (especially Poliziano) and related to narrative situations ('A wife writes to her husband', 'The husband replies to his wife'), which were not included in Fabri. Comparison of the model letters reveals some changes in phrasing and some places where Durand's material is longer or clearer than Fabri's, which might suggest a common source rather than direct copying. Untypically Durand does include some instructions for love-letters which are not the same as Fabri's, though the model letters are similar in most, but not all, respects.[31]

Estienne du Tronchet (?1510–85), secretary to Catherine de Medici, queen of France, published his *Lettres missives et familières* (1567) which was printed ten times up to 1608. It consists of 239 model letters, mainly written by du Tronchet himself, organized according to their addressees.[32] Several of the letters are preceded by an argument which explains the relationship between writer and recipient, and the main arguments of the letter. The book ends with a sequence of 'lettres amoureuses', translated from Bembo and other authors. There is no other classification of letter-types and no instruction in letter-writing is offered.

The first book of William Fulwood's *Enemie of Idleness* (1568), which was printed nine times before 1620, combines instructions on writing forty-five types of letter with examples of each type. The remaining three books, amounting to about two-fifths of the work, give model letters of various kinds, some translated from well-known writers, others apparently fictitious. For the most part Fulwood follows Durand very closely, with some omissions and some changes of order. Almost all Fulwood's model letters are translated from Durand. But Fulwood adds a great deal of didactic material, especially in the first book. He gives brief instructions for the topics to be included in each type of letter which appear to be translated from Pierre Fabri's *Le grant et vray art.* For example Fulwood follows Fabri in defining the letter as 'a declaration (by writing) of the minds of such as bee absent, one of them to another, even as though they were present'.[33] Conversely Fulwood includes many letters which are in Durand but not in Fabri. On the basis of my present knowledge I would

31 Ibid., sig. C2^r–4^v. Fabri, *Cy ensuit*, sigs. O3^v–P1^v.

32 Du Tronchet, *Lettres missives et familières* (Lyon, 1591). M. Sullivan, *Etienne Du Tronchet* (Washington, DC, 1931).

33 W. Fulwood, *The Enimie of Idlenesse* (London, 1582), sig. B1^r. Compare Fabri, *Cy ensuit*, sig. N1^r. On Fulwood and Day: K. G. Hornbeak, 'The Complete Letter-Writer in English', *Smith College Studies in Modern Languages*, 15 (1934), 1–150; Jean Robertson, *The Art of Letter Writing* (London, 1942); Lynne Magnusson, *Shakespeare and Social Dialogue* (Cambridge, 1999).

have to conclude that Fulwood had both French books before him, but perhaps he had direct access to a common source of both. Fulwood's manual provides a complete English-language manual of letter-writing, with many examples for imitation.

Angel Day's *The English Secretorie* (1586), which was printed six times before 1620, offers a general introduction to letter-writing, followed by instructions for and examples of around thirty types of letter and, in later editions, a treatise on the tropes and schemes and a guide to the secretary's conduct. Day defines the letter as 'the messenger or familiar speech of the absent, for that therein is discovered whatsoever the mind wisheth in such cases to have delivered'.[34] For Day there are many different types of letter, corresponding to the different purposes a person might wish to convey. All letters must be apt, brief, and comely. They will all have five parts, like an oration, as well as salutations, farewells, subscriptions, and outward directions, for which he provides formulae.[35] Like Erasmus, Day divides the types of letter into four categories: demonstrative, judicial, deliberative, and familiar. Day's list of letters seems to be adapted from Erasmus's list, though there are places where it seems closer to Macropedius or Hegendorff. Day includes the types of letter most often found: praising, blaming, exhorting, persuading, dissuading, reconciling, requesting, commending, consoling, advising, reprehending, amatory, accusing, defending, attacking, narrating, thanking, and delegating. His first type, the descriptive letter, looks like an innovation.

Like Erasmus, Day directs his reader's attention to the social situation underlying the letter. After establishing that praise will be one of the main topics of the letter of exhortation, and considering the nature of praise, Day invites the reader to consider the recipient of the letter.

> To apply now this praise in exhorting or counselling anyone, it behoveth we first conceive what disposition, habiliments or other matter of value are in him whom we have to deal with, furthering or convenient to such a purpose, whereunto we would exhort or persuade him and the likelihood of the same greatly to put forth or commend; or if before time he hath behaved himself any ways well, we shall encourage him in praising of that already done; and in showing that the more excellent the thing is, the more difficult it is to be attained, for *Difficilia quae pulchra*, and yet the difficulty not so great as the praise, glory and recordation thereof, shall thereby afterwards be returned honourable.[36]

[34] A. Day, *The English Secretary (1599)*, facsimile ed. R. Evans (Gainesville, Fla., 1967), sig. B1ʳ.

[35] Ibid., sigs. B1ʳ–2ᵛ, C2ʳ–D2ʳ.

[36] Ibid., sig. G4ᵛ. Compare Erasmus, *De conscribendis epistolis*, 324–6.

The summary is not elegantly composed or easy to follow, but it is worth reading because of the well-thought-out Erasmian material it contains. For each type of letter Day provides at least one example (not translated from Erasmus) with marginal notes which point out the topics of the letter and the figures of rhetoric employed. Occasionally Day adds comments on one of his examples, as here on a son's letter seeking reconciliation with his father.

> The style of this letter is vehement because the passions of him from whence it came were vehement, and is deduced as you see from the nature of *Reconciliatorie*, which as well for the submissive and lowest terms it beareth as also for the urgent petition therein contained I have rather chosen to place among the *Petitorie*. The part of *honest* herein delivered is passed in words meekest and of great obedience, wherein he studieth by all possibility to mitigate towards himself the too much severity of his father. The *Exordium* is carried by *Insinuation*, expressing the vehement affects and surcharged conceits of a mind more than ordinarily grieved.[37]

Day uses the technical vocabulary of rhetoric to analyse the effect his letter has achieved. *The English Secretorie* relies heavily on continental models but it adapts them thoughtfully to provide a complete course in humanist letter-writing for English readers.

VERNACULAR PREACHING MANUALS

Although the numbers remained rather small, preaching manuals formed a higher proportion of the total output in vernacular languages than they had in Latin. By 1620 preaching manuals had appeared in Dutch, English, French, German, Italian, and Spanish. In total fifty-four editions of twenty titles were produced.[38] The most successful books were Simon Pauli's German-language *Postilla* (1567) with thirteen editions, which I have not read, and Francesco Panigarola's Italian *Modo di comporre una predica* (1584) with six. Most of the vernacular preaching manuals first appeared between 1580 and 1620, nine of the titles achieving only

[37] Day, *English Secretary*, sig. N4$^{r–v}$.

[38] The lines of demarcation can be difficult to draw. Among the works listed by Green and Murphy I have excluded Samuel Hieron's *Preachers Plea* (1604) because it is a dialogue arguing in favour of preaching and William Perkins's *A direction for the government of the tongue* (1592) because it discusses the modest and truthful speech required of all Christians rather than the language or method of preaching, but included Leonard Wright's *A patterne for pastors* (1589), a very short tract appended to his tract on repentance *Summons for Sleepers*, because, like the works of Borromeo and Panigarola, it discusses the preacher's life and attitude to preaching, even though it does not describe preaching techniques.

one edition. Pauli's book was a gathering of materials on the Epistles and Gospels for each Sunday and feast day, rather like the works of Stapleton and Trujillo mentioned at the start of Chapter 12 above.[39]

The *Modo di comporre una predica* (1584) by Franciscan preacher and Bishop of Asti, Francesco Panigarola (1548–94) was printed six times in Italy up to 1603, with a further five editions of its French translation. Panigarola assumes that his reader is already studying classical rhetoric. Basing his words on his own experience of preaching, he focuses on the practical aspects of invention and disposition.

> Above all you must know that the person who gives good sermons always gives them to the honour of God and with the main aim of delighting the souls of the audience.[40]

The earlier chapters of his short book are arranged as a step-by-step guide to sermon composition. First one must identify the genus and subtype to which your intended sermon belongs: didascalic, deliberative (e.g. urging a fast), demonstrative (e.g. praising a saint), or judicial (e.g. confuting a heresy). Each type has three subtypes according to whether the sermon is based on a single passage from a gospel, on the whole gospel, or on comparisons between two gospels. Then you must identify the proposition of your sermon, a single word or (more usually) sentence which sums up what you want to prove. Panigarola identifies several examples of propositions for each subtype of sermon from Christian writers.[41]

Having identified the proposition you must read through all the books you have at hand in order to assemble a mass of possible material for your sermon. You should number each extract which you copy out, noting its author and its place in his work. If you have little time or a small library you must especially concentrate on St Thomas Aquinas's *Summa Theologiae*. Panigarola advises his readers to purchase only books with indexes to make this process easier. The *silva* of material assembled should then be read through three or four times. The aim is to identify the strongest material for proving the proposition and to organize it under three or four headings. Throughout this section Panigarola gives the running example of a sermon arguing that one should observe a fast in Lent. For this

[39] This is suggested by the full title of the work *Postilla: Das ist Ausslegung der episteln und evangelien an sontagen und fuernemesten festen ordentlich und richtig nach der rhetorica gefasset*.

[40] 'E sappiate sopra il tutto, che buone prediche fa, chi le fa sempre ad honor di Dio e con principalissimo scopo di giovare all'anime de' gli ascoltatori.' F. Panigarola, *Modo di comporre una predica*, in G. Aromatari (ed.), *Degli autori del ben parlare*, 5 parts (1633), ultima parte, sig. s2^{v}.

[41] Ibid., sigs. s2^{v}–5^{v}.

example he selects the headings: useful, necessary, and established by tradition, under which he groups some of the numbered material he earlier listed.[42]

At this point he turns to the structure of the sermon in seven sections: *prologhino*, introduction, proposition, proof, end of the first part, beginning of the second part, end of the whole sermon.[43] As he has already indicated the main force of the sermon will be in the proposition and proof. The introduction serves to establish a general proposition (in this case 'you ought to observe every fast') which will help in proving the proposition of the particular sermon.[44] The second part aims to provide some relief for the tired listener. It may be a story, a fable, a description, or something similar. A classical orator might call this section a digression. Both the first and second conclusion must sum up the main point of the sermon but one should avoid too much repetition and one might hold back a strong argument for the final conclusion. This is also where the strongest appeals to the emotions and to God should be made.[45] The *prologhino* must be written last. Panigarola, who often uses musical analogies, compares it to the prelude to a madrigal. Its aim is to secure the attention and favour of the audience, for example by a comparison or by speaking of the pleasure the preacher finds in speaking in this particular town or church.[46] The *Modo di comporre una predica* is an original and practical exposition of sermon-writing, whose principles could easily be extended to other forms of writing. The spirit of its approach to writing, rather than its content, connects it with the humanistic traditions of Agricola, Erasmus, and Melanchthon.

VERNACULAR MANUALS AND THE DEBATE ON CICERONIANISM

Kees Meerhoff has shown that rhetoric treatises in Italian and French became involved in the debates around the imitation of Cicero, and in particular in questions concerning the possibility of transferring Latin ideas about prose-rhythm to the vernacular.[47] These authors understood that establishing a more impressive literature in French or Italian would require both the adaptation of classical models and the imitation of the best extant vernacular writers. Writers active in the promotion of

42 Ibid., sigs. s6^{r}–t2^{r}. 43 Ibid., sig. t4^{v}. 44 Ibid., sigs. t2^{v}–4^{r}.
45 Ibid., sigs t4^{r-v}, u1^{v}–2^{v}. 46 Ibid., sigs t4^{v}–5^{r}, u3^{r-v}.
47 K. Meerhoff, *Rhétorique et poétique au XVI siècle en France* (Leiden, 1986), 4–14.

vernacular literature draw inspiration from a learned quarrel apparently concerned with different approaches to Latin pedagogy.

Pietro Bembo argued that Cicero should be the sole model for Latin prose composition in his *De imitatione*. His *Prose della volgar lingua* (1525), printed at least twelve times in the sixteenth century, insisted on the necessity of writing in Italian, in order to increase the value of one's own native tongue, as Cicero had in writing in Latin rather than Greek.[48] Bembo argues that the great weakness of Italian, its variability with place and time, should be overcome by basing the written language on the Tuscan dialect, which already has a distinguished literature. Petrarch and Boccaccio should be the models for verse and prose, assisted by imitation of Latin.[49] Bembo founds his elevation of Petrarch and Boccaccio on five qualities of writing, which he derived from Latin rhetoric: sound, number, variation, decorum, and persuasion.[50]

I Dialogi (1542) by Sperone Speroni (1500–88), printed eleven times in the sixteenth century, contained a *Dialogo della retorica*, an argument about rhetoric which summarizes or assumes a good deal of basic rhetorical doctrine, in the manner of Cicero's mature rhetorics. Brocardo, the main speaker of the dialogue, maintains the provocative views that the main purpose of rhetoric is to please (rather than to teach or move), that style is the skill which most distinguishes the orator, and that the most important genre of oratory is the demonstrative.[51] Like Bembo he takes Petrarch and Boccaccio as the principal models for imitation. He argues that in Italian rhyme and harmonious sentence construction take the place of the patterns of long and short syllables which dignify Latin verse and prose.[52] His *Dialogo delle lingue* outlined many of the arguments in favour of the vernacular which Du Bellay would use.

La Deffence et Illustration de la langue Françoyse (1549) by Joachim Du Bellay (*c.*1525–60) was printed four times independently and seven times as part of Du Bellay's *Oeuvres* in the sixteenth century.[53] Du Bellay insists that languages need to be cultivated in order to grow.

[48] P. Bembo, *Prose della volgar lingua*, in *Prose e Rime*, ed. C. Dionisotti (Turin, 1966), 1.3, pp. 79–80. In addition to the works cited in pp. 166–8 above, see F. Cornilliat *et al.*, 'Les Voies de l'imitation', in P. Galand-Hallyn and F. Hallyn (eds.), *Poétiques de la renaissance* (Geneva, 2001), 415–88.

[49] Bembo, *Prose*, 1.12, 15, 2.3, pp. 105–6, 111–14, 132–5.

[50] Ibid., 2.9–19, pp. 145–75.

[51] S. Speroni, *Dialogo della retorica*, in *Opere* (Venice, 1740; repr. Manziana, 1989), 205, 212–15, 217, 236, 239. Meerhoff, *Rhétorique et poétique*, 82–102.

[52] Speroni, *Dialogo della retorica*, 223–34.

[53] J. Du Bellay, *La Deffence et Illustration de la langue Françoyse*, ed. J.-C. Monferran (Geneva, 2001),47–9. T. Cave, *The Cornucopian Text* (Oxford, 1979), 54–77. Meerhoff, *Rhétorique et poétique*, 108–34.

French at the present day is uncultivated but not incapable.[54] Du Bellay quotes Cicero's insistence that Latin is as good as Greek and cites the unfinished *Orateur françois* by Etienne Dolet (1509–46).[55] The successful translation of classical works of philosophy, history, poetry, and oratory has shown the potential of French, but translation will not be enough to develop the language; original poetry and oratory in French are required.[56] Du Bellay uses ideas inherited from rhetoric as the basis of his argument. Knowledge and *copia* will be required for invention; tropes, figures, and rhythm for style. Original poetic composition will contribute a special liveliness and *enargeia* to the language.[57] Since no existing French models are suitable, French literature will have to be developed by imitation of Latin and Greek authors. This should involve a careful choice of the model suited to one's own talent, and imitation of the aims and methods of their writing rather than copying their words and phrases.[58] The nature of the French language will have to be respected; the music of rhyme and the harmony of French pronunciation will have to become as rich for us as quantity was for the Greeks and Romans.[59] Du Bellay's aim was to encourage the writing of poetry and oratory in French; his inheritance from classical rhetoric provided him with the arguments and techniques for doing this.

Peter Ramus's Latin *Ciceronianus* (1557), which I mention here because it discusses the use of the vernacular, was printed ten times up to 1617. Ramus follows Erasmus in preference to Bembo in asserting that one should imitate the best features of all classical writers, rather than restricting oneself to Cicero.[60] He treats Cicero's life, and in particular his translation and imitation of Greek models, as a pattern for French writers. In parallel with Quintilian, Ramus believes that the French language can be enriched through translation. He urges French writers to imitate the best features of all good classical authors. But he also calls for the study and imitation of existing French writers, especially the poets of the Pléïade. Ramus rejects part of Cicero's over-exuberant Asianism along with the rules for quantitative prose, but he insists that Cicero's sentence composition was unequalled in skill. He aims to understand this harmony in terms of balance and repetition rather than by analysing patterns of long and short syllables. Ramus makes this move independent of his promotion of

[54] Du Bellay, *La Deffence*, 1.1–3, pp. 73–82.
[55] Ibid. 1.12, pp. 115–17.
[56] Ibid. 1.4–5, pp. 83–5.
[57] Ibid. 1.5–6. pp. 85–91.
[58] Ibid. 1.7–9, 2.3–4, pp. 91–9, 129–38.
[59] Ibid. 2.7–10, pp. 148–64.
[60] M. Fumaroli, *L'Age de l'éloquence* (Geneva, 1980), 454–60. Meerhoff, *Rhétorique et poétique*, 34–45.

French prose; it evidently helps the assimilation of Latin rhetorical techniques and fits in with the approach of Speroni and Du Bellay. Ramus's commitment to writing in vernacular languages was reflected in the French version of his *Dialectique* (1555) printed four times, in Fouquelin's *La rhétorique françoise* (1555) printed twice, and in the English, German, and Dutch translations of his dialectic and rhetoric.[61]

Meerhoff has also shown that humanist techniques of textual analysis began to be applied to vernacular texts. Barthélemy Aneau (*c.*1505–61) provided notes to his *Chant natal* (1539) showing how he had imitated and varied materials from Marot and the Bible. Basing himself on Melanchthon's logic and rhetoric, in his *Quintil Horacien* (1550) Aneau analyses the underlying logic and especially the errors in Du Bellay's *Deffence et Illustration.* He writes a French logical and rhetorical analysis in his commented translation of St Eucher's *Epistola paraenetica.*[62] When Ramus prepared his French-language *Dialectique* (1555) he enlisted the help of Pléïade poets in translating the illustrative quotations from Latin literature into French. Antoine Fouquelin went a step further in choosing illustrations for his French version of Talon's *Rhetoric* from the works of the Pléïade poets.[63] The commentator E. K. remarks on Spenser's imitation, and notes rhetorical figures in the first edition of *The Shepheardes Calendar* (1579). The Ramist Abraham Fraunce quotes a few passages from Spenser (and many from Sidney) to illustrate the teaching in his *Lawiers Logike* and *Arcadian Rhetorike* (both 1588). Hoskins's manuscript *Directions for Speech and Style* (*c.*1599) discusses the tropes and figures on the basis of examples from Sidney. William Temple wrote a Latin analysis and criticism of the logical structure of Sidney's *Apology for Poetry.*[64]

RHETORIC IN VERNACULAR COURTESY BOOKS

One indication of the cultural importance of rhetoric in the sixteenth century was the discussion of often quite technical rhetorical issues in major vernacular treatises on polite conversation and the behaviour and

[61] Green and Murphy, *Renaissance Rhetoric STC*, 368.

[62] K. Meerhoff, *Entre logique et littérature* (Orleans, 2001), 39–61; *Rhétorique et poétique*, 135–9, 147–54.

[63] Meerhoff, *Rhétorique et poétique*, 234–9.

[64] J. Hoskins, *Directions for Speech and Style*, ed. H. Hudson (Princeton, 1935). William Temple, *Analysis of Sir Philip Sidney's Apology for Poetry*, ed. and tr. J. Webster (Binghamton, NY, 1984). P. Mack, 'Renaissance Habits of Reading', in S. Chaudhuri (ed.), *Renaissance Essays for K. S. Datta* (Calcutta, 1995), 1–25.

education of courtiers. For Baldassare Castiglione (1478–1529) whose *Il Libro del cortigiano* (1528) went through sixty-two Italian editions and a further sixty editions in other languages before 1620,[65] the ability to speak and write well was one of the chief requirements for the courtier.

> I think that what the courtier mainly requires in order to write and speak well is knowledge, because someone who knows nothing and has no thoughts in his head which deserve to be understood, can neither write nor speak them. Then he needs to arrange in good order what he has to say or write; then express his thoughts effectively in words, which in my opinion should be suitable, carefully chosen, impressive, and well joined together, but above all should still be part of ordinary popular usage. For the words create the grandeur and solemnity of an oration, if the orator has good judgement and takes care, and knows how to choose the words which best signify what he wants to say, and also how to amplify it, and how, as if shaping wax to the form he desires, to arrange them in such parts and with such order as to make known the dignity and splendour of his thoughts at first glance, like paintings displayed in good natural light.[66]

While observing rhetoric's division into invention, disposition, and style, Castiglione puts the main emphasis on choosing and arranging words so as to present one's thoughts clearly and impressively. Above all the courtier must show grace and avoid affectation in his writing. The qualities of his speaking and writing must suit the occasion. He must not always be serious, but must be able to please and joke.

> And then when he speaks about something obscure and difficult I want him with carefully distinguished words and thoughts to explain his meaning cleverly, and to make every doubtful thing clear and plain in a manner that is scrupulous, without pedantry. In the same way when it is appropriate he should know how to speak with vehemence and to arouse the emotions which our minds have within them, inflaming and moving them as the need

[65] P. Burke, *The Fortunes of the Courtier* (Oxford, 1995), 40–2, 55–6, 158–62.

[66] B. Castiglione, *Il Libro del cortigiano*, 1.33: 'Quello adunque che principalmente importa ed è necessario al cortigiano per parlere e scriver bene, estimo io che sia il sapere; perché chi non sa e nell'animo non ha cosa che meriti essere intesa, non po né dirla né scriverla. Appresso bisogna dispor con bell'ordine quello che si ha a dire o scrivere; poi esprimerlo ben con le parole: le quali, s'io non m'inganno, debbono esser proprie, elette, splendide e ben composte, ma sopra tutto usate ancor dal populo; perché quelle medesime fanno la grandezza e pompa dell'orazione, se colui che parla ha bon giudicio e diligenzia e sa pigliar le più significative di ciò che vol dire, ed inalzarle, e come cera formandole ad arbitrio suo collocarle in tal parte e con tal ordine, che al primo aspetto mostrino e faccian conoscer la dignità e splendor suo, come tavole di pittura poste al suo bono e natural lume.'

arises; sometimes with such simplicity of sincerity that it seems that nature herself speaks to our minds, making them tender and almost drunk with sweetness.[67]

The courtier needs the kind of facility in different types of speaking which rhetoric teaches but he must never strain for any effect, always concealing his art, as an orator would.[68] Like contemporary rhetoricians Castiglione's speakers are much concerned with imitation and with the question of how to employ (and improve) the vernacular. Imitation is necessary in order to learn how to write, but the model chosen should suit the gifts of the student, who should imitate the procedures and intentions rather than simply the words of the model.[69] The view that all Italians should write in Tuscan, imitating Petrarch and Boccaccio, is opposed by the idea of speaking your own current Italian, choosing especially words in popular use, but using your own judgement to add words from other languages where they can enrich your expression.[70] The question of how to imitate Latin prose-rhythm is raised but Emilia closes the discussion before it can be developed.[71] *Il libro del cortigiano* (1528) was the most successful and influential courtesy book, with more than forty sixteenth-century editions, and was translated into Spanish (1534), French (1537), English (1561), German (1566), and Latin (1571).

Sir Thomas Elyot (*c.*1490–1546) in *The Book named the Governor* (1531), which was printed eight times in the sixteenth century, combines a humanist educational programme with a digest of the moral knowledge required in a counsellor. The duty of the tutor is to observe the nature of the pupil and apply his teaching to increasing the pupil's virtues and reducing his vices.[72] The young nobleman must learn Latin and Greek and must read a wide range of poetry, especially Homer, Virgil, and Ovid.[73] He should study classical and humanistic dialectic and rhetoric, especially Aristotle, Agricola, Quintilian, Cicero, and Erasmus. These studies will help him to learn ethics, politics, and expression from

[67] Ibid. 1.34: 'E quando poi parlerà di cosa oscura o difficile, voglio che e con le parole e con le sentenzie ben distinte esplichi sottilmente la intenzion sua, ed ogni ambiguità faccia chiara e piana con un certo modo diligente senza molestia. Medesimamente, dove occorrerà, sappia parlar con dignità e veemenza, e concitar quegli affetti che hanno in sé gli animi nostri, ed accenderli o moverli secondo il bisogno; talor con una simplicità di quel candore, che fa parer che la natura istessa parli, intenerirgli e quasi inebbriargli di dolcezza.'

[68] Ibid. 1.26, 28, 40.

[69] Ibid. 1.26, 32, 36–8.

[70] Ibid. 1.29–31, 35.

[71] Ibid. 1.38.

[72] T. Elyot, *The book named the Governor*, 1.6.

[73] Ibid. 1.7.

his reading in oratory, history, and philosophy.[74] The disquisitions on the virtues, combining moral axioms and narratives, which fill books 2 and 3 of the work collect the material obtained by a rhetorical and ethical reading of classical and modern texts. Elyot's assumption throughout is that the boy will learn in Latin but that his practical work as a counsellor will be conducted in English.

Galateo by Giovanni Della Casa (1503–56) was printed twenty times in Italian and eleven times in two Latin translations (1578, 1595) before 1620. Della Casa sees conversation as one of the primary aspects of good manners. Speaking at length, especially to tell stories, is one of the best ways of contributing to conversation. In telling a story one should plan what one is going to say in advance, add lively descriptions, and employ carefully chosen, commonly used, and appropriate words. Old, new, and ambiguous words are to be avoided. Charm is achieved through proportion, grace, and decorum.[75]

Stephano Guazzo's *La civil conversazione* (1574), which was printed twenty-four times in Italian, eight times in French (1579), twice each in English (1582) and German (1591), and nine times in Latin translation (1585) before 1620, emphasizes the importance of conversation in acquiring knowledge, through listening and questioning, and in learning how to express oneself.[76] One should concentrate on the meaning one wants to convey rather than the words, which should be suited to the audience, meaningful, and effective. Simple expression will always be better than excess but just as the common people use proverbs, allegories, and similes in ordinary speech so some admixture of art will make what we say more pleasing. One should avoid excessive brevity and excessive *copia*.[77] Imitation is necessary as a way of enriching one's knowledge and style but one should not copy from too many places. Rather than everyone trying to write in Tuscan, Italian authors should use their own local language, taking care to write and speak clearly and well, and using words from other languages where they help.[78] Even in Montaigne's *Essais* (1580, 1588, 1595) three chapters are largely and two others partly concerned with questions of rhetoric.[79]

[74] Ibid. 1.8.
[75] G. Della Casa, *Galateo overo de' costumi* (Florence, 1944), 22–8.
[76] S. Guazzo, *La civil conversazione*, ed. A. Quondam, 2 vols. (Modena, 1993), i. 84–5.
[77] Ibid. i. 93–5.
[78] Ibid. i. 96–101.
[79] Montaigne, *Essais*, 1.10, 51, 3.8; 1.24, 25 (1595 numbering).

NATIONAL SPECIALITIES: THE ENGLISH STYLE MANUAL

Although all the vernacular traditions depend on the Latin mainstream, particular languages did develop specialities. In German, as we have seen, it was the notarial formulary; in French it was the manual of *seconde rhétorique*, describing the rules for the different forms of vernacular poetry. In English, while only four manuals were really successful, several different works included a manual of tropes and figures. Richard Sherry's *A Treatise of Schemes and Tropes* (1550, two editions), Henry Peacham's *The Garden of Eloquence* (1577, two editions), the third book of George Puttenham's *The Arte of English Poesie* (1589, one edition), together with the third book of Wilson's *Art of Rhetoric* (1553, eight editions), the later editions of Day's *English Secretorie* (1592, five editions before 1620), and the Ramist rhetoric manuals of Fenner (1584, two editions) and Fraunce (1588, one edition) put into circulation a total of twenty-one editions of a treatise on tropes and figures in English. All these treatments of the tropes and figures depended heavily on continental manuals, such as Mosellanus's *Tabulae de schematibus et tropis*, Melanchthon's *Institutiones rhetoricae*, and Susenbrotus's *Epitome troporum ac schematum*. The English manuals also regularly borrowed from each other: Wilson using Sherry; Peacham relying on Sherry and Wilson as well as Susenbrotus. Puttenham and Day usually work directly from Susenbrotus. There are a few signs of particular Latin-based figures being adapted to different uses in English, but for the most part the English manuals translate from their classical and continental predecessors.[80]

COMPLETE RHETORICS IN THE VERNACULAR

Some mid-sixteenth-century vernacular manuals covered the whole syllabus of rhetoric or dialectic. In Italy there was Cavalcanti's outstanding *La retorica* (1558), as well as adaptations and translations of Latin manuals. In French the same need was fulfilled by Fabri's *Le grant et vray art de pleine rhétorique* (1521), discussed in the section above on the dependence of vernacular rhetorics on the Latin tradition, which combines a survey based on *Rhetorica ad Herennium* with a letter-writing manual and a *seconde rhétorique*.

[80] Mack, *Elizabethan Rhetoric*, 84–102. Skinner, *Reason and Rhetoric in the Philosophy of Hobbes* (Cambridge, 1996), 51–67.

Rhetorica en lengua castellana (1541) by the Zaragozan monk Miguel de Salinas (?1501–1567), printed in Alcalá de Henares by Joan de Brocar among a group of humanistic and rhetorical works, was intended to assert and develop the maturity of the Spanish language. Salinas bases his work on classical and renaissance Latin sources and on the Latin rhetoric and Spanish grammar of Antonio de Nebrija (1444–1522).[81] Following Quintilian Salinas defines rhetoric as 'the art of speaking well'. The aim of the orator, adapting Cicero, is 'to persuade or to cause belief in what he intends through teaching, proving something not only without pain but also in a delightful and pleasing way, and finally to move the wills of the audience'.[82] Salinas covers the five skills of the orator, giving most attention, under invention, to the contents of the six parts of the oration. He devotes seven chapters to narration, including accounts of descriptions of persons and things, and, within the section on confirmation, discusses the three genres, status-theory, and three subtypes of deliberative (exhortation, consolation, and petition), which suggests a debt to letter-writing manuals. This section also describes different forms of argumentation. The section on the conclusion discusses amplification and the emotions, especially pity, indignation, and love.[83] Salinas's account of the tropes and figures is based on Nebrija.[84] He gives a pair of examples from Spanish literature which he probably took from Nebrija.[85] The last third of the work comprises: a short summary of rhetoric, suggested titles and plans for practising rhetoric, a discussion of *copia* of words and things based on Erasmus, and a discussion of the method of collecting religious examples and *sententiae* into a commonplace book, including a list of headings for the pages of the book.[86] Here Salinas adds up-to-date and practical teaching to his compendium of classical rhetorical doctrine. The book was printed only once.

Francesco Sansovino (1521–86) in *L'arte oratoria* (1546), reprinted three times in expanded editions, follows the order of *Rhetorica ad Herennium*. The first book includes the types of rhetoric, the five skills, and, as part of invention, the six parts of the judicial oration (including status-theory). The second book describes the topics of deliberative and demonstrative oratory, disposition, memory, and delivery. The third book is

[81] M. de Salinas, *Rhetórica en lengua castellana*, ed. E. Sánchez García (Naples, 1999), pp. v–xxiv, xxxv–xxxix. A. de Nebrija, *Artis rhetoricae compendiosa coaptatio* (Alcalá de Henares, 1515); *Gramática de la lengua castellana*, ed. A. Quilis (Madrid, 1989).

[82] 'Rhétorica es arte de bien hablar . . . El fin del rhetórico es persuadir o hazer creer lo que intenta con ayuda de enseñarlo, prouándolo y no solamente sin pesadumbre, pero aún deleitable y apaziblemente y en fin, mover las voluntades de los oyentes.' Salinas, *Rhétorica*, 20.

[83] Ibid. 98–111.

[84] Ibid. 116–34.

[85] Ibid. 124, 128.

[86] Ibid. 146–209.

concerned with style, including the styles of the Tuscan classics, imitation, amplification, the topics of arousing pity, and the tropes and figures.[87] Sansovino typically gives a brief summary of each doctrine, followed by examples, usually from Petrarch and Boccaccio, but sometimes Italian translations of passages from Cicero's speeches, sometimes with short commentary.[88] For the figures, for example, he often simply names the figure and appends examples to show its form and effect.[89] This combination of short precepts and abundant vernacular examples resembles later Ramist manuals. With a little help from a teacher one could learn rhetoric from this textbook, but it might be more effective in showing someone who had already studied the subject in Latin how it could be adapted to Italian. The second and two subsequent editions of the dialogue *Ragionamenti della lingua toscana* (1546) by Bernardino Tomitano (1517–76) include in their third and fourth books discussions of the importance of rhetoric, the nature of the art, the three genres, status-theory, topics of the person, issues of imitation, and the resources of style,[90] but as in Cicero's *De oratore* the main doctrines are mentioned and debated rather than being set out fully enough to train the reader.

In the 1550s Thomas Wilson (1524–81) composed English-language manuals in order to make dialectic and rhetoric easily available to readers of English.[91] While he fully covers the traditional syllabus of both subjects he follows the humanists in insisting on the close relations between them. Students need to master dialectic's topics of invention before they can benefit from rhetorical training.[92] Wilson's comparison between the two arts concentrates on similarity, locating their differences mainly in issues of style and audience.

> Both these arts are much like, saving that Logic is occupied about all matters and doth plainly and nakedly set forth with apt words the sum of things by way of argumentation. Again of the other side Rhetoric useth gay painted sentences and setteth forth those matters with fresh colours and godly ornaments and that at large.[93]

[87] F. Sansovino, *L'arte oratoria* (Venice, 1546), sigs. *6^{v}, G5^{r}–7^{r}, K7^{r}–8^{v}.

[88] e.g. ibid., sigs. A1^{v}–4^{r} (Italian examples of genres), A5^{r}–B3^{r} (Italian and Roman proems and *exordia*), E7^{v}.

[89] e.g. ibid., sigs. K2^{v}–3^{r}.

[90] B. Tomitano, *Quattro libri della lingua thoscana* (Padua, 1570), sigs. u2^{r}–6^{r}, x3$^{r–v}$, z6^{r}–8^{r}, Aa6^{r}–Bb2^{v}.

[91] T. Wilson, *The Rule of Reason*, ed. R. Sprague (Northridge, 1972), 1–3.

[92] T. Wilson, *The Art of Rhetoric (1560)*, ed. P. Medine (University Park, PA, 1994), 49, 65, 145. R. H. Wagner, 'Wilson and his Sources', *Quarterly Journal of Speech,* 15 (1929), 525–36. Wagner, 'Thomas Wilson's *Arte of Rhetorique*', *Speech Monographs,* 27 (1960), 1–32. P. Medine, *Thomas Wilson* (Boston, 1986), 55–74.

[93] Wilson, *Rule of Reason*, 11; Medine, *Thomas Wilson*, 41–54.

The Rule of Reason (1551), which was printed seven times, provides a complete course in Aristotelian dialectic, from the predicables to the sophisms but with some important humanist inflections. Wilson gives prominence to the topics, taking the definitions of logic and topic, the list of topics, the diagram, and some of the treatment of individual topics from Rudolph Agricola, but supplementing this with maxims from Boethius.[94] Wilson's discussions of definition, division, and eight topics for handling a simple question derive from Melanchthon.[95]

The Art of Rhetoric (1553), which was printed eight times, is organized according to the five skills of the orator, with invention divided between accounts of the three genres of oratory, which focus on the main topics of each genre and provide (sometimes lengthy) speeches as examples of each type, and of the seven parts of the oration. Wilson arrives at seven parts by treating the proposition ('a pithy sentence, comprehending in a small room the sum of the whole matter'), and the division ('an opening of things wherein we agree and rest upon, and wherein we stick and stand in traverse, showing what we have to say in our own behalf') as two separate sections, as well as separating confirmation and confutation.[96] The discussion of deliberative oratory is filled out with discussions of exhortation, commendation, and comfort, which are taken over from Erasmus's *De conscribendis epistolis*.[97] Wilson adds sections on amplification, vivid description, similitudes, examples, and fables, which are based on *De copia*.[98] He also adds a substantial section on humour.[99] In contrast to the treatment of dialectic, the precepts are presented rather briefly, with much space given over to long examples (some of them translated from Erasmus); the treatment of the figures of speech is rather brief and disorganized and the figures of thought are not presented helpfully. Wilson neither copies slavishly, nor really innovates. His work makes classical and humanist teaching on all aspects of rhetoric and dialectic easily available to English readers without Latin.

In the 1560s Orazio Toscanella performed an important service in translating Cicero, Quintilian, Agricola, and Aphthonius into Italian. His classical translations appeared in thirteen editions, far more than any other translator. His folio *Armonia di tutti i principali retori* (Venice, 1569) begins with a large fold-out spread enabling the reader to take in the whole art of

[94] Wilson, *Rule of Reason*, 8, 90–1, 93, 99–100. Agricola, *De inventione dialectica*, 9, 25, 26, 57–9, 62–5, 193.
[95] Wilson, *Rule of Reason*, 37–45.
[96] Wilson, *Art of Rhetoric*, 50.
[97] Ibid. 100–20.
[98] Ibid. 147–60, 203–5, 213–22 with Medine's notes.
[99] Ibid. 164–83.

rhetoric (including some variants from different authorities) at a glance.[100] Synthesizing Aristotle, Cicero, and Quintilian he then offers diagrams of the topics of deliberative, judicial, and demonstrative oratory and of Aristotle's account of the emotions.[101] Then he provides a series of Lullian diagrams which enable discourse to be generated mechanically.[102] The work, which was printed three times, closes by explaining that there is no space for a discussion of style.[103]

VERNACULAR PHILOSOPHERS ON RHETORIC: PATRIZI AND BACON

Dieci dialoghi della retorica by Francesco Patrizi (1529–97), which was printed once before 1620, in Venice in 1562, is a Platonically inspired attack on rhetoric which asserts the primacy of the more creative use of language in poetry. Patrizi argues that there is little agreement among the famous rhetoricians, that rhetoric has no subject-matter of its own, that its only use is in now outmoded democratic societies, and that it is in fact a part of dialectic.[104] The work may be symptomatic of a new confidence in Platonic circles since to revive Plato's attack on rhetoric would have seemed hopeless a generation before. Cardinal Du Perron, by contrast, had recognized that deliberative oratory belonged mainly to democratic societies but had suggested a special role for royal eloquence in times of civil war, because at such times the people had to be made to understand for themselves what was at stake.[105]

Francis Bacon (1561–1626) in *The Advancement of Learning* (1605) urges King James I to promote higher level study and research by surveying the state of knowledge in all fields and identifying areas of weakness, to which more efforts could be devoted.[106] Among the general weaknesses in learning Bacon mentions an excessive concern with words, and specifically Ciceronianism, but he also points to the usefulness of

[100] O. Toscanella, *Armonia di tutti i principali retori... posta in registro* (Venice, 1569).
[101] Ibid., sigs. A1^{r}–H1^{v}, O1^{r}.
[102] Ibid., sigs. I2^{r}–N2^{r}.
[103] Ibid., sig. R2^{v}.
[104] F. Patrizi, *Della retorica dieci dialoghi* (Venice, 1562), sigs 9^{r}–10^{v}, 22^{v}–25^{v}, 40^{v}–42^{v}, 59^{v}–61^{v}. C. Vasoli, 'Francesco Patrizi and the Double Rhetoric', *New Literary History*, 14 (1983), 539–51. *Francesco Patrizi da Cherso* (Rome, 1989).
[105] Du Perron, *Oeuvres diverses* (Paris, 1633), 759–60. La Charité, 'Les Trois Institutions', 47–8.
[106] F. Bacon, *The Advancement of Learning*, ed. M. Kiernan (Oxford, 2000). M. Malherbe, 'Bacon's Method of Science'. B. Vickers, 'Bacon and Rhetoric', in M. Peltonen (ed.), *The Cambridge Companion to Bacon* (Cambridge, 1996), 75–98, 200–31.

verbal skill in disseminating knowledge, and he finds it to be a less serious fault than the scholastic preoccupation with logical minutiae and fruitless cavillations.[107] He is also critical of Ramus for oversimplifying subjects, and of the practice of disputation (122–7). The influence of rhetoric on Bacon's thinking is shown in his classification of four types of intellectual art: inquiry or invention; examination or judgement; custody or memory; elocution or tradition (107), which clearly reflect a combination of the five skills of the orator with the division of logic into invention and judgement. Bacon's discussion of these arts reflects sixteenth-century rhetorical ideas. He places great emphasis on the topics of invention, which he regards as a method of recovering what you already know rather than a way of finding new knowledge (111–13); he advocates the use of commonplace books (118); and he argues that axioms and aphorisms are helpful in testing, creating, and conveying knowledge (124, 126–7).

Bacon composed a new and thought-provoking definition of rhetoric ('to apply reason to imagination for the better mooving of the will', 127), which helpfully links it with faculty psychology. He uses the traditional comparison with the closed and open hand to develop a more detailed explanation of the connections and differences between rhetoric and logic:

> Logicke handleth reason exact, and in truth, and Rhetoricke handleth it, as it is planted in popular opinions and manners: And therefore Aristotle doth wisely place Rhetoricke as between Logicke on the one side and Morall or Civile Knowledge on the other, as participating of both: for the Proofes and Demonstrations of logicke are toward all men indifferent, and the same: but the Proofes and perswasions of Rhetoricke, ought to differ according to the Auditors. (129)

Bacon declares that rhetoric has generally been very well cultivated, in the theories of Aristotle and Cicero and in the practice of Demosthenes and Cicero (127), but identifies three minor areas where further work could be done: refutations of common errors in ethical arguments, axioms for and against commonly made arguments, and formulae for expressing commonly required ideas (129–31). Some of Bacon's other works (such as the *Colours of Good and Evil*, published with the *Essays* in 1597 and the manuscript *Promus of Formularies*) were intended to fill these gaps. Because he felt that the principal rules of rhetoric had already been set out effectively, Bacon did not compose rhetoric treatises of his own. But his major work the *Novum Organum* was intended to indicate ways in which new, reliable knowledge could be acquired through observation of

[107] Bacon, *Advancement*, 21–3; subsequent references in the text.

particulars and the gathering of the conclusions of such observations into more general axioms. The ideas of the *Advancement* acquired a wider circulation when they were expanded and translated into Latin as *De dignitate et augmentis scientiarum* (1623).

Both the vernacular rhetoric treatises and the discussions of rhetorical issues in guides to ethical and courtly behaviour indicate the importance of rhetoric in renaissance culture. But Latin remained the principal medium of instruction and of innovation in rhetoric. With the exception of three Italian manuals and some of the more reflective discussions (for example, by Castiglione, Patrizi, and Bacon) the work produced in the vernacular is derivative, firmly based on classical or renaissance Latin textbooks. Perhaps the innovation of Italian-language manuals in the sixteenth century makes up for the relatively small contribution of Italy to rhetoric in Latin after 1480, at least in comparison with the Netherlands, France, and Germany. French-language rhetoric was dominated by letter-writing and arts of poetry; German rhetoric by letter-writing and formularies for notaries. England had letter-writing manuals, surveys of rhetoric and dialectic, and textbooks on the tropes and figures. Usable surveys of the whole of classical rhetoric, of letter-writing, and of sermon composition were available in the principal vernacular languages of Western Europe by the end of the sixteenth century.

14

Conclusion

Renaissance Rhetoric

The humanist project of improving knowledge of the ancient world was the primary cause of the increase in the study of rhetoric in the renaissance. Humanists promoted classical rhetoric because it taught pupils to understand and use the full resources of classical Latin. Rhetoric offered privileged access to ancient writers' understanding of language and its effective use in the world. At the same time other technological, social, and intellectual factors also supported and shaped the development of renaissance rhetoric.

After 1460 the growth of printing ensured that a wider range of ancient rhetorical texts was available throughout Europe, including newly discovered texts, improved editions, and new commentaries. The rapid spread of printing and the international trade in printed books also favoured the production of new textbooks by enabling successful works to be made available much more rapidly throughout Europe than had been possible in the manuscript age.

Reforms in education and the foundation of new schools encouraged production of rhetoric textbooks and new developments in rhetorical theory. Humanist ideas gave rhetoric an important place in the middle and higher levels of grammar schools. Erasmus and other leading humanists wrote textbooks on aspects of rhetoric (such as letter-writing, tropes and figures, *copia,* and proverbs) specifically for grammar schools. Soarez's highly successful *De arte rhetorica* was composed for a specific place in the Jesuit curriculum, capping pupils' study of Latin literature and style in the humanities class and preparing them for the reading of texts by Aristotle and Cicero in the following year in the rhetoric class. Early in the sixteenth century in northern Europe professors of logic and Greek, such as Melanchthon and Latomus, argued for more instruction in rhetoric in universities and wrote university-level textbooks to prepare for the study of classical rhetorical texts.

The renaissance fascination with educational theory promoted the study of rhetoric. Rhetoric and dialectic came to be regarded as propaedeutics for further education, training pupils to argue and communicate effectively but also offering other subjects models of organization. Humanist writings on the education of the prince and the role of the educated counsellor presented skill in rhetoric as an essential attainment for effective and benevolent government.

Humanism's promotion of the study of Greek presented teachers of rhetoric with a special problem. On one side rhetorical theory was Greek in origin and, as with other subjects, newly recovered Greek texts, such as Aristotle's *Rhetoric* and the Hermogenean corpus, offered new intellectual resources which needed to be absorbed. But on the other side, unusually, Latin rhetoric provided a complete body of teaching, particularly by Cicero and Quintilian, which most humanists were habituated to. Greek rhetoric texts first made an impact on renaissance rhetoric early in the fifteenth century, but it took almost 150 years and the efforts of George Trapezuntius, Sturm, Soarez, and many commentators on Aristotle before Greek rhetorical doctrines, especially in relation to style, epideictic, and the arousal of emotions, found a secure place in Latin textbooks of rhetoric. Most humanist writers found classical rhetoric far more to their taste than scholastic (or even Aristotelian) logic, but some, including Vives and Ramus, criticized the fundamental doctrines of rhetoric, such as the five skills of the orator, the three genres of oratory, and the three levels of style, while several others found that rhetoric needed to be adapted to modern circumstances. Melanchthon, for example, added a fourth genre, the didascalic, while authors of letter-writing manuals identified several types of letter suited to practical communication needs (such as recommendation, request, consolation, encouragement), which were later absorbed into full textbooks of rhetoric. Reflection on contemporary preaching and reading of St Paul prompted some writers to identify five types of sermon. Partly for practical reasons and partly on the basis of newly discovered Greek texts, far more attention was given to epideictic oratory in later renaissance manuals.

The record of printing gives a very clear indication of the importance of rhetoric in the renaissance, but it also suggests some temporal limits. As we saw in Chapter 2, very large numbers of classical and modern rhetoric texts, amounting in some decades to over 200 editions, were printed between 1520 and 1570. The same sources suggest a very steep decline in the production of Ciceronian and early sixteenth-century manuals after 1590. We do not yet understand the reasons for this. It seems that there was a revival of scholastic logic in the late sixteenth century. If the logicians reclaimed more of the syllabus of the arts course in northern Europe, that could have reduced demand for rhetoric texts. Or perhaps the growth in editions of Soarez and Talon after 1570 meant that new, simplified textbooks of the whole of rhetoric were now replacing classical (and other renaissance) manuals. But earlier in the century publication of many new manuals seems to have prompted more rather than less printing of classical manuals; the huge increase in publication of Erasmus, Melanchthon, and Agricola in the 1520s and 1530s preceded the very large numbers of Ciceronian manuals, especially *De oratore*, *Partitiones oratoriae*, *Topica*, and Quintilian's *Institutio oratoria*, produced between 1530 and 1560.

Both the pattern of printing and the study of individual manuals suggest a significant geographical element to renaissance rhetoric. Whereas Italian scholars made the first steps in the discovery, editing, and printing of texts, in promoting the study of rhetoric, and in establishing many of its key preoccupations, by the final quarter of the fifteenth century intellectual leadership in rhetoric had passed to northern Europe. Most important renaissance rhetoricians, including Agricola, Erasmus, Melanchthon, Ramus, Talon, Vossius, and Caussin, came from and worked in the Netherlands, France, and Germany. Parisian fashions in the study of rhetoric dominated northern Europe and the Iberian peninsula. Sixteenth-century Italy largely stood apart from these developments, although it made innovative contributions at the fringes of the subject: in the interpretation of Aristotle's *Rhetoric*, in the debate around Ciceronianism, in vernacular rhetoric, in poetics, and in preaching. No textbook of the whole of rhetoric composed in Italy after 1480 achieved more than ten editions or was printed outside Italy.

Humanists especially favoured the use of rhetoric to interpret classical texts. Valla, Erasmus, and others saw the possibilities of applying the same grammatical and rhetorical techniques to the study of the Bible and the early Christian church. Rhetoric manuals incorporated discussions of allegory and the interpretation of scripture. This type of study, which tended to undermine authority and encourage the reassessment of traditional practices, together with dismay at clerical corruption and resentment of the temporal power of the Church, contributed to the Reformation division of Christian Europe. The reformers employed rhetoric to spread their ideas; Melanchthon, in particular, includes many examples with a Protestant flavour in the rhetoric textbooks which he wrote, initially for his teaching in Wittenberg. Many of the writers discussed in this book were Protestants or had Protestant sympathies at some stage. Between 1530 and 1560 Protestants also wrote several new preaching manuals.

One consequence of the Reformation was the political and intellectual division of Europe. Catholic bishops encouraged training in rhetoric and the composition of Catholic rhetoric textbooks as part of their reaction to Protestantism, because they regarded the greater effectiveness of Protestant preaching as one of the causes of the spread of heresy. For these (and for missionary) reasons, Jesuit schools placed great emphasis on rhetorical education. So in one way Reformation and Counter-Reformation policies encouraged rhetoric. But the division of Europe meant that good Catholics could no longer acknowledge their intellectual debts to Melanchthon or Erasmus. Increasingly schools and universities required rhetoric texts to endorse the religion prevailing locally. It seems likely that the intellectual development of rhetoric was one of the many casualties of the division of Europe at the Reformation.

This study has identified seven characteristics of renaissance rhetoric, most of them related to the historical motivating forces discussed in the preceding paragraphs. In the first place, from Loschi in the 1390s to Caussin in 1619, renaissance rhetoric involved close reading of classical texts, in order to identify the ways in which Cicero (especially), Virgil, and others used the resources of language identified in rhetoric. Grammar-school teachers were instructed to point out figures of rhetoric in their teaching of Latin authors. Most renaissance rhetoricians devoted as much time to commentary on texts as they did to teaching rhetorical theory. Their textbooks are filled with examples showing the use of particular doctrines by important Roman authors. Agricola invented the genre of the dialectical commentary and based much of his teaching on logical analysis of classical texts. Agricola, Erasmus, and Melanchthon promoted the commonplace book as a way for pupils to record axioms and stories from their reading in order to reuse them in their own compositions.

Secondly renaissance rhetoric renewed the connection between rhetoric and dialectic. Humanist dialectic focused on the use of logic in practical arguing, especially as it appeared in classical Latin orations and poems. Where scholastic logic had developed into a theoretical investigation of problems in interpreting a quite restricted range of sentences, renaissance logic aimed to show how arguments could most effectively be made using the full resources of neo-classical Latin. Humanist logicians emphasized the role of the topics of invention in finding materials suitable for persuading, moving, and pleasing an audience. Their manuals analysed passages from classical literature to show how arguments discovered through the topics and formulated according to the rules of logic could be used most effectively in practical communication. They regarded the syllogism as one form, among several others, in which arguments could be expressed, rather than as the formal guarantee of correct inference. They insisted that rhetoric should take advantage of the techniques of dialectic.

The association between rhetoric and dialectic raised questions about the conservatism of rhetoric teaching and made possible new manuals of the whole of rhetoric. Because ancient rhetoric brought together such a wide range of different aspects of speaking (e.g. the nature of the audience, the arguments to employ, choice of words, verbal patterns, emotional manipulation, self-presentation, gesture, tone of voice) it was very hard for later writers to criticize even relatively ossified elements (such as the three types of oration) because of the risk of accidentally losing important elements of the whole structure. Thus, many medieval and renaissance rhetoricians made their adaptations to modern requirements in specialized subsections of the subject, such as letter-writing manuals or treatises on poetry. But the fact of considering rhetoric and dialectic together, and even more of writing manuals of both subjects, as several sixteenth-centuries authors did, led writers to question established doctrines, for example by asking why dialectic and rhetoric handled invention in different ways, whether there should be a difference in the forms of argument employed in the two subjects, and why the list of figures was so long and disorganized. The close connection between rhetoric and dialectic favoured by renaissance authors prompted new thinking about both subjects.

Thirdly, humanists re-established the study of arousing emotion as an element in rhetorical training, partly as a result of giving new attention to Aristotle's *Rhetoric*. Where the classical Latin rhetorical manuals had tended to discuss emotion only in connection with the conclusion of the speech and largely in relation to the need for the orator to feel the emotion he wished to convey to the audience, Agricola, Melanchthon, and their followers suggested an argumentative basis for arousing emotions, which enabled students to use the topics of invention to discover material suited for moving a particular audience. They founded their discussion of emotion on analysis of Roman speeches and poems. Earlier in the period they referred their readers to book 2 of Aristotle's *Rhetoric* for a more thorough theoretical treatment; by the late sixteenth and early seventeenth centuries they summarized Aristotle's doctrines in detail and adapted them to Christian purposes by adding accounts of other emotions, such as love of God and one's neighbour, which preachers would need to arouse.

Fourthly, renaissance rhetorical training revived the study of disposition. Where classical textbooks of rhetoric had taken the four- (or six-)part oration as the only appropriate form, and by organizing their schemes of invention accordingly had in effect reduced disposition to discussing when the order of the four parts might be varied or when one of them might be omitted, renaissance textbooks presented many alternative structures, several of them based on analysis of classical texts. Thus, for example, the *progymnasmata* gave recipes for fourteen different types of training exercise, while the letter-writing manuals presented twenty or more different types of letter, to supplement the three genres of oration found in the classical manuals. Agricola explained that the writer would need to decide the suitable form for a text when all the materials had been assembled and when proper consideration had been given to the purpose of the work, its audience and their likely reactions, the persona of the writer, and the context. Vives gave instructions for writing in a number of humanist genres, such as description, history, poetic fiction, precepts of an art, and commentary. Later renaissance writers added instructions for writing description and various types of deliberative oratory derived from the letter-writing manuals to their manuals of the whole of rhetoric.

Fifthly, as a result of the success of Erasmus's work, *copia* became an important element in renaissance education. Through *copia* of words pupils were trained to express an idea in many different ways to increase their stylistic resources and to make them aware of the effects of different forms of expression. *Copia* of things taught pupils to devise new material on the basis of a pre-existing sentence. Together both kinds of *copia* encouraged the writing of highly amplified passages in which considerable density of expression was combined with a playful approach to language. This in turn prepared readers for the abundant and exuberant style of writing which we find, for example, in Rabelais, Lyly, Nashe, and Andrewes.

Sixthly, again under the influence of Erasmus, renaissance rhetorical training gave particular emphasis to collecting, composing, and using *sententiae*, proverbs, descriptions, examples, and comparisons. Pupils were trained to observe these elements in their reading, to collect them in notebooks for reuse, to write new texts employing them, and to construct new expressions of their own on the model of what they found in their reading. The *progymnasmata* gave instructions for, and examples of, compositions using these elements and suggested supplementary material to be discovered through the topics. Erasmus, Ravisius Textor, Pedro Mexia, and many others produced works collecting examples of proverbs, stories, and axioms from classical literature as resources for modern writing. This strand in renaissance rhetoric is an important starting point for the new literary genre of the essay.

A seventh characteristic is the great importance which renaissance manuals give to style and particularly to the tropes and figures. As we saw in Chapter 10, renaissance authors produced many new handbooks of the tropes and figures, to collect and supplement what they learnt from *Rhetorica ad Herennium* and Quintilian. Schoolteachers were instructed to point out the figures and tropes in the texts they read with their pupils, and to discuss the ways in which classical authors used these resources of style. The absorption of the lessons of Hermogenes, one of the Greek texts which were new to Western Europe, provided an alternative way of thinking about style to the three levels of style described in the classical Latin rhetoric textbooks. The style manual illustrates the pressures which moulded later renaissance rewriting of rhetoric. On one side there was an impulse to be more expansive, to include more figures than anyone else, and to give more examples from classical literature and more commentary; on the other there was the pedagogical motivation to produce texts which were so short and simple that they could easily be learnt by heart, in order that students could keep them in mind as they read their texts.

Related to these seven characteristics of renaissance rhetoric, and to some extent overlapping with them, we may distinguish five common features of later renaissance rhetoric, which we could regard as developments from earlier renaissance rhetoric. First, several of the later textbooks, notably the works of Talon, but also the preaching manuals, give much more importance to delivery than we find in earlier renaissance rhetorics. In Talon this consists more in reporting the ideas of Quintilian and Cicero's later manuals than in devising new doctrines, but the preaching manuals use Bible text and personal experience to reflect on the best way to prepare to deliver a sermon. The sermon manuals also prompt and reflect further attention to the speaker's self-presentation (*ethos*) in later manuals.

Secondly, as Hardison, O'Malley, and Vickers have shown,[1] later renaissance rhetoric puts much greater emphasis on epideictic oratory than there was in Roman rhetorical works. The recovery of the work of Menander Rhetor may have encouraged this; his work is certainly referred to in some of the later renaissance textbooks.

Thirdly, starting on the dialectical side, later manuals, especially by Melanchthon, Ramus, and Sturm, show much more interest in issues of method.[2] Method was linked to ways of presenting material best adapted to a reader's understanding. Melanchthon's method is connected to the short list of questions suggested for the explanation of a simple concept. Ramus's three laws of method concentrate on defining a subject accurately and organizing its presentation from the most general principles to specific instances, through definition and division and without extraneous

[1] O. B. Hardison, *The Enduring Monument* (Chapel Hill, NC, 1962). A. Leigh De Neef, 'Epideictic Rhetoric and the Renaissance Lyric', *Journal of Medieval and Renaissance Studies*, 3 (1973), 203–31. J. W. O'Malley, *Praise and Blame in Renaissance Rome* (Durham, NC, 1979). B. Vickers, 'Epideictic and Epic in the Renaissance', *New Literary History*, 14 (1982–3), 497–537.

[2] N. W. Gilbert, *Renaissance Concepts of Method* (New York, 1960).

material. Rhetorical interest in method seems to coincide with encyclopedism and the aim of teaching pupils a wide range of subjects as efficiently as possible.

Fourthly, rhetorical training and later rhetoric manuals become involved in the debate about whether or not Cicero is the only model in Latin prose and the question of the importance and correct manner of imitation.[3] By the end of the period there seems to be a consensus that pupils should study Cicero carefully, though he is not the only suitable model, and that true imitation consists in learning from the ideas and techniques of an author rather than copying his sentence structures or restricting oneself to his vocabulary.

Finally, in the sixteenth century vernacular rhetoric became much more prominent. Although teaching was conducted in Latin in schools and universities, and although Latin remained the European *lingua franca* of intellectual life, there was more recognition that most practical and political life (and most preaching) would be conducted in the vernacular. The Reformation was probably an important cause of this development. By 1600 good surveys of the whole of rhetoric (and also manuals of letter-writing and preaching) were available in many European vernacular languages. Although learned culture remained effectively bilingual, the movement towards conducting at least school education in the vernacular was well under way. Increasingly the fruits of humanist training were to be sought in Italian, French, Spanish, and English literature rather than in Latin.

How did renaissance rhetoric differ from medieval rhetoric? We are still learning too many new things about both sides of this comparison to give a confident answer. The characteristics I have listed above will give medievalists some basis for comparing what changed and what remained the same. Medieval rhetoric was taught through five main types of textbook: texts of and commentaries on *Rhetorica ad Herennium* and *De inventione*; letter-writing manuals (*artes dictaminis*); preaching manuals; textbooks for the composition of poetry (such as Geoffrey de Vinsauf's *Poetria nova*); and treatises on the tropes and figures (such as Bede's *Liber de schematibus et tropis* and Marbod of Rennes's *De ornamentis verborum*).[4]

[3] M. L. McLaughlin, *Literary Imitation in the Italian Renaissance* (Oxford, 1995). T. M. Greene, *The Light in Troy: Imitation and Discovery in Renaissance Poetry* (New Haven, Conn.,1982). V. Pineda, *La imitación como arte literario en el siglo xvi español* (Seville, 1994).

[4] Good starting points on medieval rhetoric would be J. J. Murphy, *Rhetoric in the Middle Ages* (Berkeley, Calif., 1974); J. Murphy (ed.), *Medieval Eloquence: Studies in the Theory and Practice of Medieval Rhetoric* (Berkeley, Calif., 1978); J. Ward, *Ciceronian Rhetoric in Treatise, Scholion and Commentary* (Turnhout, 1995); V. Cox and J. Ward

As we have seen, renaissance writers made alterations to most of these types. Many new classical texts were discovered, circulated widely through printing, and commented on. New versions of manuals on letter-writing, preaching, and the tropes and figures were produced, which reflected better knowledge of the classical texts and adaptation to contemporary circumstances. Most significantly, especially in northern Europe, hundreds of new manuals of rhetoric were composed, widely circulated, and used as the basis for teaching. A few of these manuals can be connected with the medieval arts of poetry (for example, Erasmus's *De copia* teaches amplification in ways that partly parallel the *Poetria nova*) but for the most part they resulted from collaboration with dialectic and from attempts to absorb the teaching of newly discovered classical textbooks, especially Greek ones. On one side, none of the medieval rhetorical textbooks was much printed. On the other hand, Guarino's methods of teaching retain many medieval elements. The classical texts studied and the writing exercises undertaken at the Elizabethan grammar school show considerable continuity with their medieval forebears, and some differences in approach and in the writing textbooks employed. The most important changes brought about during the renaissance were the result of two centuries of development rather than of a sudden break with the past.

Renaissance rhetorical training taught techniques for reading. The graduates of renaissance schools were more active as readers than as writers. Schoolboys were expected to collect Latin vocabulary, phrases, sentences, and narratives from their reading in order to keep them ready for reuse in their own compositions. Instruction and practice in compiling commonplace books inculcated the habit of asking of any passage read, first, is this striking enough to record, and second, under which of my headings should I place it? Both these kinds of reading have fairly been described as reading in fragments, but the montage of material in the commonplace book also suggests new connections between different works and between different sections of the same work, a form of reading based on theme rather than temporal sequence.

The intimate connection between reading and writing compelled students to read as fellow-practitioners, observing the way in which the writer used a particular trope or figure, whose name they knew, and which they too employed. Reflecting on the ways in which different writers used the

(eds.), *The Rhetoric of Cicero in its Medieval and Renaissance Commentary Tradition* (Leiden, 2006); R. Copeland and I. Sluiter (eds.), *Medieval Grammar and Rhetoric* (Oxford, 2009); M. Woods, *Classroom Commentaries* (Columbus, Ohio, 2010); and their bibliographies.

same technique suggested conclusions about the qualities of their writing. Training in techniques of amplification was reinforced by teachers pointing out stylistically elaborated passages in Cicero and Virgil. In their own reading pupils would notice passages of amplification and ask themselves about the writer's purpose in working up some passages and leaving others briefer and plainer. Being taught to construct and notice, for example, descriptions, comparisons, speeches for a character, and commonplaces suggested ways to understand the contribution of different elements to a scene or chapter.

In contrast to the fragmentation involved in some types of rhetorical reading, other aspects of their training helped readers notice structures in texts. Dialectical analysis exposed the chains of syllogisms underlying a passage or attempted to show how a complete speech or poem presented an argument in response to a question. Practice in composing letters and *progymnasmata* made pupils aware of a wider range of possible structures for texts than the classical four-part oration. Structure was also a concern for teachers in their commenting on Terence, Cicero, Virgil, Ovid, and Horace. Renaissance rhetoricians and teachers believed that the principles had always to be tested and improved by applying them to reading the great classical authors.

Reading texts rhetorically always involved thinking about the writer's purpose in writing and the way in which the writer's consideration of the likely responses of the audience shaped the way stories and arguments were presented. Renaissance authors of rhetoric textbooks and preaching manuals gave particular attention to self-presentation and arousing emotions in the audience. Awareness of these processes in the writer's mind adds to the resources of the reader. Rhetoric characteristically connects close observation of linguistic form with comment on its effect on an audience. This grip on the consequences of form, together with the fact that it was widely taught, enabled rhetoric to provide tools of analysis to other forms of discourse. For example, Patricia Rubin has argued that Vasari's categories for discussing painters are based on rhetoric, while Quentin Skinner has pointed out the impact of rhetorical ideas and terminology on Machiavelli and renaissance political thought.[5] There are now many fine studies of the impact of renaissance rhetoric on other

[5] P. Rubin, *Giorgio Vasari: Art and History* (New Haven, Conn., 1995), 156–8, 332–3, 387–92. Q. Skinner, *The Origins of Modern Political Thought*, 2 vols. (Cambridge, 1978), i. 23–48, 152–86.

fields, for example on art criticism,[6] on the growth of science,[7] and on French and English literature.[8]

This history could not have been written without Green and Murphy's *Renaissance Rhetoric Short-Title Catalogue* or without numerous studies by members of the International Society for the History of Rhetoric. No doubt I have missed some studies and resources which would have improved my knowledge. At the same time, writing this history and asking my ISHR colleagues for guidance on particular issues has made me even more aware than before of what still remains to be done. Some essential work is in progress as I write,[9] but, in the spirit of suggestions to young researchers, I will conclude the history with a list of twenty projects (and genres of project) whose fruits I would have wished to have used and which would greatly enhance our knowledge of renaissance rhetoric:

- More studies on rhetoric within the educational system in particular places (and in particular of documents of composition exercises).

[6] J. Spencer, 'Ut Rhetorica Poesis: A Study in Quattrocento Theory of Painting', *Journal of the Warburg and Courtauld Institutes,* 20 (1957), 26–44. M. Baxandall, *Giotto and the Orators* (Oxford, 1971), 97–139; *Painting and Experience in Fifteenth Century Italy* (Oxford, 1972), 122–4, 131–7, 150–1. C. van Eck, *Classical Rhetoric and the Visual Arts in Early Modern Europe* (Cambridge, 2007).

[7] B. Vickers, 'Epideictic Rhetoric in Galileo's *Dialogo*', *Annali dell'Istituto e Museo di Storia della Scienza di Firenze,* 8 (1983), 69–102; 'The Royal Society and English Prose Style: A Reassessment', in B. Vickers and N. Struever, *Rhetoric and the Pusruit of Truth* (Los Angeles, 1985), 1–76. Jean Dietz Moss, *Novelties in the Heavens: Rhetoric and Science in the Copernican Controversy* (Chicago, 1993). Jeanne Fahnestock, *Rhetorical Figures in Science* (New York, 1999). Jean Dietz Moss and William Wallace, *Rhetoric and Dialectic in the Time of Galileo* (Washington, DC, 2003).

[8] e.g. T. Cave, *The Cornucopian Text* (Oxford, 1979). F. Lestringant (ed.), *Rhétorique de Montaigne* (Paris, 1985). J. Supple (ed.), *Montaigne et la rhétorique* (Paris, 1995). M. Fumaroli, *L'Age de l'éloquence* (Geneva, 1980). Pierre Zoberman, *Les Cérémonies de la parole* (Paris, 1998). Claudine Jomphe, *Les Théories de la dispositio et le Grand Œuvre de Ronsard* (Paris, 2000). P. France, *Racine's Rhetoric* (Oxford, 1965); *Rhetoric and Truth in France: Descartes to Diderot* (Oxford, 1972). M. Joseph, *Shakespeare's Use of the Arts of Language* (New York, 1947). B. Vickers, 'Shakespeare's Use of Rhetoric', in K. Muir and S. Schoenbaum (eds.), *A New Companion to Shakespeare Studies* (Cambridge, 1971), 83–98. Russ McDonald, *Shakespeare and the Arts of Language* (Oxford, 2001). B. Vickers, *Classical Rhetoric in English Poetry* (London, 1970). Thomas O. Sloane and R. B. Waddington (eds.), *The Rhetoric of Renaissance Poetry* (Berkeley, Calif., 1974). W. J. Kennedy, *Rhetorical Norms in Renaissance Literature* (New Haven, Conn., 1978). T. O. Sloane, *Donne, Milton and the End of Humanist Rhetoric* (Berkeley, Calif., 1985). B. Vickers, *In Defence of Rhetoric* (Oxford, 1988), 294–339, 375–434. N. Rhodes, *The Power of Eloquence and English Renaissance Literature* (Basingstoke, 1992). C. Bates, *The Rhetoric of Courtship in Elizabethan Language and Literature* (Cambridge, 1992). J. Richards, *Rhetoric and Courtliness in Early Modern Literature* (Cambridge, 2003).

[9] I am thinking especially of Lawrence Green's work on renaissance commentators on Aristotle, of Manfred Kraus's studies of the use of Aphthonius in the renaissance, of Kees Meerhoff's work on the rhetorical teaching of Melanchthon and his followers, and of Judith Rice Henderson's studies of renaissance letter-writing manuals.

- More work on renaissance commentaries on classical rhetoric textbooks.
- More work on renaissance rhetorical commentaries on classical texts, especially Cicero and Virgil.
- Study of the reception and influence of *De oratore* in the renaissance.
- Study of the reception and influence of Quintilian in the renaissance.
- More studies of the rhetorical doctrines of George Trapezuntius and their influence.
- Studies of the handbooks of *elegantiolae* and effective construction of Latin sentences.
- New edition and analysis of Valla's *Elegantiae.*
- More work on all aspects of Perotti's grammar.
- More work on rhetorical aspects of Melanchthon's commentaries on the Bible and on classical literature.
- New study of Sturm's rhetorical textbooks and their influence.
- Study of the evolution of Talon's rhetoric textbook.
- Study of changes in the presentation of Ramus's work, after the death of Ramus, including commentaries.
- Study of the evolution of Ramus's critiques of Ciceronian rhetoric and Quintilian.
- New study of the Senecan style in the late sixteenth century, especially in relation to Lipsius.
- Study of the links between renaissance treatises on poetics and rhetoric textbooks.
- Studies of the use of rhetorical and dialectical principles in Bible commentaries in the sixteenth and early seventeenth centuries.
- More studies of Renaissance German-language rhetoric.
- A hypertext to show the interrelations between the treatment of particular figures in renaissance Latin and vernacular works on the figures and tropes, and their sources.
- Studies of the revival of scholastic logic in the late sixteenth century and its implications for rhetoric, including the causes of the decline of Ciceronian rhetoric after 1590.

Bibliography of Secondary Literature

For classical texts I have used standard Oxford Classical Texts and Loeb editions. For primary texts printed in the renaissance I have relied on L. D. Green and J. J. Murphy, *Renaissance Rhetoric Short-Title Catalogue 1460–1700* (Aldershot, 2006). The specific edition of a renaissance text which I have cited can be discovered through the index, in which my main treatment(s) of each author are indicated in bold. Studies indicating further research topics listed in the conclusion are not included here.

Abbott, Don P., *Rhetoric in the New World* (Columbia, SC, 1996).

Adamson, Sylvia (ed.), *Renaissance Figures of Speech* (Cambridge, 2007).

Akkerman, Fokke, and A. J. Vanderjagt (eds.), *Rodolphus Agricola Phrisius* (Leiden, 1988).

Alessio, G. C., 'L'Ars dictaminis nel Quattrocento italiano: eclissi o persistenza?', *Rhetorica,* 19 (2001), 155–74.

——'Il *De componendis epistolis* di Niccolò Perotti e l'epistolografia umanistica', *Res publica litterarum,* 11 (1988), 9–18.

Augustijn, Cornelius, *Erasmus: His Life, Works and Influence* (Toronto, 1991).

Ax, W. (ed.), *Von Eleganz und Barbarei* (Wiesbaden, 2001).

Baldwin, T. W., *Shakspere's Small Latine and Lesse Greeke*, 2 vols. (Urbana, Ill., 1944).

Baños, Pedro Martín, *El arte epistolar en el Renacimiento europeo 1400–1600* (Bilbao, 2005).

Barker, William, *The Adages of Erasmus* (Toronto, 2001).

Barozzi, L., and R. Sabbadini, *Studi sul Panormita e sul Valla* (Florence, 1891); repr. in L. Valla, *Opera omnia*, ii (Turin, 1962).

Bataillon, M., *Erasme et l'Espagne* (Paris, 1937); repr. and enlarged (Geneva, 1991) .

Bath, Michael, *Speaking Pictures: English Emblem Books and Renaissance Culture* (Harlow, 1994).

Baxandall, Michael, *Giotto and the Orators* (Oxford, 1971).

—— *Painting and Experience in Fifteenth Century Italy* (Oxford, 1972).

—— *Words for Pictures* (New Haven, Conn., 2003).

Berwald, O., *Philipp Melanchthons Sicht der Rhetorik* (Weisbaden, 1994).

Besomi, O., and M. Regoliosi (eds.), *Lorenzo Valla e l'umanesimo italiano* (Padua, 1986).

Bezares, Luis E. Rodríguez-San Pedro (ed.), *Historia de la Universidad de Salamanca,* ii (Salamanca, 2004).

Bietenholz, Peter (ed.), *Contemporaries of Erasmus,* 3 vols. (Toronto, 1985–7).

Binns, J. W., *Intellectual Culture in Elizabethan and Jacobean England* (Leeds, 1990).

Black, Robert, *Humanism and Education in Medieval and Renaissance Italy* (Cambridge, 2001).
Brennan, Joseph X., 'The Epitome Troporum ac Schematum of Joannes Susenbrotus: Text, Translation and Commentary', Ph.D. dissertation, University of Illinois, 1953.
Briscoe, Marianne, *Artes Praedicandi* (Turnhout, 1992).
Bruyère, Nelly, *Méthode et dialectique dans l'oeuvre de La Ramée* (Paris, 1984).
Burke, Peter, *The Fortunes of the Courtier* (Oxford, 1995).
Büsser, Fritz, *Heinrich Bullinger (1504–1575): Leben, Werk und Wirkung*, 2 vols. (Zurich, 2004–5).
Cairns, Francis, 'The Poetices libri septem: An Unexplored Source', *Res Publica Litterarum,* 9 (1986), 49–57.
Calboli, Gualtiero, 'From Aristotelian λέξις to elocutio', *Rhetorica,* 16 (1998), 47–80.
——, 'The Metaphor after Aristotle', in D. C. Mirhady (ed.), *Influences on Peripatetic Rhetoric* (Leiden, 2007), 123–50.
Camargo, Martin, *Ars Dictaminis, Ars Dictandi* (Turnhout, 1991).
—— 'Latin Composition Textbooks and *Ad Herennium* Glossing: The Missing Link?', in V. Cox and J. O. Ward (eds.), *The Rhetoric of Cicero* (Leiden, 2006), 267–88.
Camporeale, Salvatore I., *Lorenzo Valla: umanesimo e teologia* (Florence, 1972).
Carruthers, Mary, *The Book of Memory* (Cambridge, 1990).
Cave, Terence, *The Cornucopian Text* (Oxford, 1979).
Chomarat, Jacques, *Grammaire et rhétorique chez Erasme*, 2 vols. (Paris, 1981).
Classen, Joachim, *Antike Rhetorik im Zeitalter des Humanismus* (Munich, 2003).
Coigneau, Dirk, '*De const van Rhetoriken*', in J. Koopmans (ed.), *Rhetoric-Rhétoriqueurs-Rederijkers* (Amsterdam, 1995), 123–40.
Conley, Thomas M., *Rhetoric in the European Tradition* (New York, 1990).
——,'Some Renaissance Polish Commentaries on Aristotle's Rhetoric and Hermogenes' *On Ideas*', *Rhetorica,* 12 (1994), 265–92.
Copeland, Rita, and Ineke Sluiter, *Medieval Grammar and Rhetoric* (Oxford, 2009).
Cornilliat, François, *Or ne mens: Couleurs de l'éloge et du blâme chez les 'Grands Rhétoriqueurs'* (Paris, 1994).
——, and Jean-Claude Mühlethaler, 'Les Voies de l'imitation', in P. Galand-Hallyn and F. Hallyn (eds.), *Poétiques de la renaissance* (Geneva, 2001), 415–88.
Cox, Virginia, *The Renaissance Dialogue* (Cambridge, 1992).
—— and J. O. Ward (eds.), *The Rhetoric of Cicero in its Medieval and Early Renaissance Commentary Tradition* (Leiden, 2006).
Croll, Morris W., *Style, Rhetoric and Rhythm*, ed. J. M. Patrick and R. O. Evans (Princeton, 1966).
Daly, Peter M., *The English Emblem and the Continental Tradition* (New York, 1988).

D'Ascia, Luca, 'La retorica di Giorgio Trebisonda e l'umanesimo ciceroniano', *Rinascimento,* 29 (1989), 193–216.

DeCoursey, M., 'Continental European Rhetoricians 1400-1600', in E. Malone (ed.), *British Rhetoricians and Logicians 1500–1660 First Series, Dictionary of Literary Biography,* 236 (2001), 309-43.

Dellaneva, J. (ed.), *Ciceronian Controversies* (Cambridge, Mass., 2007).

Eden, Kathy, *Friends Hold All Things in Common: Tradition, Intellectual Property and the* Adages *of Erasmus* (New Haven, Conn., 2001).

Engelhardt, G., 'Medieval Vestiges in the Rhetoric of Erasmus', *PMLA* 63 (1948), 739–44.

Faral, E., *Les Arts poétiques du XIIe et du XIIIe siècle* (Paris, 1924).

Farris, G., *Umanesimo e religione in L. G. Traversagni* (Milan, 1972).

Fehrenbach, Richard, and E. S. Leedham-Green (eds.), *Private Libraries in Renaissance England,* 5 vols. (Binghamton, NY, 1993–8).

Feingold, Mordechai, J. S. Freedman, and W. Rother (eds.), *The Influence of Peter Ramus* (Basel, 2001).

Flynn, Lawrence J., 'The *De arte rhetorica* (1568) of Cyprian Soarez S.J.: A Translation with Introduction and Notes', Ph.D. thesis, University of Florida, 1955.

Fois, Mario, *Il pensiero cristiano di Lorenzo Valla* (Rome, 1969).

Freedman, Joseph S., 'The Career and Writings of Bartholomew Keckermann', *Proceedings of the American Philosophical Society,* 141 (1997), 305–64.

——, 'The Diffusion of the Writings of Petrus Ramus in Central Europe c.1570–c.1630', *Renaissance Quarterly,* 46 (1993), 98–152.

Fumaroli, Marc, 'Genèse de l'épistolographie classique: Rhétorique humaniste de la lettre', *Revue d'histoire littéraire de la France,* 78 (1978), 886–905.

——, *L'Age de l'éloquence* (Geneva, 1980).

—— (ed.), *Histoire de la rhétorique dans l'Europe moderne 1450–1950* (Paris, 1999).

Galland-Hallyn, P., and F. Hallyn (eds.), *Poétiques de la Renaissance* (Geneva, 2001).

Gallo, E., *The Poetria Nova and its Sources in Early Rhetorical Doctrine* (The Hague, 1971).

García, L. Alburquerque *El arte de hablar en público: Seis retóricas famosas* (Madrid, 1995).

Garin, Eugenio, *L'Educazione in Europa 1400–1600* (Bari, 1957).

—— (ed.), *Il pensiero pedagogico dello Umanesimo* (Florence, 1958).

—— *Italian Humanism* (Oxford, 1965).

George, Edward, 'Rhetoric in Vives', in *Ioannis Lodovici Vivis Valentini Opera omnia,* i (Valencia, 1992), 113–77.

Gilbert, N. W., *Renaissance Concepts of Method* (New York, 1960).

González, J. M. Núñez, *El ciceronianismo en España* (Valladolid, 1993).

Gordon, Alex, *Ronsard et la rhétorique* (Geneva, 1970).

Goyet, Francis, 'Les Analyses de discours dans le livre XIII des *Parallela*', in S. Conte (ed.), *Nicolas Caussin: Rhétorique et spiritualité* (Berlin, 2007), 221–68.

Grafton, Anthony T., and L. Jardine, *From Humanism to the Humanities* (London, 1986).
Green, Lawrence D., 'Classical and Medieval Rhetorical Traditions in Traversagni's *Margarita eloquentiae*', *Quarterly Journal of Speech,* 72 (1986), 185–96.
—— *John Rainolds's Oxford Lectures on Aristotle's Rhetoric* (Newark, NJ, 1986).
—— 'Aristotelian Rhetoric, Dialectic and the Traditions of Antistrophos', *Rhetorica*, 8 (1990), 5–27.
—— 'Aristotle's *Rhetoric* and Renaissance Views of the Emotions', in P. Mack (ed.), *Renaissance Rhetoric* (Basingstoke, 1994), 1–26.
—— 'Renaissance Commentators on Aristotle's *Rhetoric*', in W. Fortenbaugh and D. Mirhady (eds.), *Peripatetic Rhetoric after Aristotle* (New Brunswick, NJ, 1994), 320–48.
—— 'Aristotle's *Rhetoric* and Renaissance Conceptions of the Soul', in G. Dahan and I. Rosier-Catach (eds.), *La Rhétorique d'Aristote: Traditions et commentaires* (Paris, 1998), 283–97.
—— 'Grammatica movet', in P. Osterreich and T. Sloane (eds.), *Rhetorica Movet: Studies in Honour of H. F. Plett* (Leiden, 1999), 73–115.
—— and James J. Murphy, *Renaissance Rhetoric Short-Title Catalogue 1460–1700* (Aldershot, 2006).
Grendler, Paul, *Schooling in Renaissance Italy* (Baltimore, 1989).
—— *The Universities of the Italian Renaissance* (Baltimore, 2002).
Grigera, L. López, *La retórica en la España del Siglo de Oro* (Salamanca, 1994).
Hammerstein, N. (ed.), *Handbuch der deutschen Bildungsgeschichte*, i (Munich, 1996).
Hardison, O. B., *The Enduring Monument* (Chapel Hill, NC, 1962).
Harsting, Pernille, 'The Golden Method of Menander Rhetor. The Translations and the Reception of the *Peri epideiktikôn* in the Italian Renaissance', *Analecta Romana Instituti Danici,* 20 (Rome, 1992), 139–57.
—— 'More Evidence of Menander Rhetor on the Epithalamium: Angelo Poliziano's Transcription in the Statius Commentary (1480–81), Re-edited with a Discussion of the Manuscript Sources and Earlier Editions', *Cahiers de l'Institut du Moyen-Age Grec et Latin,* 72 (2001), 11–34.
Hartfelder, Karl, *Philipp Melanchthon als praeceptor Germaniae* (Berlin, 1889).
Hathaway, Baxter, *The Age of Criticism: The Late Renaissance in Italy* (Ithaca, NY, 1962).
Heath, Malcolm, *Hermogenes On Issues: Strategies of Argument in Later Greek Rhetoric* (Oxford, 1995).
Henderson, Judith Rice, 'Erasmus on the Art of Letter-Writing', in J. J. Murphy (ed.), *Renaissance Eloquence* (Berkeley, Calif., 1983), 331–55.
—— 'Despauterius's *Syntaxis* (1509): The Earliest Publication of Erasmus's *De conscribendis epistolis*', *Humanistica Lovaniensia,* 37 (1988), 175–210.
—— 'Erasmian Ciceronians: Reformation Teachers of Letterwriting', *Rhetorica,* 10 (1992), 273–302.
—— 'Humanism and the Humanities', in C. Poster and L. Mitchell (eds.), *Letter-Writing Manuals and Instruction* (Columbia, SC, 2007), 141–77.

Herrick, Marvin T., *The Fusion of Horatian and Aristotelian Criticism 1531–1555* (Urbana, Ill., 1946).
—— *Comic Theory in the Sixteenth Century* (Urbana, Ill., 1950).
Hollier, D., and H. Bloch (eds.), *A New History of French Literature* (Cambridge, Mass., 1994).
Hornbeak, Katherine G., 'The Complete Letter-Writer in English', *Smith College Studies in Modern Languages,* 15 (1934), 1–150.
Hotson, Howard, *Commonplace Learning: Ramism and its German Ramifications 1543–1630* (Oxford, 2007).
Howell, Wilbur S., *Logic and Rhetoric in England 1500–1700* (Princeton, 1956).
Huisman, Gerda C., *Rudolph Agricola: A Bibliography* (Nieuwkoop, 1985).
Jardine, Lisa, *Erasmus, Man of Letters* (Princeton, 1993).
Jiménez, A. Martín, 'Rhetoric, Dialectic, and Literature in the Work of Francisco Sánchez, *El Brocense*', *Rhetorica* 13 (1995), 43–59.
—— *Retórica y literatura en el siglo XVI: El Brocense* (Valladolid, 1997).
Kallendorf, Craig (ed.), *Humanist Educational Treatises* (Cambridge, Mass., 2002).
Kennedy, George A., *The Art of Rhetoric in the Roman World* (Princeton, 1972).
—— *Greek Rhetoric under Christian Emperors* (Princeton, 1983).
—— *Classical Rhetoric and its Christian and Secular Tradition from Ancient to Modern Times*, 2nd edn. (Chapel Hill, NC, 1999).
Knape, J., *Philipp Melanchthons Rhetorik* (Tubingen, 1993).
Knox, Dilwyn, 'Order, Reason and Oratory: Rhetoric in Protestant Latin Schools', in P. Mack (ed.), *Renaissance Rhetoric* (Basingstoke, 1994), 63–80.
Kraus, Manfred, 'Aphthonius and the Progymnasmata in Rhetorical Theory and Practice', in David Zarefsky and Elizabeth Benacka (eds.), *Sizing up Rhetoric* (Long Grove, Ill., 2008), 52–67.
Kristeller, Paul O., *Renaissance Thought and its Sources* (New York, 1979).
La Charité, Claude, 'Les Trois Institutions oratoires de Henri III', *Renaissance et Réforme*, 31/4 (2008), 43–66.
Lane Ford, Margaret, 'The Importation of Printed Books', in L. Hellinga and J. B. Trapp (eds.), *The Cambridge History of the Book in Britain*, iii (Cambridge, 1999), 179–201.
Lanham, Richard, *A Handlist of Rhetorical Terms* (Berkeley, Calif., 1991).
Lares, Jameela, *Milton and the Preaching Arts* (Pittsburgh, 2001).
Lausberg, Heinrich, *Handbuch der literarischen rhetorik*, 3rd edn. (Stuttgart, 1990).
—— *Handbook of Literary Rhetoric* (Leiden, 1998).
Leedham-Green, Elisabeth, *Books in Cambridge Inventories*, 2 vols. (Cambridge, 1986).
López, Jorge Fernández, 'Rhetorical Theory in Sixteenth-Century Spain: A Critical Survey', *Rhetorica,* 20 (2002), 133–48.
McConica, J. K. (ed.), *The History of the University of Oxford*, iii. *The Collegiate University* (Oxford, 1986).
McGinness, Fred, *Right Thinking and Sacred Oratory in Counter-Reformation Rome* (Princeton, 1995).

Mack, Peter, 'Rudolph Agricola's Reading of Literature', *Journal of the Warburg and Courtauld Institutes,* 48 (1985), 23–41.
—— *Renaissance Argument: Valla and Agricola in the Traditions of Rhetoric and Dialectic* (Leiden, 1993).
—— 'Renaissance Habits of Reading', in S. Chaudhuri (ed.), *Renaissance Essays for K. S. Datta* (Calcutta, 1995), 1–25.
—— 'Ramus Reading: the Commentaries on Cicero's *Consular orations* and Vergil's *Eclogues* and *Georgics*', *Journal of the Warburg and Courtauld Institutes,* 61 (1998), 111–41.
—— *Elizabethan Rhetoric* (Cambridge, 2002).
—— 'Melanchthon's Commentaries on Latin Literature', in G. Frank and K. Meerhoff (eds.), *Melanchthon und Europa,* ii (Stuttgart, 2002), 29–52.
—— 'Rhetoric, Ethics and Reading in the Renaissance', *Renaissance Studies,* 19 (2005), 1–21.
—— 'Vives's Contributions to Rhetoric and Dialectic', in C. Fantazzi (ed.), *A Companion to Juan Luis Vives* (Leiden, 2008), 227–76.
McLaughlin, Martin, *Literary Imitation in the Italian Renaissance* (Oxford, 1995).
Maclean, Ian, 'Philosophical Books in European Markets 1570–1630: The Case of Ramus', in J. Henry and S. Hutton (eds.), *New Perspectives in Renaissance Thought: Essays in Memory of Charles B. Schmitt* (London, 1990), 253–63.
McManamon, John, *Pierpaolo Vergerio the Elder: The Humanist as Orator* (Binghamton, NY, 1996).
Magnusson, Lynne, *Shakespeare and Social Dialogue* (Cambridge, 1999).
Malherbe, A., *Ancient Epistolary Theorists* (Atlanta, Ga., 1988).
Malosse, P.-L., *Lettres pour toutes circonstances: Les Traités épistolaires du Pseudo-Libanios et du Pseudo-Démétrios de Phalère* (Paris, 2004).
Mann Phillips, Margaret, *The Adages of Erasmus: A Study with Translations* (Cambridge, 1964).
Margolin, J. C., *Erasme: Précepteur de l'Europe* (Paris, 1995).
Marsh, David, 'Grammar, Method and Polemic in Valla's *Elegantiae*', *Rinascimento,* 19 (1979), 91–116.
—— *The Quattrocento Dialogue* (Cambridge, Mass., 1980).
Martí, A., *La preceptiva retórica española en el Siglo de Oro* (Madrid, 1972).
Maskell, Dan, and R. Sayce, *A Descriptive Bibliography of Montaigne's Essais* (London, 1983).
Meerhoff, Kees, *Rhétorique et poétique au XVI siècle en France* (Leiden, 1986).
—— 'The Significance of Philip Melanchthon's Rhetoric in the Renaissance', in P. Mack (ed.), *Renaissance Rhetoric* (Basingstoke, 1994), 46–62.
—— 'Logique et éloquence: Une révolution ramusienne?', in K. Meerhoff and J.-C. Moisan (eds.), *Autour de Ramus* (Montreal, 1997), 87–132.
—— *Entre logique et littérature* (Orleans, 2001).
—— 'L'Enseignement des lecteurs royaux pour l'éloquence et la philosophie: De Latomus à Ramus', in A. Tuilier (ed.), *Histoire du Collège de France,* i. *La Création 1530–1560* (Paris, 2006), 293–352.

—— 'Jean Sturm et l'introduction de l'humanisme du Nord à Paris', in Arnold Matthieu (ed.), *Johannes Sturm (1507–1589): Rhetor, Pädagoge und Diplomat* (Tübingen, 2009), 109–29.
—— and Michel Magnien (eds.), *Ramus et l'université* (Paris, 2004).
—— and J.-C. Moisan (eds.), *Autour de Ramus: Le Combat* (Paris, 2005).
Mercer, R. G. G., *The Teaching of Barzizza* (London, 1979).
Monfasani, John, *George of Trebizond* (Leiden, 1976).
—— *Collectanea Trapezuntiana* (Binghamton, NY, 1984).
—— 'Humanism and Rhetoric', in A. Rabil, jun. (ed.), *Renaissance Humanism: Foundations, Forms and Legacy*, 3 vols. (Philadelphia, 1988), iii. 171–235.
Montagne, V., 'Jean Sturm et Valentin Erythraeus', *BHR* 63 (2001), 477–509.
—— 'Le *De suavi dicendi forma* de Jean Sturm: Notes sur la douceur du style à la Renaissance', *BHR* 66 (2004), 541–64.
Montefusco, Lucia Calboli, *La dottrina degli status nella retorica greca e romana* (Hildesheim, 1986).
——, 'Ciceronian and Hermogenean Influences on George of Trebizond's *Rhetoricorum libri V*', *Rhetorica,* 26 (2008), 139–64.
—— 'Les Catégories stylistiques du discours dans les *Rhetoricorum libri V* de George de Trébisonde', in idem (ed.), *Papers on Rhetoric IX* (Rome, 2008), 165–83.
—— 'Les Formes d'argumentation dans les *Rhetoricorum libri V* de George de Trébisonde', forthcoming.
Montes, Francisco Javier Alejo, *La Universidad de Salamanca Bajo Felipe II: 1575–98* (Burgos, 1998).
Mortari, V. Piano, 'Dialettica e Giurisprudenza', *Annali di storia del diritto,* 1 (1957), 293–401.
Moss, Ann, *Printed Commonplace-Books and the Structuring of Renaissance Thought* (Oxford, 1996).
—— *Renaissance Truth and the Latin Language Turn* (Oxford, 2003).
Mouchel, C., *Cicéron et Sénèque dans la rhétorique de la Renaissance* (Marburg, 1990).
Murphy, James J. (ed.), *Three Medieval Rhetorical Arts* (Berkeley, Calif., 1971).
—— *Rhetoric in the Middle Ages* (Berkeley, Calif., 1974).
—— and M. Davies, 'Rhetorical Incunabula STC', *Rhetorica,* 15 (1997), 355–470.
Nauta, Lodi, *In Defense of Common Sense* (Cambridge, Mass., 2009).
Navone, P., 'La "Doctrina loquendi et tacendi" di Albertano da Brescia. Censimento dei manoscritti', *Studi Medievali,* 35 (1994), 895–930.
Nims, Margaret (tr.), *Poetria nova of Geoffrey of Vinsauf* (Toronto, 1967).
Norton, Glyn (ed.), *The Cambridge History of Literary Criticism*, iii. *The Renaissance* (Cambridge, 1999).
O'Malley, John W., *Praise and Blame in Renaissance Rome* (Durham, NC, 1979).
Ong, Walter, *Ramus: Method and the Decay of Dialogue* (Cambridge, Mass., 1958).
—— *Ramus and Talon Inventory* (Cambridge, Mass., 1958).

Pade, Marianne (ed.), *On Renaissance Commentary* (Hildesheim, 2005).
Patterson, Annabel, *Hermogenes and the Renaissance: Seven Ideas of Style* (Princeton, 1970).
Peltonen, Marku (ed.), *The Cambridge Companion to Bacon* (Cambridge, 1996).
Percival, W. K., 'The Place of the *Rudimenta Grammatices* in the History of Grammar', *Res Publica Litterarum,* 4 (1981), 233–64.
—— 'The Influence of Perotti's *Rudimenta* in the Cinquecento', in Sesto Prete (ed.), *Protrepticon* (Milan, 1989), 91–100.
—— 'A Working Edition of the *Carmina Differentialia* by Guarino Veronese', *Res Publica Litterarum,* 17 (1994), 153–77.
—— *Studies in Renaissance Grammar* (Aldershot, 2004).
Pereira, Belmiro Fernandes, 'A edição conimbricense da *Rhetorica* de Joachim Ringelberg', *Peninsula,* 1 (2004), 201–13.
—— *Retórica e Eloquência em Portugal na época do Renascimento* (Coimbra, 2005).
Pigman, G. W., III, 'Imitation and the Renaissance Sense of the Past: The Reception of Erasmus' *Ciceronianus*', *Journal of Medieval and Renaissance Studies,* 9 (1979), 155–77.
—— 'Versions of Imitation in the Renaissance', *Renaissance Quarterly,* 33 (1980), 1–32.
—— 'Barzizza's Studies of Cicero', *Rinascimento,* 21 (1981), 123–63.
Poster, Carol, and Linda Mitchell (eds.), *Letter-Writing Manuals and Instruction from Antiquity to the Present* (Columbia, SC, 2007).
Quint, David, 'Humanism and Modernity: A Reconsideration of Bruni's *Dialogues*', *Renaissance Quarterly,* 38 (1985), 423–45.
Rademaker, C. S. M., *Life and Work of G. J. Vossius (1577–1649)* (Assen, 1981).
Reynolds, L. D., and N. Wilson, *Scribes and Scholars*, 2nd edn. (Oxford, 1974).
Ridder-Symoens, H. de (ed.), *A History of the University in Europe*, ii. *Universities of Early Modern Europe* (Cambridge, 1996).
Risse, W., *Die Logik der Neuzeit*, i. *1500–1640* (Stuttgart, 1964).
Roaf, Christine, 'Bartolomeo Cavalcanti, 1503–62: A Critical and Biographical Study', D.Phil. dissertation, Oxford, 1959.
Roberts, Julian, 'The Latin Trade', in J. Barnard and D. F. McKenzie (eds.), *The Cambridge History of the Book in Britain*, iv (Cambridge, 2002), 141–73.
Robertson, Jean, *The Art of Letter Writing* (London, 1942).
Russell, Donald A., *Criticism in Antiquity* (London, 1981).
Sabbadini, Remigio, *Storia di Ciceronianismo* (Turin, 1885).
——, *Le scoperte dei codici latini e greci*, 2 vols. (Florence, 1905–14; corr. repr. 1967).
Santangelo, G., *Le epistole 'De imitatione' di Giovanfrancesco Pico della Mirandola e di Pietro Bembo* (Florence, 1954).
Schindling, Anton, *Humanistische Hochschule und freie Reichsstadt: Gymnasium und Akademie in Strassburg 1538–1621* (Wiesbaden, 1977).
Schmidt, C., *La Vie et les travaux de Jean Sturm* (Strasbourg, 1855).
Schneider, B., *Die mittelalterlichen greichisch-lateinischen Uebersetzungen der Aristotelischen Rhetorik* (Berlin, 1971).

Schoeck, R. J., *Erasmus of Europe: 1501–36* (Edinburgh, 1993).
Scott, I., *Controversies over the Imitation of Cicero* (New York, 1910; repr. Davis, Calif., 1991).
Sealy, Robert J., *The Palace Academy of Henri III* (Geneva, 1981).
Seidel Menchi, S., *Erasmo in Italia* (Turin, 1987).
Sharratt, Peter, 'The Present State of Studies on Ramus', *Studi francesi,* 47–8 (1972), 201–13.
—— 'Nicolaus Nancelius, *Petri Rami Vita*', *Humanistica Lovaniensia*, 24 (1975), 161–278.
—— 'Petrus Ramus and the Reform of the University', in P. Sharratt (ed.), *French Renaissance Studies 1540–1740* (Edinburgh, 1976), 4–20.
—— 'Recent Work on Peter Ramus', *Rhetorica*, 5 (1987), 7–58.
—— 'Ramus 2000', *Rhetorica*, 18 (2000), 399–455.
Shuger, Debora, *Sacred Rhetoric* (Princeton, 1988).
Simon, Joan, *Education and Society in Tudor England* (Cambridge, 1966).
Skinner, Quentin, *Reason and Rhetoric in the Philosophy of Hobbes* (Cambridge, 1996).
Sonnino, Lee, *A Handbook to Sixteenth Century Rhetoric* (London, 1968).
Spitz, L. W., and B. Sher Tinsley, *Johann Sturm on Education* (St Louis, 1995).
Tracy, James D., *Erasmus of the Low Countries* (Berkeley, Calif., 1996).
Ueding, Gert (ed.), *Historisches Wörterbuch der Rhetorik*, 9 vols. (Tübingen, 1992–2007).
Vaillancourt, Luc, *La Lettre familière au 16e siècle* (Paris, 2003).
van der Poel, Marc, 'The Scholia in Orationem Pro Lege Manilia of Rudolph Agricola', *Lias,* 24 (1997), 1–35.
Van Houdt, Toon, Jan Papy, G. Tournoy, and C. Matheeussen (eds.), *Self-Presentation and Social Identification: The Rhetoric and Pragmatics of Letter-Writing in Early Modern Times* (Louvain, 2002).
Vasoli, Cesare, *La dialettica e la retorica dell'Umanesimo* (Milan, 1968).
—— 'Francesco Patrizi and the Double Rhetoric', *New Literary History*, 14 (1983), 539–51.
—— *Francesco Patrizi da Cherso* (Rome, 1989).
Verdú, J. Rico, *Le retórica española de los siglos XVI y XVII* (Madrid, 1973).
Vickers, Brian, *Classical Rhetoric in English Poetry* (London, 1970).
—— 'Epideictic and Epic in the Renaissance', *New Literary History,* 14 (1982–3), 497–537.
—— *In Defence of Rhetoric* (Oxford, 1988).
Waddington, Charles, *Ramus: Sa vie, ses écrits et ses opinions* (Paris, 1855).
Wagner, Russell H., 'Wilson and his Sources', *Quarterly Journal of Speech,* 15 (1929), 525–36.
—— 'Thomas Wilson's *Arte of Rhetorique*', *Speech Monographs,* 27 (1960), 1–32.
Walker, D. P., *The Ancient Theology* (London, 1972).
Ward, John O., 'Artificiosa Eloquentia in the Middle Ages', Ph.D. thesis, University of Toronto, 1972.

Ward, John O., 'Renaissance Commentators on Ciceronian Rhetoric', in J. J. Murphy (ed.), *Renaissance Eloquence* (Berkeley, Calif., 1983), 126–73.

—— *Ciceronian Rhetoric in Treatise, Scholion and Commentary* (Turnhout, 1995).

Weinberg, Bernard, *A History of Literary Criticism in the Italian Renaissance*, 2 vols. (Chicago, 1961).

Wels, V., *Triviale Künste* (Berlin, 2000).

Wengert, T., and P. Graham (eds.), *Melanchthon and the Commentary* (Sheffield, 1997).

Wenzel, S., 'The Arts of Preaching', in A. Minnis and I. Johnson (eds.), *The Cambridge History of Literary Criticism*, ii. *The Middle Ages* (Cambridge, 2005), 84–96.

Wiedenhofer, S., *Formalstrukturen humanistischer und reformatorischer Theologie bei Philipp Melanchthon*, 2 vols. (Munich, 1976).

Witt, R. G., *Coluccio Salutati and his Public Letters* (Geneva, 1976).

——, 'Medieval "Ars Dictaminis" and the Beginnings of Humanism: A New Construction of the Problem', *Renaissance Quarterly,* 35 (1982), 1–35.

—— *In the Footsteps of the Ancients: The Origins of Humanism from Lovati to Bruni* (Leiden, 2000).

Woodward, W., *Studies in Education during the Age of the Renaissance* (Cambridge, 1906).

Woods, Marjorie Curry, *Classroom Commentaries: Teaching the* Poetria nova *across Medieval and Renaissance Europe* (Columbus, Ohio, 2010).

Yates, Frances, 'The Ciceronian Art of Memory', in *Medioevo e Rinascimento: Studi in Onore di Bruno Nardi*, ii (Florence, 1955), 873–903.

—— *The Art of Memory* (London, 1966).

Glossary of Rhetorical and Dialectical Terms

This glossary provides definitions of the technical terms used in this book, in senses in which they would have been used in the renaissance. For many of these definitions I am indebted to R. A. Lanham, *A Handlist of Rhetorical Terms* (Berkeley, Calif., 1991), who points out (p. v) that different authorities sometimes define particular figures differently. Where I have been aware of choosing between different views I have named the author I have followed. Like Lanham's book, Gideon Burton's website 'Silva rhetoricae' at http://rhetoric.byu.edu provides useful information and definitions about a much wider range of rhetorical terms. One could also consult G. Ueding (ed.), *Historisches Wörterbuch der Rhetorik*, 9 vols. (Tübingen, 1992–2007) and H. Lausberg, *Handbuch der literarischen rhetorik*, 3rd edition (Stuttgart, 1990), translated as *Handbook of Literary Rhetoric* (Leiden, 1998).

Acryologia Use of an inappropriate or illogical word.

Addubitatio Self-questioning or appearance of inwardly debating an issue.

Aetiology Figure of thought, including a cause or reason.

Allegory A mode of writing in which one physical element or character consistently stands for a specific abstract quality; sometimes called 'an extended metaphor'. Also a way of reading abstract meaning from a narrative by interpreting individual characters or objects as abstract qualities. Usually regarded as one of the tropes.

Amplification Use of heightened language; making a subject seem more impressive by using comparisons.

Anadiplosis Repeating the last word of one line or sentence as the first word of the next.

Anaphora Successive lines, phrases, or sentences begin with the same word.

Antimetabole Repeating two words in successive phrases, but in reverse order (e.g. you should eat to live rather than live to eat).

Antiphrasis A word or idea is understood through its contrary; naming a quality or object with a word signifying the opposite.

Antistrophe Successive lines, phrases, or sentences end with the same word.

Antithesis Expressing contrary ideas one after the other.

Antonomasia Replacing a proper name with a descriptive phrase or vice versa.

Aposiopesis Hesitating, as if overcome by emotion.

Apostrophe Interrupting a text to address directly a god, abstract figure, or character; usually introduced by 'O', followed by the name of the addressee.

Argumentation, forms of The forms in which arguments are set out. Aristotelian dialectic recognized four forms (syllogism, induction, enthymeme, and example), of which the first two were regarded as perfect; the latter two defective. Stoic logicians put forward different forms of argumentation (e.g. if it is light, it must be day; but it is light; therefore it must be day), which Aristotelians called 'hypothetical syllogism'.

Ars dictaminis Medieval genre of treatises on letter-writing.

Asianism A florid style of oratory, identified and defended by Cicero.

Asteismus Surprising and absurd joke.

Asyntedon The omission of conjunctions.

Atticism A very restrained style of oratory, favoured by Cicero's critics.

Barbarism An error in the use of an individual word, of a type likely to be committed by a non-native speaker; divided into various species by grammarians.

Catachresis Trope, a thing without a name is provided with one through a sort of metaphor; also a far-fetched metaphor.

Categories From Aristotle's logic, a set of ten classes (substance, quantity, quality, relative, place, time, stance, having, doing, being affected) into which all words can be divided according to the type of existence they denote.

Chreia One of the exercises of the *progymnasmata*, in which a saying or action is explained through a set of topics.

Climax A step-by-step figure in which the end of one phrase becomes the starting point for the next, in the form 'A to B, B to C, C to D'.

Collectio Form of argumentation, according to George Trapezuntius a five-part argument: proposition, reason, confirmation of the reason, elaboration, and conclusion (*Rhetoricorum libri V* (Paris, 1528), 223–5).

Colon Mid-length element of a complex sentence, part of the theory of sentence composition.

Commonplace A pre-prepared and highly developed argument on a general theme, such as the benefits of peace or the dangers of leaving crimes unpunished.

Commonplace book An exercise book, with headings, generally of a moral nature, at the top of each page. Students enter phrases and stories from their reading in their commonplace books so as to keep them ready for reuse when they need to write about, for example, justice, temperance, or peace.

Communicatio Request for advice about how to proceed, from judges or opponent.

Complexio Latin word for dilemma, used in Cicero, *De inventione* 1.29.45.

Composition Artistic construction of a sentence.

Composition and division One of the fallacies, which depends on interpreting a word in two different ways, as in 'Five is two and three; therefore five is two, and five is three'.

Concessio The speaker grants a point to the opposing counsel, usually in preparation for a stronger response; can be used to give the impression of evenhandedness.

Conclusion Also known as peroration, the final section of the oration in which the speaker sums up the key points made and appeals to the audience.

Confirmation The section of the speech containing the arguments in favour of the speaker's position; the fourth part of a six-part oration, or, as Confirmation and Refutation, the third part in the four-part scheme.

Conjectural issue Part of status-theory; the type of judicial case in which the defence denies that the accused committed the act and the orators argue about the facts of the case.

Consequences Doctrine of medieval logic, which sets out the inferences which follow from a particular type of premise and analyses the conditions in which this occurs.

Contradictories Part of the square of contraries, from Aristotle's *De interpretatione*; the opposition between a universal proposition and a particular proposition, differing in quality, for example, between 'all horses are white' and 'some horse is not-white'.

Contraries Part of the square of contraries; the opposition between two universal propositions, differing in quality, for example, between 'all horses are white' and 'no horses are white'.

Conversion Part of Aristotle's teaching on the syllogism, from *Prior Analytics*, in which later figures of the syllogism are shown to derive from the first figure.

Copia Abundance of expression, one of the aims of invention.

Correctio The speaker gives one expression and then corrects it with another (often harsher), with the effect of emphasizing the more severe expression.

Cursus A medieval system for marking the end of a Latin prose phrase or sentence with one of three set patterns of long and short syllables, based on the rules of Latin poetry; not favoured by the humanists.

Declamation An exercise in public speaking, presented by pupils as part of their training or by a master as a display of skill.

Decorum The doctrine of suiting style to subject-matter and oration to audience.

Definition (1) in rhetoric, a part of status-theory, which applies when both orators agree on the facts of the case and on the intentions of the defendant, but they argue about whether this act meets the definition of the alleged crime; (2) in dialectic and rhetoric, one of the topics of invention. In Aristotelian theory a definition is made up of the genus to which something belongs and its *differentia*.

Deliberative One of the three genres of classical rhetoric; orations which debate public policy.

Delivery Fifth of the skills of the orator; the art of delivering an oration, using voice and gesture.

Demonstration Full and convincing proof, also the art of constructing reliable bodies of knowledge.

Demonstrative Genre of classical rhetoric; speeches of praise and blame; also called epideictic.

Dialectic Persuasive argument; in the renaissance most commonly a synonym for logic, but sometimes used to denote argument which is persuasive but not fully reliable.

Dialyton Omission of conjunctions; also called asyntedon.

Diasyrmus Joking dismissal of opponent's opinion.

Didascalic genre Fourth genre of rhetoric, proposed by Melanchthon, to include speeches which aim to instruct an audience.

Differentia One of the Aristotelian predicables; the property which distinguishes one species from the other members of its genus; if man is defined as 'rational animal'; 'rational' is the *differentia.*

Dilemma Form of argumentation; the speaker offers the opponent two alternatives (which are meant to be the only two possibilities in that situation) and then shows that both of them lead to the same result.

Disposition Second of the skills of the orator; the art of arranging the material found through invention in the most effective way.

Disputation University exercise in arguing about a particular proposition, required for graduation in a particular subject, governed by rules taught as part of logic.

Division (1) Third part of a six-part oration, in which the speaker sets out the points of agreement and disagreement with the opponent, before arguing the points at issue; (2) logical technique of dividing a whole into its parts or a genus into its species; one of the topics of invention.

Dubitatio The speaker pretends to be unsure about a particular point.

Elocutio Third of the skills of the orator; the art of finding the most effective expression for the materials found for the speech.

Enargeia Vivid description, using words to bring something before the eyes of the audience.

Energeia Vigour of expression.

Enigma A thought hidden in obscurity; obscure expression; may be a fault of style or an ornament.

Enthymeme One of the Aristotelian forms of argumentation; a defective syllogism, in which either one of the propositions is missing or one or more of the propositions is uncertain.

Enumeratio Form of argumentation, in which all the possibilities are set out and all but one are eliminated.

Epanalepsis The same word at the beginning and end of a line, phrase, or sentence.

Epanodos Repetition of a word; sometimes with a different meaning.

Epicheireme Form of argumentation, involving premises which are not reliable.

Epideictic Genre of rhetoric; speeches of praise and blame.

Epithet Qualifying a noun with an appropriate adjective.

Ethos Speaker's self-presentation; character of the speaker.

Exclamatio Exclamation expressing emotion.

Exordium First part of the oration; aims to make the audience well-disposed, attentive, and receptive.

Expolitio Evidently embellishing a passage.

Exposition Agricola's term for language in which the speaker sets out material to an audience which follows willingly.

Figures of the syllogism Aristotle divides the syllogism, on the basis of arrangement of the terms in the three propositions, into three figures and various moods of each figure.

Figures of thought Part of *elocutio*; stylistic ornaments which depend largely on the attitude which the speaker presents to the audience in a particular sentence.

Figures of words Part of *elocutio*; stylistic ornaments which depend on features of the words and sounds employed.

Five skills or tasks of the orator Invention, disposition, style (*elocutio*), memory, and delivery.

Four-, five- or six-part oration The classical structure of the oration; Aristotle identifies four parts (*exordium*, narration, confirmation and refutation, conclusion); Cicero distinguishes also division (sometimes seen as part of narration) and treats confirmation and refutation as separate parts.

Genus One of the Aristotelian predicables; the higher level class to which a group of species belong.

Gradatio Latin term for climax.

Grammatical figures Ornaments which are related to faults of expression, to the organization of sentences or to changes in words required to adapt them to poetry.

Homoeoptoton The same sound at the end of a series of words.

Homoeosis Greek term for similitude.

Homoeoteleuton The same sound ends a series of words or phrases or sentences; overlaps with homoeoptoton.

Hypallage Word apparently misused, usually with comic intention.

Hyperbaton Change in expected word-order.

Hyperbole Trope; extravagant exaggeration.

Hypophora Asking questions and answering them at once; also called *subiectio.*

Hypothetical syllogism Form of argumentation, which involves establishing an inference based on a condition (e.g. 'if it is light, it is day') and then drawing implications from it (e.g. 'But it is not day, so it cannot be light').

Hypotyposis Vivid description.

Hysteron proteron The last element of the sentence or phrase is placed first.

Ideas of style Hermogenes's seven characteristics of style (subdivided in some cases): clarity, grandeur, beauty, rapidity, character, sincerity, and force. See p. 41.

Induction Form of argumentation which moves from particular events to establish general principles; if all the species of a genus can be shown to have a certain property then it may be inferred that that property belongs to the genus.

Insolubilia In medieval logic, a class of sophisms which involve elements of contradiction which seem impossible to resolve, for example, the truth value of the statement 'I always tell lies'.

Interrogatio The speaker asks a question, which conveys the point and does not expect a reply.

Invention First of the skills of the orator; the art of finding the material to make one's case.

Irony Trope, implying a meaning opposite to what the words used apparently mean.

Isocolon A series of phrases of equal length in a sentence.

Judicial One of the three genres of rhetoric; speeches made in court cases.

Licentia Figure of thought; speaking with freedom and boldness.

Logos One of Aristotle's three forms of persuasion; the use of words and reason.

Memory Fourth skill of the orator; describes techniques for memorizing the speech.

Metalepsis Trope; expressing an equivalence between two words which seem remote from each other because the intermediate connecting word is left unstated.

Metaphor Trope; one word is replaced by another, chosen because of some sort of parallelism; ideally presenting the two as parallel says something new about the idea which would have been expressed by the original word.

Method Order of working; in logic a way of discovering or presenting material; in Melanchthon a short list of questions designed to help the speaker explore an idea quickly and clearly.

Metonymy Trope, the replacement of one word with another contiguous to it, typically cause replaced by effect, proper name by epithet (or vice versa).

Modal proposition A proposition which is modified by a condition usually stated before it, for example, 'It is possible that some horses are red'.

Moods of the syllogism Syllogisms are divided into figures (on the basis of the patterning of the propositions) and subdivided into moods (on the basis of the quantity and quality of the propositions).

Mycterismus Open derision, involving gesture as well as words.

Narratio Second part of the oration, in which the speaker sets out the facts of the case.

Occupatio Stating that you will not say something; often going into such detail about what you will not say that you have in fact covered the main points.

Onomatopoeia Trope, inventing a word which sounds like the thing it signifies.

Oppositio Form of argumentation in which an opposite conclusion is drawn from a hypothetical proposition (for example, 'If it is day, we must work; but it is night, so we can rest').

Parenthesis Inserting a phrase or sentence within another complete sentence.

Paroemia Proverb, expression in common use marked with novelty.

Paronomasia Play on words; usually replacing one word with another which is very similar but not identical in sound; extended to include playing on the different meanings of a single word.

Parrhesia Greek term for *licentia*, speaking with freedom.

Pathos One of Aristotle's three types of persuasion, arousing an emotional response in the audience.

Period Complex Latin sentence.

Periodic style Style described in rhetoric manuals in which a longish sentence is made up of a series of elements of roughly equivalent length.

Periphrasis Replacing an unstated word with a phrase describing it.

Permissio Figure of thought; leaving some points to the judgement of the jury or the opponent (Quintilian 9.2.25).

Petitio Fourth element of the medieval letter described in the *ars dictaminis*, in which the writer makes a request of the addressee.

Pleonasmus Evident and unnecessary repetition within a phrase.

Polyptoton Repetition of the same word in different cases or of the same root word with different endings or other modifications.

Polysyntedon Use of many conjunctions.

Post-predicaments Sections from Aristotle's *Categories* which occur after the categories themselves: the square of contraries, meanings of prior, and kinds of change.

Predicables Five coordinating words of Aristotelian logic, defined in Porphyry's *Isagoge*: genus, species, property, *differentia*, accident.

Predicaments Latin word for categories.

Progymnasmata Set of writing exercises.

Property One of the predicables; something which always belongs to a subject.

Proposition (1) A logical statement, in the basic form A is B, which must specify quantity (universal or particular) and quality (affirmative or negative). It can be modified to make a modal proposition; (2) in rhetoric, a statement of the main argument of the speech; sometimes treated as the third part of the six-part oration.

Prose-rhythm the arrangement of sound quantities (long and short syllables, as in Latin poetic metre) at the end of a sentence so as to give a pleasing sense of completion; the arrangement of sentences into clauses of similar length and patterning. See Cicero, *Orator* 44.149–71.238.

Prosopopeia A speech written for an animal, object or abstraction, or the *progymnasmata* exercise of writing a speech for a character or object.

Quadrivium Second stage of the seven liberal arts, the four arts connected with number: arithmetic, geometry, music, and astronomy.

Quality (1) One of the Aristotelian categories, covering things which can be perceived about a substance, both sense perceptions and more abstract qualities; (2) in relation to the proposition, whether the proposition is affirmative or negative; (3) a part of status-theory, when the defence admits that the defendant performed a certain action, but denies that it is of the nature alleged by the prosecution, for example, one might admit striking a fatal blow, but claim that one did so in self-defence.

Quantity (1) One of the Aristotelian categories, covering things connected with number and spatial extension; (2) in relation to the proposition, whether the proposition is universal ('all horses') or particular ('some horses').

Ratiocinatio Ciceronian five-part form of argumentation: (1) foundational argument; (2) proof of the foundational argument; (3) particular statement about the thing you wish to prove; (4) proof of that statement; (5) conclusion (Cicero, *De inventione* 1.34.58–9).

Refutation Fifth part of the six-part oration, in which the orator attacks the arguments against his view.

Relatives Aristotelian category; properties which imply a reciprocal relation, such as mother and daughter or half and twice.

Salutation Greeting at the start of the letter, especially in the *ars dictaminis*.

Sententia Pithy and memorable phrase, often a moral axiom or a proverb.

Similitude A comparison in which one thing is said to be like another; sometimes (as in Agricola) restricted to a comparison involving four terms, just as A is to B, so C is to D.

Simplex conclusio Form of argumentation; a simple inference which necessarily follows, for example, 'since I was out of the country when the crime was committed, I could not have done it' (Cicero, *De inventione* 1.19.45).

Sophisms Misleading arguments, as listed and analysed by Aristotle in *Sophistical Refutations*.

Sorites Form of argument not discussed in the Aristotelian tradition, in which propositions involving quantities are attacked, by repeatedly questioning them in relation to quantities which are increased or decreased by single units; so, for example, if a 60-year-old man is old, is a fifty-nine-year-old . . . is a one-year-old?

Species One of the predicables; a defined group at a lower level than a genus.

Square of contraries Aristotelian doctrine relating different qualitative and quantitative expressions of the same basic proposition.

Status-theory Theory of invention, in the judicial genre, in which arguments are suggested according to the point of conflict between prosecution and defence.

Style Third skill of the orator; see *elocutio*.

Subalterns Part of the square of contraries, the relation between universal and particular propositions of the same quality (for example, between 'No horses are white' and 'Some horses are not-white').

Subjectio (1) Figure: the speaker poses a question and answers it; (2) in George Trapezuntius a form of argumentation, in which you ask what can be said against your opinion and show by a series of questions that this opposing opinion must be wrong (*Rhetoricorum libri V* (Paris 1538), 212–15).

Substance First of the Aristotelian categories, covering things which exist independently.

Superscription Part of the art of letter-writing; the address to the recipient.

Supposition Semantic theory developed in medieval logic, analysing the different ways in which a term is understood to refer to things in the world.

Syllogism A form of argumentation discovered by Aristotle in *Prior Analytics*; an arrangement of three propositions (involving three terms, each of which appears in two of the propositions), in which, if the first two are true, the third must necessarily also be true on formal grounds.

Synecdoche Trope; part is named where whole is meant, or vice versa.

Synthesis Figure related to quantity, when two words are joined to make one, usually for metrical reasons (Scaliger, *Poetices*, 4.40).

Three genres of rhetoric judicial, deliberative, and demonstrative (or epideictic).

Three levels of style High, middle, and low.

Three aims of the orator According to Cicero, the orator aims to teach, move, and please the audience.

Tmesis Grammatical figure; a word is interposed between the two parts of a compound word. For Scaliger, the division of one word into two, for metrical reasons, *Poetices*, 4.40.

Topical difference According to Boethius, the rules of inference which comprise the topics are divided into groups marked by the topical differences, which generally appear in each rule. Boethius's topical differences are definition, genus, species, etc., which others call the topics.

Topical maxim According to Boethius, the topics contain rules of inference (the topical maxims) which provide support for plausible arguments.

Topics In Cicero and in renaissance dialectic, a list of headings (such as definition, genus, species, cause, effect, circumstances, opposites) which can be used to generate arguments. By applying each of these headings to the subject of the speech the orator will explore the subject and think of possible arguments.

Topics of deliberative oratory Classification of arguments likely to be helpful in political debates, primarily the honourable and the useful.

Topics of person List of headings for describing a person, for example, in a demonstrative oration, including family, nation, education, virtues, deeds.

Trivium First stage of the seven liberal arts; the three arts of language: grammar, rhetoric, and logic.

Trope A subset of the figures, some of which involve a change in the meaning of the word used.

Valediction Final part of the letter, where the writer bids farewell to the recipient.

Violatio According to George Trapezuntius, a form of argumentation in which we show that an argument made by the opponent in fact favours our side (*Rhetoricorum libri V* (Paris, 1538), 220–1).

Index

The book is indexed by author rather than title, except for anonymous works, which are listed by title. For authors who wrote several major rhetoric texts, there are separate entries for titles after the author's name. Bold text indicates the main treatment(s) of a particular text or author. Classical authors and figures of rhetoric are indexed only when there is discussion or example and not when they are part of a list.

Printed and bound by CPI Group (UK) Ltd, Croydon, CR0 4YY